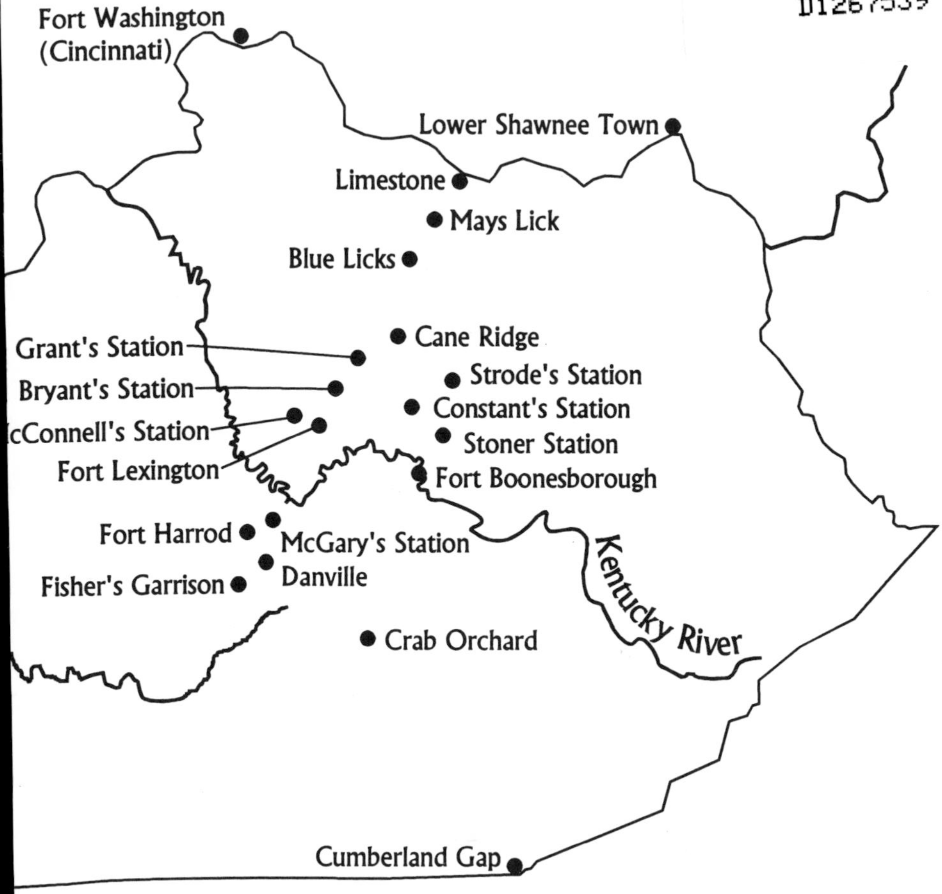
Fort Washington
(Cincinnati)
Lower Shawnee Town
Limestone
Mays Lick
Blue Licks
Cane Ridge
Grant's Station
Bryant's Station
Strode's Station
Constant's Station
cConnell's Station
Stoner Station
Fort Lexington
Fort Boonesborough
Fort Harrod
McGary's Station
Danville
Fisher's Garrison
Kentucky River
Crab Orchard
Cumberland Gap

The Buzzel About Kentuck

The Buzzel About Kentuck

Settling the Promised Land

Edited by

CRAIG THOMPSON FRIEND

THE UNIVERSITY PRESS OF KENTUCKY

Publication of this volume was made possible in part by a grant from the National Endowment for the Humanities.

Scholarly publisher for the Commonwealth,
serving Bellarmine College, Berea College, Centre
College of Kentucky, Eastern Kentucky University,
The Filson Club Historical Society, Georgetown College,
Kentucky Historical Society, Kentucky State University,
Morehead State University, Murray State University,
Northern Kentucky University, Transylvania University,
University of Kentucky, University of Louisville,
and Western Kentucky University.

Editorial and Sales Offices: The University Press of Kentucky
663 South Limestone Street, Lexington, Kentucky 40508-4008

99 00 01 02 03 5 4 3 2 1

Library of Congress Cataloging-in-Publication Data

The buzzel about Kentuck : settling the Promised Land / Craig Thompson Friend, editor.
p. cm.
Includes bibliographical references and index.
ISBN 0-8131-2085-3 (cloth : alk. paper)
1. Kentucky—History—To 1792. 2. Kentucky—History—1792-1865.
3. Frontier and pioneer life—Kentucky. I. Friend, Craig Thompson.
F454.B89 1998
976.9—dc21 98-27466

This book is printed on acid-free recycled paper
meeting the requirements of the American National Standard
for Permanence of Paper for Printed Library Materials.

Manufactured in the United States of America

Contents

List of Illustrations

Foreword

The images of frontier Kentucky have remained etched in the national consciousness. Those enduring views of the First West featured a land not populated by American Indians, an Eden waiting to be claimed, a place of milk and honey. To this Heaven on Earth, first came small bands of Long Hunters who then told of the wealth waiting to be won, and settlers from beyond the mountains soon followed. Daniel Boone, wilderness scout, Daniel Boone, Indian fighter, and Daniel Boone, frontier leader, all became part of the picture. Families braved the dangers, fought hostile forces, built their cabins, and found their dreams. Small yeoman farmers, with their brave and hearty families at their side (if not always visible), lived a good life in the promised land. A few grew wealthy in the rural world and, with the labor of their mostly happy slaves, soon prospered. Out of all that burst forth a new state. So went the image.

But it was a false picture in so many aspects. Many of the parts of that society were covered over with fresh historical paints, hiding the reality of the original oils of memory. Yes, there was much of what the early rhetoric promised. It was a land rich in game, with fertile soils and the rest. But the rhetoric and the vision and, later, the writings of those who chronicled the era also obscured much. The Native American presence and viewpoint, the physical hardships and danger, the mental challenges, the roles of women, children, and blacks, the unfulfilled promises, the lawsuits, the frustrations—all that and more might still be a part of the early picture but would be buried away in some dark, unlit corner of the frontier tapestry spread before Americans.

When I wrote an article surveying the status of writing on Kentucky history, over a decade and a half ago, few of the new waves of historical inquiry had swept across the study of the frontier. Yet, it seemed to me at the time, the sources cried out for just such a study. Some well-used materials could easily yield new insights if given a fresh look; some utilized items simply awaited an eager historical explorer; some accepted and older outlooks needed questioning and challenging.

History too abhors a vacuum, and new historians have moved into the field. More recent studies have shown that the earlier interpretations no longer can serve as faithful guides to frontier and early antebellum Kentucky. A whole series of recent books and articles demonstrate that while there is much very sound in those previous accounts, there is much more to know and to understand. Despite two centuries of writing, the images and the realities of early Kentucky remain as far distant from each other as the seacoast was to those on the frontier, beyond the mountains.

This collection represents an important new study in that evolving reexamination of the early frontier. The result is a nuanced portrayal of a perplexing and complex world, one evolving and changing, one that brings the reality closer and into clearer focus. These essays sometimes support, often refute, and usually redefine ideas about this society and those who lived in it. They demonstrate which parts of the older story still ring true and which ones are hollow echoes of the frontier as it existed.

The Buzzel About Kentuck presents a view of the frontier based on a wider concept of what affected those early European-Americans and African Americans—the American Indian context, the ties to the East, the national markets, the world situation. This book emphasizes the lives of those often ignored on the frontier—settlers south of Green River, workmen, free blacks, African American churchgoers, and women generally. These essays also stress that the western frontier was not specifically of one historical moment. In Kentucky, different frontier societies developed in different ways at different times, according to a whole series of economic, financial, migratory, and governmental factors. There was a frontier not of time but of actions for a century after 1750, and beyond.

These scholars and their essays represent a large part of the core of exciting work being done on the trans-Appalachian west. When you combine their fresh insights with good scholarship and an important subject, the result is what this work is—a significant new look at Kentucky and the early American frontier.

James C. Klotter

Acknowledgments

Part of the joy of researching and writing history is when one realizes that others are engaged in similar pursuits and share interest in the same questions. *The Buzzel About Kentuck: Settling the Promised Land* is testimony to such moments. Some of the contributors are scholars with whom I have shared panels at meetings of the Southern Historical Association and the Society for Historians of the Early American Republic. Others have become cherished colleagues whose interest in my work pales when compared with my respect for their own. Still others are people I have never met, recommended for their dedication to serious scholarship. Without their hard work, flexibility, attention to details, and, most important, common interest in the history of early Kentucky, this collection would never have come together. To them I am most grateful.

The task of compiling and editing such diverse essays was more demanding than I expected. Without the encouragement and assistance of several people, I would have become disheartened by the magnitude of the project. A friend, Thomas Appleton, has always recharged my ebbing enthusiasm and is the best proofreader I know. In the spring of 1996, Sue Miller and Mark Roy studied historical editing with me and found needed corrections and improvements in several of the articles. I am especially indebted to Sue, who spent many hours typing and indexing. I commend my colleagues at Georgetown College for honoring my "Do Not Disturb" sign and granting me the solitude to complete the task. I am indebted to Jennifer Harr for the maps herein and to David Pollack and Gwynn Henderson for helping me find her. I want to acknowledge three scholars—Elizabeth Perkins, Gail Terry, and Matthew Schoenbachler—who were unable to contribute to this volume. Their interactions with me at conferences and over the phone partially inspired this collection; their participation is missed.

That leaves friends and family, who make it easy for me to pursue my historical interests. Although I knew her before the inception of this project, I have a newfound appreciation for my friendship with Blair Pogue, and I wish her the best. I thank Gaylord and Billie Friend for their undying support. My sisters, Rebecca and Dixie, have always lifted my spirits. My friend, Roderick Turner, reminds me often of balancing my scholarly interests with the joy of just living, for which I could never be thankful enough. Finally, Theda Perdue has been a constant adviser and confidant for the past nine years. Her unwavering interest in my projects has made my pursuit of history enjoyable and rewarding.

Chronology

Virginian representatives and Indians "on Ohio" meet at LoggsTown.	1754	Colonial representatives meet at lower Shawnee Town.
The Great War for the Empire erupts between England, France, and their respective Indian allies.	1756	
The Great War for the Empire concludes with the Treaty of Paris. England establishes Proclamation Line prohibiting colonists from entering trans-Appalachia.	1763	
	1769	Daniel Boone makes first excursion into Kentucky.
Battle of Point Pleasant results in Indian cession of lands south of the Ohio.	1774	James Harrod and party erect Fort Harrod.
American Revolutionary War erupts.	1775	Daniel Boone and party construct Fort Boonesborough. Richard Henderson forms Transylvania Company.
Continental Congress approves Declaration of Independence.	1776	Virginia consolidates western territory into Kentucky County.
	1779	Robert Patterson and party build Fort Lexington.
	1780	Virginia divides Kentucky County into Fayette, Lincoln, and Jefferson Counties.

	1781	Large numbers of Virginia Baptists, fleeing Anglican establishment, arrive.
	1782	Shawnee rout pioneers at Battle of Blue Licks.
American Revolutionary War concludes with Treaty of Paris.	1783	John Brown arrives.
Confederation Congress passes first Northwest Ordinance.	1784	John Filson publishes *The Discovery, Settlement and Present State of Kentucke.*
Constitutional Convention meets in Philadelphia.	1787	John Bradford prints first issue of the *Kentucky Gazette.*
George Washington elected first president.	1789	George Nicholas arrives.
	1790	Kentucky's population reaches 73,677.
Kentucky becomes fifteenth state.	1792	George Nicholas completes first state constitution.
	1793	John Breckinridge arrives.
Battle of Fallen Timbers ends Shawnee threat to settlements south of the Ohio River.	1794	
	1795	State assembly enacts first land allocation law for Green River country.
John Adams elected president. Pinckney's Treaty guarantees use of the Mississippi River.	1796	
	1797	State assembly enacts second land allocation act for Green River country.

U.S. Congress passes Alien and Sedition Acts.	1798	Kentucky Resolutions pass state assembly.
	1799	John Breckinridge leads adoption of second state constitution.
Thomas Jefferson elected president.	1800	State population reaches 220,955.
		Matthew Lyon arrives.
	1801	Cane Ridge revival occurs in Bourbon County.
Spanish governor of New Orleans closes port to American trade.	1802	State assembly establishes the Kentucky Insurance Company to protect trade and issue transferable notes.
U.S. government purchases Louisiana Territory and secures Mississippi River trade.	1803	
Lewis and Clark depart on westward expedition.	1804	
	1806	John Robert Shaw publishes his autobiography. Bank of Kentucky chartered.
James Madison elected president.	1808	
	1810	State population reaches 406,511.
	1811	Henry Clay takes seat as War Hawk in U.S. House of Representatives.
War of 1812 erupts.	1812	
War of 1812 concludes with Treaty of Ghent.	1814	Thornton Blackburn is born in Maysville.

First steamboat travels from New Orleans to Louisville.	1815	Lexington's wartime economic boom collapses.
James Monroe elected president.	1816	
	1818	State assembly charters forty-six banks.
Panic of 1819 hits.	1819	
Missouri Compromise passes U.S. Congress.	1820	State population reaches 564,317. State assembly passes replevin law to aid debtors.
Santa Fe trail opens.	1821	
Monroe Doctrine proclaimed.	1823	
	1824	State assembly abolishes Court of Appeals because it refused to uphold replevin law.
John Quincy Adams elected president by House of Representatives.	1825	
Andrew Jackson elected president.	1828	
	1830	State population reaches 687,917.
	1831	Lucie and Thornton Blackburn flee from Louisville.

Introduction
The Buzzel About Kentuck

CRAIG THOMPSON FRIEND

In 1982, while appraising scholarship on Kentucky, state historian James C. Klotter lamented the "relative dearth of good historical works" about the early decades of the Bluegrass State. The pronouncement came as a surprise. Frontier Kentucky has engrossed academics and the public alike since John Filson mythologized it in 1784. Kentuckians traditionally have supported a variety of historical sites and activities that emphasize the state's early years. And historians have produced many studies that channeled public attention to securing the state's heritage, whether through reconstruction and restoration of material culture or by the accumulation of libraries and archives. Still, Klotter understood that public interest had not metamorphosed into scholarly scrutiny. He urged a future generation of historians "to re-study and revise the old masters."[1]

Since the mid-1980s, a new generation of historians and archaeologists has begun to address some gaps that Klotter identified in the historiography. *The Buzzel About Kentuck: Settling the Promised Land* is the first collection of articles since Klotter's review to focus exclusively on early Kentucky and to take up his charge. This volume serves as a benchmark in the shifting focus of scholarship on early Kentucky.

Ironically, the new wave of academic interest poses a query first uttered by a Virginia clergyman in 1775 on the eve of Euro-American colonization of the region: "What a buzzel is this amongst people about *Kentuck?*"[2] The question implies that there was something more to the region's role in early America than we had previously understood and that there is something more to the new wave of interest represented by the essays herein.

The ten articles of the collection, as the subtitle indicates, interpret the "settling of the promised land." The premise that Kentucky was a region of tremendous opportunity was one shared in the mid-1700s by Indians and Euro-Americans. By the 1790s, Jeffersonian Republicans had appropriated it as an ideal that the American West could become a yeoman republic, one rooted in the agrarian patterns that they believed undergirded a virtuous nation. This "agrarian myth" has weighed heavily on Kentucky historians, from John Filson to Frederick Jackson Turner to Thomas D. Clark and Patricia Watlington.

The promise of Kentucky as evinced in this collection, however, differs from that presented by previous historians. In fact, the contributors come to no consensus about the nature of early Kentucky or the promise that it held, but they do agree that settlers' lives and communities were more complex than has been portrayed. After a discussion of the historiographical context for these essays, this introduction ventures an interpretive framework by which, despite their diversity, the articles may be understood as a single corpus.

In 1784, with the publication of *The Discovery, Settlement and Present State of Kentucke,* land speculator John Filson established Kentucky's situation in American historiography even as he sought to make its place in American history. Accompanied by a "Map of Kentucke" that emphasized the excellent topography, extensive river systems, existing trails, and regions of fine and abundant cane, Filson's book set before East Coast Americans the image of a western Edenic garden, one ripe for cultivation by farmers. In the final pages of the book, Filson included "The Adventures of Col. Daniel Boon," a romanticized celebration of the frontiersman that solidified Boone's place in the pantheon of national heroes and Kentucky's frontier character in the mythology of the new nation.[3]

In the late eighteenth century, other western promoters wrote descriptions for their patrons that reinforced Filson's portrait. Harry Toulmin published *A Description of Kentucky in North America* in 1793; Gilbert Imlay's *A Topographical Description of the Western Territory of North America* arrived four years later, with a complete reprint of Filson's text as an appendix.[4] Toulmin, in particular, encouraged the vision of a yeoman republic. His ideal of the Kentucky farm was a thirty-acre homestead where the family planted, harvested, produced, and consumed within the household.[5] This vision of the self-sufficient Kentucky yeoman farmer was etched early into the region's historiography. Yet, neither Toulmin nor Imlay was a historian in the modern sense of the term: they did not view the settlement of Kentucky with a critical eye. Still, when coupled with Filson's work, their interpretations of the agrarian promised land became the most readily available literature on the topic.

Filson and the others wrote not only from their ambitions to sell land or promote a way of life. They held assumptions about the role of the trans-Appalachian West shared by many Americans. Published only one year after Filson's history, Thomas Jefferson's *Notes on the State of Virginia* (1785) reinforced the prevailing image of Kentucky.[6] The work extolled the virtues of the West—openness, simplicity, innocence, newness, and rusticity—and made an appeal for the creation of an agrarian republic in which self-sufficiency would lead to political virtue and disinterestedness. Amid the emerging patriotism of the post-revolutionary era, Jefferson and Filson viewed trans-Appalachia as a blank slate on which the free, republican institutions of a new nation could expand and become an American West populated by Toulmin's yeoman ideal.

Of course, a Jeffersonian portrait of Kentucky did not go unchallenged. With the escalation of partisan politics in the new nation, an author's definition of nationalism often reflected his political loyalties. In 1812, Humphrey Marshall published *The History of Kentucky,* a scathing retrospective of the men who directed Kentucky's political development.[7] As a Federalist, Marshall found himself in the political minority as early as 1793, when he first gained a seat in the state legislature. Two years later the state assembly appointed him to the United States Senate, a position he held until voted out with the Jeffersonian "revolution of 1800." Marshall had many axes to grind, particularly against Jeffersonians like John Breckinridge, George Nicholas, and John Brown. He exerted significant energy depicting many of his enemies as conspirators against the federal government and, consequently, Kentucky's early history as one at odds with a united nation.

Marshall's interpretation of the past made Mann Butler's 1834 *A History of the Commonwealth of Kentucky* more significant than it might have been. Butler wrote his narrative with particular attention to "impartial truth" and condemned Marshall's text because "every man and party of men, who came into collision with Mr. Marshall or his friends, in the exciting and exasperating scenes of the Kentucky story, have been essentially and profoundly misrepresented by him. . . ."[8] Butler did not revert to a more Jeffersonian rendering; he instead broke the cycle of partisan interpretations, addressing much of Marshall's bias and tying Kentucky's history to the larger national portrait of the United States.

In 1847, Daniel Drake wrote *Pioneer Life in Kentucky*, and, although it remained unpublished until 1870, the book expanded on the nationalistic themes of Butler. Because Drake held such abiding love for his mother and because he experienced the frontier through the lens of family life, his story was more attentive to the concerns that would later intrigue modern social historians. For example, in an 1834 public lecture reproduced as an appendix, Drake exalted pioneer families, giving equal regard to the roles of pioneer women and children as to those of frontiersmen. Still, the patriotic fervor was evident. Drake wrapped Kentucky's settlers in the mantle of national heroism, equating their sacrifices with those of the military: "We should plant willows over the spots once fertilized with their blood," he challenged his audience, "and the laurel tree where they met the unequal war of death, and remained conquerors of the little field."[9]

As the century progressed, the nationalism that had characterized earlier histories evolved into chauvinism. One of the most influential arguments set forth was the "germ theory," an observation that American institutions and patterns arrived intact from their Teutonic origins via the Anglo-Saxon heritage. Herbert Baxter Adams most effectively argued this theory, one that reflected contemporary assumptions that American history was the story of the progress of democracy and that peoples of Anglo-Saxon ancestry were destined to spread equality across the continent and possibly farther.

Unlike Jefferson, Filson, and others of the late eighteenth century, historians of the late nineteenth century were not enthralled with trans-Appalachia. America had grown beyond the Mississippi River and survived a civil war that had erupted because of that expansion. That the West had moved beyond Kentucky was, for Kentucky historiography, fortunate. Historians reinterpreted the region as eastern and sought its place within the germ theory. In *Kentucky: Pioneer Commonwealth* (1885), Nathaniel S. Shaler depicted the state as an extension of Virginian culture and one of the sole repositories of the Anglo-Saxon tradition: "All the Western States, as well as those of the South, have been settled by immigrants from several older States, generally with more or less admixtures of people drawn from foreign sources. . . . In Kentucky, on the other hand, we shall find nearly pure English blood, mainly derived from districts that shared the Virginian conditions."[10] Most amusing is Shaler's difficulty situating Kentucky as a western or southern state, for Kentuckians still bicker about their regional identity. But, more important, Shaler identified the state as a key player in the continuity of American tradition, for as its residents migrated farther west, they spread germs of democracy that had been nurtured in the Bluegrass State.

To glorify the triumph of Anglo-Saxon heritage as emphatically as they did, historians targeted the traditions and customs of "lesser" civilizations as proof of the need to extend American culture. We see hints of such distinctions in Shaler's work, although his attentions were directed more toward European cultures. Among most historians, American Indians most directly faced the brunt of these comparisons. Since 1607, many Euro-Americans had seen Indians as barriers to their own economic betterment. By the 1840s, however, Indians stood in the way of much greater designs—the spread of liberty and democracy, the manifest destiny of a nation. Lewis Collins's *History of Kentucky* (1847) reflected much of the emerging jingoism of the era. Collins opened his narrative puzzling about the presence of "ancient monuments" in the Ohio River valley. Jefferson had speculated on these mounds in *Notes on the State of Virginia,* concluding that they served as burial sites. Collins refused to accept that the Shawnee, Wyandot, and Cherokee, whom Boone and other long hunters encountered on the "dark and bloody ground," had the wherewithal to build such structures. He argued that an earlier race of humans superior "in arts, in civilization, and in knowledge" had occupied the region before the "rude tribes" of the frontier period. When contrasted with the "brave and simple race of [white] hunters and farmers" who had "love for order, the respect for law, and the passionate attachment to their kindred race," the baser Indians of Kentucky and farther west deserved little consideration and no claim to the land.[11]

The culmination of these historiographical trends was Theodore Roosevelt's six-volume *The Winning of the West,* published between 1889 and 1896. He situated American expansion as a continuation of European migration, especially that of English, Celtic, and Germanic peoples, and identified Indians as obstacles to the growth of a great nation. Within those mobility patterns, Kentucky held an important role as the first wedge into the West, the initial phase of the "conquest of a continent."[12] Roosevelt's interpretation evidenced the expansionist mentality of late-nineteenth-century Americans.

The dominance of this patriotic history meant that any challenger to the interpretation would struggle to be heard. In fact, when Frederick Jackson Turner presented his essay, "The Significance of the Frontier in American History," at a meeting of the American Historical Association in 1893, few historians gave him much credence. Nevertheless, Turner's work turned Kentucky and American historiography on their heads. He refocused the historical interpretation of America from the germs of European civilization to the contributions of western frontier societies. He described a "democratizing" process by which European institutions of the colonial era became more "American" as settlers transported them through successive frontiers. As a prime example of this process, Kentucky was "a frontier free from the influences of European ideas and institutions."[13] In contrast to Shaler's depiction of Kentucky as an incubator for American institutions of European origin, Turner suggested that the early trans-Appalachian frontier (and those that emerged farther west) filtered European traditions and reformed them into a uniquely American culture.

Turner represented a new wave of historians who researched and wrote history as a vocation. Consequently, their interaction with other academics exposed them to new scientific and economic theories that colored their writings. Turner did see America moving forward, as had his predecessors, but he interpreted that progress through Darwinian models of evolution. Thus, he could portray the frontier as successive stages on which American institutions evolved within each new environment. In a sense, Turner was an early practitioner of geographical history on a grand scale. His study, like those of modern geographical historians, "invariably begins with location."[14] He sought to understand how human relationships with the western landscape shaped cultural development. Specifically, he concluded that democracy and individualism originated on the frontier, rather than in Germanic Europe, and became an "effective force . . . with western preponderance under [Andrew] Jackson and William Henry Harrison, and it meant the triumph of the frontier."[15] By rooting his thesis in the rhetoric of place, Turner established forever his standing in American historiography; for who can write of the frontier without dealing with location? It is probable that we will never escape his long shadow.[16]

Yet, Turner faced a problem with which all historians who pose historical models must grapple—the exceptions. He was not oblivious to this: "with all these similarities [among various frontiers] there are essential differences due to the place element and the time element."[17] Obviously, Turner did not escape the reality that once each frontier came under greater scrutiny, the differences would threaten to overwhelm the similarities and, consequently, his thesis. Still, he embraced the likenesses and left the variations for future generations to debate.

In Kentucky historiography, one of Turner's students, Thomas Perkins Abernathy, was among the first to accept the challenge and attack the frontier thesis. In *Three Virginia Frontiers* (1940), he reevaluated Kentucky's settlement as a struggle between classes. Instead of a frontier that created equality and democracy, Abernathy found powerful land speculators and aristocratic planters dominating Kentucky's formation, just as they controlled earlier frontiers.[18] Rather than the optimistic perspective of Turner, whose frontier thesis developed just as industrial capitalism began to alter the American countryside, Abernathy's interpretation reflected more cynical ideas about political and economic equality in America—ideas fashioned by the trials of the Depression.

In the decade before World War II, Thomas D. Clark began his studies of Kentucky's past. Clark understood well the glaring problem with Turner's thesis: "The pattern of expansion was never uniform over any considerable geographical area, nor within any large segmented part of the more localized social organization. The movement bore telltale marks of the traditional origins of people and institutions—the flavor and coloration of the peculiar traditions of traditional Europe, England, and the eastern Atlantic Coast."[19]

But it was in the consensus-building atmosphere of World War II and the early Cold War that Clark's interpretation coalesced. As he picked apart Turner's grand thesis, Clark pushed forward a theme of continuity despite diversity, stressing the stability of American institutions, the persistence of national character, and the homogeneity of American culture. He understood that, despite their differences, Americans agreed on certain principles, and he introduced these themes into his works repeatedly. In *A History of Kentucky,* for example, he emphasized land-ownership and the tradition of private property as central foundations of Kentucky society; he identified the development of local and state governments as necessary countermeasures to the expansion and antagonisms of the federal government; and he depicted the democratic practices of petitioning government and universal male suffrage as integral to understanding Kentuckians' long struggle for statehood.[20]

The mood of the nation changed in the 1960s and 1970s. Rapid social changes jolted the consensus view of the late 1940s and 1950s, and historians renewed their awareness of tensions in American society, especially class conflict. Lowell Harrison's work reflected the transitional nature of the times: his work preserved much of the consensus model, but also recognized the forces altering American society. In *John Breckinridge: Jeffersonian Republican* (1969), Harrison acknowledged that economic disparities were integral to the political development of the state; for example, he portrayed the constitutional convention of 1799 as a contest between "a wealthy, conservative element" and "a poorer, discontented class." Yet, he would not completely back away from a consensus interpretation. Although a class of poor, unhappy persons had agitated for a new constitution, few changes were made in the document; yet, "popular discontent was sufficiently satisfied so that it was half a century before another convention met."[21] Whether Harrison understood the decline of public agitation as general acceptance of the goals of conservative leaders or as a concession to those with power is never clear.

Harrison led the way into an intense reevaluation of Kentucky's politics during the early republic. In 1972, when Patricia Watlington published *The Partisan Spirit: Kentucky Politics, 1779-1792,* the continuity and consensus of Clark's studies no longer held relevance. Watlington presented the story of Kentucky's first constitution as one of "partisans" and "patricians." Her separation of interests along economic lines mirrored the increased social concerns of the 1960s about poverty and distribution of wealth. In Watlington's analysis, the patricians, acting out of self-interest, managed political hegemony in Kentucky. Eventually they split into two political camps, but both continued to identify with and actively pursue the interests of their own class.[22]

Similarly, in 1979, Joan Wells Coward analyzed early Kentucky politics, in particular, the constitutional conventions of 1792 and 1799. In *Kentucky in the New Republic: The Process of Constitution Making,* Coward elaborated on Watlington's theme. She characterized the 1792 constitution as an effort by the elite to protect republican government from democratic tendencies. By the second constitutional convention of 1799, Kentuckians of all ranks had wearied of the restraints of the first constitution and compromised to "maximize their access to economic and political opportunity."[23] Yet, Coward concluded that despite their agreement to broaden representation, the elite still maintained oligarchic control through reestablishment of the county court system and protection of slavery.

Watlington's and Coward's studies illustrate another concern of the generation of historians who emerged in the 1970s—the political dynamics and relations of government. The Vietnam War and Watergate revealed an exceptionally powerful executive branch, and as historians questioned the credibility of this "imperial presidency," they also became more critical of the historical role of government. Both Coward and Watlington interpreted Kentucky's elites as extensions of Eastern political circles; the processes of constitution making were attempts to bind a wayward western state to the new federal polity.

This theme was most apparent in Mary K. Bonsteel Tachau's *Federal Courts in the Early Republic: Kentucky, 1789-1816* (1978). She portrayed the federal courts in Kentucky as links to the nation "by promulgating a familiar and predictable law and by interpreting public policies in ways that secured the national experience in self-government."[24] Although she avoided explaining the story in terms of conflicting economic groups, Tachau's description of the federal court's personnel was a who's who of Kentucky's economic and social elite. Like the 1792 and 1799 constitutions, the federal court operated as a means to regulate Kentucky's populations, even as it protected their interests.

Since the early 1980s, American and Kentucky historiography have again undergone dramatic change. Dismissing the narrow focus of political studies, new social historians have begun to explore the entire human experience, especially the lives of ordinary people. A proliferation of nonpolitical histories has ensued: community and family studies, women's history, African American studies, environmental history, "new" labor history, "new" political history, "new" economic history. Although interpretations may be reminiscent of older historiographical camps, what makes these fields of study unique is that, beyond the choice of subject, researchers employ techniques and sources from the social sciences to create more analytical portraits of the past.

When Klotter wrote his survey of Kentucky historiography in 1982, the new social history had yet to exert its influence on the profession. Since the mid-1980s, public interest in early Kentucky has resurged, partially attributable to the state's bicentennial celebration in 1992 and to the 1993 centennial of Turner's frontier thesis. Coincidentally, scholarly popularity has also grown. Since the 1960s, social historians have pored over the records of East Coast societies and have produced a solid body of historiographical interpretations for colonial and revolutionary America. Kentucky, Tennessee, and the Old Northwest present the next big challenges. More thorough analyses of the patterns and idiosyncracies of these regions will answer many questions about the themes of the early republic, including democratic and republican tendencies, evolving gender and racial roles, and the market revolution.

Over the last decade, students of early Kentucky have taken up those themes with renewed vigor. Since 1988, they have averaged one dissertation a year, many of which are poised for publication.[25] The first was Stephen Aron's *How the West Was Lost: The Transformation of Kentucky from Daniel Boone to Henry Clay* (1996). Aron traced the transition of the region from a hunters' paradise to a "broken promised land" by exploring the economic development of Kentucky and by touching on the environment, Native American relations, the roles of women, and the situation of the poor.[26] The human complexity of his narrative spoke to the usefulness of social history in filling many of the gaps that Klotter found in Kentucky's historiography.

The essays in *The Buzzel About Kentuck: Settling the Promised Land* exemplify the new social history. In inviting contributors, I sought scholars engaged in new methodologies and materials. I also wanted articles that, in some manner, broke beyond the borders of Kentucky and involved readers in the themes of the early republic. The essays in this volume meet the criteria: they deal either with the broader context of Kentucky in the new nation or with circumstances that made the region unique within that context. While the essays in this collection cover a wide range of topics, they do not cover all the issues in the history of early Kentucky. Combined with other recent scholarship, however, they permit us to comprehend the breadth of experiences found in the trans-Appalachian promised land.

Whatever their historiographical perspectives, historians have remained interested in early Kentucky because it has seemed an anomaly in the new nation. Its physical distance portended political and cultural disconnection. Despite its membership in the early republic, Kentucky appeared not truly incorporated into it, no more so than any other region west of the Appalachians at the turn of the century. Rumors of secession rumbled across the state on several occasions. Stephen Aron expresses it best: even when Kentucky separated from Virginia and became a state in 1792, "the act of political consolidation was not the same as the fact."[27] Its geographical remoteness exacerbated the coarseness of its culture and distanced Kentucky from the political, social, and economic milieux of American society.

Yet, migrants sought to maintain citizenship in American society even as they physically distanced themselves from it. When, in the mid-1770s, Daniel Boone led settlers through the Cumberland Gap, they carried with them two interrelated concerns: how to survive in Kentucky and how to retain their cultural heritage. Part One of this volume, titled "Dependence and Autonomy," explores those anxieties among the region's earliest settlers.

Euro-Americans and their African American slaves were not the first to face the dilemmas of living in Kentucky. During the 1740s and 1750s, American Indians migrated into the Ohio River valley to escape the pressures of white settlement elsewhere. As A. Gwynn Henderson describes in "The Lower Shawnee Town on Ohio: Sustaining Native Autonomy in an Indian 'Republic,'" residents enjoyed an independence and sovereignty that would have been denied them closer to British colonial societies. During the 1740s and 1750s, they profited commercially and diplomatically by playing British and French authorities against each other. By the 1760s, however, their continued participation in European trade and diplomacy slowly threatened their capacity to live on their own terms, eventually forcing the Shawnee and their allies to reject Christianity and colonial commerce just as Euro-American interest in trans-Appalachia increased. Like Indian relations with Europeans elsewhere, as trappers, traders, and colonial administrators constrained native customs, the residents of lower Shawnee Town became obsessed with their political autonomy, legitimacy, and security.[28]

For the Shawnee and their allies, control of Kentucky's hunting lands was a question of self-determination. Their animosity toward and attacks upon white and black settlers were, like their renunciations of Christianity and commercial trade, efforts to protect political and cultural sovereignty. On the eve of the Revolutionary War, as the excursions of Boone and others "opened" the West to Euro-American settlement, Indian renunciation of colonial American ways resulted in violent conflicts between pioneers and regional native peoples for control of Kentucky and delayed large-scale white migration for nearly two decades.[29]

The imperial contests of the 1740s and 1750s were not unique to Kentucky. Exchange networks based on imperial designs developed between Indians, Europeans, and African slaves of the lower Mississippi River valley in the early eighteenth century. By the 1750s, those native peoples faced a similar predicament to that of the Indians of the Ohio River valley. In contrast, the simultaneous European settlement of Louisiana did not permit Indians to dismiss so easily the foreign presence.[30] Indians of the Southeast likewise had to address immediately the rise of Creole populations amongst themselves. As one historian explained, "Had whites remained a small and weak population [in the Southeast], the shifting cycles of conflict along the frontier might have lasted a good deal longer." The Shawnee and their allies, therefore, enjoyed a grace period that Indians closer to white settlement did not.[31]

Increased tensions not only indicated a distancing between Europeans and the residents of lower Shawnee Town, but they also affected most Indians of the Northwest. The Miami, in what would become Indiana, lost much of the French support that had made their negotiations with the English so successful. Only the Revolutionary War slowed English demands, but the results of that conflict proved even more troublesome. For native residents of Vincennes, the "Virginians and the government of the United States would destroy the world of the French and the Piankashaw far more effectively than the British government contemplated in the early 1770s."[32]

But it was Kentucky where such dramatic change immediately occurred. The wedge of white settlement that became Kentucky separated natives into northern and southern tribes, and severely crippled their exchange networks. The waves of settlers who entered the region as the revolutionary crisis subsided did not face the daunting task of settling *among* Indians; they instead had to outlast native reprisals from outside the territory.[33]

In the minds of eighteenth-century Americans, Indian reluctance to share Kentucky with long hunters from Virginia and North Carolina romanticized the promised land. Gradually, the trickle of white Americans and their black slaves into the region became a steady stream. Nancy O'Malley, in her analysis of "Frontier Defenses and Pioneer Strategies in the Historic Settlement Era," explores how early settlers designed forts and stations to secure autonomy and economic opportunity while protecting themselves from Indian attack. Studying the architectural and spatial characteristics of these rudimentary structures, O'Malley determines that their purposes transformed as the dynamics between Euro-Americans and American Indians changed. When the Indian threat faded, therefore, white settlers did not simply abandon forts and stations in a mad dash for land acquisition; rather, the complex collaborative patterns of communal dependence that protected settlers evolved as economic opportunities beckoned.

The pioneers who inhabited these defensive structures were enticed to Kentucky by land speculators who excited people to risk uprooting themselves and their families for the promise of the American Eden—a garden of great potential beckoning to the farmers of the new nation. Even when promoters like Gilbert Imlay exaggerated the region's advantages, few who actually migrated to Kentucky openly contradicted the reports, leaving future homesteaders to deduce that the region was the promised land they had envisioned. As Daniel Blake Smith concludes in "'This Idea in Heaven': Image and Reality on the Kentucky Frontier," settlers arrived with expectations that were nearly impossible to achieve—a theme as applicable to Henderson's Indians as to O'Malley's pioneers. On one end of a continuum of expectations were wealthy land speculators like Richard Henderson who wished to profit both monetarily and politically; on the other end were women and children who migrated involuntarily and hoped merely to survive. As they discovered the limitations and the dangers of life west of the Appalachians, these settlers faced an empty promised land.

For many Kentuckians, those early decades were tumultuous and unpredictable. Still, despite the challenges to their expectations, migrants did enjoy some opportunities in the rough-and-tumble atmosphere of early Kentucky: unregulated and unrestricted squatting rights (at least until a new state government and federal courts could intervene); universal male suffrage in the 1792 state constitution, protecting patterns of democratic participation that had arisen through militia organizations; and community formation as settlers migrated in family and neighborhood groups to new homes in Mayslick, Strode's Station, and other locations.[34]

By the 1790s, even these opportunities became less certain. The decline of the Indian "menace" lessened the need for collective action. Increased population pressures reduced the availability of good land. And the arrival of wealthier planters and merchants threatened to erode democratic opportunity. Consequently, the declension of the American Eden pushed many Kentuckians into overt challenges such as interest in James Wilkinson's plans of insurrection in the late 1780s; formation of reactionary groups (for example, participation in the Cane Ridge revival of 1801); petitioning and effigy-burning (as did the Lexington Democratic Society during the 1790s); or violence (for example, the torching of the Fayette County land records in 1803).[35]

Kentucky's pioneer era only faintly resembled that of other regions settled during the 1780s and 1790s. In central New York, Euro-Americans came upon a land that, like Kentucky, had largely been abandoned by native residents. Unlike Kentucky, however, where the dominant Indian nation, the Shawnee, had chosen to reject American culture and settlement, the Iroquois of New York enjoyed extensive commercial relations with white Americans and hesitated to retaliate. Central New Yorkers, released from the need to hide in forts and stations, more aggressively pursued the formation of their society.[36]

A closer parallel may be drawn between Kentucky's pioneer era and the settlement of Illinois. Waves of European hunters and traders made first contact with the Illinois and Kickapoo Indians. The latter eventually rejected the trade, like their Shawnee neighbors to the east, and chose to restrict violently further Euro-American encroachment. Kentucky militias struck at the Kickapoo in the 1790s; Anthony Wayne's victory at the Battle of Fallen Timbers in 1794 weakened Kickapoo alliances with the defeated Indians. Still, whites had to wait until the War of 1812, when the Kickapoo finally agreed to peace, to settle places like Sugar Creek. Again, however, the absence of Indian habitation in Kentucky proved a distinguishing feature of its pioneer era.[37]

The hazards and anxieties of Kentucky pioneer life seemed more complicated by what settlers perceived as neglect by first the Confederation Congress and then by the federal government. In the 1780s, in particular, the Confederation viewed Kentucky as undeserving of military protection because of the absence of an immediate native presence. While George Rogers Clark and his troops engaged Indians in the Old Northwest, settlers of Kentucky had to rely on their own defensive structures—the forts and stations about which O'Malley writes—and address their own disappointments—as Smith relates. Their success at outlasting native attacks and overcoming psychological barriers made the small groups of settlers of the 1770s and 1780s the vanguard of a tremendous wave of migrants in the 1790s. Again, the federal government appeared disinterested in Kentuckians' needs. It hesitated to negotiate opening the Mississippi River to their trade; it passed a whiskey tax that struck the corn farmers of the region. Rumors of secession circulated.[38]

Although disillusionment and disenchantment was evident, Kentucky had not lost its appeal. While for some settlers the promise of Kentucky seemed to fade, others were optimistic and opportunistic. The designs and activities of these gentry politicians, yeoman farmers, and urban laborers are the subjects of Part Two, "Enacting Expectations."

As the new nation expanded westward, concerns about its political and economic direction abounded. A Jeffersonian republic was far from certain and, in many places, those in power had yet to decide whether they wanted to be "Fathers of the People" or "Friends of the People." William Cooper's decision to join the Hamiltonian ranks in New York demonstrated how difficult and unpredictable the choice between Republicans and Federalists could be.[39] In Ohio, Jeffersonians had to employ evangelical Christian rhetoric to convince settlers of the need to support republican reform.[40]

The gentry who led Kentucky's development in the 1790s, however, had strong ties to Thomas Jefferson and James Madison; their problems arose from neither rhetorical inadequacies nor partisan indecisiveness. In "Kentucky *in* the New Republic: A Study of Distance and Connection," Marion Nelson Winship explores their efforts to bind Kentucky to a republican vision of the nation despite their geographical separation from the political center. While distance played a role in Kentuckians' autonomy over their own lives, it also provided the structure and discourse necessary for the gentry to relate to the emerging nation, especially the rhetoric of geographical distance found in their complaints about poor commercial routes and inadequate protection from the Indians. Gentry politicians like John Breckinridge, George Nicholas, and John Brown expected to reinforce connections with Jeffersonian Republicans in Philadelphia and assure the establishment of a republican state in Kentucky. Their activities, epitomized by Democratic-Republican Societies, the Kentucky Resolves, and the 1792 and 1799 state constitutions, were part of a Jeffersonian plan for American development. The political prominence of Kentucky's Jeffersonians boded well for a republic based upon yeoman farming.

The network of political associations established by the gentry paralleled a web of economic markets that would eventually alter their world. Connection to distant markets was not new: Henderson's examination of the lower Shawnee Town reveals commercial relations between native peoples and Europeans in the 1750s. The arrival of Euro-Americans into Kentucky, combined with new native rejection of their culture, however, reversed the commercial proclivities of the region's residents. O'Malley and Smith both recognize pioneer communities characterized by self-sufficiency and, although commercial opportunity was available, as Smith's depiction of land promoter Richard Henderson clearly attests, most early settlers tended toward subsistence farming.[41]

Elsewhere in the early republic, an economic transformation seemed to be under way. In the Mississippi Territory, where numerous ethnic cultures had built extensive commercial networks, the shift to a plantation economy in the 1790s and early 1810s was not difficult.[42] Along the North Shore of Massachusetts, colonial developments—a resident mercantile class, its accumulation of capital, and the masses of potential urban laborers—made a rapid transition to industrialization easier.[43] As a plethora of historians have lately concluded, the early republic saw urban and rural capitalism take root across the new nation.[44] Not until after Jefferson secured usage of the Mississippi River in 1803, however, could Kentuckians aspire to pursue the same course.

Still, their economy was neither stagnant nor rudimentary. For the waves of people that arrived in the 1790s and early 1800s, subsistence farming became one small facet of an increasingly complex economic structure. In "'Work & Be Rich': Economy and Culture on the Bluegrass Farm," I suggest that in their desires to pursue profit and in their expectations to meet the moral demands of their culture, farmers in central Kentucky solidified a social structure based on land-ownership and drew more clearly the distinctions between landed and unpropertied Kentuckians. The resulting economic patterns of the Bluegrass were a delicate balance of subsistence and commercial production that required a farmer to fulfill his proper role in a community and that required society to support him in his pursuits.

Settlers south of the Green River did not face such moral questions, at least not initially. In his analysis of "Opportunity on the Frontier South of the Green," Christopher Waldrep explains that in the 1790s and 1800s emigrants arrived fully involved in capitalistic activities. Waldrep argues that the frontier experience had little effect on the development of society in western Kentucky—that before their arrival, settlers already understood and accepted the hierarchical society and capitalistic economy of commercial America and willingly recreated it in western Kentucky. His brief study of Matthew Lyon within the article extends his argument to the political realm, reinforcing Winship's idea that distance was not a disruptive factor in the transplanting of eastern patterns to Kentucky.

The ease with which political and economic elites entrenched themselves in Kentucky society did not mean they would rule unchallenged. By 1799, the constitution of 1792, which had assured political equality, came under attack as insufficient by those to whom it granted suffrage. Efforts to ensure the promise of individual independence harbored within Jeffersonian expectations belied the discrepancies of wealth and land-ownership that had arisen. In "'The Poor Men to Starve': The Lives and Times of Workingmen in Early Lexington," Stephen A. Aron describes how, always dependent upon the needs and pocketbooks of more wealthy Lexingtonians, black and white laborers yearned for the independence of property ownership, or at least comfortable existences. While some men successfully escaped their meager situations, widespread consumption of alcohol and white resentment against free blacks and "hired-out" slaves intimated increasing discontent and concern. As Lexington's fortunes waned in the mid-1810s, so too did the opportunities available to laborers.

The declining circumstances of Lexington's workingmen signaled changing social patterns after the turn of the century. An influx of merchants, lawyers, bankers, and other middle-class entrepreneurs during the 1790s metamorphosed the pioneers' world of the 1770s and 1780s. Although Kentuckians began the transition to a more capitalist society later than most other regions of the new nation, by the War of 1812 they had not only caught up, but dominated in some rural and urban capitalistic pursuits—hemp cultivation, salt and saltpeter production, and the manufacturing of bagging and rope.[45]

The economic and political changes of the era challenged Kentucky's social construction. The essays in Part Three, "A Revised Promised Land," relate how women and African Americans found within those changes new opportunities. Many settlers who had eagerly expected to find a promised land realized that its acquisition was more difficult than they had imagined. One response was the revivalism of the early 1800s. The camp meeting became a "symbolic re-enactment of community formation," an effort to fight a perceived declension of those positive qualities of Kentucky life in the 1770s and 1780s.[46] Itinerant preachers encouraged participants to reevaluate and change their lives, their neighbors' lives, and their communities "within new boundaries of self-control and self-exploration."[47] Whether surrounding a stump speaker in the woods or listening to a pulpit preacher in the local church, revival participants enjoyed greater individual expression and equality before denominational officials—patterns reminiscent of the democratic orientation of pioneer life. Revivalism released people, if only momentarily, from the frustrations of expectations unattained or promises unfulfilled.

Despite the uplifting quality of evangelicalism, it posed significant challenge to many of the tenets of late eighteenth- and early nineteenth-century America: class privilege, generational hierarchy, slaveholding, gendered spheres, and racial separation. The democratizing effects of evangelical Christianity, while offering new opportunities for Aron's workingmen, black slaves, white women, and others on the margins, strained traditional social structures. In Kentucky, therefore, a region where traditional hierarchies had yet to solidify, evangelicalism held particular relevance to societal formation.[48]

In "The Beginnings of Afro-American Christianity among Kentucky Baptists," Ellen Eslinger interprets the Second Great Awakening as a catalyst for black Christianity in Kentucky. She determines that African Americans who were members of larger slaveholdings were more likely to participate in the new revivalism and reaped benefits, including some degree of racial equality as protected by evangelical congregations. As black Kentuckians embraced Christianity, they created new patterns of community, thereby redefining themselves and their culture.

Similarly, Blair A. Pogue finds evangelicalism relevant to gender relations. In "'I Cannot Believe the Gospel that is So Much Preached': Gender, Belief, and Discipline in Baptist Religious Culture," Pogue describes the influences of theological doctrines on the region's men and women. Her essay stresses the role of personal belief—an often overlooked consideration in history. As a result of the Great Revival of 1801, religious individuals wrestled with issues of personal belief and theological orthodoxy; even more secular individuals, like Aron's workingmen, were swayed momentarily to turn from intemperance and immorality to become more introspective. Among Baptists, such intensified self-examination led to occasional inversions of gender roles and the enforcement of doctrine through church discipline. To verify their beliefs, Baptist men and women, often unwittingly, responded in radical ways to church doctrine, challenging gender patterns well into the 1850s.

During the early 1800s, the subtle transformations in racial and gendered relationships hinted of even larger changes within Kentucky. Soon after the War of 1812, Aron's workingmen experienced the economic downturn that affected much of the nation. Across the state, propertied citizens sought to secure status by pushing unpropertied and poorer citizens to the bottom of the social ladder. The issue of debtor relief, paramount to restoring the promise of Kentucky, heightened economic and social tensions. State representatives, encouraged by small farmers who had borrowed heavily from local merchants or banks, wanted to grant debtors more time to pay loans. Other assemblymen sought to protect the monied interests. During this Relief War, the state court of appeals struck down the attempts of relief proponents who, in return, maneuvered to replace the court. A cultural crisis exacerbated by anxieties over social and economic inequality on one side and fear of a collapse of constitutional order on the other, the Old Court/New Court struggle was the moment at which the Jeffersonian orientation of Kentucky unraveled. In a coup of rhetoric, proponents of commercial growth successfully coopted their opposition's claim to guardianship over independence and traditional republican principles, squelching the dream of a Jeffersonian, agrarian West.[49]

Thus, the yeoman promised land of Kentucky, which had begun to fade in the 1790s, disintegrated in the 1820s. Kentuckians had struggled through the dangers of the frontier, the difficulties of establishing farms and communities, the trials of economic decline, and personal battles about belief, and now the Edenic promise seemed remote. In greater numbers, white Kentuckians looked westward for new gardens to create.

Similarly, for black Kentuckians, the ideal lay elsewhere. Karolyn Smardz studies the lives and adventures of two Kentucky slaves in "'There We Were in Darkness,—Here We Are in Light': Kentucky Slaves and the Promised Land." Increased emphasis on industrial and commercial development altered the patterns of everyday life for every person. Hired-out slaves, like Thornton Blackburn, worked in the towns and cities of the region, congregated with free blacks and other hired-outs, and began to experience some measure of self-determination.[50] When the opportunity arose in 1831, Blackburn and his wife fled Louisville. Their quest for freedom eventually took them to Canada, but they never truly escaped their connections to Kentucky—whether chased through Ohio and Michigan by their former owners or aiding other Kentucky runaways in their Toronto home. A fitting conclusion to this collection, Smardz's study relates most poignantly the continued appeal of the ideal of the promised land.

In America, the garden of opportunity was always evolving, both geographically across the continent and temporally across the years. The peoples of Kentucky—the myriad populations at lower Shawnee Town, station-building pioneers, daydreaming land speculators, wealthy gentry, struggling yeomen, impoverished tenants, inebriated workingmen, enslaved blacks, men of commerce, the dispossessed, the pietistic—were part of a constantly mobile population that sought, found, lost, and moved across space and time in search of the promised land. Their stories are told in the pages that follow.

Notes

The author wishes to thank Tom Appleton and Karen Guest for their readings of this introduction and helpful comments.

1. James C. Klotter, "Clio in the Commonwealth: The Status of Kentucky History," *Register of the Kentucky Historical Society* 80 (1982): 3-4.

2. John Brown Sr. to William Preston, 5 May 1775, Lyman Draper Manuscript Collection, 4QQ15, State Historical Society of Wisconsin, Madison.

3. John Filson, *The Discovery, Settlement and Present State of Kentucke* (Wilmington, Del.: James Adams, 1784); idem, "Map of Kentucke" (Philadelphia: T. Rook, 1784); Willard Rouse Jillson, *Filson's Kentucke* (Louisville: John P. Morton, 1929), 143-44; John Mack Faragher, *Daniel Boone: The Life and Legend of an American Pioneer* (New York: Henry Holt, 1992), 5-6.

4. Harry Toulmin, *A Description of Kentucky in North America: To Which Are Prefixed Miscellaneous Observations Regarding the United States* (London: n.p., 1793); Gilbert Imlay, *A Topographical Description of the Western Territory of North America, Containing a Succinct Account of Its Soil, Climate, Natural History, Population, Agriculture, Manners, and Customs* (New York: Samuel Campbell, 1797; London: J. Debride, 1797).

5. See particularly Harry Toulmin, "Comments on America and Kentucky," *Register of the Kentucky Historical Society* 47 (1949): 3-20, 96-115. Toulmin moved to Kentucky to experience the yeoman lifestyle himself, but the fact that he rented his thirty-acre farm for eighteen pounds a year suggests how little commitment he had to the ideal and how distant he was from those who invested all they had to create such a farm; Imlay, *A Topographical Description of the Western Territory*, 173.

6. Thomas Jefferson, *Notes on the State of Virginia* (Paris: Philippe-Denis Pierres, 1785); William Peden, "Introduction," in *Notes on the State of Virginia*, ed. William Peden (Chapel Hill: Univ. of North Carolina Press, 1955), xi-xxv.

7. Humphrey Marshall, *The History of Kentucky Including an Account of the Discovery, Settlement, Progressive Improvement, Political and Military Events, and Present State of the Country*, 2 vols. (Frankfort: Henry Gore, 1812).

8. Mann Butler, *A History of the Commonwealth of Kentucky* (Louisville: Wilcox, Dickerman, 1834), vii, ix.

9. Daniel Drake, *Pioneer Life in Kentucky: A Series of Reminiscential Letters*, ed. Charles D. Drake (Cincinnati: Robert Clarke, 1870), 244.

10. Nathaniel S. Shaler, *Kentucky: Pioneer Commonwealth* (Boston: Houghton-Mifflin, 1885), 22-23.

11. Lewis and Richard H. Collins, *History of Kentucky*, 2 vols. (Covington, Ky.: Collins, 1878), 1: 247, 273. Several historians wrote county histories in the late nineteenth century that also reflected this jingoism; see George W. Ranck, *History of Lexington, Kentucky* (Cincinnati: Robert Clarke, 1872); William Henry Perrin, *History of Bourbon, Scott, Harrison, and Nicholas Counties, Kentucky* (n.p., 1882); and idem, *History of Fayette County* (Chicago: O.L. Baskin, 1882).

12. Theodore Roosevelt, *The Winning of the West: An Account of the Exploration and Settlement of Our Country from the Alleghanies to the Pacific*, 6 vols. (New York: G.P. Putnam's Sons, 1889), 1: 22.

13. Frederick Jackson Turner, "The Significance of the Frontier in American History," *Annual Report of the American Historical Association for the Year of 1893* (Washing-

ton, D.C.: n.p., 1894); idem, "Contributions of the West to American Democracy," in *The Frontier in American History* (New York: Henry Holt, 1921), 253; idem, "Western State-Making in the Revolutionary Era," *American Historical Review* 1 (1895-96): 70-87, 251-69.

14. Carville Earle, "Introduction: The Practice of Geographical History," in *Geographical Inquiry and American Historical Problems* (Stanford: Stanford Univ. Press, 1992), 6.

15. Turner, "Significance of the Frontier," 217.

16. For an insightful discussion of Turner's lingering influence and recent challenges, see John Mack Faragher, "The Significance of the Frontier in American Historiography," in *Rereading Frederick Jackson Turner: "The Significance of the Frontier in American History" and Other Essays*, ed. John Mack Faragher(New York: Henry Holt, 1994), 225-41.

17. Turner, "Significance of the Frontier," 210.

18. Thomas Abernathy, *Three Virginia Frontiers* (Baton Rouge: Louisiana State Univ. Press, 1940); idem, "Democracy and the Southern Frontier," *Journal of Southern History* 4 (1938): 3-13.

19. Thomas D. Clark, *Frontier America* (New York: Charles Scribner's Sons, 1959), 3.

20. Idem, *A History of Kentucky*, rev. ed. (Lexington: John Bradford Press, 1960), especially chaps. 5 and 6.

21. Lowell H. Harrison, *John Breckinridge: Jeffersonian Republican* (Louisville: Filson Club, 1969), 93, 108.

22. Patricia Watlington, *The Partisan Spirit: Kentucky Politics, 1779-1792* (New York: Atheneum Press, 1972).

23. Joan Wells Coward, *Kentucky in the New Republic: The Process of Constitution Making* (Lexington: Univ. Press of Kentucky, 1978), 163.

24. Mary K. Bonsteel Tachau, *Federal Courts in the Early Republic: Kentucky, 1789-1816* (Princeton: Princeton Univ. Press, 1978), 199.

25. Among the pertinent dissertations produced in recent years are Ellen Eslinger, "The Great Revival in Bourbon County, Kentucky" (Ph.D. diss., University of Chicago, 1988); Fredrika Johanna Teute, "Land, Liberty, and Labor in the Post-Revolutionary Era: Kentucky as the Promised Land" (Ph.D. diss., Johns Hopkins University, 1988); Sandra VanBurkleo, "'That Our Pure Republican Principles Might Not Wither': Kentucky's Relief Crisis and the Pursuit of 'Moral Justice,' 1818-1826" (Ph.D. diss., University of Minnesota, 1988); Stephen A. Aron, "How the West Was Lost: The Transformation of Kentucky from Daniel Boone to Henry Clay" (Ph.D. diss., University of California at Berkeley, 1990); Elizabeth A. Perkins, "Border Life: Experience and Perception in the Revolutionary Ohio Valley" (Ph.D. diss., Northwestern University, 1992); Gail S. Terry, "Family Empires: A Frontier Elite in Virginia and Kentucky" (Ph.D. diss., College of William and Mary, 1992); Craig Thompson Friend, "Inheriting Eden: The Creation of Society and Community in Early Kentucky, 1792-1812" (Ph.D. diss., University of Kentucky, 1995); Matthew G. Schoenbachler, "The Origins of Jacksonian Politics: Central Kentucky, 1790-1840" (Ph.D. diss., University of Kentucky, 1996); Blair A. Pogue, "Baptist Religious Culture, Gender, and Race in Virginia and Kentucky, 1780-1860" (Ph.D. dissertation-in-progress, College of William and Mary); Marion Nelson Winship, "The Virginia Planter beyond the Appalachians: A Study of Colonial Chesapeake Influence in

Early National Cultures, North and South of the Ohio River" (Ph.D. dissertation-in-progress, University of Pennsylvania).

26. Stephen A. Aron, *How the West Was Lost: The Transformation of Kentucky from Daniel Boone to Henry Clay* (Baltimore: Johns Hopkins Univ. Press, 1996).

27. Ibid., 194.

28. See Kevin Gosner, *Soldiers of the Virgin: The Moral Economy of a Colonial Maya Rebellion* (Tucson: Univ. of Arizona Press, 1992), 9-10.

29. Also see A. Gwynn Henderson, "Dispelling the Myth: Seventeenth- and Eighteenth-Century Indian Life in Kentucky," *Register of the Kentucky Historical Society* 90 (1992): 1-25.

30. Daniel H. Usner Jr., *Indians, Settlers, and Slaves in a Frontier Exchange Economy: The Lower Mississippi Valley before 1783* (Chapel Hill: Univ. of North Carolina Press, 1992).

31. Joyce E. Chaplin, *An Anxious Pursuit: Agricultural Innovation and Modernity in the Lower South, 1730-1815* (Chapel Hill: Univ. of North Carolina Press, 1993), 281.

32. Andrew R.L. Cayton, *Frontier Indiana* (Bloomington: Indiana Univ. Press, 1996), 69.

33. Colin G. Calloway, *The American Revolution in Indian Country: Crisis and Diversity in Native American Communities* (New York: Cambridge Univ. Press, 1995), 1-25.

34. For discussions of land speculation and profit, see Stephen Aron, "Pioneers and Profiteers: Land Speculation and the Homestead Ethic in Frontier Kentucky," *Western Historical Quarterly* 23 (1992): 179-98; idem, "Significance of the Frontier in the Transition to Capitalism," *The History Teacher* 27 (1994): 271-76; Neal O. Hammon, "Settlers, Land Jobbers, and Outlyers: A Quantitative Analysis of Land Acquisition on the Kentucky Frontier," *Register of the Kentucky Historical Society* 84 (1986): 241-62.

Little has been done on the democratic precedents for the first state constitution. Two preliminary efforts are Ellen Eslinger, "The Problems of Governing Virginia's Kentucky Frontier" (paper presented at the Southern Historical Association, Louisville, 1994); and Harry S. Laver, "'Chimney Corner Constitutions': Democratization and Its Limits in Frontier Kentucky," *Register of the Kentucky Historical Society* 95 (1997): 337-67.

Likewise, scholars have only begun to explore community formation in frontier Kentucky; see Ellen Eslinger, "Migration and Kinship on the Trans-Appalachian Frontier: Strode's Station, Kentucky," *Filson Club History Quarterly* 62 (1988): 52-66; and Gail S. Terry, "Sustaining the Bonds of Kinships in a Trans-Appalachian Migration: The Cabell-Breckinridge Slaves Move West," *Virginia Magazine of History and Biography* 102 (1994): 455-76.

35. Disillusionment also manifested in animosity toward the federal government; see Patricia Watlington, "Discontent in Frontier Kentucky," *Register of the Kentucky Historical Society* 65 (1967): 77-93; and Mary K. Bonsteel Tachau, "The Whiskey Rebellion in Kentucky: A Forgotten Episode in Civil Disobedience," *Journal of the Early Republic* 2 (1982): 439-59.

36. Alan Taylor, *William Cooper's Town: Power and Persuasion on the Frontier of the Early American Republic* (New York: Alfred A. Knopf, 1995), 32-40.

37. John Mack Faragher, *Sugar Creek: Life on the Illinois Prairie* (New Haven: Yale Univ. Press, 1986), 10-36.

38. Cayton, *Frontier Indiana*, 70-97.

39. Taylor, *William Cooper's Town*, 154-59.

40. Andrew R.L. Cayton, "'Language Gives Way to Feelings': Rhetoric, Republicanism, and Religion in Jeffersonian Ohio," in *The Pursuit of Public Power: Political Culture in Ohio, 1787-1861*, eds. Jeffrey P. Brown and Andrew R.L. Cayton (Kent, Ohio: Kent State Univ. Press, 1994), 31-48.

41. Studies of commercial activities of early pioneers, beyond speculation in land, include Elizabeth A. Perkins, "The Consumer Frontier: Household Consumption in Early Kentucky," *Journal of American History* 78 (1991): 486-510; Gary A. O'Dell, "The Trotter Family, Gunpowder, and Early Kentucky Entrepreneurship, 1784-1833," *Register of the Kentucky Historical Society* 88 (1990): 5-23; and Craig Thompson Friend, "Merchants and Markethouses: Reflections on Moral Economy in Early Kentucky," *Journal of the Early Republic* 17 (1997): 553- 74.

42. Christopher Morris, *Becoming Southern: The Evolution of a Way of Life: Warren County and Vicksburg, Mississippi, 1770-1860* (New York: Oxford Univ. Press, 1995), 23-41.

43. Daniel Vickers, *Farmers and Fishermen: Two Centuries of Work in Essex County, Massachusetts, 1630-1850* (Chapel Hill: Univ. of North Carolina Press, 1994), 262-324.

44. Among the many books on this economic transformation are Allan Kulikoff, *The Agrarian Origins of American Capitalism* (Charlottesville: Univ. Press of Virginia, 1992); Charles Sellers, *The Market Revolution: Jacksonian America, 1815-1846* (New York: Oxford Univ. Press, 1991); and Christopher Clark, *The Roots of Rural Capitalism: Western Massachusetts, 1780-1860* (Ithaca: Cornell Univ. Press, 1990).

45. Tench Coxe, *A Statement of the Arts and Manufactures of the United States of America for the Year 1810* (Philadelphia: A. Cornman, 1814), 2-43.

46. Eslinger, "Great Revival in Bourbon County," 9; Samuel S. Hill, "Cane Ridge Had a Context: Let's See What They Were," in *Cane Ridge in Context: Perspectives on Barton W. Stone and the Revival*, ed. Anthony L. Dunnavant (Nashville: Disciples of Christ Historical Society, 1992), 117-30. For context on central Kentucky before the revival, see Ellen Eslinger, "Some Notes on the History of Cane Ridge prior to the Great Revival," *Register of the Kentucky Historical Society* 91 (1993): 1-23.

47. A. Gregory Schneider, "From Democratization to Domestication: The Transitional Orality of the American Methodist Circuit Rider," in *Communication and Change in American Religious History*, ed. Leonard I. Sweet (Grand Rapids, Mich.: William B. Eerdmans Publishing, 1993), 142; Christopher Waldrep, "The Making of a Border State Society: James McGready, the Great Revival, and the Prosecution of Profanity in Kentucky," *American Historical Review* 99 (1994): 457- 87.

48. Christine Leigh Heyrman, *Southern Cross: The Beginnings of the Bible Belt* (New York: Alfred A. Knopf, 1997); Nathan O. Hatch, *The Democratization of American Christianity* (New Haven: Yale Univ. Press, 1989).

49. For the constitutional and legal context of the relief crisis, see Sandra F. VanBurkleo, "'The Paws of Banks': The Origins and Significance of Kentucky's Decision to Tax Federal Bankers, 1818-1820," *Journal of the Early Republic* 9 (1989): 457-87; Schoenbachler, "The Origins of Jacksonian Politics."

50. A worthwhile overview of the position of blacks in Kentucky's early society is Juliet E.K. Walker, "The Legal Status of Free Blacks in Early Kentucky, 1792-1825," *Filson Club History Quarterly* 57 (1983): 382-95.

PART ONE

Dependence and Autonomy

By the late 1730s, lower Shawnee Town had been established along the banks of the Ohio River, with the bluffs of Kentucky in the distance. In his mural, Robert Dafford depicts a winter scene at the village: men and women in customary clothing and jewelry, women carrying sticks to their huts, and wooden-frame residences covered with tree bark and animal hides. Courtesy of Portsmouth Murals Inc., Portsmouth, Ohio

The Lower Shawnee Town on Ohio
Sustaining Native Autonomy in an Indian "Republic"

A. GWYNN HENDERSON

On June 13, 1752, the council at LoggsTown between commissioners of the colony of Virginia and the Indians "on Ohio"—the Six Nations, Shawnee, Delaware, and Wyandot—concluded. Also in attendance was an agent of the Ohio Land Company, Christopher Gist, and two representatives from Pennsylvania, George Croghan and Andrew Montour. The colonial commissioners obtained a reaffirmation of the 1744 Treaty of Lancaster in which the Six Nations ceded to Virginia the lands bordering the upper Ohio River. The commissioners also secured from the Indians the "Liberty of setting a fixed Trade to supply them with necessities" and "Leave to build Two Forts." The commissioners gave a large present of goods to the various attending nations to seal the agreement.[1]

Because the Twightwees did not attend the council, the colonial commissioners directed William Trent, an Indian agent and trading partner with Croghan, to deliver the Twightwees' share of the goods to Pickawillany, their village on the Great Miami River.[2] On June 21, accompanied by Montour as interpreter, Trent started west along the overland traders' path that linked LoggsTown to the other Indian villages "on Ohio."[3] Loaded on their pack horses was a "very large present of goods" for the Twightwees that undoubtedly included standard items in the Indian trade such as gunpowder, bar lead, gunflints, brass kettles, silver brooches, armbands, earrings, vermillion, tobacco, ready-made clothing, and kegs of rum. With bells tinkling on the animals between them, Trent and Montour journeyed toward the Twightwees' village carrying with them a string of black and white wampum, a belt of wampum to seal the gift in council, and a scarlet cloak, a hat, a jacket, a shirt, and stockings for the Twightwees' chief.[4]

Upon arrival first at the Wyandot Indian town on the Muskingum, and then at the Delaware town at Hockhocken, Trent and Montour heard disturbing rumors of an attack by the French and their Indian allies on

Pickawillany. Similar news met the men when they reached the Delaware village at the Meguck on the headwaters of the Scioto River.[5] As seasoned travelers in this Indian country—the region west of the Juniata River and east of the Wabash River—Trent and Montour may not have been surprised by the news. For several years before 1752, reports had been circulating of repeated incidents of capture and murder of traders and Indians alike.[6]

Resolving to "know the certainty" of the stories, Trent and Montour turned south after leaving the Meguck and for three days traveled the overland traders' path to the Shawnee capital situated at the confluence of the Scioto and Ohio Rivers. Women tending the fields north of town or perhaps men stationed atop the rock lookout south of the confluence may have been the first to spot the party and to spread the word of its arrival.[7] For upon entering the settlement, they received the customary visitors' salutation: "firing of guns, and whooping and hollowing" of the inhabitants, many of whom they probably knew from previous trips to the region.[8]

Given the events of the preceding few years, coupled with the attack on Pickawillany, Trent and Montour arrived in a town certainly abuzz with gossip. A harlequin crowd of people gathered: women in short shifts or calico bed-gowns wearing silver earrings asking for news of their relatives, their dark hair tied back with ribbons and their babies in their arms; men wearing black silk head scarves or roaches adorned with feathers, silver armbands and nose rings, varicolored shirts, match-coats, breechclouts, leggings, and moccasins, helping transfer the goods into Croghan's storehouse while discussing the political implications of the attack.[9] A handful of Twightwees from Pickawillany had escaped to the town, finding refuge in the homes of relatives. Similarly, Thomas Burney and Andrew McBryer, two English traders in the employ of Trent, also fled to the lower Shawnee Town, where they explained to Trent and Montour the events at Pickawillany: On June 21, about 240 French, Ottawas, and Chippewas attacked the Twightwee village and killed six persons, including the chief Old Briton (also known as La Demoiselle), and an English trader, before departing with six traders as prisoners.[10]

In the council house the day after their arrival, Trent and Montour discussed the attack with those who had escaped, chiefs of the Six Nations, and, undoubtedly, the chiefs of the lower Shawnee Town. Producing a black belt of wampum tied to a scalp, the Shawnee who had been at Pickawillany during the attack announced that they had "struck the French" and expected all their allies to do the same. The captains and Twightwee warriors also produced a string of black wampum and a large belt of white wampum. They asked for help from their allies in the protection of their families and spoke about the attack. Six Nations Indians, Trent, and Montour then planned a journey to view the destruction and assist the Twightwees who remained at Pickawillany.

Recovery of goods and people, not revenge, was the purpose behind the excursion five days later of a party of "22 men and boys, [both] whites and Indians" to Pickawillany. In his journal, Trent states that more men would have participated if not for the "quantity of liquor that had come into town."[11] After a "very tiresome and tedious journey" of a little over two weeks, the entourage returned to the lower Shawnee Town. The men had carried skins and other trade goods between "six hundred and seven hundred miles" all told, in weather so hot the "Indian dogs dropped dead as they were hunting."[12] One-third of the salvaged goods belonged to George Croghan; some of the rest likely were shared by Croghan and Trent.[13] Trent probably placed all the goods in Croghan's lower Shawnee Town storehouse for inventory and calculation of losses.

Not until a month after they had left LoggsTown did Trent and Montour finally attend to their diplomatic task. On August 4, 1752, a council was opened at the lower Shawnee Town for presentation of the LoggsTown gift to the Twightwees. Attending the council was Scarouady (an Oneida and spokesman for the Indians "on Ohio" in international councils), Six Nations members, headmen of the Shawnee divisions and possibly their "great chief" Newcommer, and Delaware representatives.[14] The young Piankashaw king and three other men attended the council as representatives of the refugees, along with the widow of Old Briton, late chief of Pickawillany. A contingent of six Cherokee that had just arrived in town also attended.

The meeting began badly. Those assembled waited for some time before it opened, and upon commencement, the Shawnee hoisted a suit of French colors, an incredible act given recent events. Incensed, Trent leaped to his feet and announced to those assembled that he considered the act "an affront to his Majesty, the King of Great Britain." Not about to conduct English business under the French king's flag, he stormed out, followed by Montour.

As soon as one of the Cherokee in attendance understood the reason for Trent's behavior, he struck the colors and threw them "away as far as he could throw them." Trent and Montour returned to the council, and the meeting proceeded. Trent presented the LoggsTown gift to the Twightwees, reinforcing the Twightwee-Virginia chain of friendship with a belt of wampum. The Six Nations, Shawnee, Delaware, and Twightwees reaffirmed their alliances to each other and to the English, sealing the commitments with strings and belts of wampum, a shell, beaver blankets, feathered pipes, and twists of tobacco. Finally, the Cherokee, concerned about the implications of their involvement in the deaths of several English traders, requested the Six Nations and Delaware to intercede on their behalf with the English.

The destruction of Pickawillany, Trent and Montour's visit to the lower Shawnee Town, and the conflicting native responses concerning the French illustrate the growing "international" tensions in Ohio Indian country in the mid-1700s. However, the descriptions of these events and native reactions also illustrate the geographical, economic, and cultural significance of the lower Shawnee Town and the role it played during this period. Native economic and cultural considerations led the Shawnee and Six Nations Iroquois to found the town at the confluence of the Scioto and Ohio Rivers. In the region surrounding the mouth of the Scioto River were rich natural resources and access to aboriginal and European trade routes. Here they could control their own future. Many of the town's inhabitants had lived in close proximity to Europeans at one time or another and had watched as European settlements steadily encroached on native lands. They carried these memories with them to the lower Shawnee Town. The town's inhabitants permitted the Pennsylvania traders to come and build trading houses, but they traded with others as their needs and economics dictated. Within Indian country, they were not so distant as to be outside of European trading spheres, but they were far enough from European settlements to safeguard their native autonomy.

Far from the political centers of Europe, England and France struggled for control of the lands that lay between the Wabash River and the Appalachian Mountains. Only a decade before, in the late 1730s, the region had not interested the French. They considered its furs inferior to those of Canada and limited their presence to a few garrisoned forts—Vincennes, Ouiatanon, and Miamis—that existed mainly to facilitate trade and communication. Because French settlers were few and located west of the Wabash River, settlement was not an issue.[15]

By 1748, however, the French became concerned about the inroads the English had made in the region and about how to safeguard their communication routes between their Canadian and Louisiana colonies. English influence at native towns like the lower Shawnee Town threatened those routes and, consequently, the French empire in North America.[16] Pennsylvania traders, foremost among them George Croghan, had expanded the English trading boundary some five hundred miles beyond the frontier of English settlement on the Juniata River to the Wabash-Maumee route, the eastern boundary of French trade.[17]

Control of the Ohio Valley depended in no small measure on control of the valley's native inhabitants. But the European powers found this difficult. The imperialistic concerns of France and England held little sway over the region's population. Indians were interested in retaining the valley as their home. They were concerned with limiting European settlements west of the mountains, confining all trade in the Ohio region to three posts, reducing prices and the number of traders, and restricting liquor.[18]

Native responses to events in the mid-1700s appeared unpredictable to Europeans; never, it seemed, were their native allies steadfast. But Indian responses did not reflect the capricious "changes of heart" of a united people. They represented the actions, agendas, and decisions of different factions gaining political control within consensus-style, tribal political systems. This contributed as much to their shifting allegiances as did the actions of their European "allies." To the native peoples "on Ohio," including the inhabitants of the lower Shawnee Town, this was simply the appropriate way to conduct life.[19]

The Ohio Valley was a good place to live, rich with the resources slash-and-burn farmer-hunters required: fertile soil, a mosaic of mixed hardwood forests, flat grassy plains, canebrakes, salt and freshwater springs, and clear streams. Deer, bear, elk, and bison wandered the countryside; wild plants and nut-bearing trees were abundant. Chert-bearing bedrock and clay-bearing river banks provided the essential materials for tools and durable containers.

Many of the nations living in the region had moved into the area comparatively recently. In response to pressure from European settlement in the east, Delaware and Six Nations Iroquois settled in the upper Ohio Valley in the 1730s and continued moving westward during the next two decades. As threats of Iroquois raids subsided, the Wyandot moved south into the region from along Lake Erie. The Miami and Shawnee peoples returned to a region known to their ancestors long before Europeans arrived in the hemisphere: the Miami moving southeastward into the area, and the Shawnee, characterized as much by their migratory habits as by their conservatism, entering from the east as well as from the south and northwest. Some may never have left.[20]

Ancient homeland or not, the region was a safe haven from the problems that native groups had experienced living among or near Europeans. All had witnessed European colonization and the threats to native culture associated with it—the European diseases brought to native communities, the disruption of society and loss of integrity and pride as liquor became more prevalent, the competition for natural resources, and the escalation of the deerskin trade. By moving to the Ohio Valley, they could escape the detrimental effects of European culture and society; they could remain or become again sovereign peoples, maintaining the ways of their forefathers and raiding their ancient enemies to the south. Native peoples believed they could continue to hunt, plant, and harvest in the Ohio Valley and perform the rituals that accompanied these activities. They could limit European contact, yet still trade for the items of European technology that they desired. Away from European settlement, they had the distance they needed to find ways to sustain native autonomy and deal with Europeans on native terms.

Within this land of promise, in the late 1730s, Shawnee and Six Nations Iroquois established the lower Shawnee Town that Trent and Montour visited in the summer of 1752. As a "factory" for the Pennsylvania traders, an economic hub at the western terminus of their southern trade route, the lower Shawnee Town was a midlevel diplomatic center and the primary village of the mid-1700s for the Shawnee. At the confluence of the Scioto and Ohio Rivers, it sat astride three important trade, travel, and communication routes: the Warriors' Path, the major north-south Indian trail that may have had great antiquity; the overland Pennsylvania traders' path to Muskingum and Pickawillany, which led north and northwest from the town; and the Scioto and Ohio River systems, which offered access both north-south and east-west.[21] Located as it was on flat ground at the rivers' confluence, the lower Shawnee Town locale held rich horticultural potential; in the opinion of George Croghan in 1765, the soil was too rich for anything but hemp, flax, and Indian corn.[22] Large by Ohio Valley standards in August 1749 (sixty houses and a council house), the population of the town apparently more than doubled over the next year and a half. It is estimated that by January 1751, the town's multiethnic population numbered somewhere between twelve hundred and fifteen hundred people.[23]

French officials in Canada, their interests escalating in the Ohio Valley in the 1740s and 1750s, became concerned with the formation of what they considered to be renegade or uncontrollable Indian settlements, like the Shawnees' LoggsTown, the Twightwees' Pickawillany, or the Wyandot's Sandusky. Like those settlements, in the words of the French minister in 1749, the lower Shawnee Town was a "sort of republic, with a fairly large number of bad characters of various nations."[24] Historian Richard White concludes that Indian "republics" of the 1740s and 1750s, including the lower Shawnee Town, developed in response to a change in the delicate balance of power between the French and the native peoples of the *pays d'en haut* (the upper country of Canada).[25] According to White, such towns were characteristically new, multiethnic, and autonomous. As new settlements, they were founded generally by peoples whose original homelands were situated outside the region. Thus, in many instances their claims to surrounding territories did not go uncontested. As multiethnic settlements, Indian republics were made up of a variety of smaller disparate social groups: village fragments, extended families, or individuals. The intermarriage and ethnic diversity within these settlements created a multitude of new kinship and social situations, adding layers of ethnic, social, and village relationships. Thus, the potential for factionalism and the development of different European responses may have been even greater in these villages than in traditional single-ethnic villages. As autonomous communities, these republics existed politically beyond the control of the French, British, and even the Six Nations at Onondaga, and their residents were responsible only to themselves. Thus, they had the freedom to make decisions based on their own needs, traditions, and cultural proscriptions, and they could ally themselves with whomever they wished or change their alliances when it suited their needs.

The historical record that describes the lower Shawnee Town and its inhabitants is richest between King George's War in 1748 and the outbreak of the Seven Years' War in 1756.[26] The native peoples living in this republic were active, equal players in Indian country. They attempted to attain the best advantages for themselves and approached situations in a manner consistent with their culture, society, and history. Little wonder, then, that the Europeans interpreted them as allies and then as enemies—a fickle, inconsistent, shifting, undependable, uncontrollable republic. The French told them not to trust the British, while the British told them not to trust the French. In truth, the peoples living in the lower Shawnee Town republic were wary of both. They relied on their own evaluations of situations and considered their own interests when choosing courses of action. The Europeans' "unreliable" allies were simply autonomous tribal peoples pursuing a rational policy of diplomatic maneuvering, an approach expected of any sovereign peoples involved in international relations.

The lower Shawnee Town was a "super village," at least twice as big as its protohistoric or prehistoric predecessors and larger than most contemporary Indian settlements in the region. Its inhabitants were a diverse lot, a mixture of indigenous peoples, Europeans, Africans, and the offspring of their unions. Permanent native residents, transient French and English traders on business, native and European captives, relatives visiting from Shawnee towns located up the Ohio or even farther away, and diplomats and spies of all nationalities spent time in the town.

The Shawnee were the settlement's largest ethnic contingent. This nation as a whole was made up of five separate and independent political units, or divisions: Pekowi, Kishpoko, Mekoche, Chalaka, and Thawikila. Each division took responsibility for particular aspects of tribal welfare. The Pekowi oversaw tribal ritual; the Kishpoko directed warfare; the Mekoche had jurisdiction over medicine and health; and the Chalaka and Thawikila controlled political affairs. The chief of the nation, therefore, could only come from the Chalaka or Thawikila divisions.[27]

A Shawnee town received its name as a derivation of the name of the division that occupied it. Though the native name for the lower Shawnee Town has not survived, scholars suspect it was "Chillicothe," the name of the town the inhabitants founded after moving from the lower Shawnee Town in 1758. In this case, the powerful Chalaka division apparently founded the village. If so, the continued use of the name implies a centrality of the Chalaka to Shawnee culture and politics.[28]

Each of the five divisions had its own chief and its own history of affiliations with other groups, Shawnee and non-Shawnee alike. In their migrations the Shawnee never moved as a whole; they moved as divisions or as a combination of two or more divisions. Even small bands drawn from the divisions could move as they chose. This relationship among the divisions suggests that the Shawnee may have been an "ethnic confederacy" that over time had institutionalized its ethnic commonalities.[29]

After the town's founding, other Shawnee divisions joined the settlement, which contributed to the social and political mix of the village. Undoubtedly, at its height, members of most if not all of the five divisions lived in this largest Shawnee settlement. In 1745, part of Peter Chartier's group of Shawnee, along with Newcommer, Big Hominy, the Pride, and their kin, left western Pennsylvania and stopped for a short time at the lower Shawnee Town. By 1748, Big Hominy and the Pride had led their families back to the Ohio Valley and may have been living at the lower Shawnee Town. In 1751, Big Hominy was definitely living there. By 1752, more families had returned or arrived. Newcommer, who emerged as the Shawnee people's "great chief," lived there.[30] In addition to division chiefs and the national chief, the lower Shawnee Town probably also would have had its own peace and war chiefs. While the names of other leaders, such as Tomenibuck, Tonelaguesena, Lawachcamicky, Assoghqua—some of whom may have lived at the lower

Shawnee Town—are preserved in the documents, it is not clear what role they played in village or national politics.[31] Undoubtedly many other men were also considered important leaders, but their names are not preserved in the documents because they did not attend councils with the British and French.

Six Nations Iroquois, mostly Seneca (or Mingo as they became known in the Ohio Valley), also considered the lower Shawnee Town home and may have cofounded the town with the Shawnee. Leaders of clans, bands, or families would have lived with their relatives at the town. Men from other villages traded at the lower Shawnee Town or may have temporarily encamped there during regional crises or diplomatic meetings: Delaware from their towns up the Scioto River; missionized Indians from communities near Montreal including Iroquois from Lake of the Two Mountains, and Oneida or Mohawk from Sault Saint Louis; and others from nearly all the Indian nations of upper Canada.[32] Given this bewildering array of nations, divisions, factions, and bands settled at the lower Shawnee Town, it is not surprising that the French characterized the lower Shawnee Town as a republic.

This amalgamation of tribal peoples at the lower Shawnee Town was not as odd as it might seem. Despite their particular tribal customs as Shawnee, Mingo, Delaware, or Iroquois from Canada, the inhabitants of the lower Shawnee Town shared many basic social, political, and economic ideas. Chief among these was the importance of kinship. For tribal peoples, kinship formed the fabric of society, defining how people interacted with one another socially, politically, and economically. Whether reckoned through the mother (matrilineal like the Iroquois or Delaware) or through the father (patrilineal like the Shawnee), kinship underlay every relationship and colored every decision.[33] These people also shared origins in village-based tribal farming societies. Women mainly farmed, gathered, and managed the domestic front; men were responsible primarily for hunting, fishing, and external village affairs such as trading and politics.

Despite the presence of many ethnic groups, the lower Shawnee Town's physical situation was typical of traditional Shawnee settlements.[34] Situated downstream from the Scioto-Ohio confluence, one hundred houses were scattered along the north side of the Ohio River atop a forty-foot river bank lined with sycamores and water willows. The surrounding floodplain was very broad and wide with the closest river bluffs located either one-half mile west or four miles east of the town. Across the Ohio on the south side were forty houses located on a narrower floodplain and on the higher terraces. Here freshwater springs issued forth and the bluffs were much closer to the river. Looking out from these bluffs on a clear day, the observer could see a panoramic view of the Ohio River and several miles up the Scioto.[35]

Though no plan of the lower Shawnee Town exists, the village was probably a diffuse settlement patterned after indigenous prehistoric and protohistoric villages of the middle Ohio Valley.[36] In that case, the lower Shawnee Town may have been less a town than a district, extending along the wide Scioto River and narrower Ohio River floodplains and terraces. Smaller paths united the elements of the district—fields, habitations, trash areas, cemeteries, the council house and public space, trading houses, and major overland trails and water routes. Houses on the edges of the settlement blended into the surrounding countryside; closer to the public space at the center of the district, houses clustered closer together. Given the settlement's multiethnic character and the fact that residents would have lived near their closest kin, it is doubtful that separate ethnic enclaves existed within the village.

Some residences resembled the prehistoric or protohistoric dwellings of the region: long rectangular buildings with rounded corners constructed of frameworks of wooden posts set singly into the ground and covered with either thatch, bark, mats, or skins. Trade blankets or skins provided "doors" at the ends of the houses. Interior partitions broke up the space within each house, and hearths were located in the center of earthen floors. Pits for storage lined the walls; trash was disposed in outdoor pits or on the ground in heaps behind the house.[37] Bundles of dried food hung from the rafters. However, Europeans also described some buildings as huts, cabins, or houses—structures with squared logs and covered with bark or clapboard. A few even had chimneys.[38]

Extended families or kin-based groups occupied clusters of houses. Each family buried its dead in cemeteries near its home, interring individuals in single shallow pits. Family members erected burial structures over some of the deceased, placing ceramic vessels, arrows, stone smoking pipes, and ornaments of native manufacture such as necklaces of animal-tooth beads in the graves. They sometimes also included a few items of European manufacture, such as glass trade bead necklaces and pendants made from metal scraps.[39]

The town's public space, in the northern section of the district, included the council house and a large open area or plaza for public events. Although ninety feet long, the bark-covered council house probably resembled family dwellings.[40] At least one and probably two English trading houses stood in the settlement, undoubtedly located near either the main overland trail or the Ohio River bank where traders could beach their canoes. If modeled on the trading houses built at Pickawillany, those at the lower Shawnee Town would have looked like ordinary Euro-American log cabins.[41]

In many respects, the day-to-day lives of the inhabitants of the lower Shawnee Town probably were like those of their ancestors. The foods they grew and the animals they hunted apparently changed little in over seven hundred years. As a summer farming people, the town's womenfolk tended corn, beans, squash, gourds, tobacco, and sunflowers in fields adjacent to the village. They used digging sticks, freshwater mussel shell hoes, and possibly metal counterparts acquired in trade. In baskets made from cane and grasses, they collected wild plant foods such as hickory nuts, grapes, sumac, and pokeberry for food or medicine. They stored dried food in above-ground cribs or silos, or in ceramic jars. Such pots resembled, both in form and method of manufacture, those made in the region during the protohistoric period. Smaller, hemispherical bowls were used to serve individual food portions. As European goods became available, women of the lower Shawnee Town employed brass and iron vessels alongside traditional earthenware.[42]

Using grass nets and bone fishhooks, men and women fished rivers and streams. They collected freshwater mussels from the shoals at the confluence of the Scioto and Ohio Rivers, eating the mollusk raw or in stews, and saving the whole shells for use as hoes or spoons, or to be crushed and mixed with clay in the manufacture of ceramic vessels.[43]

Hunting was an important subsistence and economic activity that provided food, tools, and skins for family use and also for the trade that linked the lower Shawnee Town to the Pennsylvania deerskin trading network. Men hunted mainly deer, bear, elk, and wild turkey, but squirrel, fox, raccoon, and rabbits were taken, too. Alone or in small groups, hunters equipped themselves with bows and arrows tipped with either triangular chipped stone or metal arrowheads, antler tines, and cane sharpened to a point. After European contact, native hunters began to use guns. Women prepared hides with bone beamers, iron knives, and teardrop-shaped stone scrapers also used in plant processing and woodworking. From animal bone, as well as from reworked European objects like fragments of Jew's harps, they also made sharp awls and punches.

During the winter months, as they had done for centuries, families moved into small winter camps. The aged, infirmed, and those too young to travel remained behind in the village, attended by relatives. Extended families or kin-related groups of fewer than thirty persons set up camp miles from the village in narrow valleys or mountain rock shelters, away from the rivers and larger streams. They brought some food, such as corn, but subsistence activities focused mainly on hunting deer, meat and hide processing, and the collecting and processing of wild plants.[44] They returned periodically to the village with meat and hides. Many family groups journeyed into and set up their winter camps in the forested regions south of the Ohio River, soon to be known to Europeans as "Kentucke."

While basic cultural similarities tempered the ethnic differences between the town's residents, the political implications of so many different groups living in the village are apparent. Existing factions within the separate ethnic groups now overlapped by virtue of kinship through intermarriage. Completely new factions arose in response to new problems.

Within the extremely decentralized political realm of tribal society, leaders were responsible for maintaining order, settling internal disputes, coordinating trade, and negotiating alliances with other villages. Indians determined leadership by the strength of personal character and achievements, especially on what the candidate had done recently. Leadership derived from an ability to convince and lead others in economic and diplomatic issues—for example, relations with Europeans and other natives, or the alcohol problem. A leader's perceived or actual failure raised questions in the minds of his followers and caused them to turn to another. As spokesmen for kin-based groups with little influence over others, leaders in tribal societies held no extensive powers; their authority was confined to the primary community and was imbued with no sovereign political power.[45] This was leadership by consensus, not coercion. Because the tribe as an entity often proved the weakest link, each leader and his faction freely formulated their own responses to crises.[46]

Factionalism, the nature of tribal leadership, and the multiple ethnic groups represented within the lower Shawnee Town combined with European disease, competition for trade, and diplomatic maneuvering to create the republic at the mouth of the Scioto. The town undoubtedly took no actions as a whole; only the various factions acted. This is why native responses to events like the destruction of Pickawillany ran the gamut from immediate retaliation against the French to a cautious diplomatic probing. Leaders decided on appropriate courses of action to take in response to the liquor problem or European advancement, only to find that their people, in particular their young men, would not follow their leads. Consequently, tribal leaders could not present a politically united front, a common characteristic of many tribal societies.[47] Because of this very unstable political situation,

Europeans found diplomatic relations difficult to establish with native peoples, especially with the republics. Europeans expected native leaders to speak for the whole and set tribal policy, when in fact they did nothing of the kind.[48]

The diversity of the settlement's ethnic groups created a truly international atmosphere in town councils. In the realm of purely Indian affairs, the lower Shawnee Town was an "international" diplomatic center—representatives of the Cherokee, Twightwees, and Delaware traveled to this main Shawnee settlement to meet and negotiate diplomatic issues.[49]

But within the European sphere of international diplomacy, the lower Shawnee Town did not serve as a center in the same way as LoggsTown, a contemporary Shawnee republic located farther upstream on the Ohio River. At Loggstown, native leaders and English commissioners held official meetings to discuss issues, make policy decisions, and negotiate treaties. LoggsTown provided this venue because it was closer to the eastern boundary of Indian country. In addition, the Shawnee chief Kakawatcheky, who had founded LoggsTown in 1743-44, held pro-English sympathies.[50]

Between 1748 and 1752, division chiefs and the great chief from the lower Shawnee Town traveled to meetings at LoggsTown, the colonial towns of Lancaster and Carlisle in Pennsylvania, and Winchester in Virginia. At these events, spokesmen for the nations "on Ohio" were the Six Nations Iroquois chiefs, or "half kings," Scarouady and Tanaghrisson. As at other councils, the Six Nations served as the conduit through which all communication between the various parties passed. The English recognized the Iroquois as sovereign over tribes "on Ohio." As dependents of the Iroquois, other participating native peoples acquiesced to their leadership in these councils. Shawnee chiefs, therefore, acted as secondary partners at these meetings: they signed the treaties, received the presents, but had little influence in negotiations compared with Shawnee leaders later in the century.[51]

In contrast to the official councils, fewer people attended the unofficial meetings at the lower Shawnee Town. Located deep in Indian country, too far from English and French political centers, the lower Shawnee Town functioned as a second-level or regional diplomatic center. No colonial commissioners met in the village's council house. Instead, agents of the colonial governments, like Croghan and Trent, brought diplomatic news to the inhabitants. Such agents measured and reported the tenor of Indian sentiments concerning local, regional, and international affairs, but seldom made policy decisions.

At these meetings, Shawnee chiefs may have played more central diplomatic roles. Both Shawnee and Iroquois chiefs met with Pierre Joseph de Celoron in 1749; Big Hominy as well as a Mingo chief received Croghan, Montour, and Gist in 1751; and Scarouady and probably Newcommer met with Trent and Montour in 1752. Even in the councils at the lower Shawnee Town council house, however, the Iroquois retained diplomatic control as the primary speakers.[52]

Before the 1740s, and possibly beginning as early as its settlement in the 1730s, the lower Shawnee Town had been linked in trade with the French. *Coureurs de bois* may not have come to the town routinely, but men from the lower Shawnee Town did journey to Detroit to trade. Posts on the eastern boundary of French control—Ouiatanon, Vincennes, Miamis, and Detroit—offered quality goods in limited quantities and at high prices. The French interest in beaver furs, however, with a focus on the northern Indian fur trade, meant that skins and furs from the Ohio Valley region were not especially valued. Therefore, before the mid-1740s, the lower Shawnee Town and other southern native villages drew less attention from the French.

After King George's War in 1748, the situation changed. The French gained a new appreciation for the Ohio Valley as they felt their colonial interests and communications threatened. The war had severely injured French trading interests in North America: English control of the sea lanes restricted the arrival of French goods, forcing the French to raise prices. Coupled with an aggressive English trade in Ohio Indian country, the inflated prices convinced many native peoples at the lower Shawnee Town and elsewhere in the region to turn to cheaper and more readily available, albeit lesser quality, English goods.[53]

Even though the lower Shawnee Town had earned a reputation among the French as a hotbed of political intrigue whose inhabitants were not to be trusted, the French recognized that they had to retain it and the rest of the Ohio Valley's native peoples within their sphere of influence if they were to control the region. Yet, economic competition did not arrive as the French expected from the traditional British trading colonies of New York, Virginia, and Carolina. Rather, by 1749, Pennsylvania dominated the Ohio Valley trade, and the central participants were George Croghan and his partners.[54]

To English traders from Pennsylvania, the lower Shawnee Town was an economic paradise, an "Eng. facty" (English "factory" or trading post) that functioned as an international trading hub.[55] The years between 1748 and 1752 especially witnessed an escalation in the Pennsylvania deerskin trade. The inhabitants of the lower Shawnee Town became important participants. At almost any time of year, wooden canoes or pack trains of fifteen to twenty horses entered or departed the lower Shawnee Town laden with trade goods and deerskins.[56]

A number of factors combined to make the lower Shawnee Town a hub for trading. Five trading routes in the Ohio country extended from Croghan's bases near the Forks of the Ohio (confluence of the Allegheny and Monongahela Rivers) like "sticks of a fan."[57] Pine Creek, Oswegle Bottom, and the lower Shawnee Town were the main nodes on the southern route. Croghan's most valued establishments—at Pine Creek (three miles upstream from the Forks of the Ohio on the Allegheny) and at Oswegle Bottom (on the Youghiogheny River twenty-five miles from the Forks of the Ohio)—were located in the eastern portion of the network.[58] The trading house at the lower Shawnee Town sat all alone at the route's western terminus, connecting Croghan to the western reaches of Indian territory. Before Croghan established operations at Pickawillany in November 1749, the closest English trading post to the lower Shawnee Town had been the one on the Muskingum River at the end of the central route.[59] After the June 1752 destruction of Pickawillany, which had served as the terminus for his central overland trading route, the lower Shawnee Town and Sandusky, at the end of the northern route along Lake Erie, existed as Croghan's westernmost trading centers, separated by some two hundred miles.[60] From the nodes along the southern route, Croghan's traders could move unimpeded in all directions, penetrating into Indian country north of the lower Shawnee Town or south beyond the Ohio River into the interior.[61]

By 1749, English traders (probably George Croghan) had built a storehouse in the town. In August of that year, Celoron found five English traders "established . . . in the village and well sustained by the Indians."[62] His success drew more colonial entrepreneurs. In 1753, at "the request of and by direction of the Six Nations in alliance with the English," Michael Teaffe and Robert Callender built a "trading house."[63] When a flood destroyed much of the lower Shawnee Town in the early 1750s, Croghan and Trent moved their business to the south side of the Ohio River, following most of the townspeople as they relocated their settlement into what is now Kentucky.[64] In these log cabin trading houses, the upper story or loft was used as a place to stow skins and combustible material, with trade carried on below.[65]

Traders did not have to leave the settlement to make a profit; native people from surrounding towns brought goods to the lower Shawnee Town for trade. The furs and skins of deer, elk, bison, bear, beaver, raccoon, fox, cat, muskrat, mink, and fisher filled storehouses. Native peoples also offered food and sometimes personal services in exchange for utilitarian and ornamental items of European manufacture—knives, saddles, hatchets, beads, brooches, strouds, ruffled and plain shirts, coats, and rum.[66] Canoes filled with skins moved up the Ohio River to LoggsTown, where the workers loaded the goods onto packhorses. After crossing the mountains, skins were transferred into wagons for a fourteen-day journey to Philadelphia to be shipped to London.[67]

The deerskin trade was the lower Shawnee Town's primary source for guns, metal tools, and other items of European manufacture. Increasingly, natives wore glass beads, silver earrings, armbands, and brooches, rather than traditional beads and pendants made from shell, animal teeth, or animal bone. Cloth match-coats, strouds, blankets, skirts, and shirts supplemented moccasins and garments manufactured from animal skins. And, where they had once smoked tobacco in stone pipes made from Ohio pipestone or catlinite, the inhabitants of lower Shawnee Town began to use as well clay pipes of European manufacture. Even traditional gender roles changed in response to the deerskin trade. While primarily men traded at the town, some women's names appear on the traders' lists. Women who exchanged deerskins at the lower Shawnee Town may have done so for their male relatives, but it is also possible that they caught and prepared smaller animal furs for their own profit.[68]

Trade had been an important aspect of native culture for hundreds of years before Europeans even began to consider trans-Atlantic travel and exploration. It was couched in reciprocity and a social context: restricted and controlled by the village leaders, integrated into the social fabric of the culture, and linked to kinship and trading partners across the generations. Trade carried social connotations and responsibilities, following a native protocol based on reciprocal exchange between relatives, almost like gift-giving.[69] Archaeologists have documented the exchange of exotic materials like copper and marine shell by Ohio Valley peoples as early as the late archaic period, circa 1000 B.C.[70] Indians used items such as marine shell, obsidian, mica, and stone that could be carved like catlinite or pipestone in ritual and ceremonial contexts. The earliest Spanish explorers to the Southeast documented native peoples engaged in a brisk exchange of durable and nondurable goods such as salt, deerskins, feathers, bows, and medicinal plants.[71] Even European items like glass beads and brass or copper ornaments reworked from kettles found their way into the Ohio Valley more than a century before the first European traders appeared.[72] Thus, by the 1740s, when French and then English arrived in the valley with goods to trade, the native peoples were prepared.

But the dynamics of trade—the people with whom they traded and the framework within which exchange was carried out—had changed by the 1740s and 1750s. The meaning of the exchange became divorced from traditional native contexts.[73] Now, each person could trade as an individual outside the boundaries of kinship. Indians were now producers of skins for a worldwide mercantile economy. Influenced by fashion tastes a continent away and connected to the markets of Philadelphia and London, reciprocity as a medium of exchange disappeared. Credit, a pattern established wherever the Europeans operated in North America, replaced it.[74] Extended from the London merchant to the Philadelphia middleman to the trader to the Indian hunter residing at the lower Shawnee Town, credit increased the price of goods each time the merchandise changed hands, placing the highest price on the Indians.[75]

The Pennsylvanians with whom they traded during this period conducted commerce differently from most other Englishmen. The English fur trade at Hudson Bay in Canada drew native men to far-flung posts. In New York, Indian middlemen went to the interior villages and returned to posts at Albany and Oswego with skins and furs from Indian territory. In the Ohio Valley, as in the Piedmont region of the Carolinas, colonial traders followed native peoples to their settlements to exchange goods for skins and to build trading houses in their midst.[76]

Croghan stationed at least two men at each of his posts to carry on local trading operations, which peaked in the winter and summer. As they guarded Croghan's trading interests, a small contingent of colonials may have become year-round residents of the lower Shawnee Town, perhaps taking native wives. A vile and wretched lot, many of the traders of the period were men of bad reputation who saw the Indian trade as a way to make large profits.[77] These traders took advantage of the minimal restrictions and regulations that Pennsylvania colonial officials placed on the deerskin trade. Few shared character with George Croghan, who learned native languages and treated Indians with respect, receiving in return a native name and a fictive kinship relation.

Whereas English trade at Hudson Bay and Albany gave native peoples more control over the nature, duration, and type of interactions they had with Europeans, a different sort of dynamic developed between native peoples and traders in the Ohio Valley. It is not clear how much of the trading at the lower Shawnee Town was conducted according to Indian protocol and how much was controlled by the traders. However, despite the absence of governmental regulation and the increasing prominence of Pennsylvania traders in the town's economic and social life, colonials could misbehave only up to a certain point. Though it was a Pennsylvanian trading hub, the lower Shawnee Town still sat in Indian country, hundreds of miles from English settlement and far from the security of European powers. The traders were on foreign soil in a village that during the summer months could have bustled with over one thousand people. Traders had to observe some Indian customs.[78]

Because the English and the French competed for their attentions, native peoples still controlled to some degree how trade was conducted. But their desire for European goods meant that they could not choose not to trade, and they could not control when they would trade. The native need for European goods at the lower Shawnee Town, like native peoples in trade elsewhere, was an inelastic one: they used what they needed and consumed no more.[79] Thus, demand for durable goods—items that would wear out over time but that were not immediately consumable—declined as the native peoples acquired what they needed. Only the demand for alcohol remained constant.

Alcohol, mainly rum but also brandy and other spirits, was ubiquitous in the lives of native peoples. A standard trade item and an important element of diplomatic councils and political transactions, liquor was used to open and seal treaty negotiations, maintain alliances, and create new ones. Although liquor was an element of gift-giving rituals, it also led to drunkenness and contributed to social problems.[80] It eroded the civility necessary to maintain community, contributed to an increase in violence and death, and undermined native health. Alcohol made individual Indians less reliable hunters and allies. Over the long term, alcohol destabilized village economics and led communities into poverty.[81]

Indians brought their concern about the liquor trade to the Ohio Valley. It had been such a problem in earlier homelands that several Shawnee leaders in the 1730s asked Pennsylvania authorities to restrict and control the liquor trade.[82] Colonial officials issued proclamations and the Indians made the same request again in the 1740s.[83] But native peoples could not agree on how to address the liquor problem. Some wished to stop the trade in liquor completely; others wanted to limit quantities and regulate sales.[84] Older leaders spoke for temperance and pushed to stop the liquor trade, but the nature of native leadership made them powerless to intervene or control people. Additionally, since liquor was fully integrated into the commerce of the Pennsylvania traders, interrupting the trade in alcohol would have threatened trade in other goods.[85]

As inhabitants of a large native settlement, an English trading hub, and a midlevel diplomatic center, the lower Shawnee Town residents may have been more acutely aware than others of the effects of liquor on the individual and its deleterious consequences in native society. And for the same reasons, liquor may have been more pervasive in the lower Shawnee Town than in other towns. This may have been another factor that contributed to the French characterization of the settlement as a republic.

How much impact French and English imperial concerns had on the day-to-day lives of inhabitants at the lower Shawnee Town is hard to measure, since native perspectives and points of view must be pieced together from documents generated by Europeans. Certainly their concerns about controlling the liquor trade, negotiating fair prices for their deerskins, and keeping strong their diplomatic relationships with the English suggest that their daily lives were affected to a certain degree. Many statements, however, make it clear that during the period from 1748 to 1752, French and English imperial concerns were just some of the issues confronting the residents of the lower Shawnee Town. They continued to live much as they did before the age of European imperialism. Native-generated conflicts with the Southern Indians were played out.[86] In fact, representatives from the lower Shawnee Town did not attend a 1751 council in LoggsTown because of lingering conflict with the "Southward Indians."[87] Parties raided the Cherokee and Catawba to the south and harassed the Piankashaws, Wea, and other tribes to the west.[88] To ensure good harvests and productive hunts, the inhabitants of the lower Shawnee Town attended to their communal rituals and ceremonies. And they still danced.[89]

Despite their distance from the eastern English settlements and the western French forts, the inhabitants of the lower Shawnee Town had frequent and lasting contact with Europeans within their own town. Europeans and their trade goods had become elements of native life. Their impact on the daily lives of the lower Shawnee Town inhabitants, and an indication of how well the natives sustained their autonomy, perhaps can be measured best by examining the inroads European goods made into native material culture.[90] The wide variety of items of European manufacture found in the trash pits at the lower Shawnee Town reflects the inhabitants' response to the impact of European culture.

It is clear that residents were integrating goods of European manufacture into their native way of life by the mid-eighteenth century. Guns, clay smoking pipes, brass kettles, and clothing were becoming more and more important to their way of life. In some cases, they substituted European-made items for those of native manufacture. For example, large iron pots may have been used instead of ceramic vessels in the processing of salt or in making maple sugar.[91] They wore fewer bone and shell ornaments, choosing instead glass beads, silver earrings and brooches, and pierced fragments of brass used as pendants. They replaced bone, shell, and stone tools with ones of iron, brass, or copper.

But they also used native items side by side with those of European manufacture. Both the arrows of their ancestors as well as European firearms were used in hunting. They cooked in earthenware vessels and metal kettles, used stone scrapers and iron knives, wore native shoes and European cloth. While Shawnee conservatism and the town's autonomy helped in many ways to preserve a native way of life, change still took place. Engraved shell gorgets were no longer placed with the dead, but a few objects of European manufacture, like strings of glass beads or a metal pendant, made their way into graves. Although the absence of gorgets may indicate unavailability due to the collapse of protohistoric trading networks, it also may reflect subtle changes within a religious system inherited from the late prehistoric and protohistoric periods.

The use of both native-made items and European trade goods, and the persistence of settlement and subsistence practices, native technologies, and many native burial customs, reinforce the notion that even in the 1750s inhabitants of the lower Shawnee Town remained an independent people in charge of their own destiny.[92] Residents had not yet become dependent on firearms and other functional items. They were not yet bound so closely to economic relationships with the Europeans that their self-sufficiency was undermined. Although their traditional way of life was changing, these people were still free, still equal players in the events taking place in Indian country.

One element of European culture that apparently had little impact on the inhabitants of the lower Shawnee Town was European religion. No Christian missionaries settled among the Shawnee, although Moravians, Presbyterians, and Baptists all made attempts.[93] The only documented visit of missionaries to the lower Shawnee Town was that of Father Bonnecamps, who passed through with Celoron in 1749 and who was not on a native preaching mission. Indifference to Christianity became more evident some years later. In 1773, Baptist minister David Jones attempted to preach in Chillicothe along the Scioto River where the lower Shawnee Town inhabitants had removed following the fall of Fort Duquesne in 1758. He had been warned by others on his trip that the Shawnee were not receptive to preachers. Though disappointed, he was not surprised that his request was not granted.[94]

Native residents "on Ohio" sifted through and claimed those features of European religion most useful to their own cultural developments. In a study of nativistic movements and Pan-Indianism during the last half of the eighteenth century, a period referred to as the "Indians' Great Awakening," Gregory Evans Dowd suggests that militant religious nativism germinated in the towns along the Ohio that Celoron visited in 1749. The town with the largest and most vociferous inhabitants Celoron encountered was the lower Shawnee Town, which provides some tantalizing suggestions as to the role residents of the lower Shawnee Town may have played in these developments.[95]

In 1754, native residents in Indian territory, including those of the lower Shawnee Town, turned on European commerce and threw out the English traders.[96] The action forewarned of the native response to English settlement in the Ohio Valley and particularly in Kentucky in the 1770s. One of the key characteristics of any native republic is autonomy; the residents of the lower Shawnee Town were determined to sustain theirs.

Notes

The author would like to thank Michael D. Green and David Pollack for providing encouragement, helpful insights, and useful criticisms of this manuscript. Portions of this article were previously published in A. Gwynn Henderson, "Dispelling the Myth: Seventeenth- and Eighteenth-Century Indian Life in Kentucky," *Register of the Kentucky Historical Society* 90 (1992): 1-25.

1. "Treaty of Logg's Town, 1752: Commission, Instructions, &c, Journal of Virginia Commissioners, and Text of Treaty," *Virginia Magazine of History and Biography* 13 (1905): 143-74; and Randolph C. Downes, *Council Fires on the Upper Ohio: A Narrative of Indian Affairs in the Upper Ohio Valley until 1795* (Pittsburgh: Univ. of Pittsburgh Press, 1940), 59-62. Representatives from the lower Shawnee Town did not attend this council because of a conflict with the "Southward Indians"; *Minutes of the Provincial Council of Pennsylvania,* 10 vols. (Harrisburg: Theodore Fenn, 1851), 5: 531. For a short biographical sketch of George Croghan, well-known Pennsylvania trader, colonial diplomat, and Indian agent, see Lois Mulkearn, ed., *George Mercer Papers, Relating to the Ohio Company of Virginia* (Pittsburgh: Univ. of Pittsburgh Press, 1954), 478-81. Andrew Montour, son of a Frenchman and an Indian woman, served colonial officials as interpreter on numerous occasions; see ibid., 481-84. Christopher Gist was an explorer for the Ohio Company of Virginia and later one of its traders; see ibid., 471-72.

2. "Twightwees" was the English name for the Miami. Their town of Pickawillany gained more prominence after 1748 as George Croghan worked to make it a center for Indian trade; see Albert T. Volwiler, *George Croghan and the Western Movement, 1741-1782* (Cleveland: Arthur H. Clark, 1926), 71-74; and Nicholas B. Wainwright, "An Indian Trade Failure: The Story of the Hockley, Trent, and Croghan Company, 1748-1752," *Pennsylvania Magazine of History and Biography* 72 (1948): 358-66. For a biographical sketch of William Trent, see Mulkearn, *George Mercer Papers,* 569-73.

3. The events are recorded in William Trent's journal of 1752; see Charles A. Hanna, *The Wilderness Trail, or the Ventures and Adventures of the Pennsylvania Traders on the Allegheny Path, with Some New Annals of the Old West and the Records of Some Strong Men and Some Bad Ones,* 2 vols. (New York: G.P. Putnam's Sons, 1911), 2: 291-98; and Alfred T. Goodman, ed., *The Journal of Captain William Trent From Logstown to Pickawillany, A.D. 1752* (Cincinnati: Robert Clark, 1871).

4. See Volwiler, *George Croghan,* 29; Mulkearn, *George Mercer Papers,* 26; Hanna, *The Wilderness Trail,* 2: 294-95. For descriptions of the gifts they carried for use in the council, see Goodman, *Journal of Captain William Trent,* 94-96.

5. For major tribal affiliations of the inhabitants of these towns, see Mulkearn, *George Mercer Papers,* 11, 15, 486, 495.

6. See Downes, *Council Fires on the Upper Ohio,* 53-59; Hanna, *The Wilderness Trail,* 2: 155; *Minutes of the Provincial Council of Pennsylvania,* 5: 455, 481, 483, 497, 522; "The French Regime in Wisconsin," in *Collections of the State Historical Society of Wisconsin,* ed. Reuben Gold Thwaites, 31 vols. (Madison: Wisconsin Historical Society, 1855-1931), 18: 90-92; Volwiler, *George Croghan,* 69, 71-73; Wainwright, "An Indian Trade Failure," 359, 363.

7. See A. Gwynn Henderson, Christopher A. Turnbow, and Cynthia E. Jobe, *Indian Occupation and Use in Northern and Eastern Kentucky during the Contact Period (1540-1795): An Initial Investigation* (Frankfort: Kentucky Heritage Council, 1986), 136.

8. See Mulkearn, *George Mercer Papers,* 16-17. As Croghan's close trading partner, Trent would have been familiar with the lower Shawnee Town, even though this 1752 visit may have been his first. Documents place him trading with Croghan in the Ohio country in the winter of 1751-52; see Wainwright, "An Indian Trade Failure," 371.

9. Native apparel in 1752 may have resembled that described by Rev. David Jones, *A Journal of Two Visits Made to Some Nations of Indians on the West Side of the River Ohio in the Years 1772 and 1773* (1774; reprint, New York: H.O. Houghton, 1865), 83-84.

10. Burney and McBryer were the only two English traders who escaped. For a brief biographical sketch of Thomas Burney, see Mulkearn, *George Mercer Papers,* 492. For descriptions of the French attack on Pickawillany, see Volwiler, 78-79; R. David Edmunds, "Old Briton," in *American Indian Leaders: Studies in Diversity,* ed. R. David Edmunds (Lincoln: Univ. of Nebraska Press, 1980), 1-20; and Goodman, *Journal of Captain William Trent,* 86-88.

11. Undoubtedly this liquor was watered-down rum brought in by the Pennsylvania traders in exchange for summer skins and small furs. For the dynamics of Indian drinking and trade, see Peter C. Mancall, *Deadly Medicine: Indians and Alcohol in Early America* (Ithaca: Cornell Univ. Press, 1995), 69-70.

12. The round-trip distance from the lower Shawnee Town to Pickawillany as the

crow flies is about 260 miles; see Helen Hornbeck Tanner, ed., *Atlas of Great Lakes Indian History* (Norman: Univ. of Oklahoma Press, 1987), map 9. Perhaps the unseasonably hot weather or a less-than-direct route precipitated Trent's statement concerning the distance his party traveled.

13. Volwiler, *George Croghan,* 79.

14. For Scarouady's role in Ohio Valley affairs, see Michael N. McConnell, *A Country Between: The Upper Ohio Valley and Its Peoples, 1724-1774* (Lincoln: Univ. of Nebraska Press, 1992), 61-112, especially 70-75.

15. Volwiler, *George Croghan,* 20-22.

16. See W.J. Eccles, "The Fur Trade and Eighteenth-Century Imperialism," *William and Mary Quarterly,* 3d ser., 40 (1983): 341-62; Francis Jennings, *Empire of Fortune: Crowns, Colonies, and Tribes in the Seven Years War in America* (New York: W.W. Norton, 1988), 8-45; McConnell, *A Country Between,* 46-112; and Richard White, *The Middle Ground: Indians, Empires, and Republics in the Great Lakes Region, 1650-1815* (New York: Cambridge Univ. Press, 1991), 187-268.

17. For boundary of English settlement, see Volwiler, *George Croghan,* 21; regarding the development of Pennsylvania's Indian trade, see ibid., chaps. 1 and 2; and Wainwright, "An Indian Trade Failure."

18. These concerns, plus the demand that all future councils be held at Croghan's trading house in Aughwick, were clearly stated in the minutes of the Treaty of Carlisle in 1753; see Volwiler, 81-82; *Minutes of the Provincial Council of Pennsylvania,* 5: 675-76.

19. Shawnee allegiance to Europeans did fluctuate over time, reflecting the changes in sentiment based on historical events and colonial actions as much as it reflected the sentiments of the different Shawnee factions; see *Minutes of the Provincial Council of Pennsylvania,* vol. 5.

In the 1730s and early 1740s, French documents described a people apparently firm in the French sphere. In 1732, they were described as "not enduring the English"; "The French Regime in Wisconsin," 17: 156. In 1736, they were "still rejecting the English"; see ibid., 17: 242-43. But they delayed their move to Detroit, which concerned French officials. In 1739, Shawnee accompanied Charles le Moyne, Second Baron de Longueuil, on his journey to raid the Chickasaw. In 1742, the French described them as having been "tampered with by the English" and portrayed them as "docile as [they are] inconstant"; ibid., 17: 471, 419.

By the mid-1740s, Shawnee allegiance to France, which had never been "fast," began to shift toward the English. English correspondence of 1744 voiced concern over how secure the Shawnee were to the English, due to their frequent intercourse with the French and their inconstancy; Downes, *Council Fires on the Upper Ohio,* 38-39. In 1745, Chartier's band of Shawnee, along with those of Newcommer, Big Hominy, and the Pride, plundered eight English traders; "The French Regime in Wisconsin," 17: 448-49. When the French arrived at the lower Shawnee Town to collect the prisoners, there was only one trader, an indication to the French that the Shawnee were not to be trusted. A diary of the French trip shows the conflict between factions within the town; Anonymous Diary of a Trip from Detroit to the Ohio River, 22 May-24 August 1745, Archives of the Seminary of Quebec, Quebec, Canada.

French letters of 1747 described the Indians as "devoted to the English" and suggested that the lower Shawnee Town was involved in a conspiracy to destroy the French; "The French Regime in Wisconsin," 17: 474-88. In 1748, Shawnee leaders apologized to colonial commissioners for listening to the French, known as the Chartier Incident; Downes, *Council Fires on the Upper Ohio,* 43; *Minutes of the Provincial Council in Pennsylvania,* 5: 310-16. French letters of 1749 bemoaned that a "lack of French trade goods and the antipathy of most of the other Indian nations to them" caused some Shawnee to settle at the mouth of the Scioto River; "The French Regime in Canada," 18: 20-22. The following year, Pierre Joseph de Celoron, Sieur de Blainville, also lamented the state of affairs in his journal of 1749: "The nations of these localities are very badly disposed to the French, and are entirely devoted to the English. I do not know in what way they could be brought back. If our traders were sent there for traffic, they could not sell their merchandise at the same price as the English sell theirs, on account of the many expenses they would be obliged to incur"; Rev. A.A. Lambing, ed., "Celoron's Journal," *Ohio Archaeological and Historical Society Publications* 29 (1920): 482.

In 1750, the French were convinced that Croghan was planning a conspiracy, focused at Pickawillany and the lower Shawnee Town; "The French Regime in Wisconsin," 18: 58-59. In 1751, the Shawnee cordially received the English, but the French understood them to be "good friends"; for the English perspective, see Gist's journal in Mulkearn, *George Mercer Papers;* for the French, see Theodore C. Pease and E. Jenison, eds., *Anglo-French Boundary Disputes in the West, 1749-1763* (Springfield: Illinois State Historical Society, 1940), 372. French letters of 1752, however, described the "perfidy" of the Shawnee and others on the "Beautiful River," whose statements the previous year seemed "premeditated to deceive, their feelings of attachment for [those] rebles [sic] who are connected [to them] by blood." The Indians of the whole valley were described as "all English"; "The French Regime in Wisconsin," 18: 109. In the minutes of the Treaty of LoggsTown in 1752, the Shawnee guaranteed they would have no more to do with the French. And after the destruction of Pickawillany, one faction at the lower Shawnee Town was prepared to "take up the hatchet" against the French. However, less than a month later, another Shawnee faction hoisted the French colors before the council with Trent and Montour in August 1752.

20. Similarities of house construction, village plan, and material culture between protohistoric aboriginal sites and the four sites that represent the archaeological manifestation of the lower Shawnee Town—Bentley, Forest Home, Thompson, and Laughlin—point to settlement continuity, indicating that the Shawnee were longtime residents of the region; see A. Gwynn Henderson and David Pollack, "The Thompson Site," in *Fort Ancient Cultural Dynamics in the Middle Ohio Valley,* ed. A. Gwynn Henderson (Madison, Wis.: Prehistory Press, 1992), 31. For discussions of native groups moving into the Ohio Valley at this time, see McConnell, *A Country Between,* 9-20; White, *The Middle Ground,* 146-47, 186-89. For a discussion of Shawnee migration and conservatism, and their longtime presence in the region, see Jerry E. Clark, *Shawnee Indian Migration: A System Analysis* (Ph.D. diss., University of Kentucky, 1974), especially 45-49, 58-63, and 93-97; Ermine Wheeler Voegelin, *Mortuary Customs of the Shawnee and Other Eastern Tribes,* Indiana Historical Society Prehistory Research Series, 2 vols. (Indianapolis: Indiana Historical Society, 1944), 2: 227-444. Voegelin also discusses Shawnee conservatism; ibid., 291-92, 300, 378. For a discussion of Shawnee migration broken down by division, see Noel W. Schutz Jr., *The Study of Shawnee Myth in an Ethnographic and Ethnohistorical*

Perspective (Ph.D. diss., Indiana University, 1975), 319-456. For a review of late prehistoric and protohistoric Ohio Valley native occupations and their association with the Shawnee, see Henderson et al., *Indian Occupation,* 168-70.

21. William E. Myer, "Indian Trails of the Southeast," *Bureau of American Ethnology Annual Report* 42 (1928): 727-857. Also, Mitchell's Map of 1755 in Lloyd Arnold Brown, *Early Maps of the Ohio Valley* (Pittsburgh: Univ. of Pittsburgh Press, 1959), 95-96, and fig. 25.

22. Reuben Gold Thwaites, ed., *Early Western Travels, 1748-1846,* 32 vols. (Cleveland: Arthur H. Clark, 1904-1907), 1: 134.

23. On the basis of the 1749 descriptions of Celoron and those of Father Bonnecamps, the expedition's chaplain, only three native towns were of notable size—LoggsTown, Pickawillany, and the lower Shawnee Town. LoggsTown came closest in size to the lower Shawnee Town, with fifty cabins and ten English traders. The lower Shawnee Town was the largest, with sixty cabins, though only five English traders were present. Only Kuskuskies, a town in the interior, was described as having more residents (eight hundred men versus eighty men at the lower Shawnee Town), but Kuskuskies was a district of several villages. Celoron's journal is reprinted in Lambing, "Celeron's Journal," 335-96, and 481-83; Bonnecamps' may be found in Reuben Gold Thwaites, ed., *The Jesuit Relations and Allied Documents,* 73 vols. (Cleveland: Burrow Brothers, 1896-1901) 69: 181-83. Calculating the number of inhabitants of the lower Shawnee Town is difficult. Charles Callender assumed four people per warrior to arrive at his figure of twelve hundred people living in the lower Shawnee Town in 1751; see Callender, "Shawnee," in *Handbook of North American Indians: Northeast,* ed. Bruce G. Trigger, 20 vols. (Washington, D.C.: Smithsonian Institution, 1978), 15: 622-35. Henry F. Dobyns employed an estimate of five per warrior to calculate native populations. Using his estimate results in a total of fifteen hundred residents; *Their Number Become Thinned: Native American Population Dynamics in Eastern North America* (Knoxville: Univ. of Tennessee Press, 1983).

24. Quote from French correspondence of 1748-49 in "The French Regime in Wisconsin," 18: 20-22; also see Theodore Pease and E. Jenison, *Anglo-French Boundary Disputes in the West, 1749-1763* (Springfield: Illinois State Historical Society, 1940), 49. The names "the Lower Shawonese Town," "the lower Shawanees town," "Lower Shanna Town," "the Lower Town," "the Shannoah town," or "Shawnoah" were English variations; see Hanna, *The Wilderness Trail,* 2: chap. 5; Brown, *Early Maps,* fig. 25. The French had their own names: Saint Yotoc, which may be a corruption of "Scioto," "Sinhioto," "Sononito," "Sonnioto," "Scioto," and "Cenioteaux"; O.H. Marshall, "De Celoron's Expedition to the Ohio in 1749," *Magazine of American History* 2 (1878): 129-50; Ermine Wheeler Voegelin, *An Ethnohistorical Report on the Indian Use and Occupancy of Royce Area 11, Ohio and Indiana,* 2 vols. (New York: Garland Press, 1974), 1: 261.

25. White, *The Middle Ground,* 186-222.

26. See Henderson et al., *Indian Occupation,* 21-62.

27. Callender, *Handbook of North American Indians,* 622-35. Discussion of the five divisions of the Shawnee may be found in James H. Howard, *Shawnee! The Ceremonialism of a Native Indian Tribe and Its Cultural Background* (Athens: Ohio Univ. Press, 1981).

28. Callender discusses the five Shawnee divisions and the various possible town names that resulted; also see Howard, *Shawnee!,* 25-30. Evidence for why the lower

Shawnee Town was probably called Chillicothe by the inhabitants may be found in Hanna, *The Wilderness Trail,* 1: 145-46, and 2: 129; also James Mooney, "Chillicothe," in *Handbook of American Indians North of Mexico: Part One,* ed. F.W. Hodge, Bureau of American Ethnology Bulletin #30 (Washington, D.C.: Smithsonian Institution, 1912), 267-68. Schutz suggests that the Mekoche, not the Chalaka, division originally settled the town. If so, the town's name would not have been Chillicothe; Schutz, *Study of Shawnee Myth,* 367-70. According to tradition, the national chief was a member of the Chalaka or Thawikila divisions; see Clark, *Shawnee Indian Migration,* 79; Howard, *Shawnee!,* 26-27.

29. Clark, *Shawnee Indian Migration,* 63, 71-80; Voegelin, *Mortuary Customs,* 255-56.

30. For statements about the Shawnee's "great chief," see *Minutes of the Provincial Council of Pennsylvania,* 5: 497, 685; Pease and Jenison, *Anglo-French Boundary Disputes,* 372; Mary C. Darlington, ed., *History of Colonel Henry Bouquet and the Western Frontiers of Pennsylvania* (privately printed, 1920), 27. For movements of the other chiefs, see *Minutes of the Provincial Council of Pennsylvania,* 5: 311, 352; Mulkearn, *George Mercer Papers,* 17; Hanna, *The Wilderness Trail,* 2: 139.

31. See the list of three Shawnee who attended the Treaty Council in Lancaster in 1748 and the fifteen Shawnee who attended the Treaty Council in 1753 at Carlisle; *Minutes of the Provincial Council of Pennsylvania,* 5: 318, 685.

32. See Celoron's Journal of 1749 in Lambing, "Celeron's Journal"; and Bonnecamps' Journal of 1749 in Thwaites, *The Jesuit Relations,* for a description of the inhabitants at the lower Shawnee Town.

33. Marshall Sahlins, *Tribesmen* (Englewood Cliffs, N.J.: Prentice-Hall, 1968), explores the salient characteristics of tribal societies worldwide.

34. Clark, *Shawnee Indian Migration,* 176.

35. For contemporary descriptions of the lower Shawnee Town's physical setting, see Mulkearn, *George Mercer Papers,* 16-17; Henderson et al., *Indian Occupation,* 21-22; Rev. Neander M. Woods, *The Woods-McAfee Memorial* (Louisville: Courier-Journal Job Printing, 1905), 429-30.

36. Contemporary Kittanning on the upper Ohio River was organized in a similar manner; McConnell, *A Country Between,* 25-26. For settlement patterns, see Henderson et al., *Indian Occupation,* 202-6; and A. Gwynn Henderson, David Pollack, and Christopher A. Turnbow, "Chronology and Cultural Patterns," in *Fort Ancient Cultural Dynamics in the Middle Ohio Valley,* ed. A. Gwynn Henderson, Monographs in World Archaeology #8 (Madison, Wis.: Prehistory Press, 1992), 273-75. For houses, see Lee H. Hanson Jr., *The Hardin Village Site,* Studies in Anthropology #4 (Lexington: Univ. of Kentucky Press, 1966); Henderson et al., *Indian Occupation,* 207-10; and for houses, Henderson et al., "Chronology and Cultural Patterns," 253-79.

37. For descriptions of the culture of the Shawnee and other Ohio Valley inhabitants, see Clark, *Shawnee Indian Migration;* Henderson et al., *Indian Occupation,* 201-10; and David Pollack and A. Gwynn Henderson, "Toward a Model of Fort Ancient Society," in Henderson, ed., *Fort Ancient Cultural Dynamics in the Middle Ohio Valley,* 285-91. Also see McConnell, *A Country Between,* 25-33; Howard, *Shawnee!;* and Callender, *Handbook of North American Indians.*

38. Henderson et al., *Indian Occupation,* 54-55; Reuben Gold Thwaites and Louise

Phelps Kellogg, eds., *Documentary History of Dunmore's War 1774* (Madison: Wisconsin Historical Society, 1905), 117-18; Woods, *Woods-McAfee Memorial,* 429- 30.

39. For descriptions of the items buried with the dead at the lower Shawnee Town, see David Pollack and A. Gwynn Henderson, "Contact Period Developments in the Middle Ohio Valley" (paper presented at the Society for American Archaeology, Pittsburgh, 1983); and idem, "A Mid-Eighteenth Century Historic Indian Occupation in Greenup County, Kentucky," in *Late Prehistoric Research in Kentucky,* eds. David Pollack, Charles Hockensmith, and Thomas Sanders (Frankfort: Kentucky Heritage Council, 1984), 22; and Voegelin, *Mortuary Customs,* 272-74.

40. Gist called it a "kind of state-house" with dimensions as "about 90 feet"; see Mulkearn, *George Mercer Papers,* 16.

41. Goodman, *Journal of Captain William Trent,* 39-40. Despite the fact that neither Celoron, Bonnecamps, nor Gist describe a trading house at the lower Shawnee Town in 1749 or 1751, the number of traders and the amount of trade carried out at the town implies there was one by 1749; see Kenneth P. Bailey, ed., *The Ohio Company Papers, 1753-1817* (Arcata, Calif.: privately printed, 1947), 61, 136.

42. For a description of late prehistoric archaeology in Kentucky, see William E. Sharp, "Fort Ancient Farmers," in *Kentucky Archaeology,* ed. R. Barry Lewis (Lexington: Univ. Press of Kentucky, 1996), 161-81. For a description of materials found archaeologically at the lower Shawnee Town, see Pollack and Henderson, "A Mid-Eighteenth Century Historic Indian Occupation"; Henderson et al., *Indian Occupation,* 131-35. For a description of late prehistoric and protohistoric subsistence in the Ohio Valley, see Jack Rossen and Richard B. Edging, "East Meets West: Patterns in Kentucky Late Prehistoric Subsistence," in *Current Archaeological Research in Kentucky,* ed. David Pollack (Frankfort: Kentucky Heritage Council, 1987), 225-34; Jack Rossen, "Botanical Remains," in Henderson, *Fort Ancient Cultural Dynamics in the Middle Ohio Valley,* 189-208; Emanuel Breitburg, "Vertebrate Faunal Remains," in ibid., 209-41. The remains of charred Northern Flint corn and the remains of elk, deer, and turtle have been documented archaeologically for the lower Shawnee Town; see Pollack and Henderson, "A Mid-Eighteenth Century Historic Indian Occupation." Celoron's journal also provides evidence for the continued pursuit of wild game, though he observed in 1749 that "waste had destroyed the abundance of game"; Lambing, "Celeron's Journal," 366.

43. Pollack and Henderson, "A Mid-Eighteenth Century Historic Indian Occupation."

44. Christopher A. Turnbow and Cynthia Jobe, "The Goolman Site: A Late Fort Ancient Winter Encampment in Clark County, Kentucky," in Pollack et al., *Late Prehistoric Research in Kentucky,* 25-49; and James E. Fitting and Charles E. Cleland, "Late Prehistoric Settlement Patterns in the Upper Great Lakes," *Ethnohistory* 16 (1969): 289-302; Henderson et al., *Indian Occupation,* 201-6.

45. Sahlins, *Tribesmen,* 20-22.

46. Ibid., 16.

47. Ibid., 16-17.

48. See ibid.; Elizabeth M. Brumfiel and John W. Fox, eds., *Factional Competition and Political Development in the New World* (Cambridge: Cambridge Univ. Press, 1994); and Winifred Creamer and Jonathan Haas, "Tribe Versus Chiefdom in Lower Central America," *American Antiquity* 50 (1985): 738-54, regarding principles of tribal political

organization and factionalism in general. For a discussion of native leadership and factions specifically for the Ohio Valley in the 1740s and 1750s, see McConnell, *A Country Between,* 25-46.

49. See *Minutes of the Provincial Council of Pennsylvania,* 5: 692, 702-3, 734 regarding an international native council held at the lower Shawnee Town in 1753.

50. See ibid., 5: 314.

51. Regarding the Six Nations' relationship to other native peoples "on Ohio," see McConnell, *A Country Between,* 56-112, especially 56-58 and 82. For later in the century, see Gregory Evans Dowd, *A Spirited Resistance: The North American Indian Struggle for Unity, 1745-1815* (Baltimore: Johns Hopkins Univ. Press, 1994); and R. David Edmunds, *The Shawnee Prophet* (Lincoln: Univ. of Nebraska Press, 1983).

52. See Lambing, "Celeron's Journal"; Thwaites, *The Jesuit Relations;* Croghan's deposition of 1777 in William P. Palmer, ed., *Calendar of Virginia State Papers and Other Manuscripts, 1652-1781,* 11 vols. (Richmond: State Librarian, 1875), 1: 276; Mulkearn, *George Mercer Papers,* 16-17, 25; and Hanna, *The Wilderness Trail,* 292-98.

53. Wainwright, "An Indian Trade Failure," 345; Dunbar Rowland and A.G. Sanders, eds., *Mississippi Provincial Archives, French Dominion, 1749-1763* (Baton Rouge: Louisiana State Univ. Press, 1984), 77.

54. Pease and Jenison, *Anglo-French Boundary Disputes,* 128; "The French Regime in Wisconsin," 18: 11-12; Volwiler, *George Croghan,* 39-41.

55. See Mitchell's Map of 1755 and figure 25 in Brown, *Early Maps,* 95-97.

56. The Pennsylvania trading system of the late 1740s and early 1750s is described in Volwiler, *George Croghan;* and in John W. Jordan, ed., "Journal of James Kenny," *Pennsylvania Magazine of History and Biography* 37 (1913): 1-47, 152-201. In 1749, no good fall skins were brought in, but Philadelphia was flush with prosperity and the market was strong, so credit was liberally extended in the Indian trade. April and May 1750 witnessed a bumper crop in skins, but by the time they were sold in London in 1751, their value had fallen. Prices did not improve during 1752, which sank traders like Croghan and Trent deeply into debt. The winter of 1750-51 was a severe one and possibly a factor that affected the amount of skins brought in from the region in the spring of 1751. Also contributing to the economic situation was the order in 1750 by the French that their traders undersell the English in the places where they both traded; see Wainwright, "An Indian Trade Failure," 357, 360, 374-75.

57. Volwiler, *George Croghan,* 34-37.

58. Volwiler outlines Croghan's Ohio country trading post network, listing eight locations stretching across Pennsylvania and Ohio; ibid., 33-37. Croghan's home, located five miles west of Harris' Ferry (now Harrisburg), was the eastern terminus. When the French and Indians drove the Pennsylvania traders out of the Ohio country in 1754, Pine Creek and Oswegle Bottom were valued at £300 each. The LoggsTown and Muskingum storehouses were valued at £150. The lower Shawnee Town storehouse was valued at £200; Bailey, *Ohio Company Papers,* 61. It is possible that, had it not been destroyed in 1752, Pickawillany may have eclipsed the lower Shawnee Town as a Pennsylvanian trading factory.

59. Volwiler, *George Croghan,* 34-38; Edmunds, "Old Briton," 10.

60. See Tanner, *Atlas of Great Lakes Indian History,* map 9, 40-41.

61. Volwiler interprets a January 1753 incident—when Croghan and Lowery's trad-

ers were taken captive by the French some two hundred miles south of the lower Shawnee Town—as evidence that the town served as a node from which Pennsylvania traders fanned out in all directions; Volwiler, *George Croghan,* 37-38; *Minutes of the Provincial Council of Pennsylvania,* 5: 663. Croghan's trade may have extended into central Kentucky twenty years before Daniel Boone's arrival.

62. See Lambing, "Celeron's Journal," 370.

63. Bailey, *Ohio Company Papers,* 136.

64. Henderson et al., *Indian Occupation,* 59.

65. See Goodman, *Journal of Captain William Trent,* 39-40, for a description of the trading house interior arrangement.

66. For lists of goods traded to the Indians, see Volwiler, *George Croghan,* 30; Bailey, *Ohio Company Papers,* 40, 169-71; and *Minutes of the Provincial Council of Pennsylvania,* 5: 151-52, 197, 406. For trade items found at the Bentley site, one of the four sites that represent the archaeological manifestation of the lower Shawnee Town on the south side of the Ohio River in Greenup County, Kentucky, see Pollack and Henderson, "A Mid-Eighteenth Century Historic Indian Occupation"; and idem, "Contact Period Developments in the Middle Ohio Valley." A discussion of the impact of the deerskin trade in the region may be found in James P. McClure, "The Ohio Valley's Deerskin Trade: Topics for Consideration," *The Old Northwest* 15 (1990): 115-33.

67. See Jordan, "Journal of James Kenny."

68. Bailey, *Ohio Company Papers,* 120.

69. Bruce G. Trigger, *Natives and Newcomers: Canada's "Heroic Age" Reconsidered* (Montreal: McGill-Queen's Univ. Press, 1985), 186-94; Sahlins, *Tribesmen,* 9, 23, and chap. 5.

70. Richard W. Jefferies, "Hunters and Gatherers after the Ice Age," in Lewis, *Kentucky Archaeology,* 61-62, 75.

71. John R. Swanton, *The Indians of the Southeastern United States* (Washington, D.C.: Smithsonian Institution, 1979), 736-42.

72. Hanson, *The Hardin Village Site;* idem, *The Buffalo Site—A Late Seventeenth-Century Indian Village Site (46PU31) in Putnam County, West Virginia,* Report of Archaeological Investigations #5 (Morgantown: West Virginia Geological and Economic Survey, 1975); E.A. Hooten and C.C. Willoughby, *Indian Village Site and Cemetery Near Madisonville, Ohio* (1920; reprint: Millwood, N.Y.: Krause Reprints, 1974); Robert F. Maslowski, *Protohistoric Villages in Southern West Virginia* (paper presented at the Second Uplands Conference, James Madison University, Harrisonburg, Va., 1984); Jeffrey R. Graybill, *The Eastern Periphery of Fort Ancient (A.D. 1050-1650): A Diachronic Approach to Settlement Variability* (Ph.D. diss., University of Washington, 1981); Henderson et al., *Indian Occupation,* 212-15.

73. James H. Merrell, *The Indians' New World: Catawbas and Their Neighbors from European Contact Through the Era of Removal* (Chapel Hill: Univ. of North Carolina Press, 1989), 38-40, 64-65.

74. Volwiler, *George Croghan,* 31.

75. Wainwright, "An Indian Trade Failure," 343-44.

76. For discussion of New York trade, see Volwiler, *George Croghan,* 19. For Hudson Bay fur trade, see Arthur J. Ray, *Indians in the Fur Trade, Their Role as Hunters, Trappers, and Middlemen in the Lands Southwest of Hudson Bay, 1660-1860* (Toronto: Univ. of

Toronto Press, 1974), 141-42; Arthur J. Ray and D.B. Freeman, *"Give Us Good Measure"* (Toronto: Univ. of Toronto Press, 1978). For discussion of Piedmont Indian trade, see Merrell, *Indians' New World.*

77. *Minutes of the Provincial Council of Pennsylvania,* 5: 630, 749.

78. McConnell, *A Country Between,* 39-41; White, *The Middle Ground,* 211-12. Merrell provides an excellent discussion of the culture of trade in the Carolina Piedmont; see *Indians' New World,* chap. 2.

79. Ray, *Indians in the Fur Trade,* 141-42; Trigger, *Natives and Newcomers,* 186-94.

80. See Mancall, *Deadly Medicine,* for a consideration of all facets of native peoples and alcohol.

81. Ibid., chap. 4.

82. Downes, *Council Fires on the Upper Ohio,* 31-39. The sale of liquor was such a problem that some natives took an oath to stop drinking rum for four years.

83. Ibid., 30-35; McConnell, *A Country Between,* 44; Mulkearn, *George Mercer Papers,* 558. Pennsylvanian proclamations about liquor were made in 1747 and 1749; *Minutes of the Provincial Council of Pennsylvania,* 5: 194-96, 397-98. For the liquor problem in 1748, see ibid., 5: 357. Scarouady's comments about liquor control made at the Council of Carlisle in 1753 may be found in ibid., 5: 676. For an aside from the 1753 Council's commissioners deploring the alcohol trade, see ibid., 5: 684.

84. See *Minutes of the Provincial Council* 5: 357, for colonial observations and the Indian chiefs' responses.

85. Mancall, *Deadly Medicine,* chap. 5.

86. McConnell, *A Country Between,* 49-50.

87. See Croghan's statement in his journal in *Minutes of the Provincial Council of Pennsylvania,* 5: 531, about the "Southward Indians" who had come to the "Lower Towns" to war, thus preventing the chiefs from attending.

88. Ibid., 5: 696-706, 6: 153; Mulkearn, *George Mercer Papers,* 544n, 556n; Thwaites, *Early Western Travels,* 18: 90.

89. Anonymous Diary of a Trip from Detroit to the Ohio River, 4; Mulkearn, *George Mercer Papers,* 121-22. Amidst the commotion at LoggsTown resulting from the news that the French were on their way to attack the English on Ohio, Trent complained in 1753 about the Shawnee attendance to their dancing: "I am obliged to wait here till the Shawnese finish their Dance, which is likely to hold these five or six days. They seem to think of nothing but their dancing"; Darlington, *History of Colonel Henry Bouquet,* 39; and, "They are the most indefatigable dancers"; Jones, *Journal of Two Visits,* 77-78.

90. See Homer G. Barnett, "Culture Process," *American Anthropologist* 42 (1940): 21-48; Ralph Linton, "Acculturation and the Processes of Culture Change," in *Acculturation in Seven American Indian Tribes,* ed. Ralph Linton (New York: Appleton Century, 1940), 463-82; Edward H. Spicer, "Types of Contact and Processes of Change," in *Perspectives in American Indian Culture Change,* ed. Edward H. Spicer (Chicago: Univ. of Chicago Press, 1961), 517-43; John R. White, "Historic Contact Sites as Laboratories for the Study of Culture Change," *The Conference on Historic Site Archaeology Papers* 9 (1975): 153-63; and Pollack and Henderson, "Contact Period Developments in the Middle Ohio Valley," for discussions about the circumstances under which native peoples accept non-native goods.

91. Pollack and Henderson, "Contact Period Developments in the Middle Ohio

Valley," 20.

92. Ibid., 21-22.

93. Dowd, *A Spirited Resistance,* 40.

94. Jones, *Journal of Two Visits,* 54, 62-65.

95. Dowd, *A Spirited Resistance,* 24.

96. Bailey, *Ohio Company Papers,* 4.

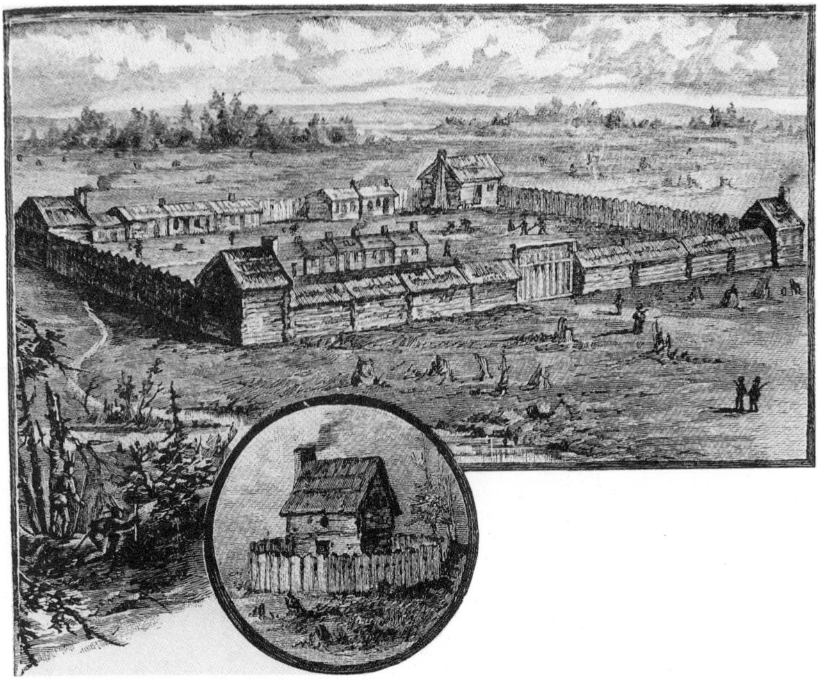

Nineteenth-century historians of Kentucky took particular interest in the fort and station construction of the 1770s and 1780s. In 1886, Z.F. Smith rendered his version of Fort Lexington, built in 1779 on the plain-like expanse of the inner Bluegrass region. Below the drawing of the fort is a sketch of the blockhouse which preceded it. Z.F. Smith, *History of Kentucky* (Louisville: Courier-Journal Printing Co., 1886)

Frontier Defenses and Pioneer Strategies in the Historic Settlement Era

NANCY O'MALLEY

Colonel William Whitley, who first brought his wife and two small children to Kentucky in 1775, conceded the threat to his family's survival in his recollections: "time went on very smooth with us until the Spring 76 when the Indians took Callaways & Boones daughters and that alarmed us . . . so that we moved to Harrodsburg . . . where I remained until sometime March in which time James McDonald was killed at Drennon's Lick leaving a wife & one child. Shortly after this time William Ray was killed at the Shawney springs. . . . This was the first person I ever seen Scalpt."[1] With the onset of the Revolutionary War, settlers quickly realized that they were in dangerous and exposed circumstances, far from the security of eastern settlements and subject to unexpected attacks from Native American tribes and, occasionally, British troops. Their response was not to abandon attempts to settle in the new unclaimed lands of Kentucky, but to devise a system of defense that allowed them to satisfy the requirements of colonial land claim laws and still protect themselves. The system embodied features borrowed from earlier frontiers—safety in numbers, erection of physical barriers, a vigilant patrol system—that worked remarkably well considering the limited numbers of settlers involved. Yet, its effectiveness was uneven, and it occasionally failed to prevent significant loss of life. This system was so specifically tailored to wartime conditions that once hostilities ceased, settlers completely abandoned it.

The concept of the frontier has prompted much research, debate, and discussion among historians, anthropologists, geographers, folklorists, and other scholars.[2] While historians have placed much emphasis on Frederick Jackson Turner's famous frontier hypothesis (and its debunking), social scientists have sought appropriate theories in ecological models. All of the theoretical attempts tend to focus on only a few variables, however; and all seek regularities that supposedly represent natural migration laws. As Ellen

Eslinger points out when speaking of frontier social structure, "The laws remain elusive, yet it has become increasingly clear that certain factors do influence who migrates when and where. It is also clear that some of these factors operate widely and affect a major proportion of all migrations."[3]

No one theory can adequately explain the complexities of frontier settlement. To survive on the frontier, the Kentucky pioneer had to be flexible and adaptable. Roles varied, depending on whether the individual was married or single, male or female, a parent or childless, adult or child. From a purely practical standpoint, the pioneer family had to construct a place to live where it was sheltered from the elements, could procure enough to eat, and could protect itself from hostile threats. As parents, pioneers naturally sought to provide sustenance and protection for their children, but they also were concerned with developing acceptable value systems. Adult men, married and single, served as soldiers and placed their own lives at risk for the greater good; adult women demonstrated a considerable amount of self-reliance at all times, particularly when their men were away at war. Children often took on adult responsibilities for the sake of the family. To some extent, the role of each family member was bounded by cultural expectations and mores, but the frontier demanded flexibility in defining and fulfilling that role.

The station and fort network enabled frontier settlers to fulfill both the roles thrust upon them by the greater society in which they lived and those dictated by the events and conditions of the frontier. Never wholly arbitrary, the decisions that settlers made and the solutions they crafted drew upon a longstanding tradition—adaptability reinforced by strong cultural patterns of kinship and interpersonal relationships, bound together for the common good, and in search of expedient solutions to short-term problems. The result was that during a relatively short period, settlers successfully adapted to a difficult situation without losing sight of the ultimate goals of settling. Hence, as soon as possible, settlers unceremoniously abandoned the stations and forts that served them so well during the taming of the Kentucky frontier for their more overarching dreams of greater prosperity, stability, and security for their families.

Although no one theory satisfactorily explains these complexities, the combined application of several theoretical positions can generate useful and insightful interpretations. Dating of documented stations and forts in the Inner Bluegrass region indicates that settlement of the Kentucky frontier was a series of "pulses" in which the entry of settlers into Kentucky waxed and waned. Four chronological periods—the Pre-Revolutionary (1773-1777), Revolutionary (1778-1782), Post-Revolutionary (1783-1785), and Post-

Frontier (after 1785)—with specific characteristics are evident, differentiated by the conditions under which settlers constructed stations and forts. These periods also fit nicely into three distinct sequential phases theorized by geographer J.C. Hudson and modified by geographer Michael J. O'Brien.[4] The first phase, "colonization," is exemplified by the stations of the Pre-Revolutionary Period. As colonists migrated into an area, populations filled in unoccupied spaces and increased the density of settlement, resulting in the spatial manifestation of "spread," the second phase. Stations classified under the Revolutionary Period are representative of the spread phase. The third phase, "competition," occurred with the Post-Revolutionary and Post-Frontier Periods. Because earlier settlers had annexed the best tracts, this stage is characterized by increased competition for land. These later two periods witnessed the replacement of forts and stations with small towns and crossroads communities that served a dispersed population of rural farms.

The Kentucky frontier was a powerful lure to the yeoman farmer who found himself on the lower rungs of eastern social ladders. Scarcity of land, resistance to established religious authorities, and the urge for greater prosperity all fueled the movement to western lands with most settlers coming from Virginia, North Carolina, and Pennsylvania.

Before 1773, Kentucky (then known as Fincastle County, Virginia) had been explored by various people, but the only official surveys made were two made for John Fry by Colonel George Washington in the Big Sandy River drainage in 1770.[5] In 1773, Captain Thomas Bullitt led a party of about thirty-five men to make surveys in the Falls of the Ohio area. To receive the grants, he had to enter the claims in the books of the Fincastle County surveyor, William Preston. But when he attempted to do this, Preston refused to record them, saying that, because the land was not cleared of Indian rights by treaty and the claims had not been officially surveyed by duly authorized deputies, they were illegal.[6] Bullitt appealed to Lord Dunmore, governor of the Virginia colony, resulting in two grants recorded as military warrants. Also in 1773, two parties, one led by James Harrod and the other by the McAfee brothers, made surveys in the present county of Mercer.

Surveying renewed in 1774 when Governor Dunmore released a statement that allowed veterans of the French and Indian War to claim Kentucky lands wherever they desired, thereby skirting the problem of Indian rights to territories. James Harrod returned with thirty-one men, laid out the town that later became Harrodsburg, and surveyed claims as far south as Knob Lick in present Boyle County and as far east as the Kentucky River.

In late May 1774, William Preston sent his own surveyors, many of whom had accompanied Bullitt, to Kentucky under the leadership of John Floyd. They resurveyed patents at the Falls of the Ohio, then split into two groups: one under Hancock Taylor moved west to the Fort Harrod area; the other under Floyd surveyed in the vicinity of Bullitt's Lick in present Bullitt County. They rendezvoused along Elkhorn Creek in late June and surveyed additional tracts. An anticipated August 1 meeting at James Harrod's settlement failed when Shawnee killed two of Harrod's men and induced the remaining Harrod party to return east to the settlements. Two Preston surveying groups, headed by James Duncan and John Floyd, reached the deserted cabins separately and departed without making contact. Indians ambushed a third group in late July, killing one man on the site and mortally wounding leader Hancock Taylor. A concerned Preston sent Daniel Boone and Michael Stoner to guide the remaining two groups back to the eastern settlements.

While these early explorers and surveyors established the patterns of settlement, Colonel Richard Henderson's 1775 purchase of the territory south of the Ohio River between the Kentucky and Cumberland Rivers resulted in the founding of the region's most important settlement. Henderson's Transylvania Company paid two thousand pounds sterling to the Cherokee for the rights to the lands.[7] Colonial governments immediately challenged the legality of the purchase. Henderson did not succeed in gaining legal title, but until his purchase was officially nullified, the activities of his land company significantly influenced Kentucky settlement. Fort Boonesborough, established in April 1775 on the Kentucky River in present Madison County, became headquarters for the land company, served as communications entrepôt, and provided sanctuary for hundreds of settlers through the settlement era.

Despite settlers' confinement within the walls of Fort Harrod, Boonesborough, and other fortified settlements, a focus on agricultural pursuits early set the stage for how Kentucky's frontier was perceived and settled. Early arrivals, recognizing that the soils of central Kentucky were uncommonly rich and fertile, claimed these areas first. Vegetational cover was considered a good indicator of underlying soil quality. Settlers divided the land into first-, second-, and third-rate categories, depending on its usefulness for farming. As a result, these designations were used for determining property taxes. The presence of walnut, sugar maple, ash, cherry, buckeye, honey and black locust, coffee, elm, mulberry, hackberry, oak, hickory, and yellow poplar trees identified highly fertile soils, as did large stands of native cane, which provided good forage for livestock. In his study of historical botany, Julien

Campbell explains, "The Bluegrass forests were distinctive from the rest of Kentucky in the dominance of walnuts (open sites), sugar maple (shady sites) and ashes (drier sites), all of which are typical of richer soils."[8]

The richness of wild game was also commonly noted by early settlers. In 1795, a visitor, Rev. David Barrow, described the abundance of the region:

> Our common kind of birds were very scarce I am told when the country was first settled but they have greatly increased such as Partridges; the gray mocking bird and kill dee are very rarely to be seen. They have no whipoorwills off from the cliffs. They have an abundance of woodpeckers, crows and ravens. Their woodcocks have white or what some call ivory bills. They have plenty of pheasants in places also wild geese and ducks are plentiful in the fall season on the Ohio. Wild turkeys are much reduced on the settlements but plentiful in the borders. It is the same with deer, bear, etc. They have no rats or common mice except in the neighborhood of the boat landings. There are but few hares and no fox squirrels but the like of gray and ground squirrels I have never seen before.[9]

An important ingredient for survival was the exploitation of deer, bison, bear, elk, and turkey. Smaller mammals, fowl, and fish were taken for various purposes; for example, long hunters commonly trapped otter and beaver for their pelts.[10] This largesse did not remain unchanged over time, as the pressure of additional immigration altered the patterns of wildlife, driving some species into extinction or to less crowded environs, and expanding habitat niches for others. Some species succumbed to the increased competition of domesticated livestock; others were eradicated as pests. Settlers themselves created great waste in taking game. Henderson mentioned this problem in his 1775 journal. He tried with little success to institute some controls on settlers' wasteful practices. "We found it very difficult at first and indeed yet to Stop great waste in killing meat," complained Henderson; "Others & indeed all at times shoot, cripple and Scare the game, without being able to get much. . . . Others of wicked and wanton dispositions would Kill three four five or a Dozen Buffaloes and not take a half horse Load from them all."[11]

While settlers chose a tract of land for its soil quality and abundant game, they constructed residences according to access to water. Stations and forts were always located near one or more freshwater springs, permanent sources of water throughout the year. The springs were usually located outside the stockaded enclosure rather than in it, although a few sites departed from this pattern. On several occasions, the spring's location outside the enclosure created difficulties for settlers who ran short of water during Indian attacks or sieges. Occasionally, covered walkways were built to the spring to provide some protection from attack while gathering water. Generally, however, a visit to the station spring exposed the water gatherer and necessitated an armed accompaniment. The inconveniences of building a station around a spring were not limited to exposure. Springs were seldom located on level ground, most emanated from ridge slopes, rock ledges below the brow of a ridge, subterranean caves, or artesian sources that produced what were called "boiling springs." Thus, they posed hazards of flooding and muddiness during particularly wet seasons. Because livestock as well as human inhabitants used the springs, sanitation was also an issue. Although fouling of water sources was common, a strongly running spring cleaned itself out periodically.

Once settled, pioneers turned to land acquisition. Often several men claimed the same tracts, a situation that made a good many lawyers wealthy from the lawsuits that arose. The land claim process was fraught with complexities. As Neal O. Hammon accurately noted, "According to the custom of the time, a person who marked off a tract of vacant land and made some sort of improvement on the claim had a legal preemption to that tract for a period of three years. During that time the land was no longer considered vacant, so it could not be claimed by anyone else. Within that three-year period, the claimant was expected to have sufficient time to have that tract legally surveyed, enter the survey, and pay the requisite fees in order to obtain a patent."[12] By purchasing land claims made by others, many settlers saved the costs and risks of marking the land themselves, but they became dependent on the honesty of the person selling the claim. Known as "outlyers" or "land jobbers," frontier speculators like Daniel Boone and James Harrod insured the legality of the claims they offered; less scrupulous characters often made cabin improvements and sold lands with no intention of ever having them formally surveyed or paying any fees. Consequently, claimants often had to buy out others with claims to the same tract, sometimes paying for lands several times over. The situation became so problematic that in 1779 and 1780 several land courts were held in Kentucky to resolve land disputes.[13] Well into the nineteenth century, however, county circuit courts continued to hear land suits that stemmed from the claiming practices of the frontier settlement era.

At the time of Kentucky's settlement in the 1770s, Native American tribes such as the Shawnee were living in permanent villages along and north of the Ohio River.[14] They considered Kentucky part of their territory, using it for winter hunting camps and for gathering various natural products such as salt. Since their permanent villages were located a considerable distance from central Kentucky, where Euro-American settlement first took place, their raids tended to involve relatively limited numbers of warriors and were generally not lengthy excursions. While a few notable sieges took place in Kentucky, settlers knew that the most common experiences they would have with American Indian enemies would be ones of short duration that could often be withstood from within the confines of a fort or station.

Death at the hands of American Indian warriors was most likely if a settler was caught away from his settlement. Hunting game, surveying and clearing land, and other activities that exposed the settlers were far more likely to result in fatalities. An incident recalled by William Whitley was just such a case. In 1777, fourteen-year-old William Ray was clearing land with his older teenage brother and two other men near the Shawnee Springs where his stepfather, Hugh McGary, later built a station. A band of Shawnee warriors captured William, tomahawked and scalped him, and probably killed or took captive another of the party. William's brother, James, survived the attack by outrunning the Indians to Fort Harrod; an older man named Coomes hid until the party left.[15]

Danger also loomed during the punitive raids that settlers meted out to their enemies. Operating on the premise that an effective defense is a serious offense, the settlers launched numerous attacks, often engaging Indian raiding parties as they returned north. On several occasions, General George Rogers Clark organized expeditions to the Ohio country to destroy native villages and corn crops, kill Indians, and take prisoners. Deaths among the adult male population of Kentucky reduced the number of able fighting men; widows and orphans frequently became dependent on others for sustenance. Hugh McGary, living in Fort Harrod, wrote an impassioned petition to the Virginia General Assembly in 1779, mentioning that "our fort is already filled with widows and orphans; their necessities call upon us daily for supplies."[16]

Forts and stations answered the need for defense and were specifically suited to the nature of the danger. The Kentucky system of frontier protection was a network of defensible residential stations interspersed among larger defensible forts. John Filson's 1784 map illustrates the stations and forts, as well as the trails that ran between them. Documentary literature relating to the frontier settlement period of Kentucky frequently describes aspects of station and fort construction, plans, and architecture. Some of the pioneers interviewed by Reverend John Dabney Shane, a Presbyterian minister of the 1840s, drew plans of the stations they frequented. Historians also have rendered their own artistic reconstructions of the appearances of stations and forts. As is often the case in historical documentation, descriptions are usually not detailed, and questions remain concerning specific characteristics. Nevertheless, the documentary record provides substantial data that is useful in reconstructing how stations looked and were perceived.

Additionally, the exact meanings of the terms "fort" and "station" varied. The differences in their usage, however, gradually became less distinct as the frontier became more settled. "Fort" generally referred to a large, communally occupied, stockaded enclosure that provided a place of public sanctuary. Notable examples are Fort Harrod, Fort Boonesborough, and the Lexington Fort—sites established by groups of settlers and subject to very transient and shifting occupancy. Although no private individual or family controlled the fort, one man commanded respect and generally was considered the leader. The term "station" applied to defensible residential sites, often very similar in appearance to forts. Single families claiming unoccupied tracts of land established these stations throughout the region. Other families often joined the founding family for safety reasons, but the station was a privately held and controlled site. "The perturbed state of that period, and the savage state of the country, which was in entire wilderness," explained land promoter Gilbert Imlay, "made the object of the first emigrants that of security and sustenance which produced the scheme of several families living together in what were called stations."[17] Families that lived in stations were frequently related by blood, marriage, or friendship as Ellen Eslinger discovered in her study of Strode's Station in present Clark County.[18] Such sites were generally smaller than forts, and living conditions were not as unpleasant. Issues of sanitation, crowding, and deprivation existed at both stations and forts, but the latter generally experienced more social unrest as settlers of differing convictions, moral values, and behavioral codes lived together in confined and intimate association. Stations were not as safe as forts, but many settlers preferred more amenable company and proximity to their own land claims. Jane Stevenson, who came to the Lexington Fort in 1779, moved to McConnell's Station because of her distaste for some of the settlers she and her children encountered: "There were every sort of people there . . . that was what took us away."[19]

The distinction between stations and forts was not made by everyone. Stations were sometimes called forts although the reverse generally was not true; Fort Harrod, Fort Boonesborough, and the Lexington Fort were never called stations. Other sites, like Bryan's Station in Fayette County, attained the size of a fort, but continued to be called a station by most settlers, as attested to in this description by Gilbert Imlay.

These stations were a kind of quadrangular, or sometimes oblong forts, formed by building log-houses connectedly, only leaving openings for gateways to pass as they might have occasion. They were generally fixed in a favourable situation for water, and in a body of Good land. Frequently the head of some party of connections who had a settlement and pre-emption right, seized upon these opportunities to have his land cleared, which was necessary for the support of the station, for it was not only prudent to keep close in their forts at times, but it was also necessary to keep their horses and cows up, otherwise the Indians would carry off the horses, and shoot and destroy the cattle.[20]

While public forts were always stockaded, defensibility varied considerably between stations. Minimally, a station could be composed of one or more cabins in which families shuttered themselves. Other stations were "forts in miniature" with cabins organized in a rectangular or square plan forming an enclosure.[21] External walls from each cabin, including two walls of each corner bastion cabin, and stockading between the cabins formed a solid enclosure within which families and their livestock could take sanctuary.

If they survive in any form at all, station and fort sites exist with few exceptions as archaeological sites. Many have been destroyed by cultivation, urban construction, or other factors. Of the large forts in the central Kentucky area, only Fort Boonesborough still exists. Limited excavations and documentary research on this site indicate that at least one-third has eroded away, but significant deposits still exist.[22] Both the Lexington Fort and Fort Harrod have been destroyed by urban construction. The survival rate of station sites is not fully known because only limited excavations have been undertaken at a few locales. Over 150 stations have been documented in the history of the twelve counties of the Inner Bluegrass region where settlement was earliest and most intense. Of the approximately sixty specific locations that are suspected, only a few have been verified by archaeological excavation.[23] Even less is known of station sites in the Outer Bluegrass and around the Falls of the Ohio.

Archaeological investigations of frontier forts and stations have, to date, been limited in scope. Excavations that have yielded cultural features dating to their pioneer settlement occupation have been conducted at Fort Boonesborough in Madison County, John Grant's Station in Bourbon County, and Hugh McGary's Station in Mercer County. Artifacts recovered and features documented at these sites relate to limited station occupations and, in all but McGary's Station, to continued habitation of the sites into the nineteenth century. Some preliminary observations can be made from these limited investigations.

As previously explained, settlement of the Kentucky frontier was a series of pulses—chronological periods whose study provides further insight into the nature of stations and forts. The Pre-Revolutionary Period, dating from 1773 to 1777, is characterized by the earliest extensive surveys on the Kentucky frontier. Stations established during this period were usually small sites, very crudely constructed, and often with minimal defensive capability. Fifteen stations were established during this period in the Inner Bluegrass region. Most of these were occupied by men who came to survey claims and make preliminary improvements. Families headed for the larger forts at Harrodsburg and Boonesborough. Surveying parties usually only stayed long enough to choose land, mark it, build an improvement cabin, and raise a corn crop, before returning east to their families.

The large forts were all stockaded enclosures. Unlike the military forts of the eastern settlements that borrowed European architectural plans with diamond-shaped bastions and thick rammed earth walls, most of the large forts and stations in Kentucky were ordered along very different lines. Except for the fort built at Lexington under the direction of John Todd in 1781 and the short-lived Fort Jefferson far away in western Kentucky in 1780, the large forts and stations formed their enclosures with cabins arranged in a square or rectangle, connected by short sections of stockading. The corner cabins were usually called blockhouses, bastions, or "bast-ends," and generally had an overhanging second story. Cabins along the walls were usually one or one and a half stories with shed roofs that sloped entirely to the inside. In 1791, Benjamin Van Cleve described Fort Harrod during his visit:

> The outline of the fort is a square of 264 feet. The S.W. and S.E. corners are blockhouses about 25 by 44 feet each. In the N.W. corner is a spring on the eastern side is another spring. The south line of the fort on the hill is a solid row of log cabins, each 20 by 20 with a blockhouse at each end. The east, north and west sides are stockades. Gates of stout timbers, ten feet wide, open on the west and on the north sides . . . the doors are secured by heavy bars—The pickets are round logs of oak . . . more than a foot in diameter. They are set four feet in the ground, leaving ten feet clear and the earth rammed tight. They are held together with stout wall pieces pinned in through holes with inch tree nails [pegs] on the side.
>
> The corner buildings are blockhouses, the upper stories extend two feet from the wall on each side providing for gunfire along the walls. . . . Seven story-and-a-half cabins are between the block house giving a space of ten feet between the buildings. A small single-room cabin of one story is to the right of the east corner and is built as a school. . . . The cabins are 20 by 20 . . . built of round logs, a foot in diameter, chinked and jointed with clay, in which straw has been mixed as a binder. The doors and the window shutters are of oaken puncheons, secured by stout bars on the inside with a latchstring of leather hanging out.
>
> The eave bearers are the end logs which project over to receive the butting poles,

against which the lower tier of clapboards rest in forming the roof. The trapping is the roof timbers composing the gable ends and the ribs upon which the course of clapboards lie. The weight poles are those small logs on the roof which weigh down the clapboards upon which they lie and against which the next course is laid. The knees arme pieces of heart timber laid above the butting poles to prevent the poles rolling off.

The walls of this fort are none of them bare, some are chinked with white clay, in which straw has been used as a binder, but several of the houses have entire walls covered with mortar and rubbed down smooth.[24]

Van Cleve did not mention all the details known about the original fort, actually describing its appearance some fifteen years after its construction. His account of the stockading is particularly interesting because other accounts indicate that stockading was not always impenetrable. When James Ray lived in the fort, he was pinned down by enemy gunfire behind a stump that stood next to the fort stockade. Calling for help, he was rescued by settlers inside the enclosure who dug under the stockade to save him.[25] Accounts of other sites such as Bryan's Station in Fayette County mention that some of the puncheons or upright members forming the stockade could be removed to allow access.[26] The chinking or mortar mentioned by Van Cleve also was used to fill in gaps between the stockade log members. In one case, failure to maintain the chinking at Bryan's Station cost a man his life when an Indian sharpshooter placed a well-aimed shot through a hole in the stockade.[27]

The Fort Boonesborough excavations produced cultural features associated with the Pre-Revolutionary Period. The base of a stone chimney and a remnant of hard-packed dirt floor were excavated, yielding artifacts that date to the late eighteenth century. While the entire cabin foundation was not exposed, the orientation of the fireplace indicated that the hearth faced roughly northeast or east (to the interior of the cabin). The chimney is located northwest of two postmolds that align in a northeast-southwest direction. Postmolds are soil stains that indicate where wooden posts once stood. These posts, which measured approximately fourteen inches in diameter, were seven feet apart and oriented more or less perpendicular to the adjacent river. They could have served as pivot posts for a gate, as part of the stockade, or as support for an interior facility inside the enclosure. Plans of the fort drawn by pioneers indicate that the enclosure had two gates, one in each long side. The orientation of the two excavated postmolds would not correspond to the orientation of the long walls if the fort sat parallel to the Kentucky River. They could have been part of the shorter wall on the southeast end of the fort. If that was the case, their relationship to the chimney base suggests that the cabin was part of the long wall running northwest-southeast, labeled as the front wall of the fort on Richard Henderson's sketch.

Also excavated at Fort Boonesborough was a large hearth, filled with domestic and wild animal bones. A single glazed redware sherd with a decorative green stripe suggests a late eighteenth-century date. The list of species identified is similar to the types of animals taken for food by the pioneers: black bear, pig, white-tailed deer, buffalo, cow, turkey, elk, and channel catfish. In particular, the probable identification of buffalo suggests that because buffalo were hunted out relatively quickly, this feature was made before the mid-1780s.

The numbers of settlers coming and going between the eastern settlements and the Kentucky frontier were significant by the opening of the Revolutionary War. Even though the war began a year earlier, its effect on Kentucky was not pervasively felt until 1777 when Indian attacks, sanctioned by the British, intensified. The Kentucky area was nearly emptied of settlers in the year of the "terrible sevens." As wartime conditions dictated a much more defensive posture on the part of the settlers than had previously been required, the Pre-Revolutionary Period of settlement came to a close.

The Revolutionary Period dated from 1778 to 1782. Despite wartime conditions, emigration to Kentucky intensified, evidenced by the fifty-seven stations established in the Inner Bluegrass region during these years. Documentary evidence suggests that many of the stations were fortified. The settlers who built these stations had been living in the larger forts. As they moved out to establish their own residences, other pioneers arrived to take their places. Although leaving the large forts meant less security, the settlers' desires to continue improving and clearing land and the better living conditions at the smaller stations outweighed the dangers.

Spencer Records, who moved to Kentucky in 1783, wrote a description and drew a simple plan of a stockaded station of the Revolutionary Period based on his personal observations.

> As I have mentioned forts and forting, I will for the information of those that never saw a stockade fort, describe one, and lay down a plat thereof. In the first place the ground is cleared off the size they intend to build the fort, what was an oblong square. . . . Then a ditch was dug three feet deep, the dirt being thrown out on the inside of the fort. Logs, twelve or fifteen inches in diameter and fifteen feet long, were cut, and split open. The top ends were sharpened, the butts set in the ditch with the flat sides all in, and the cracks broke with the flat sides of others. The dirt was then thrown into the ditch and well rammed down. Port holes were made high enough that if a ball should be shot, it would pass overhead. The cabins were built far enough from the stockade to have plenty of room to load and shoot. Two bastions were constructed

at opposite corners . . . with port holes about eighteen inches from the ground. The use of these bastions was, to rake the two sides of the fort, should the Indians get close up to the stockades, so that they could not shoot them from the portholes in the sides. Two gateways were made fronting each other . . . with strong gates and bars so that they could not be forced open. Some forts called Stations, were built with cabins all set close together, half-faced, or the roof all sloping one way with high side out, raised eight feet high, and overlaid with split logs. The upper story was over jutted two feet, and raised high to have plenty of room to load & shoot, with port-holes both above and below. The use of the over-jut was to prevent the Indians from climbing up, should they get close to the wall, and from it they could shoot down on them. Such was Bryant's Station.[28]

The stockaded enclosures required some form of ingress and egress, a need commonly supplied by gates that swung on pivots. William Clinkenbeard, who lived at Strode's Station, explained that "Right between Stephen Bile's and Matthias Spahr's houses, on the east side, was a big gate, swung like a water gate, on pivots, but with the lower half the heaviest, so that it kept down, made so that it could be propped up with a stick, and wagons and sleds, wood, and corn, or anything could be taken in."[29] The Stoner settlement in Clark County contained fortified houses built by fifteen families in 1783, centering around a large two-room fortified log house erected by Edmond Ragland. According to a descendant of the Tracy family who lived in this settlement,

All of the houses in this colony were built of unhewn logs, except Wyatt Hulett's and Edmond Ragland's, and with the exception of Mr. Ragland's, was only one story high, being about seven feet from floor to joist, with loft above. Floors were made of slabs or puncheons split out of the wood; with one side hewn smooth with broad ax. Doors were made of same put together with wooden pins and hung with wooden hinges. Instead of using rafters and sheeting for support of roof, they used what they called "rib poles." These were put on across the building in the opposite direction from which the roof was intended to run, and about two feet apart, each rib pole being raised higher than the other, by means of end logs. These end logs, of course, become shorter as the rib poles went up until the last end logs would not be more than four feet long. The roof was made of four feet boards, put on two double, and fastened in place by straight edge logs laid across each course of boards, the first of these roof logs was fastened in place by being pinned to the first rib pole, the next was kept in place by scatches one end resting against the first roof log and extending to the second, and so on to the top or comb.[30]

Although cabins within forts and stations were constructed of logs, the details and quality of their construction varied. Some were divided into rooms by partitions, and some were heated by fireplaces that also served cooking purposes. Excavations at Hugh McGary's Station have, to date, yielded some evidence of subterranean pits and one feature that involved a considerable amount of burning, possibly a hearth built either in association with a cabin or outside in the open. The pits could have been used as storage cellars until they soured and then for trash disposal. The use of fireplaces for heat and food preparation necessitated the construction of chimneys, generally located on a gable end of the cabin. The same Tracy provides a description of how settlers built chimneys in the Stoner settlement: "A few of the chimneys . . . were built entirely of stone . . . others were built up four, five, or six feet with stone and then finished with sticks and mortar, these sticks for chimney building were riven out about the size, or a little larger than tobacco sticks, the chimney was then built up after the fashion of a chicken coop, and the space between the sticks was plastered with a stiff mortar made of yellow clay, and some chimneys were built from the foundation with mud and sticks and then protected from the fire by large flat rocks set up at the back and sides of the fire place."[31]

Omitted from accounts of stockaded fort and station construction is the relative location of chimneys to the stockaded enclosure. If they were located on the inside of the enclosure, seemingly more secure from tampering, they may have represented a greater fire hazard. Artistic reconstructions rendered in the late nineteenth and early twentieth centuries consistently show the chimneys on the inside of the stockade. None of the consulted pioneer accounts, however, specifically indicate where the chimneys were placed relative to the stockade.

Facilities other than residential cabins are also occasionally uncovered. Storage sites were sometimes located inside the enclosure, sometimes outside. Bryan's Station contained a cabin that was built to hold a large quantity of dried meat, or jerky, prepared for one of George Rogers Clark's punitive campaigns.[32] It was later used as a school. Other storage facilities were excavated pits or cellars for foodstuffs. At Fisher's Garrison in present Boyle County, John Hinton was killed in 1781 while retrieving "simblins" (a type of squash) from a storage pit outside the stockade.[33] Corn, flax, and other harvested products were sometimes stored in cribs built near the fields.[34] Also, blacksmithing facilities were associated with some of the forts and stations; Fort Boonesborough is documented as having had an area designated for blacksmithing. Recent archaeological investigations at Hugh McGary's Station in Mercer County recovered hand-wrought nails, unprocessed nail rod, and slag that suggest rudimentary forging activities at this site.[35]

Excavations at John Grant's Station identified a structural feature, consisting of foundation stones once stacked to form a crude pier and charred log remnants, that is interpreted as the remains of a cabin in the station's stockaded enclosure. Grant's Station was partially burned after its abandonment in 1780 and was later rebuilt and reoccupied in 1784. This feature suggests that cabins, particularly those in stations that were built early in the settlement period, may have had foundation piers at the corners or at intervals along their walls rather than completely filled-in foundations. Documentary clues provide some corroboration of this interpretation. William Clinkenbeard noted that during an attack on Constant's Station in Clark County, John Constant was taken up into the house by crawling under it and coming up through the floor after his wife "took up a puncheon"; "the house was a new log house on uneven ground and hadn't been underpinned all along. Was open [underneath] except at the corners."[36] This account is important for two reasons: it clarifies the type of foundations provided for some of the station cabins, and it indicates that cabins were sometimes floored with wooden puncheons. John Grant's Station appears to have been similarly constructed, while the cabins at Fort Boonesborough may have lacked the amenities of a wooden floor.

The settling of central Kentucky took place in a remarkably short period with the bulk of stations and forts built, occupied, and abandoned between early surveys of 1773, through the Revolutionary War's conclusion in 1783, to Anthony Wayne's treaty with the Shawnee in 1795. Settlers risked constructing smaller stations knowing that their slender hold on the Kentucky frontier was dependent on preventing Indians and their British allies from gaining control of the coveted lands. Success against the Indians was the key to claiming and gaining legal title to property. The Revolutionary Period closed in 1783, marked by the disastrous defeat of Kentucky settlers in the Battle of Blue Licks in August 1782. After 1783, Indian raids were much more sporadic. Although life became more serene in the central Kentucky region around Lexington, northern Kentucky along the Ohio River continued to be a dangerous place to settle.

With the coming of peace, settlers no longer needed a defensive network. With some exceptions, stations and forts were abandoned, often dismantled for reuse of their timbers, as more commodious and comfortable single-family dwellings were built. In a few cases, station cabins were improved and extended, but for the most part, settlers moved to new locations. The stations began to disappear from the landscape, existing only in the memories of the people who had occupied them. The very wilderness itself was cleared and modified as settlers worked to create the cultural landscape that reflected their mental template of how a civilized world should look.

Although the war with Britain ended formally with the Treaty of Paris in 1783, hostilities between settlers and American Indian tribes continued, albeit on a much reduced scale. Even the slightest increase in safety meant that stations could be less concerned with strong defenses. The Post-Revolutionary Period, from 1783 to 1785, witnessed the establishment of new structures, still called stations, but closer in character to nondefensive residences. Many settlers of this period were bound together by religious beliefs or kinship ties. Captain William Bush led a contingent of Virginia families persecuted in the east for their religious beliefs. As part of the "Traveling Church," Bush's group was just one of several that came to Kentucky for religious freedom. Primarily designed to accommodate families, stations of this period tended to have more carefully constructed cabins than did their predecessors with amenities such as chinking, better foundations, and chimneys. Stockading became less common, although the practice of several families building cabins close to one another continued.

The years after 1785 were the Post-Frontier Period, characterized by decreasing usage of the term "station" and much less concern with defensibility. Stations established in the Inner Bluegrass area during this period did not differ much from other contemporary residential sites. The use of the term seems to have been more of a linguistic holdover from the earlier periods. The Hamilton family established their station in present Franklin County in 1792, building a cabin that Alexander Hamilton described as "better than the houses of [the] two families that lived back of us." He described the house as "stronger, the chinking was pinned in, & there were port-holes to fire out at. . . . The door was of black-oak, 4 inches thick—[with] battons, pinned. Swung as gates are sometimes, on a pivot. 2 in. holes made, & then dogwood crotches put in, to [receive] a heavy bar. The 2 in. auger port-holes, so as to fire [through], right above the hinches [haunches] of any one pushing [against] the door, if they [should] get there before the door was fairly shut."[37] A few station sites actually contained substantially built houses of stone or brick rather than the ubiquitous logs of the earlier periods. The latest date for a station was 1798, when Henry Wilson relocated to Bourbon County and built a brick house. He had been on the frontier for many years and may have continued to use the term out of habit.

In the Post-Frontier Period, inhabitants of safer areas centering largely around Lexington moved forward with the process of founding towns, building nicer and more elaborate houses, and establishing mercantile, educational, and religious institutions. With this settlement pattern, the frontier truly ceased to exist in central Kentucky. Areas outside of the Inner Bluegrass, however, particularly northern Kentucky along the Ohio River, continued to experience hostilities for a number of years. In this sense, the "frontier" moved beyond the Inner Bluegrass to other regions where settlers utilized the same strategies that had worked earlier.

Notes

The author would like to thank the National Park Service for a Federal Survey and Planning Grant, administered through the Kentucky Humanities Council, which funded the initial research for the manuscript. Subsequent research was funded by the University of Kentucky, the Kentucky Department of Parks, the Kentucky Heritage Council, Mr. Ralph Anderson, the Kentucky Transportation Cabinet, Fort Boonesborough State Park Association, Madison County Historical Society, and Shelby County Development Corporation. I am further indebted to Neal O. Hammon, Frances Keightley, Corinna Balden, Ann Bolton Bevins, Mary Hammersmith, Howard Gregory, Jack Bailey, Gerald Tudor, E. Edward Montgomery, Pat Ballard, Bettye Lee Mastin, Philip DiBlasi, Ken Carstens, Edward Estes, Chontrelle Layson, the staff of the Margaret I. King Library Special Collections at the University of Kentucky, and the families who allowed me to visit sites on their properties.

1. Bayless Hardin, "Whitley Papers, Volume 9—Draper Manuscripts—Kentucky Papers," *Register of the Kentucky Historical Society* 36 (1938): 190. Also see John Ray to Lyman Draper, 20 February 1843, John Lyman Draper Manuscript Collection, 12C6, State Historical Society of Wisconsin, Madison.

2. Stephen Aron, "The Significance of the Kentucky Frontier," *Register of the Kentucky Historical Society* 91 (1993): 298-323; R.A. Billington, *America's Frontier Heritage* (New York: Holt, Rinehart and Winston, 1966); A.G. Bogue, "Social Theory and the Pioneer," *Agricultural History* 34 (1960): 21-34; R.F. Berkhofer Jr., "Space, Time, Culture, and the New Frontier," *Agricultural History* 38 (1964): 21-30; H.C. Brookfield, "Questions on the Human Frontiers of Geography," *Economic Geography* 40 (1964): 283-303; J.E. Eblen, "An Analysis of Nineteenth-Century Frontier Populations," *Demography* 2 (1965): 399-413; Reginald Horsman, *The Frontier in the Formative Years, 1783-1815* (New York: Holt, Rinehart and Winston, 1970); J.C. Hudson, "A Location Theory for Rural Settlement," *Annals of the Association of American Geographers* 59 (1969): 365-81; Ladis K.D. Kristof, "The Nature of Frontiers and Boundaries," *Annals of the Association of American Geographers* 49 (1959): 269-82; Kenneth E. Lewis, "Sampling the Archaeological Frontier: Regional Models and Component Analysis," in *Research Strategies in Historical Archaeology*, ed. Stanley South (New York: Academic Press, 1977), 151- 201; J.G. Leyburn, *Frontier Folkways* (New Haven: Yale Univ. Press, 1935); D.H. Miller and J.O. Steffen, eds., *The Frontiers* (Norman: Univ. of Oklahoma Press, 1977); Malcolm J. Rohrbough, *The Trans-Appalachian Frontier: People, Societies, and Institutions, 1775-1850* (New York: Oxford Univ. Press, 1978); Frederick Jackson Turner, "The Significance of the Frontier in American

History," *Annual Report of the American Historical Association for the Year 1893* (Washington, D.C.: Government Printing Office, 1894), 199-227; David Ward, ed., *Geographic Perspectives on America's Past* (New York: Oxford Univ. Press, 1979); Gregory A. Waselkov and R. Eli Paul, "Frontiers and Archaeology," *North American Archaeologist* 2 (1981): 309-29.

3. Ellen Eslinger, "Migration and Kinship on the Trans-Appalachian Frontier: Strode's Station, Kentucky," *Filson Club History Quarterly* 62 (1988): 52.

4. Michael J. O'Brien, *Grassland, Forest, and Historical Settlement: An Analysis of Dynamics in Northeast Missouri* (Lincoln: Univ. of Nebraska Press, 1984).

5. Samuel M. Wilson, "West Fincastle—Now Kentucky," *Filson Club History Quarterly* 9 (1935): 65-94.

6. Neal O. Hammon, "Land Acquisition on the Kentucky Frontier," *Register of the Kentucky Historical Society* 78 (1980): 297-321.

7. George Washington Ranck, *Boonesborough*, Filson Club Publication #27 (Louisville, Ky.: Filson Club, 1901).

8. Julien J.N. Campbell, *The Land of Cane and Clover: Presettlement Vegetation in the So-Called Bluegrass Region of Kentucky* (Lexington: University of Kentucky, 1985): 3.

9. David Barrow Diary, 30 July 1795, Manuscripts Division, Filson Club, Louisville.

10. "Excerpt from the Boone Papers," Draper Manuscript Collection, 3B179.

11. Richard Henderson, "Journal of Trip to Boonesborough," Draper Manuscript Collection, 1CC21-102.

12. Neal O. Hammon, "Settlers, Land Jobbers, and Outlyers: A Quantitative Analysis of Land Acquisition on the Kentucky Frontier," *Register of the Kentucky Historical Society* 84 (1986): 242.

13. Samuel M. Wilson, *The First Land Court of Kentucky, 1779-1780* (Lexington: private printing, 1923).

14. A. Gwynn Henderson, "Dispelling the Myth: Seventeenth- and Eighteenth-Century Indian Life in Kentucky," *Register of the Kentucky Historical Society* 90 (1992): 1-25.

15. Hardin, "Whitley Papers," 190.

16. Hugh McGary, Petition to the Virginia General Assembly, 1779, Draper Manuscript Collection, 4CC29-30.

17. Gilbert Imlay letter, Draper Manuscript Collection, 14CC214.

18. Eslinger, "Migration and Kinship," 52-66.

19. "Interview of Jane Stevenson by John Dabney Shane," Draper Manuscript Collection, 13CC138.

20. Imlay letter, Draper Manuscript Collection, 14CC214.

21. Willard Rouse Jillson, *Pioneer Kentucky* (Frankfort: State Journal Company, 1934), 15.

22. Nancy O'Malley, *Searching for Boonesborough* (Lexington: University of Kentucky Department of Anthropology, 1990).

23. Nancy O'Malley, *"Stockading Up": A Study of Pioneer Stations in the Inner Bluegrass Region of Kentucky* (Lexington: University of Kentucky Department of Anthropology, 1987); idem, *Searching for Boonesborough*; idem, *Hugh McGary's Station at the Shawnee Springs* (Lexington: University of Kentucky Department of Anthropology, forthcoming).

24. Willard Rouse Jillson, *Tales of the Dark and Bloody Ground* (Louisville: C.T. Dearing, 1930), 106-14.

25. Ray to Draper, Draper Manuscript Collection, 12C6.

26. "Excerpt from the Boone Papers," Draper Manuscript Collection, 22C10.

27. Interview with Mrs. John Arnold by John Dabney Shane, Draper Manuscript Collection, 22CC276-279.

28. Spencer Records Narrative, Draper Manuscript Collection, 23CC95-96.

29. Lucien Beckner, "Reverend John D. Shane's Interview with Pioneer William Clinkenbeard," *Filson Club History Quarterly* 5 (1928): 95-128.

30. Capt. B.A. Tracy, "A Scrap of Clark County History, 1890," unpublished manuscript, Kentucky Historical Society, Frankfort.

31. Ibid.

32. Map of Bryan's Station as drawn by Joseph Ficklin, Draper Manuscript Collection, 13C79.

33. Lucien Beckner, "Reverend John Dabney Shane's Interview with Mrs. Sarah Graham of Bath County," *Filson Club History Quarterly* 9 (1935): 222-71.

34. Ray to Draper, Draper Manuscript Collection, 12C6.

35. O'Malley, *Hugh McGary's Station*.

36. Beckner, "Interview with Clinkenbeard," 114.

37. Interview of Alexander Hamilton by John Dabney Shane, Draper Manuscript Collection, 11CC294.

In 1775, delegates of the Transylvania Land Company congregated in Boonesborough to organize their backwoods government—a scene that George Ranck captured in his 1901 sketch. Fort Boonesborough is visible in the left background. George W. Ranck, *Boonesborough* (Louisville: J.P. Morton & Co., 1901)

"This Idea in Heaven"
Image and Reality on the Kentucky Frontier

DANIEL BLAKE SMITH

Kentucky was first, and perhaps foremost, an idea. It was an idea born out of need and hope. The need lay in the dying soil and declining prospects of marginal Virginia and North Carolina planters looking for a fresh start somewhere else. The hope lay in the dreams and schemes of enterprising speculators, explorers, land developers, and promotional writers who saw in the trans-Appalachian West a chance to strengthen and perpetuate their claims to wealth and status. Frontier Kentucky, then, was forged out of dreams and desperation.

From these often disparate needs and hopes, restless and enterprising energies, grew very different expectations of Kentucky. For many of those looking west for another chance, Kentucky conjured up images of a yeoman republic where small, independent freeholders would people a newly opening West, thus escaping a bottled-up and declining commercial economy in the East. Leading Virginians such as James Madison and Thomas Jefferson had long envisioned America's future as a republican empire inhabited by free and equal yeoman farmers. This idyllic agricultural image required an ever-enlarging western territory. Kentucky would become, then, America's first West into which restless colonists (both poor whites and slaveholders) could move, creating an outlet for excess population while sustaining for future generations the ideal of a small farmer democracy.[1]

Jefferson tried to implement this agricultural paradise in Kentucky. In 1777 he outlined to the Virginia Assembly a land office plan that provided seventy-five acres in the new Kentucky territory to each free-born male Virginian after marriage and that allowed small farmers to buy up to four hundred acres at the county courts to be established there. Although Jefferson's vision never materialized—the speculators and private investors would quickly and dramatically recast the law to serve their own profit-seeking needs—his ideas of Kentucky as a place where ordinary farmers could get a new start, a comfortable subsistence, fired the imaginations of those considering removal.[2]

What also animated prospective settlers was the pervasive belief—for some it was a conviction—that beyond the mountains lay a land of bounteous promise, a new Eden of fertile soil and the richest flora and fauna. Ever since the adventures of Daniel Boone and other long hunters in the Kentucky territory in the 1760s, elaborate descriptions circulated depicting the West as a wild, exotic landscape full of weird rock formations, beautiful flowering meadows, large roaming buffalo herds, medicinal rock springs, and restorative air. Simon Girty called Kentucky "the land of cane and clover—spontaneously growing to feed the buffalos, the elk and the deer; there the bear and beaver are always fat."[3] Few descriptions, though, equaled that given by Felix Walker, Boone's companion during his trail-blazing trip to Boonesborough in 1775. "A new sky and a strange earth seemed to be presented to our view," Walker remembered somewhat melodramatically. "So rich a soil we had never seen before; covered with clover in full bloom, the woods were abounding with wild game—turkeys so numerous that it might be said that they appeared but one flock, universally scattered in the woods. It appeared that nature, in the profusion of her bounty, had spread a feast for all that lives, both for the animal and the rational world. . . . We felt ourselves passengers through a wilderness just arrived at the fields of Elysium, or at the garden where there was no forbidden fruit."[4]

Men of more prosaic temperament also envisioned Kentucky as a new Eden of limitless fertility. In contrast to the depleted soil of Tidewater Virginia, Kentucky offered unparalleled fecundity. As David Meade, a settler from Williamsburg, observed from his new home in the Bluegrass, "I have in view, more Corn growing, than all the crops which I made at Maycox put together for twenty Years would amount to." Here in Kentucky, Meade proclaimed, "a man upon only two hundred acres of land—might eat better meats and vegetables than he could upon five thousand pounds a year near the Atlantic."[5] Other settlers spoke wondrously of the "amazing rapidity of the vegitation, or the immense powers of the soil." Numerous letters back home urged friends and kin to "hurry . . . on to Move to the Land of Milk & Honey," to Kentucky, "this almost paradise." As one pioneer who brought his wife and family across the mountains noted dramatically, the move from Virginia to Kentucky brought a "Change to us Like that from death to Life or in other words from a Land of poverty and distress to a Land of peace and plenty."[6]

Migration is always fueled in part by alluring visions and optimistic expectations of a new land—and Kentucky offered up a rich supply of such hopeful images. But what settlers actually discovered in this "Land of peace and plenty" was something else. And that often rude reality revealed itself in countless ways: in the conflicting family feelings about migration, in the dangerous and deadly trip west, in the fearful presence of hostile Indians, and in the privation and solitude that awaited settlers on the borderlands. The yawning gap between dream and reality on the Kentucky frontier, though, began with the men and the means by which the land was first seized.

The visionary and idyllic note that was often struck in speaking about early Kentucky was not, of course, simply poetic indulgence. Flattering portraits of the new western lands were clearly aimed at promoting land sales to emigrants and private investors. Nowhere did the romantic imagination and the self-seeking profit motive merge more effectively than in the speculative land ventures that played such a large role in the settlement of Kentucky. And no one played the land-grabbing game more ambitiously than Richard Henderson. His story demands attention both in spite of his failed efforts in Kentucky and because of them. Henderson's desperate dream of transforming the Kentucky wilds into Transylvania Colony illuminates much of the hope, exploitation, and elusive promise that characterized frontier Kentucky.

Like George Washington and many other speculators, Henderson, a self-made lawyer and judge from Yadkin Valley in North Carolina, had looked longingly toward Kentucky since the mid-1760s. He had helped fund annual expeditions of Boone and other long hunters into the region. Henderson seized on land-hungry woodsmen and settlers, using them as advance men in his speculative schemes.

Before Kentucky became a scheme, it was a hunting ground. Henderson, along with other white traders, had engaged for years in an informal fur trading business with the Shawnee and Cherokee populations in the Kentucky territory. By the late 1770s what had begun as a trading relationship with the Indians had turned into increasingly provocative intimidation. Frequent skirmishes of squatters, settlers, and explorers with the Shawnee finally erupted in Lord Dunmore's War in 1774. When the war ended in the fall of 1774 with the defeat of the Shawnee at Point Pleasant, the trans-Allegheny West opened dramatically wider for migrants heading for Kentucky. And with the Shawnee abdicating their claims to the Kentucky territory, the Cherokee to the south were left as sole guardians of the land.

Richard Henderson could almost smell the profits and prospects in the negotiations after Lord Dunmore's War. Having already stockpiled huge amounts of goods—everything from corn and flour to muskets, rum, and blankets—over years of trading with the Cherokee in the Kentucky and Tennessee territories, Henderson and his partners were well prepared to cut a very ambitious deal.

In March 1775 at Sycamore Shoals in northeastern Tennessee, Henderson's ambitions were more than realized. Before more than a thousand Cherokee, Henderson traded some ten thousand pounds in goods for "title" to about 17 million acres of land in the triangular area bounded by the Kentucky River on the east, the Ohio River to the north and west, and the sources of the Cumberland River on the south. While leading chiefs such as Attakulla-kulla and Oconostota accepted the trade, younger chiefs like Dragging Canoe reacted angrily at relinquishing so much valuable hunting land for so little in trade goods. It was Dragging Canoe whose bitterness drove him to issue the prophetic warning to Henderson: white men who tried to settle this new land, he declared, would find it a "dark and bloody ground."

The truth of this prophecy did not take long to discover. Having secured one of the most impressive land deals in American history, Henderson wasted no time staking his claim to it. He prevailed on his friend Boone and thirty long hunters to blaze a road from Indian trails and animal traces from southwest Virginia and northeast Tennessee, across the mountains through the Cumberland Gap, and northward into central Kentucky. The Wilderness Road, as it was called, ended 220 miles later at Fort Boonesborough on the banks of the Kentucky River. Ten days after the road was completed, Henderson himself headed west with thirty riflemen, several slaves, a wagon train, and packhorses.

Even though he witnessed along the Wilderness Road almost as many people fleeing because of disease and Indian attacks as entering Kentucky, Henderson pressed on. In doing so, he must have known how patently illegal his Transylvanian land scheme was. It violated the Proclamation of 1763 that forbade colonial settlements west of the Appalachian mountains; it clearly trespassed on the rightful western claims of Virginia and North Carolina; and it openly ignored the Crown's right of title to all undistributed lands.

None of this seemed to restrain the enterprising Henderson. No sooner had he effectively exploited Boone's trailblazing talents than he laid political claim to his Kentucky fiefdom. On May 23, 1775, under the shade of an enormous elm tree at Boonesborough, Henderson convened the House of Delegates for Transylvania. Henderson's open-air "empire of liberty" consisted of seventeen representatives drawn from the four forts in central Kentucky. While Transylvania had the look of democracy—the delegates set up a court and militia system; provided for annual elections to a colonial assembly, invoking the "consent of the governed"; and created laws to preserve game and other resources from outside exploitation—it was to become in fact nothing less than the proprietary colony of Richard Henderson. Transylvania's executive power rested entirely in the proprietors instead of in an elected governor. Likewise, the proprietors had the sole right to appoint judges, sheriffs, and all other civil and military officers.

The feudal design of Henderson's visionary kingdom found theatrical expression during the last day of the legislative session. In Boonesborough, Henderson staged a formal and public observance of the ancient feudal ceremony, "Livery and Seisin"—the final "legal" transfer of the immense territory Henderson and company had purchased from the Cherokee. Standing under the enormous spreading elm tree, John Farrar, the lawyer employed by the Indians, handed to Henderson a piece of turf cut from the soil beneath them. And while both men held the symbolic soil, Farrar pronounced the cession of seisin and possession of the land, according to the terms of the deed. Henderson proudly displayed the deed, which was then immediately read publicly.

The significance of this ostentatious outdoor pageant was not lost on Henderson. "This tree," Henderson noted triumphantly in his journal, "is placed in a beautiful plain surrounded by a turf of white clover forming a green to its very stock to which there is scarcely anything to be likened." With a diameter of 100 feet, its immense expanse of cooling shade made it "the most beautiful tree that imagination can suggest . . . any time between the hours of 10 and 2 100 persons may commodiously seat themselves under its branches." So must Kentucky's wide-open expanse have appeared to Henderson a huge fertile place of natural beauty available to those enterprising enough to seize it.[7]

No doubt, this feudal spectacle in Boonesborough's amphitheater was Henderson's greatest moment. It was also his last great moment. While the picturesque scene richly revealed the pastoral dreams of Kentucky's biggest dreamer, it also signaled the beginning of the end for an illegal land venture and an anachronistic political scheme.

In the free-for-all atmosphere of early Kentucky, Henderson's huge private fiefdom found few followers. Transylvania was attacked from all quarters—from the Crown to Virginia to the settlers themselves. Within days, there was the angry response of fellow schemers such as James Harrod, who the year before had founded the first settlement in Kentucky. Harrodsburg, settled amid rich canelands and open grassland, was the personal venture of the thirty-two-year-old from Washington County, Pennsylvania. Harrod laid out the settlement as thirty-one half-acre in-lots fronting a single main street. In his relatively democratic scheme, every original member of the settlement party was given a ten-acre piece of land. Harrod and most men who had staked their claims made surveys, built crude cabins, and planted corn. These independent men took a very dim view of Richard Henderson's brash claim to a "New Independent Colony" that included nearly all of the rich land in central Kentucky. Offended by Henderson's land-grabbing bravado, Harrod's men, as well as most individual settlers, were in no mood to become rent-paying vassals to some visionary overlord whose title to the land was shadowy at best. Casting about for legal protection to their claims, Harrod's men embraced Virginia, contending that their lands lay within its charter, thus invalidating Henderson's title to them.

Henderson not only badly misjudged his fellow settlers, he foolishly believed that both Great Britain and Virginia would approve his attempt to make Transylvania the fourteenth colony. Trying to establish and legitimate Transylvania on the eve of the American Revolution was, to say the least, an exercise in bad timing. In 1775 Virginia found itself caught between an increasingly estranged Mother Country and squabbling factions in the Kentucky territory trying to resolve the land claims of Henderson and company. The result was predictable: Virginia was not disposed to surrender its western lands either to the imperial demands of the Mother Country or to scheming land adventurers like Richard Henderson. By the fall of 1776, Virginia became an independent commonwealth with its own constitution and sovereignty. Thus no impediment now existed in England or elsewhere to Virginia's territorial claims over western lands. Kentucky became a western county within the state of Virginia. Henderson's Transylvanian dream world was finally shattered. In its place Virginia brought not only legal title to the land but thousands of poor settlers whose desperation would produce yet another sort of dream.

If adventurers and schemers like Henderson and Harrod finagled and financed the opening of the Kentucky territory, thousands of ordinary families driven from deteriorating eastern lands and inspired by the prospect of a new start crossed the mountains and seized the land. At first it was a modest movement of people. In 1775, about one thousand Virginians crossed the roughly 250 miles separating Virginia from the fertile lands of Kentucky. But what began as a trickle in the 1770s became a floodtide by the 1790s. Between 1775 and 1795 more than two hundred thousand white settlers and slaves passed over the Wilderness Road into Kentucky. While the four-week trek along the road, in most places little more than a footpath, was longer, more difficult, and more dangerous than traveling down the Ohio River, the Wilderness Road was considerably cheaper. As a result, slave gangs, commoners, and the poor invariably took the overland route.

What drove most of these settlers across the mountains? Movement to Kentucky was prompted by many factors: the migration of evangelical church communities; the death of a patriarch and subsequent sale of the plantation; the decision of younger sons to head west where, they believed, better land could be found and an independent household could be established. For many, though, it was the prospect of bounty lands awarded out west to veterans of the Revolution or their heirs or assigns. Privates of the Continental Line were entitled to one hundred acres; officers could claim thousands of acres. The vast majority of these veterans came from Virginia. A sprinkling emigrated from North Carolina and Pennsylvania.

Wherever their place of origin, pioneers almost always came in families. Rarely did a single man, let alone a woman, pick up and brave alone the dangers of the wilderness. Removal was a strategic family decision and a family process. "Removal" is itself a revealing word, for many of these migrants were "re"-moving for a second or third time or more. They were, in Harriette Simpson Arnow's phrase, "seasoned borderers."[8]

William Scott served in Braddock's army as a packhorse master. According to his son Patrick, William moved thirteen times in one year before finally settling in Kentucky in 1778. "My mother carried me on her lap," Patrick remembered. "My father took a bed, opened a place at the two ends, put one child in one end and the other child in the opposite while the third, the stoutest, rode the horse (saddle bag style)."[9] Migration rates for settlers were very high. In a study of backcountry Lunenburg County, Virginia, Richard Beeman described the "phenomenal movement" of the population. From 1750 to 1769, 80 percent of the population disappeared from the county.[10] Much of this was short-distance movements involving only a few miles. Families with little property frequently picked up and moved looking for better living conditions.

The settlements these settlers created were a loose collection of isolated farmsteads covering many miles. The German traveler, Johann David Schoepf in 1784 described North Carolina backcountry farms as "scattered about in these woods at various distances, three to six miles, and often as much as ten or fifteen or twenty miles apart."[11]

While emigration required a certain amount of courage and self-reliance, the West was not peopled by a collection of rugged individuals. Most settlers migrated in family groups, often prompted by family motives. Most settlers did not simply head west on a whim but coordinated with neighborhood kin and friends for practical as well as emotional reasons. Drawing on these family connections made those ties all the more critical out on the frontier. As Ellen Eslinger discovered, Strode's Station in central Kentucky was settled primarily by a group of Berkeley County Virginians. These transplanted Virginians brought with them the protection and cohesive power of neighborhood and kinship: over 80 percent of those inhabiting Strode's Station had some relative in the station. Moreover, family and friends aided one another in key public business—witnessing wills, getting power of attorney, and resolving conflicting land titles. Indeed, there is some evidence that later-arriving settlers deliberately moved to areas where family and friends had already located. Clearly, the difficulty and danger of the trek out west and the stress of living in isolated, vulnerable stations on the frontier served to draw families closer together, making removal in every sense a collective undertaking.[12]

In a world on the margins riddled with fear and uncertainty, family life took on heightened significance. In the absence of strong government or regular church life, it was the family that nourished neighborhood and community life and created a sense of belonging. Far from being rootless individuals, settlers moved in part as an affirmation of kinship. What drove migrants west was the search for a "modest independence"—a contentment, a sense of respectability, and freedom as freeholding farm families. As Jack P. Greene has observed, "settlement on the colonial frontier involved clear attempts to transplant familiar forms of family and community life."[13]

Migration may have been a family matter, but the decision to remove was not necessarily a happy, unanimous one. In fact, movement to Kentucky, like most other westward migrations on the American frontier, was strictly patriarchal. Once a man determined to remove, a wife or mother's reluctance or a child's fear, one suspects, counted for little. Benjamin Allen, for example, remembered that his first knowledge of Kentucky came from some family friends who had just returned from a land-scouting expedition along the Ohio River. One of the men had been badly wounded from an Indian raid, which only heightened Allen's fears about going to Kentucky. "They were acquaintances and told us how it turned out, after they came back. I was at their house the next Sunday morning. My father took me up. I saw them dress Peter Johnson's wounds. It scared me from coming to Kentucky, & I didn't want to come at all." Allen was forced to swallow his fears when that same year his father brought the family out to Kentucky.[14]

Women, wives and mothers especially, often found that their doubts and reservations, too, went unheeded in the decision-making process. The result was a sad resignation at the inevitable. Almost all of Letitia Preston Breckinridge's children left Piedmont Virginia for Kentucky in the 1780s and 1790s. Her daughter Elizabeth Preston Meredith lamented, "I have just parted with my poor Dear Mother in a great dell of distress about my going to Kentucky indeed I have never meet with anything in my life that give me so much unea[si]ness as parting with my Mother." Elizabeth minced no words about her fears of Kentucky: "Thare never was a person whent to that Country with more reluctance than I shall go god only knoas how whe shall get thare though I am afraid very badly from the manner whe seem to be fixt." Elizabeth's worries were well placed. Her husband, Samuel Meredith Jr., was in debt with no income. Despite help from his family, Meredith did not improve his lot in Kentucky.[15] As Annette Kolodny has concluded, "most women who entered the wilderness at the end of the eighteenth century" did not go there on their own; they "first followed a man's lead into the forest."[16]

Removing to frontier Kentucky, then, meant very different things to men and women. But it also affected poor and well-to-do migrants in distinctive ways. For one thing, the very route suggested particular class differences. Well-to-do emigrants tended to come by boat down the Ohio River rather than by the longer, more dangerous overland paths that the common folk struggled along. And wealthier families could afford to make more deliberate, careful movements out west. A wealthy man like John Breckinridge, for example, made the transition from a comfortable life in Tidewater Virginia to the rude reality of the Kentucky frontier by doing it in stages. A full year before Breckinridge moved, he sent twenty slaves to central Kentucky and put them out to hire. By the time Breckinridge and his family arrived, his slaves were acclimated to the new environment and were ready to work on his plantation. Breckinridge also arranged through a friend to have a comfortable home in Lexington available for his family to move into while his own country estate was being constructed. Meanwhile Breckinridge's lands were being improved, as he had rented them for several years before arriving. "If I can get my Lands soon improved," he noted, "& made to look a little less like a Wilderness," the sooner he would remove to Kentucky.[17] The rich had the luxury of constructing a "civilized" persona amid the crude realities of the frontier.

For the vast majority of pioneers, though, traveling across the Appalachian mountains was a long and difficult journey, full of fear and danger. Throughout the eighteenth century the Wilderness Trail threatened many settlers with bad weather, disease, and Indian attacks. One traveler in 1784 reported that it rained and thundered eighteen of twenty-two days along the road. What was worse, an outbreak of measles in one company along the road placed everyone in jeopardy; "To go back with them was out of the question, to leave them behind certain death; we agreed to keep with them and move on slowly encamping every night by the roadside, and keeping a guard of thirty men, who by keeping a great number of fires round the encampment, and crying every five minutes as loud as they can 'all is well,' would endeavour to terrify the savages."[18]

The simple journal entries of William Calk and his party heading for Boonesborough in the spring of 1775 suggest the daily hardships of life on the trail:

> fryday ye 24th we Start early and turn out of the wagon Road to go across the mountains to go to Danil Smiths we loose Driver come to a turabel mountian that tired us all almost to death to git over it & we lodge this night on the Laurel fork of holston under agrait mountain. Roast afine fat turkey for our suppers & Eat it without aney Bread
>
> thursd 30th we set out again and went down to Elk gardin and there suplied our Selves with Seed Corn & irish taters then we went on alittel way I turned my hors to drive afore me & he got Scard Ran away threw Down the Saddel Bags & Broke three of our pouder gourds & Abrams flask Burst open a walet of corn and lost a good Deal & made aturrabel flustration amongst the Reast of the horses Drakes mair Ran against asapling & noct it down we cacht them all again & went on & lodged at John Duncans.[19]

No women or children accompanied Boone or Henderson, but soon they came in large numbers. The danger and travail they experienced along the road are palpable in some of the surviving narratives. Colonel William Whitley, for example, vividly recalled the precarious experiences of his family's month-long crossing from Virginia in 1775. "We were 33 days in the wilderness in this Unkind Season of the year," he remembered. Whitley complained of rain, hail, and snow afflicting their party, along "with the disadvantage of large Cainbrakes to wade through . . . Many times in Our travels we had to Unpack & leave the familys to find Out way to get on," he continued; "At times my wife would fall Horse and all, and at Other times, She & her children all in a pile tied together for When One went all must go in that situation."[20]

Twenty years later the Wilderness Trail was still a dangerous, debilitating trip. Moses Austin noted on a journey through Kentucky, "I cannot omitt Noticeing the many Distressed families I passd in the Wilderness." Austin was himself distressed "to see women and children in the month of December. Travelling a Wilderness Through Ice and Snow passing large rivers and Creeks with out Shoe or Stocking, and barely as many raggs as covers their Nakedness." The pioneers Austin saw were so poor they were "with out money or provisions except what the Wilderness affords, the Situation of such can better be Imagined than described. to say they are poor is but faintly express'g there Situation,—life *What is it Or What can it give,* to make compensation for such accumulated Misery?"[21]

The greatest difficulty and hardship along the trail and for years after initial settlement was the fear—and all too often, the reality—of Indian attack. In the wake of agreements with the Cherokee and the Shawnee at the end of Lord Dunmore's War, pioneers initially felt a certain amount of security—especially from the Shawnee, who had agreed not to molest whites south of the Ohio River. Indeed, until it got within five miles of present-day Richmond, Daniel Boone's party was left untouched by Indians. And then one morning just before daybreak Boone's men were ambushed by Indians. Two men, including one slave, were killed. The deadly attack not only surprised Boone's party, it cast the first shadow over "Paradise." Boone tried to put the best face on it in a hurriedly scribbled note to Henderson: "We stood on the ground and guarded the baggage till day, and lost nothing." Boone's companion, Felix Walker, was badly wounded in the skirmish. His emotional wounds seemed to penetrate deeper than his physical ones. Walker, who had at first been awestruck at the new Kentucky territory, regarded the Indian attack as a serious, even tragic jolt of reality to his frontier dreams: "But, alas! the vision of a moment made the dream of a dream, and the shadow of a shade! . . . a sad reverse overtook us . . . on our way to the Kentucky river. . . . So fatal and tragical an event cast a deep gloom of melancholy over all our prospects, and high calculations of long life and happy days in our newly-discovered country were frustrated."[22]

If for Walker the Indian attack cast a pall over the once-glorious Edenic landscape, Boone saw this early confrontation as a critical test to the perseverance of white pioneers. Amid the fearful departures of scores of settlers heading back across the mountains, Boone took a firm line. After another skirmish with the Indians, Boone wrote Henderson: "My advice to you, sir, is to come or send as soon as possible. Your company is desired greatly, for the people are very uneasy, but are willing to stay and venture their lives with you, and now is the time to flusterate their intentions and keep the country whilst we are in it. If we give way to them now, it will ever be the case."[23]

Indians found small companies of pioneers an easy mark. Thomas

Perkins guessed that more than one hundred travelers had been killed on the Wilderness Road since the summer; "Some whole companies have never been heard of." Perkins's party was never disturbed by Indian attacks, but "scarce a day but we found the marks of a defeated company," he noted.[24] Travel down the Ohio River was safer, but it was not without its ghoulish sights. Once a keelboat came floating down the Ohio River with "every person on it dead," Benjamin Allen remembered. "Found an Indian's fingers in it that had been chopped off"—presumably while trying to climb aboard.[25]

Gripped with fear of Indian attacks, scores of men fled the Kentucky territory. Richard Henderson passed close to a hundred men heading back. A few were returning for their families, but most were running from the Shawnee. Their fears frightened Henderson's own company. "The general panic that had seized the men we were continually meeting," he wrote, "was contagious; it ran like wildfire." Henderson tried to calm his men as well as prevail on those fleeing to turn and go with him to Boonesborough. But only a few could be persuaded. Henderson observed, "some hesitated and stole back, privately; others saw the necessity of returning to convince their friends that they were still alive, in too strong a light to be resisted; whilst many, in truth, who have nothing to thank but the fear of shame, for the credit of intrepidity, came on; though their hearts, for hours, made part of the deserting company."[26]

Confronted with such danger and fear, settlers crowded into forts, which were usually little more than a stockade erected to protect the hastily-built cabins. However safe settlers may have felt living inside the four forts in central Kentucky, they experienced little peace of mind. Corn could not be planted or tended to except at great danger and inconvenience. Boone had to divide the men at Boonesborough into two companies—one to act as guards and scout to protect the others, who were told to plant and cultivate corn. Still, Indians often destroyed crops, despite organized efforts by settlers to poison them by leaving crops "impregnated with Arsenic."[27] And they frequently made off with the settlers' horses—about two hundred were reportedly stolen in the spring of 1777 alone.

Settlers grew restless shut up in forts. As one traveler observed, forts served "as Beds to engender Sedition and Discord in, and as excuses for Indolence, Rags and poverty."[28] The dependent and impoverished state of the settlers, bottled up inside a few forts, was frequently noted. From Harrodsburg, Colonel Bowman observed, "They have left us almost without horses sufficient to supply the stations, as we are obligated to get all our provisions out of the woods. Our corn the Indians have burned all they could find the past Summer, as it was in cribs at the different plantations some distance from the garrisons, & no horses to bring it in on. At this time we have not had more than two month's bread,—near 200 women & children; not able to send them to the inhabitants; many of these families are left desolate, widows with small children destitute of necessary clothing."[29]

Boonesborough was no better. Josiah Collins, upon reaching the fort in March of 1778, said: "We found a poor distressed, 1/2 naked, 1/2 starved, people; daily surrounded by the savage, which made it dangerous, the hunters were afraid to go out to get buffalo meat."[30] In some cases women might safely venture out from the fort. But as one pioneer woman remembered, "if the men went out, they were sure to be killed; & had therefore to lay still."[31] As a result, settlers confessed to cowardice and fear in moving about the very territory that they were bent on possessing. As the surveyor John Floyd wrote to the governor of Virginia in 1781, "We are all obliged to live in our forts in this country, and notwithstanding all the caution we use, forty seven . . . have been killed or taken prisoners by the savages, besides a number wounded, since January." The year before he had noted, "Hardly one wek pass without some one being scalped between this [place] and the Falls and I almost got too cowardly to travell about the woods without company."[32]

The pervasive fear and cowardice led to outbursts of frustration. Arthur Hopkins, for example, revealed his impatience with settlers' Indian fears in explaining to a friend why he could not explore the country between the Green and Cumberland Rivers: It was because of the "dread of the Indiances the Men here [at Casey's Station] have been so afraid, I could not get them to venture out with me at all; they are the most dastardly sett of people I ever saw."[33]

No place, and no moment, was truly secure. This constant sense of being at risk imbued everything from the quickly assembled log cabins to family life itself with impermanence and uncertainty. Men and women not only hunted and farmed at great peril, they conducted their personal lives sometimes amidst considerable danger. Daniel Drake recalled a 1791 wedding ceremony in Mayslick that was halted because of the news of an impending Indian attack. The alarm came as all the wedding guests were assembling in Drake's house. "All the armed men mounted their horses and galloped off in a style so picturesque that I shall never forget it," Drake noted. Drake's memories as a boy growing up on the Kentucky frontier were laced with the daily threat of danger and violence. "Indian wars, midnight butcheries, captivities and horse stealings, were the daily topics of conversation," he wrote.[34]

Despite the obviously racist tone of the settlers' accounts of the Indians, their remarkably vivid, graphic descriptions of violent encounters with Indians merit attention, if only to sense white perceptions of the brutality and fear that seemed to pervade their view of life on the borderlands. Many of these encounters involved parents and children witnessing one another's torture and death. The memories no doubt lingered because they cut so deep into the psyche.

In December 1790 Benjamin Allen and his father were caught at Mud Lick Branch when young Benjamin was only sixteen. Indians captured Benjamin while they killed and scalped his father. Allen later saw his father's scalp, he recalled, "stretched on a hickory hoop at the camp."[35]

From Sarah Graham's riveting interview with John Shane, we learn about Captain Joseph Mitchell, who was coming down the Ohio in 1788 when some Shawnee stopped his boat, boarded it, and beat up several men. Mitchell's son "was burnt before his eyes."[36] There were human burnings in the battle of Blue Licks in August 1782. According to one man, "the smell of a human was the awfullest smell he had ever had in his life."[37]

One woman witnessed her husband killed by Indians in her own home, along with all but two of her children. "She got away but went back that night and laid in her husband's bosom all in a gore of blood." Another wife likewise watched her husband and child's killing, according to Graham: "Mrs. Davis had gone out in the night to bring in some clothes. Saw the Indians go in the cabin and kill her husband, and into the kitchen and kill all the negroes. There she stood in agony, saying, 'I must go in,' and then her heart would fail her and she would turn back and then go again. The Indians took four children, two boys and two girls, and sold them to the french."[38]

Indian raids were not only frightful, violent moments, they decimated families, sometimes leaving households to cope with nothing but horrible images and memories. John Floyd railed against the carnage and vulnerability of border families in the spring of 1781: "Whole families are destroyed without regard to age or sex; infants are torn from their mothers arms and their brains dashed out against trees. . . . Not a week passes, and some weeks scarcely a day, without some of our distressed inhabitants feeling the fatal effects of the internal rage and fury of these execrable hell-hounds. . . . A large proportion of the inhabitants are helpless indigent widows and orphans, who have lost their husbands and fathers by savage hands, left among strangers without the most common necessaries of life."[39]

A settler's darkest fear, one suspects, was that Indians might somehow infiltrate the cabins—in essence, destroying the family from within. For the "widow Hanks" of Mount Sterling, this horrifying scene happened in 1788. Her family lived in a double log house. One evening dogs were heard barking near the Hanks cabin. "The men, or part of the family in the larger room, noticed the barking and shut the door. Two girls were spinning hemp in the room, across the passage [the 'dog trot'] who had not noticed the conduct of the dogs, and their door was yet left open. The hemp was hung from the loft; the Indians set fire to the hemp, and the house was caught. The flames spread to the other part, and when the family could no longer remain, the door was thrown open, and they rushed out. Mrs. Hanks was shot through the body, went a little piece, kneeled down by a stump, and died."[40]

How did settlers cope with the constant pressure of danger and violence? The reactions ranged from Christian resignation to angry retaliation, insanity, and nightmares. Ann Christian tried to sound a calm religious note in responding to the Indian threat. "All the time we lived on Beargrass," she wrote Ann Fleming in the fall of 1785, "we have been all exposed to the Savages every time we were out of the Sight of this Station. The Indians have been Continually in this Country & have kill'd people all round us, but that mercifull God who had protected us all our days has preserv'd us in Safety till now."[41] Other women reacted with acts of violent retribution. Jeptha Kemper told the story of some women living near Brashear's Creek, who upon hearing Indians firing on a man out plowing in the field, recognized it was Indian fire, "and resolutely seized their hats and marched out with their guns to the conflict."[42] One of Daniel Drake's most vivid childhood memories involved the heroics of a woman seeking revenge on Indians who had attacked some travelers near Drake's village. When one of the men killed in the encounter was brought into the village "on a rude litter," the woman "broke open a chest in one of the wagons with an axe, got at the ammunition, gave it to the men and called upon them to fight. This, with the extinction of their Camp fire, led the Indians to retreat."[43]

If they could not singlehandedly confront the Indians or persuade their families to leave the territory, women sometimes quietly asserted themselves to protect their family from danger. One woman told Shane about her mother's thoughtful discretion: "[One] night she heard the indians come and take the bells off their horses. Right back of their cabin. Never woke her husband. Knew he would be too venturesome."[44]

More ominously, one senses that the violence and brutality could sometimes lead vulnerable settlers down the dark road to depression, even madness. Mrs. Davis, the woman who witnessed the killing of her husband and two children, fell victim to the fears of the dark. After the tragedy, Sarah Graham noted, Mrs. Davis's countenance "put on a change, and she got all her sleep alone in the daytime. [She] would be up & walk the room at night."[45]

Perhaps it was among children that this atmosphere of dread and bloodletting had its greatest impact. Although we know far too little firsthand about the lives of children, there are hints that the Indian threat made an indelible impression on the young. Daniel Drake recalled that all the children in his family were well aware that the Shawnee and the Wyandot were their great enemies. "The children were told at night," he observed, "'lie still and go to sleep, or the Shawnees will catch you.'" Mothers, he was told, "threatened their children at night with the wild Indians who lived beyond them." "Nearly all my troubled or vivid dreams," Drake continued, "included either Indians or snakes—the copper colored man & the copper headed snake, then extremely common. Happily I never suffered from either (except in dread)."[46]

The perception of Indians as dangerous, demonic figures was a notion deeply ingrained in children, even in their play. Patrick Scott remembered as a five-year-old growing up in Harrodsburg in 1779, finding a skull of an Indian who had been killed and buried in a nearby spot, that "We boys . . . were used to plaguing each other [with it], throwing it at one another."[47]

Conditions and perceptions such as these encouraged the development of a warrior mentality among the young male settlers. As Drake observed, "there were many young men who delighted in war much more than work and, therefore, preferred the tomahawk to the axe."[48] In a culture that already saw Indians simply as uncivilized obstacles to white settlement and possession of the land, these early brutalizing experiences only exacerbated the climate of fear and anger between the races.[49]

If fear was one essential lesson the borderland taught the pioneer, the others were surely privation and solitude. While male settlers in early Kentucky focused their energies on battling Indians, hunting, and staking out land claims, women devoted themselves to building families and communities, which was no easy task given the primitive conditions, scattered stations, and isolated homesteads that dotted the landscape. As one Baptist minister observed in 1776 while visiting Harrodsburg, one of the most prominent of early Kentucky settlements, it was "a poor town . . . a row or two of smoky cabins, dirty women, men with . . . greasy hunting shirts, leggings and moccasins. I there ate some of the first corn raised in the country, but little of it, as they had a very poor way to make it unto meal; we learnt to eat wild meat, without bread or salt."[50]

What they lived in was equally primitive. The cabins settlers built were very small structures—usually one-story log houses thirty feet by sixteen feet, with a single door, no windows, and a half-finished wood chimney. Clearly, it was a home constructed to provide only the simplest of shelter and offered its hardworking inhabitants virtually no privacy and few comforts. The first home that Drake's family lived in was simply "a covered pen or shed, built for sheep adjoining the cabin of its owner."[51] These rough-hewn cabins were eminently suitable to a poor mobile people with few belongings and little confidence in the future. The backcountry cabin, as David Hackett Fischer observes, was "an inconspicuous structure, highly adapted to a violent world where a handsome building was an invitation to disaster. In that respect, cabin architecture was an expression of the insecurity of life."[52]

Contributing as well to the crudeness of life were the primitive goods that were available to settlers, especially in the 1770s and 1780s. "Every family had to wear their own make," Jeptha Kemper recalled—spinning more hemp than flax. "They had no stores, and if they had, they had no money to take them. There was never any money in the country. . . ." Even Lexington offered little, according to Kemper. "All houses [there] but one were cabins. [Emphraim] January had the only store there. You could have put it all in one wagon."[53]

It was not just simplicity at work, but deprivation and despair. One thinks of Elijah Foley's father, Richard, whose family of six had to be supported on only six bushels of corn until he could raise more. Or the case of James Beath whose five children had to be cared for by relatives when he was captured by Indians during the Revolution and was imprisoned in Detroit. After the war Beath settled on his own Kentucky land, made improvements, but soon found himself caught between conflicting land claims. He then, according to John Hedge, "got chagrined, sold out, and moved over to Ohio, and died in less than 12 months." Finally, disappointment and privation reached their extremes in the tragic instances of suicide on the frontier. Sarah Graham told John Shane that she remembered "14 persons, that I knew their faces, [who] committed suicide."[54]

Adding to the insecurity and privation was the pervading sense of solitude on the margins. What struck most settlers, especially once the stations were abandoned for individual cabins, was the desolate loneliness of life on the frontier. Even as late as 1794, Daniel Drake poignantly recalled the sadness of their removal to the woods when his father's new land was cleared and a cabin was built. When "the day for removal arrived," he wrote, "and we left the village & public roadside, with its cavalcade of travelers, for the loneliness of the woods, [there was] a solitude which very soon was deeply felt by us all, but most of all, I think, by mother."[55] A saddle peddler, Needham Parry, also complained of the lonesomeness and great distances in the Kentucky wilds. Outside of the town of Shelby, Parry found himself taken to "the wilderness again" alone. "After I crossed Bullskin Creek," he noted in his diary, "it seemed lonesome." Between eighteen and twenty miles lay between Shelby and his destination at Captain Floyd's place. "In all this distance," he noted, "there are but two houses inhabited."[56]

Keeping a diary like Parry's, or more commonly, writing to family and friends back home, allowed literate settlers a chance to give voice to their hopes and fears on the margins. But ironically, even this simple act of communication could be undermined by the very conditions the settlers were trying to describe. John Floyd was forced to end a long letter to his kinsman back in Virginia because of the simple fact of nightfall: "I must drop my pen," he wrote, "for it is too dark to write any more, and I have no candle, and as soon as it is day, obliged to go and hunt or starve."[57] Those like Floyd who came, settled in cabins, and survived their first winter were experiencing the often difficult truth about sustaining a life on the frontier. As Drake soberly observed, "Kentucky was no longer a promise, but a possession—not an imagination, but a reality."[58]

That reality may well have meant very different things to men and women on the frontier. According to some historians, the Edenic paradise of the Kentucky frontier offered to men the chance for mastery and possession of a vast territory. Transforming the landscape with the axe and the gun served for men like Henderson and Boone as a restorative for failing fortunes and allowed them the opportunity to create abundant new Arcadias for themselves.

For women, the frontier conjured up simpler images and more prosaic tasks: above all, it denoted domesticity. And in their "cabin-bound" domesticity, often separated by many miles from their nearest neighbor, women experienced "the very real loneliness" of frontier life. They survived by preparing meals, tending to young children, and with the help of their children, planting a crop of Indian corn between the stumps of the trees felled by their husbands and fathers. So for women, frontier domesticity meant recreating a sense of home and family amid the cleared spaces of the wild. It was "an act of survival, of cabin-building and hoeing corn, not of romance or high adventure."[59]

Life in the borderlands was life *in extremis*: it was a dramatic moment in which men and women found themselves tested as never before and in so many different ways: family conflict over the move itself; the often debilitating trek westward; the brutal conflicts with Indians; the physical deprivations of meager shelter, limited food and clothing; and the more subjective challenges to a settler's faith, a sense of community, economic security, and personal identity.

Although we can only guess at it, what must have jolted pioneers most forcibly was the large discrepancy between image and reality in frontier Kentucky. While the West promised pioneering women and men opportunity and abundance, it often delivered something else. What it often delivered was a strong dose of fear—for young and old.

In the face of these dangers and obstacles why did so many persist? In good part, settlers pressed on because, one suspects, much of their lives had been an exercise in coping with duress and failure. Successful speculators like Richard Henderson may have dreamed of Kentucky as a huge arena to exploit to expand their riches. But Kentucky was primarily peopled by poor families whose dream was simply to avoid failure—for many a lifelong, futile search to escape dependency. Henderson's dream of creating his own Edenic kingdom violated the egalitarian spirit of the day, but it tapped powerfully into a basic urge among ordinary settlers: to find a new land where they could finally become freeholding, self-sufficient farmers.[60]

And so what seems to us insufferable pain and privation, fear and danger, were for those living on the margins simply the price of the ticket. But what also strengthened their resolve was a crucial measure of ignorance; if they had only known how elusive Eden was to be in Kentucky, surely many of them would have had second thoughts about taking the risk.

That ordinary settlers did not know what lay before them, even twenty years after Boone's trailblazing, is evident in Moses Austin's observations on the travelers he encountered on his journey along the Wilderness Road in 1796: "Ask these Pilgrims what they expect when they git to Kentucky," he wrote, "the Answer is Land." And then Austin recorded the typical reply of pioneers he saw when confronted with their desperate search for the elusive Eden:

> "have you any [Land]?
> "No. . . .
> "did you Ever see the Country?
> "No but Every Body says its good land.
>
> "Can any thing be more Absurd than the Conduct of man, here is hundreds Travelling hundreds of Miles, they Know not for what Nor Whither, except its to Kentucky . . . and when arriv'd at this Heaven in Idea what do they find? a goodly land will allow but to them a forbiden Land. Exhausted and worn down with distress and disappointment they are at last Oblig'd to become hewers of wood and Drawers of water."[61]

Alas, despite all their dreams, for most Kentucky settlers, the wood they would cut, the water they would drink, and, most important, the land they would seek out, squat on, and battle over, would—despite all their dreams—never become their own.

Notes

1. See Drew R. McCoy, *The Elusive Republic: Political Economy in Jeffersonian America* (Chapel Hill: Univ. of North Carolina Press, 1980).

2. Patricia Watlington, *The Partisan Spirit: Kentucky Politics, 1779-1792* (New York: Atheneum, 1972), 17-18.

3. J.W. Townsend, ed., *John Bradford's Historical Notes on Kentucky* (San Francisco: Grabhorn Press, 1932), 23.

4. Felix Walker, "Narrative of His Trip with Boone from Long Island to Boonesborough in 1775," *DeBow's Review* 41 (1854): 150-55.

5. Quoted in Fredrika Johanna Teute, "Land, Liberty, and Labor in the Post-Revolutionary Era: Kentucky as the Promised Land" (Ph.D. diss., Johns Hopkins University, 1988), 149.

6. Ibid., 159, 143.

7. William Lester, *The Transylvania Colony* (Spencer, Ind.: S.R. Guard, 1935), 95.

8. Harriette Simpson Arnow, *Seedtime on the Cumberland* (New York: Macmillan, 1960).

9. Lucien Beckner, trans., "John D. Shane's Interview with Mrs. Hinds and Patrick Scott," *Filson Club History Quarterly* 10 (1936): 177.

10. Richard R. Beeman, *The Evolution of the Southern Backcountry: A Case Study of Lunenburg County, Virginia, 1746-1832* (Philadelphia: Univ. of Pennsylvania Press, 1984), 29-30, 67-70, 81-82.

11. Johann David Schoepf, *Travels in the Confederation*, trans. and ed. Alfred J. Morrison, 2 vols. (Philadelphia: W.J. Campbell, 1911) 2: 103.

12. Ellen Eslinger, "Migration and Kinship on the Trans-Appalachian Frontier: Strode's Station, Kentucky," *Filson Club History Quarterly* 62 (1988): 52-53, 62-65.

13. Jack P. Greene, "The Colonial Southern Frontier," in *An Uncivil War: the Southern Backcountry during the American Revolution*, eds. Ronald Hoffman et al. (Charlottesville: Univ. Press of Virginia, 1985), 648; Andrew Cayton, *The Frontier Republic: Ideology and Politics in the Ohio Country, 1780-1825* (Kent, Ohio: Kent State Univ. Press, 1986), 4.

14. Lucien Beckner, trans., "John D. Shane's Interview with Benjamin Allen," *Filson Club History Quarterly* 5 (1931): 65.

15. Quoted in Teute, "Land, Liberty, and Labor," 144.

16. Annette Kolodny, *The Land Before Her: Fantasy and Experience of the American Frontiers, 1630-1860* (Chapel Hill: Univ. of North Carolina Press, 1984), 62.

17. Teute, "Land, Liberty, and Labor," 162.

18. Wade Hall, "Along the Wilderness Trail," *Filson Club History Quarterly* 61 (1987): 293.

19. Quoted in Lester, *The Transylvania Colony*, 69.

20. Ibid., 77.

21. Moses Austin, "A Memorandum of M. Austin's Journey, 1796-1797," *American Historical Review* 5 (1899-1900): 524-26.

22. Lester, *The Transylvania Colony*, 64-65.

23. Boone Papers, Lyman Draper Manuscript Collection, 17CC166-167, State Historical Society of Wisconsin, Madison.

24. Hall, "Along the Wilderness Trail," 293.

25. Beckner, "Interview with Benjamin Allen," 89.

26. Quoted in Lester, *The Transylvania Colony*, 75-76.

27. *Lexington Kentucky Gazette*, 25 March 1788.

28. Quoted in Watlington, *Partisan Spirit*, 30.

29. Lester, *The Transylvania Colony*, 265.

30. Ibid., 195-96. See also Daniel Trabue's comment on Fort Boonesborough in Chester Raymond Young, ed., *Westward into Kentucky: The Narrative of Daniel Trabue* (Lexington: Univ. Press of Kentucky, 1981), 25.

31. Lucien Beckner, trans., "John D. Shane's Interview with Mrs. Sarah Graham of Bath County," *Filson Club History Quarterly* 9 (1935): 237.

32. Neal O. Hammon, "Early Louisville and the Beargrass Stations," *Filson Club History Quarterly* 52 (1978): 159.

33. Teute, "Land, Liberty, and Labor," 200.

34. Daniel Drake, *Pioneer Life in Kentucky, 1785-1800*, ed. Emmett F. Horine (New York: Henry Schuman, 1948), 26-27.

35. Beckner, "Interview with Benjamin Allen," 89.

36. Beckner, "Interview with Sarah Graham," 233.

37. Ibid., 236.

38. Ibid., 233, 241.

39. Hammon, "Early Louisville," 159.

40. Lucien Beckner, trans., "John D. Shane's Notes on an Interview with Jeptha Kemper of Montgomery County," *Filson Club History Quarterly* 12 (1938): 155-56.

41. Hammon, "Early Louisville," 163.

42. Ibid., 157.

43. Drake, *Pioneer Life*, 26.

44. Interview with Mrs. John Morrison, Draper Manuscript Collection, 11CC152.

45. Beckner, "Interview with Sarah Graham," 241.

46. Drake, *Pioneer Life*, 27-28.

47. Beckner, "Interview with Mrs. Hinds and Patrick Scott," 170.

48. Drake, *Pioneer Life*, 26.

49. See Cayton, *Frontier Republic*; R. David Edmunds, "National Expansion from the Indian Perspective," in *Indians in American History*, ed. Frederick E. Hoxie (Arlington Heights, Ill.: Harlan Davidson, 1988), 159-78.

50. Lester, *The Transylvania Colony*, 253.

51. Drake, *Pioneer Life*, 11, 15.

52. David Hackett Fisher, *Albion's Seed: Four British Folkways in America* (New York: Oxford Univ. Press, 1989), 660.

53. Beckner, "Notes on Interview with Jeptha Kemper," 156-57.

54. Lucien Beckner, trans., "John D. Shane Interview with Elijah Foley," *Filson Club History Quarterly* 11 (1937): 259; idem, "Interview with Sarah Graham," 244.

55. Drake, *Pioneer Life*, 38.

56. "The Journal of Needham Parry," *Register of the Kentucky Historical Society* 34 (1936): 234-35.

57. Hammon, "Early Louisville," 213.

58. Drake, *Pioneer Life*, 15.

59. Kolodny, *The Land Before Her*, 47, 54, 62, 80.

60. For thoughtful explorations of this theme in early America, see Greene, "The Colonial Southern Frontier"; and Gregory H. Nobles, "Breaking into the Backcountry: New Approaches to the Early American Frontier, 1750-1800," *William and Mary Quarterly*, 3d ser., 46 (1989): 641-70.

61. Austin, "M. Austin's Journey," 525.

PART TWO

Enacting Expectations

John Breckinridge was a central player in the Jeffersonian effort to mold Kentucky's nascent culture. Along with other republicans, Breckinridge served on local, state, and national levels, bringing continuity to a region that easily could have accepted physical isolation west of the Appalachian mountains. Courtesy of The Filson Club Historical Society, Louisville, Ky.

Kentucky *in* the New Republic
A Study of Distance and Connection

MARION NELSON WINSHIP

In the histories of Kentucky in the new republic, distance has been a constant and defining dynamic. A quick way to appreciate this is to notice how historians choose to set their Kentucky scenes. Here, for instance, is the view with which Mary K. Bonsteel Tachau opened her fine study of the Kentucky federal courts: "[The Kentucky District in 1789] was a land that could be reached only after hazardous journeys along primitive trails or along the rivers. No stagecoaches penetrated the region, and the unimproved Wilderness Road, recently carved through the mountains, was too rugged for wagons. There was no mail service. . . . Communications within and away from the area were exceedingly irregular."[1]

The distances that divided Kentucky from eastern home places and centers of power were great, and we have plenty of vivid firsthand testimony to the trials of traversing them. Through two centuries now, those circumstances have been intensified and enshrined, first in memory, then in the literature of legend and history. And the tradition continues: while historians today may refine or disclaim much of the pioneer saga, we seldom tamper with the picture of a distant and isolated Kentucky—a picture that, tradition aside, rings so true to our own postelectronic expectations.

This chapter attempts to take a fresh look at the extraordinary few years during which the most basic issues of government were being hammered out in the new nation and, simultaneously and in close interconnection, in its first western state. For that purpose, I want to set aside the traditional image of distant Kentucky and to view the situation, instead, through the eyes of the men who formed (to borrow Patricia Watlington's apt phrase) the "articulate center" of Kentucky's political development.[2] These men dealt daily with the distances of the new republic, but their assumptions on the subject could hardly be more different from our own. Listen, for example, to Harry Toulmin, an English immigrant who would soon be thoroughly embroiled in Kentucky politics: "But why are we to calculate the distance of every place on the continent of America from the town of Philadelphia? It is true, we are seven hundred miles from the people of Philadelphia, but it is only seven hundred miles from men like ourselves. We are as much in the busy scenes of life as the people of Philadelphia are. . . . As to intelligence, we have a regular post, which comes and returns once a fortnight, and brings a multitude of newspapers from all parts of the continent."[3] Toulmin did not deny the distance; rather, he explained why, for men like him, there was no need to dwell on it.[4] Men like Toulmin did not live in an isolated Kentucky; theirs, whether in town or on farms nearby, was a bustling milieu and, as Toulmin's remarks suggest, they were kept pleasantly and often passionately occupied by a "multitude of newspapers" as well as by the voluminous correspondence that their busy public and private lives generated.[5] Toulmin was no ordinary newcomer: he had arrived in Kentucky armed with introductions from both Jefferson and Madison. The men who formed the articulate center of 1790s Kentucky politics—John Brown, John Breckinridge, and George Nicholas will be discussed here—arrived even better connected.

The men who viewed Kentucky as Toulmin did knew how to manage the vast distances of the Republic. They could make things happen across distance; they could even, as one of their favorite rhetorical ploys will demonstrate, use distance to make things happen. These were ingredients of personal power; in fact, I argue elsewhere that this congeries of background, experience, and talent for long-distance connection constitutes a good working definition of western success.[6] This essay, however, has a different purpose.

As we observe how these Kentucky leaders stayed in touch and in tune with eastern centers of power, in particular with Philadelphia, the metropolis and capital of the new republic, the chief political episodes of 1790s Kentucky take on a different light. Never truly local events in the first place, they reverberated across the Republic. Having traced the intricate and effective ways in which long-distance communication shaped episodes like the Democratic Society campaigns and the Kentucky Resolutions—events that have been universally understood in terms of distance and separation—I suggest a new emphasis for the title phrase of Joan Wells Coward's essential book. This paper explicates a view of "Kentucky *in* the New Republic."

For historians of early Kentucky, where virtually every adult was an immigrant, migration must obviously be part of any narrative or analysis. But migration stories are also the source of much of the tradition of distance and isolation that characterizes early trans-Appalachian history.[7] Recently, though, historians have begun to explore the possibility that westward migration, even in the earliest years of Kentucky settlement and even for the least powerful migrants, did not necessarily break the ties of kinship or loosen the bonds of society.[8] The migrants who formed the original articulate center of 1780s Kentucky politics were connected by their surveyorships and land speculations to the centers of power of an expansive Virginia. They were men, as Patricia Watlington observed, who "informed Virginia about Kentucky and Kentucky about Virginia."[9]

Turning to the men who dominated 1790s Kentucky politics, immigrants all, it is particularly useful to set the epic migration story aside and to take a fresh view of the evidence. John Brown, for example, migrated in 1783, in what might seem the pioneer mode of distance and danger: he "barely reached the gates of the fort at Crab Orchard" before an Indian party "appeared on top of the hill behind them." But (since he did safely reach the fort), the functional aspect of Brown's migration was connection, not danger. As Humphrey Marshall recalls: "No man who had yet arrived in Kentucky, if there were any afterwards, made his entrance into this country under more favorable auspices. . . ." John Brown's father was minister to the western Virginia congregation whose Kentucky-mindedness provoked his plaintive question: "What a Buzzel is this amongst People about *Kentuck*?" As Marshall notes, the elder Brown was "popular in his vocation, many of his church members had moved to Kentucky, and readily transferred to the son the friendship and regard they had for the father."[10] In addition, and perhaps above all, John Brown's uncle and mentor was William Preston, a western Virginia surveyor and land magnate, who was arguably the central figure in the development of early Kentucky. All of Preston's sons and nephews would be superbly equipped to take advantage of the fact that, as one of them succinctly put it, "Kentucky is the greatest field for Speculation, I believe, in the World."[11]

The 1793 migration of John Breckinridge, a younger first cousin of John Brown, is well enough documented to reveal the actual workings of a well-connected migration.[12] Far from setting off into wilderness isolation, the Breckinridge party stayed in contact along the way, both with family left behind and with the friends and relatives awaiting them in Kentucky. To the places where the family was expected to stop along the migration route, Kentucky friends and strangers alike sent notes asking lawyer Breckinridge to represent them in pending lawsuits or, at least, not to join the other side until they could talk with him.[13] After hearing that they were under way, a friend from Fayette County, William Russell, dispatched a messenger to wait for Breckinridge at Limestone. The messenger was to deliver some "business of importance" to Breckinridge, and they would coordinate plans for Russell and Kentucky kin to meet the migrating family. The logistical difficulties of first arrival were already taken care of: "a Carivan of horse" was arranged to carry them to the house near Lexington that had been leased for them. Migrants like Breckinridge would not need to worry about the chronic shortage of horses for hire at Limestone.[14]

John Breckinridge migrated to Kentucky well connected not only, as one might expect, to Virginia kin and persons of power, but also, more surprisingly, to Philadelphia. A striking coincidence will illustrate. In the spring of 1793, Virginia Congressmen James Madison and James Monroe were making their way home from Philadelphia. As they traveled southward, Monroe and Madison maintained constant contact with Jefferson, who was still in Philadelphia, eager to hear the results of the recent congressional elections, and thus learn the progress of the Jeffersonian republican opposition. It was in this context that Madison made his last field report to Jefferson. He had fallen "in with Mr. Brackinridge on his way to Kentucky," Madison wrote. "Mr. Brackinridge adverted to Greenup's late vote with indignation and dropped threats of its effect on his future pretensions." (In plainer English, disgusted that a Kentucky congressman had defected from the Jeffersonian position on a recent vote, Breckinridge had declared that he might challenge Greenup for the seat.) Only two weeks later, Jefferson had received and responded to Madison's letter.[15] While the Breckinridge company were still traveling west, in other words, the news was going around in Philadelphia. Moreover, it was not simply the news that John Breckinridge was "on his way to Kentucky," but the significant information that he meant to use his migration well, demonstrating his (partisan) loyalty to republican principles as he followed his own trajectory of ambition towards the arena of national politics.[16]

Given his connections and his avowedly national orientation, it seems incongruous that, just a few months after migrating to Kentucky, John Breckinridge would be the president and chief spokesman of an organization whose mission was to express distance and disaffection from the general government. Nevertheless, the seventh of October found Breckinridge hurriedly at work on a "Rough draft of resolution to be offered to the democratic society today." In this first document, as in the ones that would follow, Breckinridge the newcomer adopted the predominant western view of the last decade of Kentucky history. The citizens of Kentucky, as he put it in the traditional parlance of resolutions, had "for a series of years been anxiously hoping, that the free use of an all-important right, which they received from NATURE, and which is now wantonly and cruelly controuled and abused, would have been long since secured to them." They resolved, therefore, that a committee be appointed "to prepare an address to the inhabitants of the western country . . . and . . . a remonstrance to the President and Congress."[17] Breckinridge was given the task of composing both of these documents. In the remonstrance to the president and Congress, he employed the customary rhetoric of distance: "In colonizing this dangerous and distant desart," western settlers had always considered their right to Mississippi trade inseparable from "the country they had sought out, had fought for, and acquired." And he employed the traditional western threat of separation: though western citizens were as patriotic as any others, "patriotism, like every other thing, has its bounds."[18] At the same time, Breckinridge composed a petition to Congress protesting the excise tax. Again, he invoked the "desart": the Kentuckians were "surrounded by rugged desart." No—he could do better than that—Kentuckians were "surrounded by an almost tractless desart which is infested by savages dispersed over an extensive country whose streams we durst not navigate."[19] (Honesty eventually required Breckinridge to qualify his dramatic "tractless desart" with "almost.") The petition asked that the excise not be collected until the petitioners enjoyed "free use of the navigation of the Mississippi," or at least, that it be collected not in specie but in whiskey.[20] During the next tumultuous year of Kentucky protest, Breckinridge's language became more vehement, perhaps reaching its height in a letter to a Virginia connection in 1794. There, Breckinridge played on western themes of distance and pioneer patriotism and ended with a sarcastic version of the rhetoric of distance: in excoriating Jay's negotiations, he wrote, "we may be wrong; for we are too distant from the grand seat of information, and are much too hackneyed in the old-fashioned principles of 1776, to receive much light from the banking, funding & other new fashioned systems & schemes of policy, which are the offspring and ornament of the present system."[21] It was well-connected men like Breckinridge who could, both in public remonstrances and private letters, most effectively articulate and circulate the belligerent messages of isolation and neglect that 1790s Kentucky sent to the seat of the general government.[22] Without denying the difficult questions of motivation and sincerity, which will be discussed below, it is hard to miss the gusto with which western men like Breckinridge seemed to take on their new roles. Breckinridge probably enjoyed the somewhat alarmed reactions that he received from some Virginia connections. And I am certain he would have relished the judgment of historian E. Merton Coulter on the letter above: "burning with sarcasm and strong feeling, [it] answered all the effeminate Easterners who disagreed with him and with the Kentucky Democratic Society."[23]

For historians, the Democratic Societies of Kentucky have always been a problem. Even those who most forcefully placed the societies in the context of "burgeoning democracy" have had to admit that the most prominent men in Kentucky were their leaders.[24] This has required some fancy footwork. But the leadership of men like Breckinridge seems more anomalous than it really is. In a functional way, the apparent paradox makes perfect sense. From the collective point of view of Kentucky, the purpose of all this noisy disaffection—the petitions, the remonstrances, even the threats of disunion—was to claim the attention and support of that same government. In the distinctive dynamic of distance *and* connection, the role of well-connected men becomes clear.

The ability simultaneously to appeal to and excoriate the federal government is, not incidentally, a quintessentially western phenomenon.[25] It follows that as the men at the articulate center of Kentucky politics drafted their angry editorials and remonstrances, they became western men. That transformation brings up a difficult question. What were the motives of newly arrived, well-connected western men like Nicholas and Breckinridge? For most historians—reasonably enough, given the limitations of the sources—this has been a rather ahistorical judgment call. I have not come to a judgment on this question myself, but I can demonstrate the advantages of considering the question (as our historical subjects themselves did) in a historical and geographical context that is wider than 1790s Kentucky.

Was John Breckinridge sincere as a western man? Certainly, since he knew the secret inner workings of western rhetoric, he could not have taken it at face value. As a young man, he had witnessed the wranglings behind the formation of several new western counties. He had watched his uncle, William Preston, draft petitions and then revise them by carefully ratcheting up the customary language of distance and danger.[26] Sometimes, in these petitions, "Mountains and Rivers" were literally magnified in the text to double or triple size. This emphasis on distance and dangerous isolation would be tied to a standard argument: the petitioners had "explored this uncultivated wilderness bordering on many nations of savages and surrounded by mountains almost inaccessible to any but those very savages" in order to gain their rights from an eminently reasonable (but now strangely negligent) government. The particular request or grievance would follow. The first petition Breckinridge is known to have composed himself made sarcastic use of petitioners' inflated language and implied a somewhat cynical view of the whole democratic process. In 1786, at the request of a kinsman who needed to counter rival petitions for a division of Amherst County, Virginia, Breckinridge drafted a petition that archly declared surprise "to find the Seat of the Court House has *so late* become so inconvenient," when the situation had never been complained of before.[27]

Breckinridge, then, had come to Kentucky with an insider's view and even some practice in the rhetoric of distance that he would wield so skillfully for the Democratic Society. Like the processes of settlement and land acquisition that underpinned it, this genre of remonstrance crossed boundaries of time and space; it was abundant before and after the Revolution, and east and west of the Appalachians. Like earlier petitions to create new Virginia counties, the various documents generated and sent back east by the decade-long Kentucky statehood movement had been framed in the rhetoric of distance.[28] Therefore, although it is possible that John Breckinridge had never seen most of the petitions from the Kentucky district, when called upon by the Democratic Society, he easily fit the bill.

Did this early experience with western petitions make him cynical rather than sincere? Perhaps this is the wrong question to ask. Like other leaders of his time, Breckinridge composed each of his texts for the very practical purpose of bringing about a particular result. In September 1793, for example, he wrote a treatise for the edification of a student, in which he expounded on the patriot tradition and the unsuitability of aristocracy to a new republic and, even more, to a new country. In it, he penned for the first time without sarcasm the rhetoric of distance, writing reverently of "the first adventurers to this distant country."[29]

The political documents composed by men of the articulate center of Kentucky politics were also written for a purpose. Even while they cried distance and isolation, they were meant to connect the interests of western men and thus to help bring about the reformation of the relationship between Congress and the western country. At the same time, as (printed and reprinted in newspapers) they circulated through the republic, they would connect and strengthen the national opposition to the Federalist administration.

The practical instructions for doing this were sometimes as elaborate as the political texts themselves. Breckinridge's Democratic Society remonstrance, for example, was circulated for signatures around central Kentucky and sent on to Congress. It was also sent to the western states complete with a set of instructions to ensure that *they* could successfully connect to Congress as well: "The Remonstrance, when signed, may be transmitted to the representative in Congress from your district, or to any other member of that body, delegated from the Western Country." This should be done as soon as possible, the Lexington society advised, since it was "intended that a decision should be obtained during the present session of Congress."[30]

Public remonstrances like those that Breckinridge wrote for the Democratic Society were constructed to blend two modes of communication that would be needed to make them effective in more than one setting. There was the blunt language which, read aloud on Kentucky court days, might persuade western men from a wide variety of backgrounds to attach their signatures. And there was the polished and convoluted language in which gentlemen communicated amongst themselves. This language was equally necessary: first, to impress the most influential men on local court days; second, and just as important, for creditable presentation, rather than embarrassment, when the document reached the president and Congress. This blend of "manly vigor" and genteel expression would also suit a varied readership all across the republic. Men like John Breckinridge, with their experience in the spirited politics of an expansive Virginia, and their legal-statesmen's education, were well suited to the task.

Formal remonstrances formed important strands to the web of communications that proliferated over these western issues. Other strands, equally traditional and perhaps as efficacious, were the letters that circulated among the men of the articulate center and the Virginians in the Washington administration. The correspondence of George Nicholas, who arrived in Kentucky in 1789, will illustrate. During the momentous political seasons before his removal to Kentucky, Nicholas had kept in frequent communication with James Madison. When Nicholas removed to Kentucky, he continued to do the same. Just as Breckinridge would do in 1793, Nicholas quickly and forcefully began to press a western view. "We," the newcomer-turned-western-man warned, "have every wish to continue united to you. . . . [But] Would you be contented to the Eastward with a government which left you exposed to the ravages of a merciless enemy and which permitted another power to prevent you from enjoying the fruits of your labour . . . ?" In places, Nicholas's letter almost might have been a public remonstrance, but he also took on the role of gentlemanly informant: After warning Madison that to disgruntled Kentuckians, even an alliance with Great Britain was beginning to look good, Nicholas assumed a gentlemanly distance from his disaffected countrymen, concluding: "These are the thoughts of the most enlightened men among us, but such thoughts as they only give utterance to in whispers; because it is yet hoped and believed that you will do us justice."[31]

In this form, of which Nicholas was a master, such messages of separation and even threats of disunion were conveyed within a web of communication and common political understanding.[32] And such letters had their effect in the capital. Madison customarily shared Nicholas's letters with Secretary of State Jefferson. In the case of the letter above, Jefferson's foreign policy was actually decided by warnings conveyed by Nicholas and John Brown.[33] And, having reacted to western warnings, the administration hastened, through the customary medium of a homeward-bound congressman, to assure the western leadership of their support. When John Brown returned to Kentucky the next spring, he carried letters from Madison and Jefferson to Harry Innes and George Nicholas announcing that foreign control of Mississippi navigation would no longer be tolerated and, incidentally, urging both to enter Congress from Kentucky.[34]

The political and legal education that men like Brown, Nicholas, and Breckinridge had received at the College of William and Mary had given them, as designed, an extraordinary preparation for Virginia and national politics. During the nineties, these same men, now removed to Kentucky, stayed in touch and in tune with their Virginia political compeers, who, already national-minded in the mid-eighties, were now rapidly metamorphosing into a national opposition party. It is essential, therefore, to view the actions of the men who orchestrated the political strategy of 1790s Kentucky in the context of the extraordinary era and company in which they had learned their politics.

Two Virginia examples will illustrate. It happens to have been George Nicholas himself who, in 1785, conceived a plan that, in one historian's opinion, "may well have been the most important political insight of the time." During Virginia's debates over assessing taxes to support religion, Nicholas suggested that the pro-assessment state legislature be flooded with opposing petitions which "all hold the same language." The petitions, as Nicholas explained the strategy to Madison, would demonstrate, "An exact uniformity of sentiment in a majority of the country," that could actually deter the "majority of the Assembly from proceeding." Responding to this idea, Madison wrote up a "Remonstrance" for the purpose. Both Nicholas and John Breckinridge were among the "confidential persons" trusted to keep Madison's authorship secret while "dispatching" copies of it around the state. Nicholas himself obtained 150 signatures in a single day at Orange County June court and planned to send it to ten other counties. This campaign, conceived by George Nicholas, set in motion by Madison in Jefferson's confidence, and circulated by young legislator-lawyers like Nicholas, Breckinridge, and their friends, generated petitions with some ten thousand signatures from forty-one counties.[35]

A second example will illustrate the political style and strategy that prepared the future leaders of 1790s Kentucky. During the early days of alarmed opposition politics in 1793 (the same season when Breckinridge migrated and began his career as a western man), James Madison and James Monroe, back in Virginia, were quietly plotting a strategy to solve a problem. The problem was that the Federalists were holding successful "popular" meetings in Richmond and elsewhere, and that these were being disastrously well publicized around the republic through the partisan press. On the one hand, the "language of the towns" was "generally directed" by the Federalists, while, on the other hand, the "Country" was "much uninformed, and too inert to speak for itself." The solution: In order to set "on foot expressions of the public Mind in important Counties, and under the auspices of respectable names," Madison "suggested a proper train of ideas" (i.e., a script which he drafted) to be used at such meetings. Again, Madison's authorship must be kept secret. The goal of these manipulations, as Madison and Monroe articulated it, was to make known "the real sentiments of the people."[36]

It is salutary to place the political activities of early national Kentucky where they properly belong, in the context of the partisan political maneuvering of national Virginia. When recent historians have looked closely at the workings of 1790s Kentucky politics, they have generally seen gentry making "democratic" concessions and manipulating the populace for their own security or advantage.[37] Indeed, for scholars trained in modern social history and no longer prepared to take democratic rhetoric at its word, this may seem the only acceptable interpretation of the evidence. We cannot be whigs, so we must be progressives. But this puts us and the history of Kentucky into an awfully confining interpretive box. We can escape that confinement by reconnecting our Kentucky characters in a more dynamic, functional, and accurate way to their Virginia and national milieux. However we may judge the results of Kentucky events, it is only fair to note that all the "Jeffersonian" leaders, from Madison, Jefferson, and Monroe themselves, to colleagues and younger followers like Nicholas and Breckinridge, all worked their political strategies upon the people as well as for them, while all claimed (and perhaps believed) that they were working for the good of the Republic.

If this understanding of Jeffersonian Virginia strategies is put together with a view from inside the workings of Kentucky's leading Jeffersonians, the episode known in textbooks as the "Kentucky and Virginia Resolutions" takes a new shape. Historians have long found the meaning of the resolutions in terms of their antebellum states' rights uses or, more recently, in terms of individual civil rights.[38] Whenever historians have paid attention to what Noble E. Cunningham called the "actual instrumentalities" behind the well-known documents and basic facts of this historical event, however, they have found national scope and national intentions at work.[39] They have also found shrewd political strategizing in which the resolutions were plotted, in part, for the purpose of bringing the Federalists down and clearing the way for a Jeffersonian administration.[40] Stanley Elkins and Eric McKitrick offer particularly vivid glimpses of the political machinations involved: "We see Jefferson busily urging his spokesmen to find their voices, volunteering materials that might be useful in this or that place. . . ." And, again, "For the manifestoes of protest envisioned by Jefferson to be set in motion in the right way and the right direction, secrecy as to origin was indispensable."[41] If we can also attend to the manifestoes set in motion around the republic by western men like George Nicholas and John Breckinridge, in what they considered "the right way and the right direction," how will the Kentucky Resolutions appear?

It can be admitted that the impetus for the political activity of the summer of 1798 did come from Philadelphia, in the sense that it was Federalist acts of Congress that set the Jeffersonian passions in motion. At the close of the protracted and contentious session that produced the Alien and Sedition Acts, Congressman John Fowler wrote from Philadelphia to his Kentucky constituents entreating them "to pay particular regard to the emergencies of the times, and not be wanting to yourselves in an hour of extreme danger: if there is danger to your constitution or your government," he urged, "it may be corrected by yourselves."[42] But Kentuckians did not need this admonition; at any rate, by the time it arrived they were moving full speed on their own toward the Kentucky Resolutions.

Kentuckians were reacting to the Alien and Sedition Acts even before news of their actual passage reached the state. On June 27, the *Kentucky Gazette* printed a drastic and sweeping alien and sedition bill that had been presented in draft form to the House of Representatives two weeks before.[43] On reading this paper, both John Breckinridge and George Nicholas swung into action. For the next edition of the weekly *Gazette*, they wrote a notice calling the inhabitants of Fayette and adjacent counties to a mass meeting on August court day, where "the present critical situation of public affairs" would be considered, so that citizens could "express to their representatives [in Congress] their opinions of the measures which have already been adopted, and those which ought now to be pursued."[44]

At the same time, Breckinridge also wrote sets of resolutions for protest meetings in Clark and Woodford Counties, establishing in the process a model for the resolutions of summer meetings in half a dozen other counties. The Clark County meeting on July 24 passed resolutions that made extensive use of Breckinridge's draft.[45] Breckinridge meanwhile wrote to James Monroe four days before the Clark County meeting that the "proceedings of the general government have excited considerable discontent here."[46] The proceedings of the Clark County meeting were printed in the *Kentucky Gazette* on August 1. In the same day's paper, George Nicholas placed an intentionally inflammatory statement: he believed recent Federalist legislation violated the First Amendment, and further, that the president or any judges who had approved the act had also violated the Constitution.[47]

The largest citizens' meeting, the one that Breckinridge and Nicholas had called, was held in Lexington during the August court. There, before several thousand people, George Nicholas gave a long oration and the young Henry Clay, recently arrived in the state, a fiery one. Both Nicholas and Clay were carried on the shoulders of an enthusiastic crowd.[48] That very day, Breckinridge wrote to James Monroe that "the minds of the people" were "all fired respecting the proceedings of Congress." The people were "assembling in various parts of the state & strongly reprobating the alien & sedition Bills. . . ." Like virtually all other observers at the time, he noted the "very great unanimity" on these issues in Kentucky. And he issued a declaration—one familiar in spirit from a long western tradition: "Let the consequences be what they may, I have at present not a doubt, from the apparent temper of the people, that any, & every attempt, to enforce the two first mentioned laws, will be *publickly resisted & repelled*."

That would have made a fine peroration, but John Breckinridge could not resist adding another one. He concluded: "We are, it is true, very remote from the Seat of information, & that information imperfectly transmitted to us; but if some of the most invaluable rights of a freeman are not prostrated by those laws, we have lost our senses in this country; for it seems to be the universal belief here that such is the fact. God only knows how things may end, but I entertain the most gloomy apprehensions from the consequences; & sincerely hope I may be mistaken in the Event."[49] This ending may seem anticlimactic to us, but perhaps not to contemporaries, because it rang, though sarcastically, the great western themes of distance and disaffection.

Such letters were never intended by their authors as detailed reports from Jeffersonian *legati* on some far periphery. They were purposefully abstract. In this letter, Breckinridge did not mention his own role in orchestrating and writing scripts for citizens' meetings in Lexington or anywhere else. There was a practical aspect to this editorial choice, because the proceedings of these meetings would reach the eastern newspapers soon enough. But beyond that, these letters were composed of grand principles expressed in elegant but ringing phrases, because they were intended as fuel for partisan fires, not only at the seat of government, but in circulation around the republic. Such a letter was meant to be, at the very least, shared and read aloud in company.[50]

Busy lawyer-planter-speculator-politicians like Nicholas and Breckinridge generated a great deal of paper (now, except for the curse of Nicholas's handwriting, a gift to historians). They seldom took the time to muse on political subjects. When they did, they took pains about it, and we can be sure that they meant the letters as essays, ready to be excerpted and printed for wide circulation. The apogee of this genre would be publication in pamphlet form. George Nicholas, for example, would publish the most prominent letter-turned-pamphlet, printed in Lexington and reprinted in Philadelphia, to justify the Kentucky Resolutions. Jefferson himself would purchase copies for distribution "to such as have been misled, are candid, and will be open to the truth."[51]

All of this activity took place before the narrative of the Kentucky Resolutions, as usually framed, had even begun. That story, familiar from many other sources, may be quickly summarized. While visiting in Virginia in the fall of 1798, John Breckinridge had visited Wilson Cary Nicholas, a Jeffersonian confidant and frequent business partner to Breckinridge (and brother to George Nicholas). At Breckinridge's urging, Nicholas entrusted him with a set of resolutions, originally intended for North Carolina, that Jefferson had secretly composed to enlist state governments to combat the Alien and Sedition Acts. When informed of this development, Jefferson declared his confidence in Breckinridge.[52] In November, the resolutions as promised easily passed in the Kentucky legislature. Breckinridge made a telling change to Jefferson's document. That secret draft had declared that when the federal government exceeded its powers, each state had a "natural right . . . to nullify" and had called on every state to "take measures of its own" to make unacceptable acts unenforceable within its own boundaries. The thrust of Breckinridge's draft, in contrast, was connection rather than separate action. He omitted the term "nullification" and, in familiar western tradition, called on sister states to unite with Kentucky in pressing the next session of Congress to repeal the Alien and Sedition Acts.[53]

By mid-December, the resolutions were adding fuel to partisan fires in the United States Congress. When a Federalist congressman mentioned the recent "inflammatory resolutions, and . . . tumultuous assemblages of the people," he was quickly reprimanded by Republican Albert Gallatin, who objected that Kentucky's "tumultuous assemblies" were simply "peaceable meetings of the people to state their grievances."[54] Through newspapers, similar partisan skirmishes circulated throughout the republic.[55]

Enclosed in letters from eastern friends as well as in the newspapers sent to Kentucky subscribers, reactions to their resolutions got back to Kentucky. Negative reactions caused Kentuckians, in turn, to set defenses and counterattacks into circulation.

A scurrilous excerpt from William Cobbett's *Philadelphia Porcupine's Gazette*, for example, was reprinted in the *Frankfort Palladium*. Ostensibly drawing on the account in a Kentucky paper [unnamed], Federalist polemicist Cobbett reported that a

> mob assembled on the 24th of July, with a fellow of the name of Fishback at their head; they got pen, ink, and paper and to work they went drawing up *resolves* to the number of ten, amongst which is the following one, which, for sentiment as well as orthography, is unequalled even in the annals of American Democracy.
> Resolved that thar es sufichunt resen too beeleev and wee doe beeleev that our leebeerte es in daingur and wee plege ouerselves too eche other and too ouer cuntery that wee will defende um agents awl un constetushunal ataks that mey bee made upon um.

William Cobbett concocted this piece not from whole cloth but from a Republican newspaper report of the Clark County meeting and resolutions. That meeting, chaired by a man named Jacob Fishback, had produced ten literate and articulate resolutions based, in part, on the draft that Breckinridge himself had prepared for them. Cobbett's quoted "resolve" is the ninth Clark County resolution, transformed for porcupine effect into "frontier" phonetics.[56]

If only we could witness the scene when John Breckinridge and other prominent Kentuckians first read the conclusion of this piece by William Cobbett!

> If these sagacious and learned citizens had assembled in any place, where there had been a single magistrate of spirit and good sense, he would have dispersed them by his constables and thereby spared his country the disgrace, which their barbarous resolves are calculated to reflect on it. If this Kentucky newspaper were to fall into the hands of a person totally unacquainted with the rest of America, he would take us all for a sort of savages; and, in fact, the Kentuckians do appear to be just civilized enough to be the tools of faction, and that's all.[57]

The Federalist *Porcupine*'s Kentucky-bashing would have its effect in that state but, meanwhile, back in Virginia, the lack of official support from the other states for either the Kentucky or Virginia Resolutions was a disappointment. Jefferson, for one, was unwilling to leave it at that. Both Kentucky and Virginia ought to speak again, and it was, he thought, important that they "pursue the same tract at the ensuing sessions of their legislatures."[58] Hearing in the fall of 1799 that his friend Wilson Cary Nicholas was planning soon to travel to Kentucky on business for the estate of George Nicholas, who had died suddenly during the summer, Jefferson held a dinner meeting with Madison and Monroe to "consider a little together what is to be done." In preparation, he wrote out his "ideas" for the "resolution or declaration" that "should be passed."[59] He wanted Kentucky and Virginia to issue a threat: "to sever ourselves from that union we so much value, rather than give up the right of self-government which we have reserved, and in which alone we see liberty, safety, and happiness."[60] In somewhat moderated form, these ideas were handed to Nicholas to be carried to Kentucky. Jefferson wrote to Nicholas that he had not actually written out the resolutions for two reasons: to preserve secrecy and "because there remains still (after their late loss) a mass of talents in Kentucky sufficient for every purpose."[61]

Meeting in November, the Kentucky House soon unanimously passed a resolution (presumably prepared behind the scenes by Breckinridge, who was then speaker). The 1799 Kentucky declaration, compared with other documents generated over the Alien and Sedition laws, including the 1798 Kentucky Resolutions, is very short and seems somewhat lifeless, even grudging. (To address these issues again, the House stated, ought "be as unnecessary as unavailing," because they had already been submitted to the judgment of "our fellow citizens throughout the union.") In spite of Jefferson's wishes and in contrast to so very many documents that had issued from Kentucky in the previous dozen years, the legislature did not threaten to leave the Union; the tone, instead, was conciliatory.

But the Kentucky legislature did show passion on one count: they cared deeply about what the rest of the Union thought of them. Secure in their principles, the legislature declared in 1799 that it stood "regardless of censure or calumniation." Nevertheless, they could not help but "lament" that their 1798 resolutions had provoked such "unfounded suggestions, and uncandid insinuations, derogatory of the character and principles of the good people of this commonwealth."[62]

In keeping with their concern for the reputation of Kentucky, the legislature voted to have the public printer strike eight hundred copies of the resolution. One of these was to be sent to the governor of each state. The remaining 784 were to be "distributed equally" to the Kentucky legislators.[63] At first glance, it seems obvious that these copies were meant for local political use. But what would become of the copies sent to state governors? How many were reprinted in newspapers all over the republic?[64] Within the legislators' home districts, to what uses were the copies put? How many legislators would send copies to friends and connections outside of Kentucky, and what opinions were exchanged in the process?

To address this last question, I offer only one example, but it is a significant one. As soon as copies of the resolutions were available, John Breckinridge sent one on to Jefferson.[65] Writing again by the next post, he reported to Jefferson, "It was at the opening of the session concluded on to make no reply, but on further reflection, least no improper conclusions might be drawn from our silence, we hastily drew up the paper which I inclosed you." Breckinridge reported only in general terms: having been sworn to secrecy the year before, he knew not to implicate Jefferson in the 1799 action.[66] Jefferson, also cautious, wrote only a single line on the subject to Breckinridge, but it must have been a gratifying one: "I was glad to see the subject taken up, and done with so much temper, firmness & propriety."[67]

Early in 1800, just as Jefferson was writing his approval of Kentucky's second resolution, a fifteen-year-old Robert McAfee arrived in Lexington to read law with John Breckinridge. He was immediately taken to a "Barbacue" on a farm nearby. Writing his memoirs long after the event, McAfee would vividly recall three things about the occasion. The first was apparent in the way he introduced the event itself: "There was a Barbacue in the vicinity & great excitement against the Alien & Sedition law." Second, when an old gentleman from western Pennsylvania "attempted to give a toast reflecting [unfavorably] on General Washington, the news of whose death had only reached the country a few days before," McAfee remembered that the partisan toast was "promptly repressed, altho every man on the ground was a Jeffersonian Republican." The third impression did not take hold until the next day, when the young boy resolved that he would "never drink any more whiskey or intoxicating liquors."[68]

Leaving aside the whiskey, McAfee remembered a scene very different from what we might expect at a "barbacue"—an event traditionally linked to local power and local politicking. He gives us a vivid glimpse of Kentuckians, at the end of a famously distant and disaffected decade, in a state of local excitement over national issues. The talk at this Kentucky barbecue matched the dynamic that had been developing over a dozen years and that had animated the controversy over the Alien and Sedition laws. By 1800, Kentucky had proven what Jefferson called its Republican "temper, firmness & propriety" to a "candid world." And men at Kentucky's articulate center had acted just as historians have described Madison and Jefferson acting in this same episode: with "precision, purpose, and an assurance about the Republican future."[69]

In spite of the separating and particularizing effects of subsequent myth and scholarship, and in spite of its own rhetorical claims to the contrary, 1790s Kentucky was not distant and isolated from the new nation. Even as they remonstrated against the government at Philadelphia, Kentuckians through their spokesmen made their own claim to national and even imperial ground, while painting the reigning Federalists and their interests as small and local.[70] At the articulate center of "the boisterous political world" of early national Kentucky was a group of very well connected men.[71]

For these men, the distance from powerful Virginia was eminently manageable, and the distance from Philadelphia was, as the booster-newcomer Harry Toulmin had put it, "only seven hundred miles from men like ourselves." Men like George Nicholas and John Breckinridge acted constantly and effectively on that insight and, in the process, shaped the history of Kentucky *in* the new republic.

Notes

It is a pleasure to be exploring early Kentucky in such good company. Thanks to Steve Aron, Ellen Eslinger, Craig Friend, Liz Perkins, Blair Pogue, and Gail Terry for stimulating encounters. For editorial aid and unwavering support, I am indebted to Craig Friend, Kay Ofman, and Ed Countryman.

1. Mary K. Bonsteel Tachau, *Federal Courts in the Early Republic: Kentucky, 1789-1816* (Princeton, N.J.: Princeton Univ. Press, 1978), 14.

2. Patricia Watlington, *The Partisan Spirit: Kentucky Politics, 1779-1792* (Chapel Hill: Univ. of North Carolina Press, 1972), 43.

3. Harry Toulmin to James Leigh, 19 May 1794, in Harry Toulmin, *The Western Country in 1793: Reports on Kentucky and Virginia*, eds. Marion Tinling and Godfrey Davies (San Marino, Calif.: Henry E. Huntington Library, 1948), 134.

4. Toulmin described the journey between Philadelphia and Lexington as "the most troublesome part of [Kentucky merchants'] business." He also admitted the danger, though, tellingly, he looked on the bright side, noting that the "Wilderness" was "now reduced to a hundred miles," and "It is two years since any boats were attacked in going

down the river; and I cannot imagine any danger to those who are sufficiently precautious"; Toulmin, *The Western Country in 1793*, 125, 134.

5. For a remarkable set of essays exploring similar themes and territory, see Richard D. Brown, *Knowledge is Power: The Diffusion of Information in Early America, 1700-1865* (New York: Oxford Univ. Press, 1989). One significant difference between the Kentucky described by Tachau (1978) and that sketched by Toulmin (1794) is the implementation of the 1792 Postal Act, a subject that has gained the attention it deserves in the recent work of Richard R. John Jr., *Spreading the Word: The American Postal System from Franklin to Morse* (Cambridge, Mass.: Harvard Univ. Press, 1996).

6. Marion Nelson Winship, "Power in Motion: Western Success Stories of the Jeffersonian Republic" (Ph.D. dissertation-in-progress, University of Pennsylvania).

7. For this problem and its interpretive consequences, see Marion Nelson Winship, "The Land of Connected Men: A New Migration Story from the Early American Republic," *Pennsylvania History* (forthcoming, 1997).

8. Ellen Eslinger, "Migration and Kinship on the Trans-Appalachian Frontier: Strode's Station, Kentucky," *Filson Club History Quarterly* 62 (1988): 52-66; and Gail S. Terry, "Sustaining the Bonds of Kinship in a Trans-Appalachian Migration, 1790-1811: The Cabell-Breckinridge Slaves Move West," *Virginia Magazine of History and Biography* 102 (1994): 455-76.

9. Watlington, *The Partisan Spirit*, 43-44.

10. Ibid., 79-80; Humphrey Marshall, *The History of Kentucky, Including an Account of the Discovery, Settlement, Progressive Improvement, Political and Military Events, and the Present State of the Country*, 2 vols. (Frankfort, Ky.: George S. Robinson, printer, 1824), 1: 316-17; and John Brown Sr. to William Preston, 5 May 1775, Preston Papers, Lyman C. Draper Manuscript Collection, 4QQ15, State Historical Society of Wisconsin, Madison.

11. John Breckinridge to James Breckinridge, 29 January 1786, James Breckinridge Papers, Alderman Library, University of Virginia, Charlottesville.

12. Historians besides myself have been attracted by the richness of the sources: Lowell H. Harrison, "A Virginian Moves to Kentucky," *William and Mary Quarterly*, 3rd ser., 15 (1958): 201-13; Gail S. Terry, "Family Empires: A Frontier Elite in Virginia and Kentucky, 1740-1815" (Ph.D. diss., College of William and Mary, 1992); and, framed as communications history, Hazel Dicken-Garcia, *To Western Woods: The Breckinridge Family Moves to Kentucky in 1793* (Rutherford, N.J.: Fairleigh Dickinson Univ. Press, 1991).

13. James Brown to John Breckinridge, 20 April 1793, Breckinridge Family Papers, Manuscript Division, Library of Congress. Also, letters from John Bradford "At Mr. Meredith's," 5 May; to J. Hite, 10 May; to John Edwards, 6 May; and to William Henry, 6 May 1793, Breckinridge Family Papers.

14. William Russell to John Breckinridge, 1 May 1793, Breckinridge Family Papers; and Craig Thompson Friend, "'Fond Illusions' and Environmental Transformation along the Maysville-Lexington Road," *Register of the Kentucky Historical Society* 94 (1996): 10.

15. James Monroe to Thomas Jefferson, 22 March 1793; James Madison to Jefferson, 24 March 1793; Monroe to Jefferson, 27 March 1793; Madison to Jefferson, 12 April 1793; and Jefferson to Madison, 28 April 1793, in John Catanzariti, ed. *The Papers of Thomas Jefferson*, 26 vols. (Princeton, N.J.: Princeton Univ. Press, 1992), 25: 429, 443-44, 463-64, 533, and 619.

16. A late-summer letter from Monroe shows that his partisan political intentions were taken seriously. Writing from Madison's house to Breckinridge in Kentucky, Monroe congratulated him on his safe arrival and warned him to be ready for a partisan brouhaha that would soon reach Kentucky via the Federalist press; James Monroe to Breckinridge, 23 August 1793, in Stanislaus Murray Hamilton, ed., *The Writings of James Monroe*, 7 vols. (New York: G.P. Putnam's Sons, 1898), 1: 272-73 [original in Thomas Addis Emmet Manuscript Collection, New York Public Library].

17. "Rough Draft of Resolution To Be Offered to the Democratic Society Today," 7 October 1793, in John Breckinridge's hand, Breckinridge Family Papers, as reprinted in *Lexington Kentucky Gazette* 12 October 1793, in Thomas D. Clark, ed., *The Voice of the Frontier: Bradford's Notes on Kentucky* (Lexington: Univ. Press of Kentucky, 1993), 205.

18. "Remonstrance of the Citizens West of the Allegheny Mountains to the President and Congress of the United States," in John Breckinridge's hand, December 1793, as reprinted in Philip S. Foner, ed. *The Democratic-Republican Societies, 1790-1800: A Documentary Sourcebook of Constitutions, Declarations, Addresses, Resolutions, and Toasts* (Westport, Conn.: Greenwood Press, 1976), 363-66.

19. "To the Congress of the United States, Petition of the Inhabitants of the State of Kentucky," 4 December 1793, rough draft in John Breckinridge's hand, Breckinridge Family Papers.

20. "To the Congress of the United States, Petition of the Inhabitants of the State of Kentucky," 4 December 1793, rough draft in John Breckinridge's hand, Breckinridge Family Papers. In "The Efforts of the Democratic Societies of the West to Open the Navigation of the Mississippi River," *Mississippi Valley Historical Review* 11 (1924): 367-88, his classic essay on the western democratic societies, E. Merton Coulter correctly emphasized Mississippi navigation as the motivating goal of Kentucky's political action at this time. He also (correctly, I believe) placed this impulse within a larger purpose: "to weld together the rising opposition to Washington and the federalists" (377-78). In contrast, in her elegant study of Kentucky's massive but essentially "private determination" to resist the excise, Mary K. Bonsteel Tachau neglected the resistance which took place *through connection* to Congress, including the remonstrances and the activities of the well-connected leadership behind them; Mary K. Bonsteel Tachau, "The Whiskey Rebellion in Kentucky: A Forgotten Episode of Civil Disobedience," *Journal of the Early Republic* 2 (1982): 239-59.

21. Before sending this letter, Breckinridge took the step, unusual for him, of having a clerk copy it. This suggests he had singled out this letter as a "keeper" and may have hoped to publish it; Breckinridge to General Samuel Hopkins, 15 September 1794, Breckinridge Family Papers.

22. From the viewpoint of eastern centers of power—the usual vantage-point for early national history, though not the view being explicated in this paper—this paradox might be expressed in another way: it was western men, far from the seat of government, who could best be counted on to articulate freely and effectively open opposition to the federal administration.

23. John Nicholas to Breckinridge, 15 July 1794; Hudson Martin to Breckinridge, 19 July 1794; John Preston to Breckinridge, 15 August 1794, Breckinridge Family Papers; and Coulter, "Democratic Societies of the West," 387-88.

24. Eugene P. Link, *Democratic-Republican Societies, 1790-1800* (New York: Columbia

Univ. Press, 1942), 73-79; and Thomas Perkins Abernethy, *The South and the New Nation, 1789-1819* (Baton Rouge: Louisiana State Univ. Press, 1961), 102-35, quote on 112.

25. See the chapter called "Denial and Dependence," in Patricia Nelson Limerick, *The Legacy of Conquest: The Unbroken Past of the American West* (New York: W.W. Norton, 1987), 87-96; and Richard White, *It's Your Misfortune and None of My Own: A History of the American West* (Norman: Univ. of Oklahoma Press, 1991), 57-59.

26. Petition from the inhabitants of Montgomery County, 1779, draft in William Preston's hand; and copy of the same petition (not a draft) in Arthur Campbell's hand, Campbell-Preston-Floyd Papers, Library of Congress.

27. Petition for Amherst County for Col. William Cabell Jr., in Breckinridge's hand, 9 July 1786, Breckinridge Family Papers; emphasis is mine.

28. See, for example, the eloquent rhetoric of distance in "Extracts from the Journal of the Convention," 8 August 1785, in John Mason Brown, *The Political Beginnings of Kentucky* (Louisville: Filson Club, 1889), 238-39. The printed collections of "Kentucky" petitions, valuable as they are, create an artificial separation from the petitions that poured into the Virginia legislature from other western Virginia counties; James Rood Robertson, ed., *Petitions of the Early Inhabitants of Kentucky to the General Assembly of Virginia, 1769-1792* (Louisville: John P. Mortan, 1914); and John Frederick Dorman, ed., *Petitions from Kentucky to the Virginia Legislature, 1776 to 1791* (Easley, S.C.: Southern Historical Press, 1981).

29. "Written at the request of Mr. Reed one of the students," in Breckinridge's hand, 8 September 1793, Breckinridge Family Papers.

30. [Committee of Correspondence of the Kentucky Democratic Society], Circular Letter, 31 December 1793, in "Letters of James Brown to Presidents of the United States," *Louisiana Historical Quarterly* 20 (1937): 61-62; and Foner, *Democratic-Republican Societies*, 362-63. By 1793, this type of instruction was a traditional feature of western petitions. See, for example, "Circular Letter Directed to the Various Courts in the Western Country," 29 March 1787, in Brown, *The Political Beginnings of Kentucky*, 243. And for discussion of these efforts as self-conscious adoption of the patriot tradition of committees of correspondence, see Link, *Democratic-Republican Societies*, 45-69; and Lance Banning, *The Jeffersonian Persuasion: Evolution of a Party Ideology* (Ithaca, N.Y.: Cornell Univ. Press, 1978).

31. George Nicholas to James Madison, 31 December 1790, in *The Papers of James Madison*, ed. Charles F. Hobson and Robert A. Rutland, 17 vols. (Charlottesville: Univ. Press of Virginia, 1981), 13: 337-40.

32. A similarly complex letter from John Breckinridge to James Monroe is Breckinridge to Monroe, 15 January 1796, James Monroe Papers, ser. 1, reel 1.

33. Boyd stressed that the "ominous warning of George Nicholas, echoing and magnifying the fears of disunion John Brown had expressed three years earlier, could scarcely be ignored"; "Editorial Note: The Threat of Disunion in the West," *The Papers of Thomas Jefferson*, ed. Julian P. Boyd, 26 vols. (Princeton, N.J.: Princeton Univ. Press, 1974), 19: 513-18, quote on 514.

34. Thomas Jefferson to James [should be Harry] Innes, 13 March 1791, quoted in Boyd, "The Threat of Disunion in the West," *Papers of Thomas Jefferson*, 19: 516.

35. Norman K. Risjord, *Chesapeake Politics, 1781-1800* (New York: Columbia Univ.

Press, 1978), 209-10; "Memorial and Remonstrance against Religious Assessments," *Papers of James Madison*, eds. Robert A. Rutland, William M.E. Rachal, Barbara D. Ripel, and Fredrika J. Teute, 29 vols. (Charlottesville: Univ. Press of Virginia, 1985), 8: 295-306, 316, quote on 296; and "Copy of Remonstrance Written by Madison, August, 1785," not handwritten in Breckinridge's hand, Breckinridge Family Papers; George Nicholas to James Madison, 22 April 1785; 7 July 1785; and 24 July [1785]; and Madison to Thomas Jefferson, 20 August 1785, *Papers of James Madison*, 8: 264-65, 316-317, 326-27, 296.

36. Madison to Jefferson, 27 August 1793; and 2 September 1793, in James Morton Smith, ed., *The Republic of Letters: The Correspondence between Jefferson and Madison, 1776-1826*, 3 vols. (New York: W.W. Norton, 1995), 2: 812 and 815-16. Madison's "train of ideas" is in *The Papers of James Madison*, 15: 79-80.

37. Ellen Eslinger, "The Great Revival in Bourbon County, Kentucky" (Ph.D. diss., University of Chicago, 1988); Fredrika Johanna Teute, "Land, Liberty, and Labor in the Post-Revolutionary Era: Kentucky as the Promised Land" (Ph.D. diss., Johns Hopkins University, 1988); and Craig Thompson Friend, "Inheriting Eden: The Creation of Society and Community in Early Kentucky, 1792-1812" (Ph.D. diss., University of Kentucky, 1995).

38. James Morton Smith, *Freedom's Fetters: The Alien and Sedition Laws and American Civil Liberties* (Ithaca, N.Y.: Cornell Univ. Press, 1956); John C. Miller, *Crisis in Freedom: The Alien and Sedition Acts* (Boston: Little, Brown, 1951); and Adrienne Koch and Harry Ammon, "The Virginia and Kentucky Resolutions: An Episode in Jefferson's and Madison's Defense of Civil Liberties," *William and Mary Quarterly*, 3d ser., 5 (1948): 145-76.

39. James Morton Smith, "The Grass Roots Origins of the Kentucky Resolutions," *William and Mary Quarterly*, 3d ser., 27 (1970): 244-45. Quote from Noble E. Cunningham Jr., *The Jeffersonian Republicans: The Formation of Party Organization, 1789-1801* (Chapel Hill: Univ. of North Carolina Press, 1957), vii.

40. Cunningham, *The Jeffersonian Republicans*, 128; and Dumas Malone, *Jefferson and His Time, Volume Three: Jefferson and the Ordeal of Liberty* (Boston: Little, Brown, 1962), 402.

41. Stanley Elkins and Eric McKitrick, *The Age of Federalism* (New York: Oxford Univ. Press, 1993), 721-26, quotes on 721-723.

42. John Fowler to Fellow Citizens, 20 July 1798, in Noble E. Cunningham, ed., *Circular Letters of Congressmen to their Constituents, 1789-1829*, 3 vols. (Chapel Hill: Univ. of North Carolina Press, 1978), 1: 129. This letter was printed in the *Washington (Ky.) Mirror*, 11 August 1798.

43. During the month of June, all these had been printed and discussed in the rabidly Republican *Philadelphia Aurora*, the most likely source for *Kentucky Gazette* reprintings; Smith, *Freedom's Fetters*, 99-101, 106-9; and Smith, "Grass Roots Origins," 224.

44. Smith, "Grass Roots Origins," 222.

45. [John Breckinridge], "Resolutions Drawn for Clarke County," [July] 1798, draft in Breckinridge's hand; and [Breckinridge], "Vs. Alien and Sedition Acts Resolutions for Woodford," August 1798, draft in Breckinridge's hand, Breckinridge Family Papers; Smith, "Grass Roots Origins," 226-28; and Resolutions from the Clarke County Meeting, *Kentucky Gazette*, 1 August 1798, printed in Ethelbert Dudley Warfield, *The Kentucky Reso-*

lutions of 1798: An Historical Study (1887: reprint, New York: G. P. Putnam's Sons, 1894), 41-42.

46. John Breckinridge to James Monroe, 20 July 1798, James Monroe Papers, Manuscript Division, New York Public Library.

47. Warfield, *Kentucky Resolutions*, 44-45.

48. See Stephen Aron's fine analysis of Henry Clay's national vision as an amplification of the "Bluegrass system." I would add that, as 1790s Kentucky politics is seen in its national partisan light, it will also be easier to appreciate Henry Clay's ambitions and his "American System" as an amplification of the lives, visions, and careers of Kentucky mentors like John Breckinridge; Stephen Aron, *How the West Was Lost: The Transformation of Kentucky from Daniel Boone to Henry Clay* (Baltimore: Johns Hopkins Univ. Press, 1996), 123-49.

49. Breckinridge to Monroe, 12 August 1798, James Monroe Papers.

50. This is why George Nicholas, writing at great length to explain the mood and events of Kentucky in 1793, neither described nor mentioned the recent and well-publicized activities of the Democratic Society; George Nicholas to Madison, 15 November 1793, *Papers of James Madison*, 15: 135-38.

51. George Nicholas, *A Letter from George Nicholas of Kentucky to His Friend in Virginia, Justifying the Conduct of the Citizens of Kentucky as to Some of the Late Measures of the General Government, and Correcting Certain False Statements* (1798; reprint, Philadelphia: James Carey, 1799); Jefferson quote from Boyd, "Threat of Disunion," 19: 476n.

52. Wilson Cary Nicholas to Jefferson, 4 October 1798, quoted in Edward Channing, "Kentucky Resolutions of 1798," *American Historical Review* 20 (1915): 336.

53. Noble E. Cunningham Jr., *In Pursuit of Reason: The Life of Thomas Jefferson* (Baton Rouge: Louisiana State Univ. Press, 1987), 218-20; and James Roger Sharp, *American Politics in the Early Republic: The New Nation in Crisis* (New Haven, Conn.: Yale Univ. Press, 1993), 197.

54. Report of a December 12 Debate in the House of Representatives, *Philadelphia Porcupine's Gazette*, 14 December 1798.

55. Donald H. Stewart, *The Opposition Press of the Federalist Period* (Albany: State Univ. of New York Press, 1969), 473-76.

56. The actual resolves are printed in Warfield, *The Kentucky Resolutions of 1798*, 41-42.

57. *Porcupine's Gazette*, 21 September 1798, with a reply by "A Subscriber," *Frankfort Palladium*, 23 October 1798, quoted in Stewart, *Opposition Press*, 362-63.

58. Jefferson to Madison, 23 August 1799, in Smith, *The Republic of Letters*, 2: 1118.

59. Ibid., 1118-19; and Jefferson to Wilson Cary Nicholas, 26 August 1799, in *The Works of Thomas Jefferson*, ed. Paul Leicester Ford, 12 vols. (New York: G. P. Putnam's Sons, 1904-5), 9: 78-79.

60. Jefferson to Wilson Cary Nicholas, 6 September 1799, in Ford, *Works of Jefferson*, 9: 79-81; description of these events in Cunningham, *In Pursuit of Reason*, 218-20.

61. This was a compliment to Nicholas's late brother as well as to the articulate center of 1790s Kentucky politics; Jefferson to Wilson Cary Nicholas, 6 September 1799, in Ford, *Works of Jefferson*, 9: 79-81.

62. *Journal of the House of Representatives of Kentucky, 1799*, Early American Imprints, ser. 1, #48916, 7, 8, 33-34.

63. Ibid., 57, 33, 63.

64. In a still-valuable essay, Frank Maloy Anderson also suggests such questions; "Contemporary Opinion of the Virginia and Kentucky Resolutions," *American Historical Review* 5 (1900): 242-43.

65. Jefferson to Breckinridge, 29 January 1800, Thomas Jefferson Papers, Presidential Papers Microfilm, 65 reels (Washington, D.C.: Library of Congress, 1974), ser. 1, reel 22.

66. Breckinridge to Jefferson, 9 December 1799, copy, Breckinridge Family Papers; and [the same letter] dated 13 December 1799, Thomas Jefferson Papers, ser. 1, reel 21.

67. Jefferson to Breckinridge, 29 January 1800, Thomas Jefferson Papers, ser. 1, reel 22.

68. Robert B. McAfee, "Life and Times of Robert B. McAfee and His Family and Connections," *Register of the Kentucky Historical Society* 25 (1927): 217-18.

69. Jefferson to Breckinridge, 29 January 1800, Thomas Jefferson Papers, ser. 1, reel 22; *Journal of the House, 1799*, 33; and Elkins and McKitrick, *The Age of Federalism*, 721.

70. As, for example, in Breckinridge's 1793 remonstrance to the president and Congress against a decade-long history of "local policy of American councils," which had made no real effort to establish the "grand Territorial right" of Mississippi navigation; "Remonstrance to the President and Congress," Foner, *Democratic-Republican Societies*, 367.

71. John Nicholas to Breckinridge, 9 June 1793, Breckinridge Family Papers.

John Filson's book and map, both published in 1784, established Kentucky as a garden and enticed settlers to master it. Filson's foremost purpose was to profit from the sale of land, and the cartouche from his map substantiates that point. His dedication to George Washington, however, was not enough to boost sale of his cartographic rendering. John Filson, "Map of Kentucke" (Philadelphia: T. Rook, 1784)

"Work & Be Rich"
Economy and Culture on the Bluegrass Farm

CRAIG THOMPSON FRIEND

On his 1784 "Map of Kentucke," John Filson superimposed a watermark image of a plow under which he scribbled "Work & Be Rich." Certainly, agricultural labor was the means of survival for most Americans of the era, and the fertile lands of Kentucky had the makings of an Eden for yeoman farmers. But what Filson had in mind was an alternative version of the agrarian west—a region of profit and prosperity. As a land speculator and early promoter of trans-Appalachian settlement, Filson was hardly the type to use the word "rich" in any metaphorical sense; for example, he did not see the attainment of self-sufficiency or the embrace of republicanism as means to becoming "rich." No, Filson meant money, and, because he prefaced the words with a call to labor, we may be certain that Filson was not targeting the wealthy slaveholding planters or leisurely urban folk who would eventually come to dominate the region. "Work & Be Rich," he called to the pioneer farmers, and they responded by the thousands.[1]

"The general motive for coming here is to be a freeholder, to have plenty of rich land, and to be able to settle his children around him," noted Timothy Flint; "It is a most virtuous motive."[2] As they arrived, new settlers began the process of creating, or rather recreating, a farm. A sense of optimism biased, sometimes even blinded, settlers' expectations as to the ease of this task. As the *Kentucky Gazette* heralded in 1798,

> Look round your farms—how rich the prospect seems!
> The orchard bends, the field luxurious teems!
> Here Agriculture opens to our view,
> A land of milk and honey, rich and new.[3]

To live a full life on an independent farm, to cultivate the land and harvest the produce, to bequeath property to his children: such were the inseparable objectives toward which the pioneer strove.[4]

Filson revealed another purpose, however: to pursue profit. Realization of the first three might have occurred within the microcosm of the family farm—the house, barn, and fields that provided security and sustenance; but by adding the fourth goal to the equation, Kentucky's early farmers had to participate in the market economy, both locally and nationally. As they endeavored to "work & be rich," as they supplemented the laborious demands of farming with the opportunity to make a profit, Kentuckians crafted an agrarian culture that delicately balanced commercial participation with near-subsistence farming and traditional moral responsibilities to the community.

Filson's vision poses a conundrum for historians of the early republic. The traditional notion is that farming, in the experiences of eighteenth- and early nineteenth-century Americans, was primarily a subsistence activity; that produce was sold in the local market, but only as incidental surplus and hardly ever in quantities that led to great profit. The family farm has been portrayed as the cornerstone of the household economy, the source of individual independence, the foundation of social stability, and a subculture with unique rules and traditions that shielded it from the inchoate liberal and capitalistic currents of early America. Even historians who accept the "yeoman" farm as an active extension of commercial capitalism have not yet escaped paying homage to its supposed noble character. As Joyce Appleby has written, the farm's "cornucopian abundance acquired moral significance because it was tied to the real needs of people everywhere."[5]

This tendency to glorify the American farm becomes doubly troublesome when exploring the farms of the trans-Appalachian West. When Frederick Jackson Turner put forth his idea of successive frontiers, one of the primary actors was the farmer who, always moving to the periphery in search of fresh lands, remained one step ahead of and thus isolated from the corruption of eastern capitalism.[6] Similarly, Richard Hofstadter interpreted the western farmer as a source of cultural persistence and ideological relevance: "His well-being was not merely physical, it was moral; it was not merely personal, it was the central source of civic virtue; it was not merely secular but religious, for God made the land and called man to cultivate it."[7] For both historians, the farmer epitomized a component of American society slowly crushed under the weight of industrial capitalism.

Over the past two decades, historians have taken new interest in the farmers of the early republic, hoping to determine the origins and timing of national capitalistic growth. While their efforts have enriched our understanding of agrarian life, those same historians remain greatly divided on their conclusions.[8] One camp contends that the traditional interpretation is accurate: that early American farms were subsistent enterprises isolated from the nascent market networks of the eighteenth and early nineteenth centuries until a market revolution upset these agrarian patterns in the early antebellum years. This interpretation promotes the farm as the bastion of a household economy that secured the ideals of yeoman farming—independence, local self-sufficiency, accumulation of land to support future generations, and attention to debt and credit relations with neighbors.[9]

Another group of historians argue that, beginning in 1607, American society underwent unending capitalistic development in one form or another. As members of Britain's colonial empire, the American colonies were heavily involved in global trade, especially by the outbreak of the Revolution. Farms were mere extensions of this commercial society, and farmers actively pursued profit as budding capitalists.[10] Once again, however, the historical persona of the farmer bears the onus of some American tradition: in the first interpretation, the continuity of republicanism; in the second, leadership in the economic formation of a capitalist nation.

Moral significance, agricultural integrity, civic virtue, guardianship of a subsistence tradition, harbinger of a capitalist revolution—depending on the historian consulted, the pioneer farmer was the keeper of a specific heritage that encapsulated what it meant to be American. But is it accurate? Indeed, just what tradition or traditions did the early American farm conserve? I have chosen to explore those questions within the first American West: Kentucky during the early republic. The trans-Appalachian West became a testing site for the republican principles of the revolutionary and early national eras.[11] Endowed with very fertile lands but lacking adequate commercial and transportation routes, the Bluegrass region of Kentucky provided a suitable crucible for testing the place of the farmer in American society. Would the Bluegrass farm become a sanctuary for the values and traditions of a way of life slowly slipping into obscurity, or would it become an outpost of those economic forces bringing a market revolution to American society?

The farm served a central role in the nascent agrarian society of the Kentucky Bluegrass. The hope of sustaining wife and children proved the crucial incentive for relocating into Kentucky and retarded quick out-migrations.[12] In the mid-1790s, John Breckinridge immigrated to Kentucky to "provide *good* lands here for my children, & insure them from *want*, which I was not certain of in the old Country [Virginia]."[13] In his bequest of the land to the next generation, Breckinridge or any farmer fulfilled a moral duty within the community. Property inheritance practices bound families together in webs of obligation that sought to ensure that one's children retained the *mentalité* and social standings of their parents.[14]

Farmers had first to define what type of farm they would create for themselves and their posterity. When he arrived in Fayette County in 1794, Englishman Harry Toulmin penned his ideal of the American farm. On a thirty-acre homestead, a farmer must "plough and do other things appertaining to a farm; and if his wife or his daughter can spin either flax or wool, or cotton, enough to clothe the family," wrote Toulmin, then "unquestionably he may have an abundance."[15] Sometime before 1804 Charles Julian settled in Kentucky and wrote to friends still in Virginia about how to migrate and succeed in the "new country"—"rase mony" by trading all lands in the Old Dominion for slaves, horses, hams, wagons, gin, and Kentucky lands; invest in bonds with deeds of trust; upon arrival, "imploy your women & old negroes in spining and young in a nail manufactory"; and "[s]ell your horses that move you." At least one thousand plowable acres were necessary, according to Julian, but corn was a poor choice to plant (yet "always have plenty & some to grind into meal for market"). Rather, he encouraged animal husbandry: "sheep will do very well—wool sells at 3/ & a good mutton in Dec[embe]r sells at 3 dol[lar]s and lambs in July at 7."[16]

While the contrast between Toulmin's and Julian's descriptions exemplified Americans' varying definitions of the family farm, it also spoke to their different understandings of individual independence.[17] For men like Toulmin, the ownership of enough land to support himself and his family conferred a level of freedom and autonomy which differentiated him from those in dependence: slaves, tenant farmers, propertyless laborers, and women. To others industrious or fortunate enough like Julian to acquire larger farms, preserving and exercising this independence demanded the accumulation of wealth, leisure, and status.[18] Both men understood the importance of land-ownership to one's social identity in early America.

Yet, by 1800 fewer than half of all landholders owned the thirty acres requisite to even Toulmin's notion of a family farm. Many emigrants were handicapped by youth, poverty, or both. Young farmers in eighteenth-century America were at a disadvantage. Older, more established residents laid claim to status, wealth, power, and land in community after community.[19] During the late decades of the century, the promotions of trans-Appalachian lands by men like John Filson offered hope to younger Americans, but that opportunity was illusory. The unfortunate story has been related many times over: driven by the desire to own fertile Kentucky property, thousands of pioneers migrated to the state in the 1790s and early 1800s only to lose their dreams in a morass of title disputes.[20] Seduced by a narrow, mythic image of the Edenic garden, these pioneers ignored reality for the promise. "Can anything be more Absurd than the Conduct of man," queried Moses Austin in 1796, "here is hundreds Travelling hundreds of Miles, they know not for what Nor Whither, except its to Kentucky, passing land almost as good and easy to obtain'd."[21] By 1800, only 49.2 percent of Kentucky's heads of household owned any land in the state. While its landless rates approximated the national average, the state's land distribution was the least egalitarian of the western settlements and ranked with the more stratified societies of New York, South Carolina, and Georgia as having the most unequal distribution of wealth and property in the nation.[22] For the 50.8 percent left propertyless, Kentucky suddenly became more a quagmire than a garden. Consequently, the high land-to-labor ratio that originally enticed settlers to the Bluegrass quickly reversed to a high labor-to-land ratio, creating large numbers of tenant farmers and urban workers.

While speculation in the late 1700s made individual freeholding difficult and expensive, land nonetheless remained available to those with sufficient cash.[23] In every issue of the *Kentucky Gazette* from 1792 to 1812, at least two advertisements offered improved or unimproved in-state lands. "New comers can be at no loss (if they have Cash) to secure an Estate to their taste," related David Meade, but as a wealthy Virginia planter whose former residence sat opposite William Byrd's Westover on the James River, Meade's idea of enough "Cash" was not that of the average immigrant.[24] At the turn of the century, the federal government sold an acre of midwestern lands for two dollars; property in William Cooper's New York tract sold for three to five dollars an acre.[25] In contrast, Kentucky's land prices escalated from the beginning. In the mid-1790s, lands near the sleepy town of Millersburg in the center of the Bluegrass region already brought six to eight dollars an acre. Only remote properties outside the Bluegrass ranged between $2.75 and $3.50 an acre.[26] By 1811, John Melish observed that "very little good land is now to be had under 12 dollars per acre"; and similar sized tracts in the vicinity of Lexington had soared to two hundred dollars each.[27] Thus, Charles Julian's recommendations that settlers invest in horses, hams, wagons, gin—anything that could be promptly sold—begins to make more sense in light of the immediate need for capital, especially as those items commanded higher prices in Kentucky than in the East.

Although an independent farm was the vision, the majority of Kentuckians failed to attain its near-mythical promise.[28] For even those who could afford it, the most basic act of purchasing and owning land, unquestionably the primary objective of newly arrived white males, exposed the dualism of farming as it emerged in central Kentucky. Familial and communal obligations required older residents to pass property on to the next generation. Land, therefore, held a premarket value, a communal significance integral to the stability of society. Yet, because land early became a commodity exchanged by profiteering speculators, property also took on a monetary association that could not be ignored.[29] In a society where less than half of the householders owned land, the need for capital to purchase land and create a farm compromised aspirations to live in self-sufficiency.

An unknown visitor warned the future settler that if he did not "bring a fortune with him, he will find he must at first live low and work hard."[30] In 1792, John Wallace arrived penniless in Bourbon County with hopes of eventually buying lands, establishing a farm, and relocating his family. Instead, he became immediately dependent on his merchant brother for survival. After nine years of work as an itinerant peddler and distiller of rye whiskey, he saved only enough cash to purchase land at cheaper government rates in Ohio.[31] For many like Wallace, the bubble burst soon after they arrived. Lack of capital not only limited settlers' fortunes in Kentucky, it often left them stranded in what they came to view as a land without opportunity. If the wealthy did not "feel at home" they could return east, one traveler noted, whereas "to the family of a poor man, woman, and children it is a dreadful, I may say, almost impossible thing to return."[32] Some moved farther west in search of more easily acquired lands; others were forced into tenancy.

Many propertied residents, clearly disapproving of a large unpropertied population, encouraged migration to newer frontiers as an improvement to society in general.[33] British visitor John Melish merely reiterated the conventional wisdom that the out-migration of the landless would "improve the morals of the state, as it will purge it of many of the *pioneers*."[34] When southwestern lands opened in 1797, a refined upper class rejoiced that "the rage among the poorer class of people here appears to be for the Spanish settlements."[35]

Because many of the unpropertied continued to hold tight the dream of a Bluegrass farm, however, they chose to stay in the region and work as tenant farmers. Landlords considered them unreliable workers because they little hesitated to pack up and move on when opportunity for a farm beckoned. Robert Breckinridge warned fellow property owners that investment in tenant farmers might prove fruitless: those without land "will not remain tenants longer than they can procure 100 acres of tolerable farming land" along the frontier.[36] Yet, some evidence suggests that even after the demise of the Indian threat in 1794, many persons remained in tenancy, forgoing opportunities to migrate to newly opened lands.[37] Some of their hesitation derived from a desire to remain in the vicinity of the fertile Bluegrass region. Robert's half-brother, John Breckinridge, warned out-migrants that if they "cannot make a living from the most valuable lands in the heart of Kentucky," tenant farmers had little business moving to the frontiers, "where the land is poor, the Country unsettled & sickly."[38]

Breckinridge's concern loses its altruistic luster when we consider that he advertised for twenty tenants to lease his Mason County lands for terms of seven to fourteen years.[39] Many property owners exploited the hordes of needy who sought a place to live and work. Having invested in the purchase of lands, a speculator could increase his profits not by selling uncleared lots, but by renting at low rates to poorer settlers who cleared the land and cultivated the soil. On occasion, owners even suspended rent on the condition that tenants cleared enough acreage each year.[40] Once the land acquired new and higher value, the speculator then rented or sold, often to the very pioneers who invested their labor in fattening the landlord's purse.

Still, the institution provided opportunity to tenants as well as property owners. "Many people come from Virginia & other States very poor & are strangers," remarked Edward Harris in 1797; after a four- or five-year tenancy "ordinarily if prudent they go off on land of their own full of stock & provisions."[41] Tenancy could operate as a way station to ownership of one's own farm and therein addressed a fundamental cultural problem—how to incorporate the unpropertied into a society founded upon land-ownership. In rental agreements like those between two Lexington merchants, Thomas Hart and Samuel Price, and the fifty tenants living on their lands in Jefferson County, we find hints of this cultural rationale behind tenancy. The laborers could avoid paying rent for five years and then pay $2 per acre or four bushels of wheat per acre for the following two years; *or* they could live rent-free for three years, pay $.50 per acre the fourth year, $.75 per acre the fifth year, $1 per acre the sixth year, and $1.25 per acre the seventh year.[42] Most obviously, the agreement provided substantial profits to the landowners without much investment beyond the initial cost of the lands. But the terms also propelled lessees into the commercial economy. To pay their rent, tenant farmers had to acquire cash in exchange for their own produce or labor. The annual increase in rent found in the second option reflected expectations of fiscal improvement. Even those reluctant to abandon rudimentary farming had to grow a staple crop to meet rent demands. Tenancy, therefore, prepared future farmers for a mixed-farming economy—the production of a blend of sustenance foods and commercial crops.

The experiences of tenant farmers contrasted greatly with those of settlers who owned their own farms. Rather than enjoying the opportunity to "work & be rich," the laboring poor worked just to survive. Both groups learned that agricultural labor and commercial participation were inseparable. The pursuit of land forced all settlers into a quest for capital.

If any group seemed immune to this pull, it was a "cracker" class that neither owned land nor sought out tenancy. In 1810, Alexander Wilson observed Mason County residents who lived in "miserable huts" and excitedly told Wilson "with pride" of the rich soil, the abundance of production, and the healthiness of the country.[43] These boosters lived, nevertheless, in squalid poverty: "their own houses worse than pig-sties; their clothes an assemblage of rags; their faces yellow, and lark with disease; and their persons covered with filth"—conditions he attributed to their laziness.[44] While Wilson's general observations certainly were biased by his metropolitan perspective, his conclusion was shared by others. John Hill, a new settler in the same county, likewise noted an inclination among many of his neighbors, most "Northwardly bred," to "care for little more than a little whiskey, vinison & bread from hand to mouth," none of which required much labor.[45] Daniel Drake remembered a Maryland man named Hickman and his family who lived on his family's farm outside Mayslick. They first lived in a tree house built with "a heavy garniture of green leaves," then moved into a small stable before finally settling in a cabin. With the exception of the tree house, Drake's father constructed the habitations apparently without Hickman's assistance. Even more telling, as poor as Hickman may have been, at some point he acquired two slaves, "a negro man in middle life, and a woman rather old," and forced them to do his work in the field "under the whip to the extremist degree."[46]

Without legal claim to land and often without permission to live where they did, these squatters seemed the greatest threat to the ideal of "work & be rich," and they certainly epitomized the "pioneers" whom the elite sought to purge from society. Their inclination to avoid work was blatantly obvious and fundamentally clashed with those industrious persons determined to carve a garden out of the wilderness. John T. Lyle's father arrived in Kentucky with thirty thousand dollars, squandered the money in Lexington, remained unemployed, married and settled outside the town, and "never increased his property." He failed to establish a farm because, like so many others, he "didn't care about it."[47] Social critics interpreted such lack of industry, and the apathy and pessimism that accompanied it, as ultimately debilitating to the edenic environment itself. In February 1803, the *Kentucky Gazette* printed an "Ode to Poverty" that illustrated the point:

> But not alone of this am I complaining:
> Nature herself's so altered by thy power,
> That fields and meadows, each gay tint disdaining,
> No more to me display the gaudy flowers.[48]

The condition of this indigent class became a major concern to propertied Kentuckians. In 1795, "A Friend to the Distressed" appealed to the compassion of central Kentuckians in their dealings with the poorest of the poor. The author encouraged establishment of county committees to assist new immigrants who arrived "without the means of purchasing even bread for their subsistence" and requested farmers to construct and open one cabin on their farms for a homeless family, as the Drake family had done.[49] Two years earlier, the state assembly had initiated a similar program, requiring county courts to use funds "for the relief of such poor persons . . . incapable of procuring a living."[50] Like the tenancy system, however, poverty relief incorporated unstated goals. The law ordered justices to take poor children from their families and put them through indenture to "some art, trade, or business" where they would receive appropriate education, pay of "three pounds and ten shillings, and a decent new suit of clothes."[51] By separating children from the failure of their parents and placing them in the homes of craftsmen and merchants, the state sought to assimilate them to responsible economic participation.

Indolent crackers and tenant farmers provided a constant reminder to landed settlers that failure was an eager, albeit unwanted, visitor. Anxiety about losing one's property and livelihood simmered below the surface.[52] In 1803, for example, a small stone building that housed Fayette County's land titles burned to the ground on the farmstead of county clerk Levi Todd. Although the arsonists escaped, landed farmers of the region accused unpropertied settlers and, to protect their holdings, demanded a speedy reconstruction of property boundaries and claims.

Even to the settler with sufficient cash to purchase lands and secure title to them, the cost of starting a farm and surviving for a year or two presented real obstacles. Farm-making demanded time, energy, and money often beyond pioneers' resources. First, the Kentucky farmer had to clear the forests. Deforestation became an obsession. By 1800, the canebrakes that early identified the choicest lands in the region were nearly exhausted. As Daniel Drake recalled from his youth, when his family purchased new lands "covered with an unbroken forest" near Mayslick, father and son "charged on the beautiful blue ash and buckeye grove," taking appreciation in a tree only "in proportion to the facility with which I could destroy it."[53] Some trees did survive as grazing acreage for livestock or to supply construction materials for future buildings and fences, but farmers commonly worked on clearing a field rather than protecting the forests.[54]

Next, the farmer constructed the first of many farm buildings. An "industrious settler" expected to have a "neat farm and snug cleanly habitation."[55] A simple house was central to settlers' identity and orientation.[56] Living in rude cabins in an as yet uncleared wilderness "drew us more together, and compelled us to rely more intimately on each other," young Drake commented; in comparison to the solitude of the wilderness, the intimacy of the farmhouse "enabled us to extract from the visits & company we *did* have, a high degree of enjoyment."[57] At Mayslick, a neighborhood of five families opened their homes to travelers and each other on a regular basis. Throughout the Bluegrass, each private residence took on a communal role: "Every farmer's house was a home for all, and a temple of jollity," reminisced Mann Butler.[58] The house, therefore, became the first of many ties between family and community and, on the occasions when travelers arrived with national and international news, the world.

Yet, farm-making demanded more construction than a residence. In 1809, Nathaniel Hart projected the costs: six thousand dollars for a house, one thousand dollars for a distillery, five hundred dollars to construct a mill, another five hundred dollars for a barn. "When this is all done *if I do not break in doing it*," he concluded, "I hope to be in a situation to make money."[59] If Hart's plans seem somewhat extravagant, they were not unusual. Farmers invested in such profit-seeking businesses as part of their economic and moral responsibilities to the community. Gristmills, tanneries, fulling mills, bakeries, and distilleries connected individual farms to larger agrarian and commercial networks.

Because these endeavors addressed social and economic community needs, they tenuously straddled the line between private and public enterprise. The resulting complications were well illustrated as the grinding of corn and other grains shifted from home to mill in the late eighteenth century. The demands of mill owners, whose operations played increasingly crucial roles in local agriculture, began to clash with other communal interests.[60] In 1789, Laban Shipp's construction of a milldam on Stoner's Fork in Bourbon County elicited complaints because it blocked river access to another commercial facility, the county's only tobacco warehouse.[61] The ensuing controversy formed along the lines of agricultural interest and economic class. Larger and wealthier farmers generally opposed the milldam; their interests lay in tobacco production and exportation. Allied with them were many poor residents who fished the stream for subsistence. Smaller farmers, more dependent on the local market and home productions, supported Shipp's enterprise.[62] Without the mill, residents along Stoner's Fork faced an overland journey of nearly thirty miles to grind their corn.[63] The Bourbon County Court compromised by requiring Shipp to build locks into his milldam so that navigation and fishing along the watercourse could continue.[64]

Caution should be taken, however, not to read into the story a conflict between premarket and market worldviews similar to those that erupted in East Coast societies in the early republic. In his evaluation of riparian disputes in South Carolina, Harry Watson concluded that market-oriented planters and millers vigorously pursued their interests, and that deference did not hinder fishermen in their efforts to protect their premarket activities.[65] In a study of dams and fishing rights in Rhode Island, Gary Kulik likewise found similar tensions between market and premarket plans for the use of waterways.[66]

In the late 1780s, however, neither the plantation agriculture that represented the market mentality in South Carolina nor the "industrial" enterprises that embodied that orientation in Rhode Island had rooted in the Kentucky soil. In the Bluegrass both the mill and the tobacco warehouse served communal, agricultural capacities. Milling was less a market pursuit than a necessary extension of the farming economy and, as Nathaniel Hart's intentions demonstrate, most millers were themselves farmers. Tension between farmers and mill owners, therefore, was just not common. Tobacco warehouses also served the communal interests of an agrarian society. In 1792, the Kentucky legislature established guidelines for tobacco, hemp, and flour inspection at local warehouses. The primary concern was to ensure exportation of superior quality produce, but the warehouse also protected the commercial reputation of a community.[67] The struggle between mill owner Laban Shipp and customers of the tobacco warehouse was a clash between two components of one agricultural economy.

Still, the tale of Laban Shipp's mill does make a point: In a culture where commerce and agriculture were intertwined, the question was not whether one would take part in the market, but how one would participate. A resident might choose to participate in a gristmill subculture of less established or newly arrived farmers who depended on corn to survive, finding profit in the sale of meal. Or he might strive to expand into production of a staple crop like tobacco, one that would bring greater profits or could be used as "commodity money" in local markets. Even his unpropertied neighbors might take their fish to the stalls of local market houses. When a settler answered these questions, when he determined the type of farm he would create for himself and his posterity, he also assumed a commercial role within the community. The Shipp controversy, therefore, was a struggle between individuals as they defined and molded their agri*culture*, a pattern repeated with the formation of every American community.

Mills like Laban Shipp's were necessary because on every Bluegrass farm, the art of farming began with the cultivation of corn. "It is by the culture of Indian corn," noticed François Michaux, "that all those who form establishments commence."[68] "Gentlemen" farmers with larger properties and greater expectations were not exempt (recall Charles Julian's warning to "always have plenty & some to grind into meal for market"). Corn was particularly suited to the Kentucky soil; Patrick Scott recollected that he "could hear the corn go tick, tick—it grew so fast."[69] Citizens of Lexington and Washington advertised Kentucky's agricultural output as fifty to sixty bushels of corn per acre, compared with as little as fifteen bushels per acre in southeastern Pennsylvania.[70] Corn was seemingly prerequisite to agricultural success: "Wheat . . . is fine in quality, and in quantity averaging about 25 bushels an acre; but where the land is fallowed, from 40 to 50 are frequently had. Fallow means corn land, or land planted first with Indian corn, then with oats the second year, and with wheat the next, which is generally more abundant than when sown immediately after, or amongst the corn at the last horse-hoeing."[71] Corn not only went "tick, tick," but settlers believed that it also helped other crops grow more abundantly.

Not surprisingly, then, the pursuit of profit began with the culture of the corn. Its production dominated rudimentary commercial activity in Kentucky. Between 1799 and 1802, the profits earned from the export of Kentucky corn balanced the cost of imported English goods into the state.[72] In the latter year, so many farmers attempted to enter into the trade that prices plummeted to unprecedented levels.[73] In Mason County along the Ohio River, merchant-millers profited not only from grinding the meal, they also positioned themselves as middlemen and provided export services for farmers.[74] The culture of the corn produced sustenance early in the settlement process, became the foundation for future farming and farm-making, and early evidenced the commercial mindset of the Kentucky farmer.

The success of corn cultivation raised expectations about the rewards of farming. But the ease of corn production was misleading in its demands on both time and energy. The farmer also raised myriad vegetables for domestic consumption and wheat, oats, flax, cotton, and/or tobacco for the market. "Our spring begins the last of February," wrote Edward Harris in 1797; "we plant corn from the last week in april 'till the middle of June & some have had a good crop of corn from the ground on which flax grew the same season."[75] With the help of laborers, relatives, and neighbors, the farmer harvested crops, shelled corn, slaughtered hogs, cleared and burned brush, cut firewood, tapped maple trees, and plowed the land. He oversaw the labor of his slaves and servants, if he had them, and the home productions of his wife and family as they guarded the livestock, churned butter, salted beef, smoked pork, tallowed candles, baked bread, and spun cloth.[76] Even after the demands of the spring and summer months, the farmer spent much of the autumn and winter in farm-making: grinding meal, building sheds, shoeing horses, repairing wagons, gathering firewood, mending fences, and traveling to market, to neighbors and relatives, and (in light of the extensive litigation over land titles) probably to court.[77] The multitude of demands on time and energy often took a toll. James Flint discovered farms in the heart of the Bluegrass where workers, apparently wearied by the toils of farming, left tools "to rot in the field" and the scythe "to hang on a tree from one season to another."[78]

In the commitment to mixed farming, the Bluegrass farm militated against the use of slaves. In 1790, only 17.4 percent of Kentucky's heads of household owned slaves; within two years, slaveholders comprised 22.8 percent of the population; by 1800, 25.2 percent had acquired slaves.[79] Although men like Charles Julian purchased many acres and employed some slaves, the large scale required for efficient management of huge slave operations was not common. The few grand farms were devoted mostly to tobacco, hemp, and livestock—production which could not utilize slave labor as effectively or as profitably as would characterize the rise of cotton. Slave labor generally lacked the diversity of skills crucial to mixed-farming and counteracted the family orientation of the operation. Consequently, François Michaux recognized among Kentucky's farmers "so decided a preference to agriculture, that there are very few of them who put their children to any trade, wanting their services in the field."[80]

Within their schemes of the yeoman farm, those who did own slaves were necessarily committed to a behavior of market participation. Indeed, a cyclical model developed: slaveholding farmers needed the market to supply and maintain a labor force that, in turn, helped to produce profitable crops to sell in the market. Some money then went toward taxes on land, slaves, horses, wagons, and cattle. While farmers like Charles Julian were large landholders and aspirants to the type of farm that he championed, small farmers, men who would have seemingly preferred the patterns of Harry Toulmin's more subsistence-oriented farm, also purchased slaves and, consequently, became participants in the market economy.

Like the dualism that accompanied land acquisition, crop production, and slaveholding, livestock ownership held both premarket and market value. Many settlers owned herds of cattle, hogs, and sheep, which most often roamed without supervision. In 1802, a good milk cow cost as much as a good acre of land.[81] But the cow also served a function within the family. As Daniel Drake recalled, "Old Brindle was then a veritable member of the family, and took her slop at the cabin door, while the children feasted on her warm milk within."[82]

Before deforestation, livestock thrived on the abundance of the woodlands. François Michaux discovered hundreds of hogs, "kept by all the inhabitants," wandering forested areas. Daniel Drake and his siblings daily herded their family's cattle and sheep from nearby forests and meadows, not returning home until after nightfall on most occasions.[83] Because farmers relied on tilled acreage and the woodlands, however, they paid little attention to making and improving pasturelands.[84] The loss of cane and other wild herbage created a noticeable difference in the taste of milk and butter.[85] As forests disappeared, settlers faced problems of livestock grazing on open, treeless plains and turned increasingly to production of feed and pasturage crops.

Thus, farm-making also came to include the construction of fences and rock walls. Rail fences served to keep large animals from crops.[86] More established farmers dissected their lands with stone "plantation fences." The construction of plantation fences freed farmers to increase plowable acreage. They no longer needed to retain wooded patches for the building and repairing of rail fences.[87] Once again, farmers turned to the market: the construction of stone fences required several months and possibly years of financial investment, especially in the hiring of skilled quarrymen and stonemasons from urban labor pools.

Regardless of social standing or landholdings, Kentucky's farming families shared many patterns of life: land acquisition, clearing, farm-making, farming, and animal husbandry. Some men like John Breckinridge employed tenant workers; others like Charles Julian and Isaac Drake's resident squatter, Hickman, exploited slave laborers. Farming families also shared certain forms of behavior: attention to production for sustenance, as Harry Toulmin encouraged; acquiescence to one's communal role with the construction of a mill, as Laban Shipp demonstrated; and pursuit of profit with as simple a crop as corn, as a multitude of Kentucky farmers did at the turn of the century. The disparities between the stations of these men make only one generalization possible: they were farmers who were aware of the importance of the farm to their sustenance and of the relevance of the market in what it had to offer them.

In the Bluegrass, therefore, commerce and agriculture together defined the farm. Farmers frequently used the yields of the fields—wheat, tobacco, oats, and corn—as "commodity monies" in their transactions at local stores. As crops with market-driven values, these products directly bound the farmer to national market networks; the store owner and farmer could not dicker over the value of these commercial crops out of fear that one or the other would be cheated out of the fair market price.[88] Farmers also bartered with the fruits of farm-making: firewood, beeswax, whiskey, flour, and salt. Few persons would have created a surplus of any of these items unintentionally. Similarly, it was neither easy nor thrifty to produce an excess of the products of animal husbandry (beef, pork, veal, chicken, and turkey) or home manufactures (homespun cloth, butter, lard, candles, and sugar).[89] To suggest that farmers participated in the market only to relieve themselves of surplus products is to ignore the frugality necessary to farming success.

A brief study of the domestic production of cloth illustrates this point most clearly. In 1793, the champion of yeoman farming, Harry Toulmin, wrote how common it was "for all linen which is used in the family to be made at home."[90] Indeed, farm women domestically produced quality homespun in great quantities: country linen made from flax, linsey-woolsey woven from flax and wool, and a woolen, or sometimes cotton, broadcloth.[91] "Almost every house contained a loom," recalled Mann Butler, "and almost every woman was a weaver."[92]

Between 1792 and 1810, however, purchases of imported cloth at stores in Lexington, Washington, and Maysville grew steadily. If women produced cloth for household consumption, then why did they increasingly purchase imported cloth? As he passed a caravan of Bourbon County women taking their wool to the carding machine, James Flint noticed that "Miss does not wear the produce of her own hands."[93] To complicate the scenario further, purchases of domestic cloth also rose, as did demand for twist, lace, buttons, and needles.

In those years, Kentuckians displayed a new sense of refinement, one that included a taste for finer clothing. One visitor discovered that in rustic log cabins and crude farm cottages "are seen Ladies neatly dressed, who are, as yet, obliged to reside therein for want of better houses."[94] Domestic production of excess cloth would have wasted time, energy, and resources. Women spun broadcloth or linen with a purpose—to trade for imported cloth and sewing accessories.

The boom in the production of cloth led to a demand for new private investments that, like the gristmill, would become communal enterprises in a cooperative network. Farmers who provided carding machines or bluedying were necessary partners in this burgeoning commercial activity.[95] While the use of such craftsmen strengthened the bonds of local self-sufficiency, it should be clear by now that the goal was to reap the benefits of the marketplace.[96] From field to carding machine to loom to bluedyer to local store to market network, the domestic production of cloth demonstrates well the interconnectedness of the farm to the commercial economy. The operator of the carding machine, the bluedyer, and the store owner were not capitalist threats to the stability of farming society; rather they were contributing members to it. And because the values of homespun and other home manufactures were not market-driven, customer and merchant arrived at a premarket price through neighborly agreement, underscoring the symbiosis of the Bluegrass farm and the market.

The relationship between agriculture and commerce, upon which the structures and patterns of agrarian culture were constructed, was delicate. Overemphasis on either side of the equation was dangerous for the individual and the community, warned Aristedes, author of a series of editorials published in the *Kentucky Gazette* in 1803 and 1804. One's communal role, one's merit within the complex social structures of the early republic, correlated to one's relationship to the cooperative networks which emerged in community after community.[97] Some citizens had a responsibility to produce for market; others were to provide services for the public; while still others served supplemental roles in production and exchange. In his "Reflections on Political Economy," Aristedes harangued farmers who ignored limitations on their proper economic stations. Their merit within society declined as they pursued their own self-interests. The majority of farmers, emigrants from "the most dissapated state in the union [Virginia]," lived above their means, entrapped themselves and their families in debt, and consequently compromised the independence of their farms. "Instead of cultivating the earth to produce materials for domestic manufacture," he criticized, "they have been in the habit of consuming foreign articles altogether."[98] In their ambitions to tie their own households to larger market structures, farmers seriously threatened the stability of Kentucky's agrarian culture. Having exhausted the fruits of their labors and having spent their savings in pursuit of luxury, farmers neglected their obligations to familial and communal development: "The moral reputation became mortgaged for the fanatic productions of foreign countries, and credit ensued."[99]

Aristedes refused to blame the corruption of the yeoman farm on merchants, favorite targets of Americans disenchanted with the workings of a commercial economy. Instead, he found the farmer had diminished the wealth of the soil through his own "indolence and extravegence." Men of commerce had actually worked to harness the activities of their agrarian neighbors, opening the "*appropriate market* relative to the *farmer*," in local towns and villages.[100] Yet, the farmer had pursued production for regional and national markets, circumventing the role of merchants and merchant-millers by taking on the burden of exporting, and ultimately doing "but little good to the community."[101] Here lay the crux of the argument: Aristedes emphasized the interconnected, communal value of agriculture and commerce. Farmers had exceeded their appropriate economic and social responsibilities. They superseded the role of merchants in exportation; they purchased beyond their means and became dependent; and they neglected their responsibility to provide for the local populace. Kentucky farmers squandered their economic opportunities, as had their Virginia cousins.

To salvage the moral integrity of their agrarian culture, the editorialist encouraged the farmer to return to agricultural and domestic productions for the local market; and he called for greater pressure on merchants to provide export services for patrons. He discouraged the production of some crops, particularly wheat and corn, because of their perishable proclivities on the long river trips to New Orleans. Having wasted the opportunity to create independent homesteads, farmers could redeem themselves only by producing marketable items that would contribute to the economic stability of communities, in particular, "tobacco, hemp always in its manufactured state, whiskey, brandy, pickled beef, hides, tallow candles, tow linen, cheese, salted pork, nails and nail rods, iron and utensils."[102]

According to Aristedes, profit-making was perfectly acceptable when checked against communal obligations. In his encouragement of commercial products and domestic productions, the author reinforced farmers' inclinations to pursue profit—but only as producer, not as exporter. He argued for economic individualism within a larger context of communal responsibility; every farmer, indeed every person, had a proper role in the economic patterns of everyday life. To stretch beyond that station was to deny another his appropriate place and, at its worst, to disrupt the moral structure of the community.

Bluegrass farmers shared expectations and challenges in achieving their objectives of land acquisition, cultivation, and passage to the next generation. Charles Julian and Harry Toulmin had similar goals in mind as each described his ideal farm. Julian believed that to succeed, the farmer had to invest in commodities easily sold in the local village, employ his slaves in extra-household manufacturing, and raise the crops and livestock best suited for domestic use and market. His concern over cash prices and investment in bonds suggests a fiscal mentality that stretched beyond barter systems. As we have seen, however, it was a mentality that accompanied, rather than replaced, traditional notions of exchange.

Toulmin likewise recognized the opportunities of the emerging market economy, although he more cautiously weighed them against the independent nature of the farm. He explained that in England the farmer lived off the land "*indirectly* consuming but a small proportion in his own family," but in Kentucky the settler lived "by his farm *directly* with a view to family consumption." Still, in his calculations as to how much money would be needed, he concluded that £169 (over 42 percent) of the farmer's start-up costs could be retained "for contingencies."[103] He did not emphasize that the farmer have "enough" to provide for his family, but that he have "abundance." While reiterating the rhetoric of subsistence farming, Toulmin subtly paid tribute to a pattern of economic production beyond self-sufficiency.

In many ways the Bluegrass farms of the 1790s and early 1800s mimicked those of the Northeast that rode the crest of capitalism into the nineteenth century.[104] But it would be in error to say that Kentucky's nascent agrarian culture was a continuation of either northern or southern patterns. With connections to market networks, adequate money, and a little luck, Bluegrass settlers could aspire to "work & be rich." The intensity of corn production in the early 1800s that resulted in a collapse of corn prices is testament to the possibility of and their desire to profit. But the Appalachian Mountains were a large barrier to overcome, and alternating control of the port of New Orleans made river trade unreliable. In contrast to their counterparts in New England, the Mid-Atlantic, or the South, Kentucky farmers struggled not only to take advantage of a market network, but to secure its availability. Their distance from fiscal institutions meant inconsistent supplies of cash and greater anxieties about accumulating sufficient capital to purchase land. As Aristedes's chastisement indicated, farmers were responsible not just to themselves, but to the process of creating a new society in the trans-Appalachian wilderness.

By the early 1800s, Kentuckians had blended commerce and agriculture, had enlarged their markets, and were participating in large numbers.[105] While independence appealed to many, a desire to enjoy the fruits of their labors and achieve a higher standard of living encouraged a commercial outlook as well.[106] The musings of a Mason County resident restated the point in a more lyrical manner: "May the Lord be praised/how I am a mased/to see how things have mended/hot cake and tea/for supper I see/When mush and milk was intended."[107] The use of the term "mended" exposed the expectations that mere subsistence was just a temporary consequence of relocation; the goal was comfort and luxury.

The historiographical contest over the nature of early American farms has served historians poorly because it has created a binarism—an either/or dichotomy that polarizes the debate. When analyzing the farms of early Kentucky, we can more clearly understand how rural peoples understood the advantages of an appropriate balance between producing for sustenance and producing for profit. Although political rhetoric emphasized the importance of owning the "fruits of one's labor," many Kentuckians worked long and hard to reach a level of income in which they could "introduce luxuries . . . in any great plenty," sometimes to the chagrin of Aristedes and others who interpreted such activities as extramoral.[108] The editorialist was correct: in their efforts to protect their investments, many farmers did squander away much of the potential wealth of their labors, and with it much of the underpinnings of their own independence. But he may have been mistaken in placing the blame. Farmers merely pursued the dream that had been presented to them. Ultimately, the prophecy of "work & be rich" was not realized by the majority of settlers, who failed to acquire the land on which to pursue the promise. And for those with property, unless they operated within societal expectations about their proper roles in the economic structure, profit proved a difficult crop to cultivate.

Notes

The author would like to thank Tom Appleton, Stephen Aron, Andrew R.L. Cayton, Mary W. Hargreaves, Elizabeth Perkins, and Matthew Schoenbachler for their time and energies in offering valuable criticisms of the manuscript. Additionally, I want to acknowledge the students in my historical methods class—Gerald Atkins, Jeff Bowersox, David DeVore, Erica Elmore, David Jandl, Lane Marshall, Eric Polsgrove, and Mandy Smith—who learned how to critique papers at the expense of the professor and provided some fine ideas in the process.

1. Willard Rouse Jillson, "John Filson's Book and Map: Kentucke, 1784," *Register of the Kentucky Historical Society* 28 (1930): 283.

2. Timothy Flint quoted in Thomas R. Cox, Robert S. Maxwell, Phillip Drennon Thomas, and Joseph J. Malone, *This Well-Wooded Land: Americans and Their Forests from Colonial Times to the Present* (Lincoln: Univ. of Nebraska Press, 1985), 54.

3. *Lexington Kentucky Gazette*, 2 October 1798.

4. J.M. Powell, *Mirrors of the New World: Image and Image-Makers in the Settlement Process* (Hamden, Conn.: Archon Books, 1977), 64-65.

5. Joyce Appleby, *Capitalism and a New Social Order: The Republican Vision of the 1790s* (New York: New York Univ. Press, 1984), 42.

6. Frederick Jackson Turner, "Dominant Forces in Western Life," in *The Frontier in American History* (New York: Henry Holt, 1920), 239.

7. Richard Hofstadter, *The Age of Reform: From Bryan to F.D.R.* (New York: Vintage Books, 1955), 24-25.

8. Allan Kulikoff, "Households and Markets: Toward a New Synthesis of American Agrarian History," *William and Mary Quarterly*, 3d ser., 50 (1993): 343-55; Paul A. Gilje, "The Rise of Capitalism in the Early Republic," *Journal of the Early Republic* 16 (1996): 159-81.

9. Michael Merrill, "Cash is Good to Eat: Self-Sufficiency and Exchange in the Rural Economy of the United States," *Radical History Review* 4 (1977): 42-71; James A. Henretta, "Families and Farms: *Mentalité* in Pre-Industrial America," *William and Mary Quarterly*, 3d ser., 35 (1978): 3-32; Richard D. Brown, *Modernization: The Transformation of American Life, 1600-1865* (New York: Hill and Wang, 1976), chap. 1; Robert Mutch, "Colonial America and the Debate about the Transition to Capitalism," *Theory and Society* 9 (1980): 847-64; Winifred B. Rothenberg, "The Market and Massachusetts Farmers, 1750-1855," *Journal of Economic History* 41 (1981): 283-314; Robert A. Gross, "Culture and Cultivation: Agriculture and Society in Thoreau's Concord," *Journal of American History* 69 (1982): 42-61; Christopher Clark, *The Roots of Rural Capitalism: Western Massachusetts, 1780-1860* (Ithaca, N.Y.: Cornell Univ. Press, 1990), 17, 23-24; Daniel Vickers, "Competency and Competition: Economic Culture in Early America," *William and Mary Quarterly*, 3d ser., 47 (1990): 3-29; Charles Sellers, *The Market Revolution: Jacksonian America, 1815-1846* (New York: Oxford Univ. Press, 1991); Allan Kulikoff, "The Revolution, Capitalism, and Formation of Yeoman Classes," in *Beyond the American Revolution: Explorations in the History of American Radicalism*, ed. Alfred F. Young (DeKalb: Northern Illinois Univ. Press, 1993), 88-89; Alan Taylor, "Agrarian Independence: Northern Land Rioters after the Revolution," in ibid., 221-45.

10. Louis Hartz, *The Liberal Tradition in America* (New York: Harcourt- Brace, 1955); Charles S. Grant, *Democracy in the Connecticut Frontier Town of Kent* (New York: Columbia Univ. Press, 1961); Richard L. Bushman, *From Puritan to Yankee Character and the Social Order in Connecticut, 1690-1765* (Cambridge, Mass.: Harvard Univ. Press, 1967); Kenneth Lockridge, *A New England Town, the First Hundred Years: Dedham, Massachu-*

setts, 1636-1736 (New York: W.W. Norton, 1970); James T. Lemon, *The Best Poor Man's Country: A Geographical Study of Early Southeastern Pennsylvania* (Baltimore: Johns Hopkins Univ. Press, 1972); Joyce Appleby, "Commercial Farming and the 'Agrarian Myth' in the Early Republic," *Journal of American History* 68 (1982): 833-49; Carole Shammas, "How Self- Sufficient Was Early America?" *Journal of Interdisciplinary History* 13 (1982): 247-72; Bettye H. Pruitt, "Self-Sufficiency and the Agricultural Economy of Eighteenth-century Massachusetts," *William and Mary Quarterly*, 3d ser., 61 (1984): 333-64; Steven Hahn and Jonathan Prude, eds., *The Countryside in the Age of Capitalist Transformation: Essays in the Social History of Rural America* (Chapel Hill: Univ. of North Carolina Press, 1985); Peter C. Mancall, *Valley of Opportunity: Economic Culture along the Upper Susquehanna, 1700-1800* (Ithaca, N.Y.: Cornell Univ. Press, 1991); T.H. Breen, "Narrative of Commercial Life: Consumption, Ideology, and Community on the Eve of the American Revolution," *William and Mary Quarterly*, 3d ser., 50 (1993): 471-501.

11. For the intersections between revolutionary ideals and westward expansion, see Drew R. McCoy, *The Elusive Republic: Political Economy in Jeffersonian America* (New York: W.W. Norton, 1980), 121-22; Peter S. Onuf, "Liberty, Development, and Union: Visions of the West in the 1770s," *William and Mary Quarterly*, 3d ser., 43 (1986): 193-203; John Lauritz Larson, "'Bind the Republic Together': The National Union and the Struggle for a System of Internal Improvements," *Journal of American History* 74 (1987): 363-87; and idem, "Jefferson's Union and the Problem of Internal Improvements," in *Jeffersonian Legacies*, ed. Peter S. Onuf (Charlottesville: Univ. Press of Virginia, 1993), 340-69.

12. Lee Shai Weissbach, "The Peopling of Lexington, Kentucky: Growth and Mobility in a Frontier Town," *Register of the Kentucky Historical Society* 81 (1983): 115-33; Ellen Eslinger, "Migration and Kinship on the Trans-Appalachian Frontier: Strode's Station, Kentucky," *Filson Club History Quarterly* 62 (1988): 52-66; Gail S. Terry, "Family Empires: A Frontier Elite in Virginia and Kentucky, 1740-1815" (Ph.D. diss., College of William and Mary, 1992), 282; Robert E. Bieder, "Kinship as a Factor in Migration," *Journal of Marriage and the Family* 35 (1973): 429-39. A good overview of the kinship networks along the southern frontier in a later period is Joan E. Cashin, *A Family Venture: Men and Women on the Southern Frontier* (Baltimore: Johns Hopkins Univ. Press, 1991), especially chap. 4.

13. Quoted in Lowell H. Harrison, "A Virginian Moves to Kentucky, 1793," *William and Mary Quarterly*, 3d ser., 15 (1958): 201. Also see Harry Toulmin, "Comments on America and Kentucky," *Register of the Kentucky Historical Society* 47 (1949): 115.

14. Michael Merrill and Sean Wilentz, eds., *The Key of Liberty: The Life and Democratic Writings of William Manning, "A Laborer," 1747-1814* (Cambridge, Mass.: Harvard Univ. Press, 1993), 12.

15. Toulmin, "Comments on America and Kentucky," 114. Not surprisingly, Toulmin's own farm consisted of thirty acres that he did not own but rented for eighteen pounds sterling a year; see Gilbert Imlay, *A Topographical Description of the Western Territory of North America* (London: J. Debrett, 1797; reprint: New York: Johnson Reprint, 1968), 173.

16. Journal of Charles Julian, 1800-1818, Special Collections, Margaret I. King Library, University of Kentucky, Lexington.

17. Over the past two decades, research into economy and polity in rural areas has produced two distinct interpretations that reflect the differences in Toulmin's and Julian's

farming models. The first interpretation argues for rural economies limited in market participation and restricted by traditional notions of familial and communal reciprocity; see Merrill, "Cash is Good to Eat," 42-71; Henretta, "Families and Farms," 3-32; Clark, *The Roots of Rural Capitalism*; and Allan Kulikoff, *The Agrarian Origins of American Capitalism* (Charlottesville: Univ. Press of Virginia, 1992).

The second emphasizes farmers as individual capitalists pursuing both markets and profits; see Grant, *Democracy in the Connecticut Frontier Town of Kent*; James T. Lemon, *The Best Poor Man's Country: A Geographical Study of Southeastern Pennsylvania* (Baltimore: Johns Hopkins Univ. Press, 1972); Robert D. Mitchell, *Commercialism and Frontier: Perspectives on the Early Shenandoah Valley* (Charlottesville: Univ. Press of Virginia, 1977); and Appleby, *Capitalism and a New Social Order*.

18. Fredrika Johanna Teute, "Land, Liberty, and Labor in the Post-Revolutionary Era: Kentucky as the Promised Land" (Ph.D. diss., Johns Hopkins University, 1988), 632. For brief but very useful discussions on the changing interpretations of independence during the early republic, see Marc W. Kruman, "The Second American Party System and the Transformation of Revolutionary Republicanism," *Journal of the Early Republic* 12 (1992): 509-37; Lacy K. Ford Jr., "Frontier Democracy: The Turner Thesis Revisited," *Journal of the Early Republic* 13 (1993): 144-63; James L. Huston, "The American Revolutionaries, the Political Economy of Aristocracy, and the American Concept of the Distribution of Wealth, 1765-1900," *American Historical Review* 98 (1993): 1079-1105; and Jack P. Greene, "Independence, Improvement, and Authority: Toward a Framework for Understanding the Histor*ies* of the Southern Backcountry during the Era of the American Revolution," in *An Uncivil War: The Southern Backcountry during the American Revolution*, eds. Ronald Hoffman, Thad W. Tate, and Peter J. Albert (Charlottesville: Univ. Press of Virginia, 1985), 12.

19. Henretta, "Families and Farms," 6-9.

20. Stephen A. Aron, "Pioneers and Profiteers: Land Speculation and the Homestead Ethic in Frontier Kentucky," *Western Historical Quarterly* 23 (1992): 179-98; Neal O. Hammon, "Settlers, Land Jobbers, and Outlyers: A Quantitative Analysis of Land Acquisition on the Kentucky Frontier," *Register of the Kentucky Historical Society* 84 (1986): 241-46; Thomas D. Clark, *Agrarian Kentucky* (Lexington: Univ. Press of Kentucky, 1977), 6-10; Patricia Watlington, *The Partisan Spirit: Kentucky Politics, 1779-1792* (New York: Atheneum, 1972), 11-34.

21. George P. Garrison, ed., "A Memorandum of M. Austin's Journey from the Lead Mines in the County of Wythe in the State of Virginia to the Lead Mines in the Province of Louisiana West of the Mississippi, 1796-1797," *American Historical Review* 5 (1900): 524-25.

22. Lee Soltow, "Kentucky Wealth at the End of the Eighteenth Century," *Journal of Economic History* 43 (1983): 632-33, and appendix; idem, *Distribution of Wealth and Income in the United States in 1798* (Pittsburgh: Univ. of Pittsburgh Press, 1989), 77. For a discussion of the effects of landlessness on a large part of Kentucky's population, see Teute, "Land, Liberty, and Labor in the Post-Revolutionary Era," 620-24.

23. Aron, "Pioneers and Profiteers," 179-98.

24. Bayard Still, "The Westward Migration of a Planter Pioneer in 1796," *William and Mary Quarterly*, 3d ser., 21 (1941): 341.

25. Malcolm J. Rohrbough, *The Land Office Business: The Settlement and Adminis-*

tration of American Public Lands, 1789-1837 (New York: Oxford Univ. Press, 1968), 23, 48; Alan Taylor, *William Cooper's Town: Power and Persuasion on the Frontier of the Early Republic* (New York: Alfred A. Knopf, 1995), 328.

26. Victor Collot, *A Journey in North America* (Paris, France: Arthur Bertrand, 1826), 101; Imlay, *A Topographical Description*, 175.

27. John Melish, *Travels in the United States of America in the Years 1806 and 1807, and 1809, 1810, and 1811*, 2 vols. (Philadelphia: Thomas and George Palmer, 1812), 1: 404.

28. The yeoman ideal provided the model for agricultural fundamentalism throughout American history; see Zhaohui Hong, "Changing Interpretations of Land Speculation in Western Development: Historians and the Shaping of the American West" (Ph.D. diss., University of Maryland, 1992), 8.

29. Indeed, Fredrika Teute argued that traditional inheritance patterns contributed to the maintenance of economic inequality in Kentucky; "Land, Liberty, and Labor in the Post-Revolutionary Era," 632. Stephen Aron suggested that "because pursuit of land encouraged participation in the market, the dominance of commerce and eventually of capitalism proved less unsettling to pioneers and their posterity"; see "Significance of the Frontier in the Transition to Capitalism," *The History Teacher* 27 (1994): 271-72.

30. "Some Particulars Relative to Kentucky," in *Travels in the Old South*, ed. Eugene Schwaab, 2 vols. (Lexington: Univ. of Kentucky Press, 1973), 1: 59.

31. John C. Wallace Journal, 1786-1802, Manuscripts Collection, Filson Club Historical Society, Louisville, Ky.

32. "Some Particulars Relative to Kentucky," 60; Donald F. Carmony, ed., "Spencer Record's Memoirs of the Ohio Valley Frontier, 1766-1795," *Indiana Magazine of History* 55 (1959): 370.

33. Ford, "Frontier Democracy," 155.

34. Melish, *Travels through the United States*, 413.

35. William Lytle to John Breckinridge, 10 January 1797, Papers of the Breckinridge Family, Manuscripts Division, Library of Congress, Washington, D.C.

36. Robert Breckinridge to Samuel Beall, 18 April 1792, Beall-Booth Papers, Manuscripts Collection, Filson Club.

37. Historians have not yet determined the statewide extent of tenancy. It may have been as high as 25 percent; Teute, "Land, Liberty, and Labor," 294.

38. John Breckinridge to S. Meredith, n.d., Papers of the Breckinridge Family.

39. *Lexington Kentucky Gazette*, 21 November 1795.

40. Ibid., 7 November 1795. Also see Lewis C. Gray, *History of Agriculture in the Southern United States to 1860,* 2 vols. (1932; reprint: Gloucester, Mass.: Peter Smith, 1958), 1: 646-57.

41. R.C. Ballard Thruston, ed., "Letter by Edward Harris, 1797," *Filson Club History Quarterly* 2 (1928): 167.

42. Ibid.

43. Alexander B. Groshart, ed., *The Poems and Literary Prose of Alexander Wilson, the American Ornithologist*, 2 vols. (Paisley, Scotland: Alexander Gardner, 1876), 1: 184.

44. Ibid., 184-85.

45. John Hill to Peyton Skipworth, 4 April 1796, Peyton Skipworth Papers, Manuscripts Collection, Filson Club. Also see William Faux, "Memorable Days in America,"

part 1, in *Early Western Travels, 1748-1846*, ed. Reuben Gold Thwaites, 32 vols. (Cleveland: Arthur H. Clark, 1904-1907), 11: 187.

46. Daniel Drake, *Pioneer Life in Kentucky, 1785-1800*, ed. Emmett Horine (New York: Henry Schuman, 1948), 206-7.

47. John T. Lyle, Lyman Draper Manuscript Collection, 14CC17, State Historical Society of Wisconsin, Madison.

48. *Lexington Kentucky Gazette*, 7 February 1803.

49. "A Friend to the Distressed," *Lexington Kentucky Gazette*, 19 December 1795.

50. *Acts Passed at the First Session of the Second General Assembly for the Commonwealth of Kentucky, 1793* (Lexington: John Bradford, 1793), 45.

51. Ibid., 46. In 1808, the Kentucky Court of Appeals determined that county courts must first inform the next of kin before binding poor children into apprenticeship. *Curry v. Jenkins*, 3 Hardin 501 (1808).

52. Gordon S. Wood, *Radicalism of the American Revolution* (New York: Alfred A. Knopf, 1992), 170-71; Greene, "Independence, Improvement, and Authority," 14.

53. Drake, *Pioneer Life in Kentucky*, 165, 37-38.

54. Julian J.N. Campbell, "Present and Presettlement Forest Conditions in the Inner Bluegrass of Kentucky" (Ph.D. diss., University of Kentucky, 1980), 173.

55. Groshart, *The Poems and Literary Prose of Alexander Wilson*, 185.

56. Clarence Mondale, "Place-on-the-Move: Space and Place for the Migrant," in *Mapping American Culture*, eds. Wayne Franklin and Michael Steiner (Iowa City: Univ. of Iowa Press, 1992), 54.

57. Drake, *Pioneer Life in Kentucky*, 176.

58. Quoted in Thomas D. Clark, *A History of Kentucky*, rev. ed. (Lexington: John Bradford Press, 1960), 279.

59. Nathaniel Hart to James McDowell, 18 June 1809, James McDowell Papers, State Historical Society of Wisconsin, Madison.

60. Drake, *Pioneer Life in Kentucky*, 57-58.

61. James Rood Robertson, *Petitions of the Early Inhabitants of Kentucky to the General Assembly of Virginia, 1769-1792* (Louisville: J.P. Morton, 1914), 148-49.

62. Ellen Eslinger produced the most thorough analysis of petition signing in the Shipp's mill controversy; see "The Great Revival in Bourbon County" (Ph.D. diss., University of Chicago, 1988), 122-29. Stephen Aron likewise promoted an economic breakdown of the episode in terms of corn versus tobacco producers; *How the West Was Lost: The Transformation of Kentucky from Daniel Boone to Henry Clay* (Baltimore: Johns Hopkins Univ. Press, 1996), 117-21.

63. Robertson, *Petitions*, 148-49.

64. *Bourbon County Court Order Book A*, Kentucky Department for Libraries and Archives, Frankfort, 245, 288-89.

65. Harry S. Watson, "'The Common Rights of Mankind': Subsistence, Shad, and Commerce in the Early Republican South," *Journal of American History* 83 (1996): 13-43.

66. Gary Kulik, "Dams, Fish, and Farmers: Defense of Public Rights in Eighteenth-Century Rhode Island," in *The Countryside in the Age of Capitalist Transformation: Essays in the Social History of Rural America*, eds. Steven Hahn and Jonathan Prude (Chapel Hill: Univ. of North Carolina Press, 1985), 25-50.

67. *Acts Passed at the Second Session of the First General Assembly of the Commonwealth of Kentucky* (Lexington: John Bradford, 1792), 36; William Littell, *The Statute Law of Kentucky*, 3 vols. (Frankfort: William Hunter, 1809), 1: 378-80; G. Glenn Clift, *History of Maysville and Mason County*, 2 vols. (Lexington, Ky.: Transylvania Printing, 1936), 1: 137.

68. Andre Michaux, "Journal of Travels into Kentucky," in Thwaites, *Early Western Travels 1748-1846*, 3: 237. Also see Fortesque Cuming, "Sketches of a Tour to the Western Country," in Thwaites, *Early Western Travels 1748-1846*, 4: 170.

69. Lucien Beckner, ed., "Reverend John D. Shane's Notes on Interviews, in 1844, with Mrs. Hinds and Patrick Scott of Bourbon County," *Filson Club History Quarterly* 10 (1936): 169.

70. *Lexington Kentucky Gazette*, 16 September, 11 November 1797; James T. Lemon, *The Best Poor Man's Country*, 152. François Michaux noted the significance of corn to farmers around Washington; *Travels to the West*, 3: 196.

71. Faux, *Memorable Days in America*, 187.

72. Michaux, *Travels to the West*, 205.

73. Ibid., 239.

74. Faux, *Memorable Days in America*, 187; *Laws of Kentucky*, 2 vols. (Lexington: John Bradford, 1799), 2: 411-13; *Federal Census, 1810: Mason County, Kentucky.*

75. Thruston, "Letter By Edward Harris," 166.

76. For description of slaves' tasks on the average farm, see Joseph Hornsby Diary 1798-1804, Manuscripts Collection, Filson Club; for the role of the farmer, see Journal of Charles Julian, Special Collections, Margaret I. King Library; and for Kentucky farm women's work, see John McClelend File, Kentucky Historical Society, Frankfort. Similar farm labor patterns are found in New England; see Christopher Clark's study of gender and farmwork in *The Roots of Rural Capitalism: Western Massachusetts, 1780-1860* (Ithaca, N.Y.: Cornell Univ. Press, 1990), chaps. 2 and 3; also Jeanne Boydston, *Home & Work: Housework, Wages, and the Ideology of the Early Republic* (New York: Oxford Univ. Press, 1990), especially chaps. 1 and 2. Because smaller populations in the countryside did not support specialization, farmers and their wives had to develop skills beyond sowing and reaping; see Mutch, "Yeoman and Merchant in Pre-Industrial America," 279-302.

77. Darrett B. and Anita H. Rutman found a similar pattern of local travel in colonial Virginia; see *A Place in Time: Middlesex County, Virginia, 1650-1750* (New York: W.W. Norton, 1984), especially chap. 7. Historians note persistent needs for the services of courthouse, militia, and market even in the absence of towns; see for example Carville Earle, *The Evolution of a Tidewater Settlement System: All Hallow's Parish, Maryland, 1650-1783* (Chicago: Department of Geography, University of Chicago, 1975); Joseph A. Ernst and H. Roy Merrens, "'Camden's Turrets Pierce the Skies!': The Urban Process in the Southern Colonies during the Eighteenth Century," *William and Mary Quarterly* 30 (1973): 549-73; Merrens, *Colonial North Carolina in the Eighteenth Century: A Study in Historical Geography* (Chapel Hill: Univ. of North Carolina Press, 1964); and Charles J. Farmer, *In the Absence of Towns: Settlement and Country Trade in Southside Virginia, 1730-1800* (Lanham, Md.: Rowman & Littlefield, 1993).

78. James Flint, *Letters from America*, in Thwaites, *Early Western Travels 1748-1846*, 9: 147.

79. Joan Wells Coward, *Kentucky in the New Republic: The Process of Constitution*

Making (Lexington: Univ. Press of Kentucky, 1979), 37, 63; Gray, *History of Agriculture in the Southern United States*, 1: 482.

80. Michaux, *Travels to the West*, 200-201.

81. Ibid., 245.

82. Drake, *Pioneer Life in Kentucky*, 45.

83. Michaux, *Travels to the West*, 246; Drake, *Pioneer Life in Kentucky*, 75.

84. "Some Particulars Relative to Kentucky," 56.

85. Still, "The Westward Migration of a Planter Pioneer," 335; "Some Particulars Relative to Kentucky," 56.

86. Michael Williams, *Americans and Their Forests: A Historical Geography* (New York: Cambridge Univ. Press, 1989), 71; Michaux, *Travels to the West*, 247.

87. Carolyn Murray-Wooley and Karl Raitz, *Rock Fences of the Bluegrass* (Lexington: Univ. Press of Kentucky, 1992), 77-82.

88. For a discussion of merchant-consumer relations in early Kentucky, see Craig Thompson Friend, "Merchants and Markethouses: Reflections on Moral Economy in Early Kentucky," *Journal of the Early Republic* 17 (1997): 553-74.

89. Edmund Martin Journal (Maysville), vol. B, July 1808-February 1811, Research Library, Mason County Historical Museum, Maysville, Ky.

90. Harry Toulmin, *The Western Country in 1793: Reports on Kentucky and Virginia*, eds. Marion Tinling and Godfrey Davis (San Marino, Calif.: Henry E. Huntington Library, 1948), 96-97.

91. Butler, "Manners and Habits of the Western Pioneers," 25-26; Toulmin, "Comments on America and Kentucky," 106; Groshart, *The Poems and Literary Prose of Alexander Wilson*, 195.

92. Butler, "Manners and Habits of the Western Pioneers," 26.

93. James Flint, *Letters from America*, in Thwaites, *Early Western Travels 1748-1846*, 9: 129.

94. "Some Particulars Relative to Kentucky," 56.

95. During the 1790s, at least four bluedyers transformed plain, white homespun into calico for the citizens of Fayette County alone. Winston Coleman, ed., *Lexington's First City Directory, 1806* (Lexington: Winburn Press, 1953); William A. Leavy, "A Memoir of Lexington and Its Vicinity," *Register of the Kentucky Historical Society* 41 (1943): 310-46.

96. Carole Shammas argued that rural households often relied on artisans to complete production of home manufactures; see "How Self-Sufficient Was Early America?," 268.

97. Similar patterns existed throughout eastern America. See Mutch, "Yeoman and Merchant in Pre-Industrial America," 279-302; Richard B. Sheridan, "The Domestic Economy," in *Colonial British America: Essays in the New History of the Early Modern Era*, eds. Jack P. Greene and J.R. Pole (Baltimore: Johns Hopkins Univ. Press, 1984), 43-85; James T. Lemon, "Spatial Order: Households in Local Communities and Regions," in Greene and Pole, *Colonial British America*, 86-122; and Stephen Innes, *Creating the Commonwealth: The Economic Culture of Puritan New England* (New York: W.W. Norton, 1995).

98. *Lexington Kentucky Gazette*, 13 September 1803.

99. Ibid.

100. Ibid., 11 October 1803. For the role of commerce in early America, particularly in the West, see Peter S. Onuf, "Liberty, Development, and Union: Visions of the West in the 1780s," *William and Mary Quarterly*, 3d ser., 43 (1986): 193-203. Also see J.E. Crowley, *This Sheba, Self: The Conceptualization of Economic Life in Eighteenth-Century America* (Baltimore: Johns Hopkins Univ. Press, 1974), 2-6; Merrill and Wilentz, *The Key of Liberty*, 12-13; Breen, "Narrative of Commercial Life," 482; Elizabeth A. Perkins, "The Consumer Frontier: Household Consumption in Early Kentucky," *Journal of American History* 78 (1991): 486-510.

101. *Lexington Kentucky Gazette*, 25 October 1803.

102. Ibid., 14 March 1804.

103. Toulmin, "Comments on America and Kentucky," 113.

104. Compare the description of Kentucky's farms in this essay to that of New England farms in Howard S. Russell, *A Long, Deep Furrow: Three Centuries of Farming in New England* (Hanover, N.H.: Univ. Press of New England, 1976), 245-56.

105. J.E. Crowley demonstrated that eighteenth-century Americans held a spectrum of ideas about commerce, including benign acceptance; *This Sheba, Self*, chap. 4. Also see Edmund S. Morgan, *American Slavery, American Freedom* (New York: W.W. Norton, 1975), especially chap. 8; Christine Heyrman, *Commerce and Culture: The Maritime Communities of Colonial Massachusetts, 1690-1750* (New York: W.W. Norton, 1984); Jacob M. Price, "The Transatlantic Economy," in Greene and Pole, *Colonial British America*, 18-42; and the collection of essays in *The Economy of Early America: The Revolutionary Period, 1763-1790*, eds. Ronald Hoffman, John J. McCusker, Russell R. Menard, and Peter J. Albert (Charlottesville: Univ. Press of Virginia, 1988).

106. This commercial outlook, or rather British regulations that restricted Americans' abilities to exercise it, precipitated the Revolutionary War; see Breen, "Narrative of Commercial Life." In Gail S. Terry, "Family Empires," the dual agency of land-ownership proved crucial to the definition of an elite class (pp. 4-5). Richard L. Bushman argued that the commercial mentalities of farmers arose not from a blatant acceptance of commercialism, but from cultural circumstances, particularly the desire to refine their lives; see "Opening the American Countryside" in *The Transformation of Early American History: Society, Authority, and Ideology*, eds. James A. Henretta, Michael Kammen, and Stanley N. Katz (New York: Alfred A. Knopf, 1992), 255.

107. Attached to the inside cover of Mason County, Kentucky, Account Book 1797-1799, Manuscripts Collection, Filson Club.

108. "Some Particulars Relative to Kentucky," 59; Huston, "The American Revolutionaries, the Political Economy of Aristocracy, and the American Concept of the Distribution of Wealth," 1081; Wood, *The Radicalism of the American Revolution*, 36-38.

Although settlement south of the Green River took a different path from that of the Bluegrass, almost all Kentucky settlers of the late eighteenth century started out in log cabins in uncleared wilderness. Lewis Collins sought to capture this basic reality with his sketch of the average homestead. Lewis Collins, *Historical Sketches of Kentucky* (Covington, Ky.: Collins and Co., 1847)

Opportunity on the Frontier South of the Green

CHRISTOPHER WALDREP

In 1795, Kentucky's legislature "relieved" pioneers who had moved onto land in western Kentucky located south of the Green River. The law allowed the sale of two-hundred-acre tracts priced at thirty cents an acre to adults who actually settled on the land. In 1797, a new law further encouraged migration by providing for sales of two-hundred-acre tracts to widows, free male persons, and anyone else with a family who actually cleared, fenced, and tended two acres of corn for a year.[1] These laws had the desired effect. By 1800 the population of the Green River country had reached and exceeded thirty thousand.[2] The eager multitudes journeying to western Kentucky raised families, governed themselves, and created a society in America's mythic wilderness: the West, the frontier. Rich or poor, these pioneers came to western Kentucky committed to private property and capitalism.

Today, Americans look at any frontier experience, including that in the Green River country, through glasses fashioned by Frederick Jackson Turner. The influence of Turner's writings is so profound that it would be foolish to consider white frontier settlement without first assessing his impact on our ability to look objectively at the pioneer experience. Turner claimed that what he called the "the meeting point between savagery and civilization" promoted formation of a composite American nationality.[3] Americans emerged from their frontier experiences more independent, more committed to individualism, and more democratic than Europeans. Free land along the frontier, Turner wrote, gave political power to men who would never have played a role in government under any other circumstances. In Turner's careful and not uncritical language, pioneer life promoted a democracy "strong in selfishness and individualism" that pressed "individual liberty beyond its proper bounds."[4]

Turner's thesis has proven remarkably seductive to historians. Many have attacked Turner, but his theory still speaks to a wide variety of scholars, even those critical of his insensitivity toward nonwhites. Environmental historians, for example, find attractive Turner's bold assertion that "the stubborn

American environment" shaped society. Similarly, social historians must find themselves nodding in agreement when Turner writes that institutions and constitutional forms merely reflect more vital societal forces.[5] Perhaps more important, historians from almost any ideological position can use Turner's insights to support their positions. Radical historians (I use Hayden White's typology here) seek "a remote past of natural-human innocence from which men have fallen." Such radicals find Turner's work appealing: he reports a lost utopia, a time now passed when poor men could make something of themselves in a state of nature. Thus, when Marxists and Neo-Marxists lament what they call the rise of capitalism, they follow a Turnerian trope. Capitalism may be a term too general to have meaning, but it must include the centralization of particular core values—individualism, competition, and commercialism. The passage of fencing laws illustrates the capitalistic process, reflecting a time when the public and communal became private, individual, and commercial.[6]

Turner's student, Thomas Perkins Abernathy, tested the thesis in Tennessee. Instead of finding the frontier democracy his mentor predicted, Abernathy documented land speculators' controlling influence as they planted settlements and dominated policies and politics. "The first offspring of the West," Abernathy concluded, "was not democracy but arrant opportunism." But Abernathy still presented the pioneer as "stalwart," if "ignorant and simple," "a fitting subject for exploitation."[7] Thus, Abernathy's break with Turner was not so total as it first appeared. Abernathy and those following him discovered the frontier democrats Turner posited; they just found these generous, hospitable, and honest people defeated, exploited, and undermined by powerful economic forces beyond their control. Like Turner's original hypothesis, Abernathy's description of the honest pioneer abused by economic forces beyond his control has proven attractive, durable, and appealing.

Most recently Turner has informed the work of Stephen Aron. Aron insists that his book, *How the West Was Lost*, traces the loss of possibilities rather than of a paradise. Still, Aron finds on the frontier a system of customary common rights with a broader and more equitable distribution of land than is possible under capitalism. According to Aron, lawyers led by Henry Clay helped unseat this more equitable system when they privatized property rights.[8] At bottom Aron has a remarkably radical view of history. In his paradigm, Kentucky frontier folk were primitive communists, caring little for property rights until those rights were, unfortunately, "privatized." Daniel Boone may have cooperated with Shawnee plans to incorporate whites into their culture. But, at the same time, Aron concedes that once Boone left the Shawnee, he and other backcountry whites proved "as susceptible to a speculative spirit as gentlemen."[9] More than Abernathy, Aron recognizes that the real hazard to customary common rights came not from some elite villain, but from within the heart of each pioneer.

Abernathy and Aron agree on one thing: grand theories like Turner's must be tested against particular situations. Scholars working in the colonial Chesapeake have found that new democratic institutions and opportunities emerged early on that frontier, much as Turner claimed.[10] But that does not prove that Turner's theory of frontier democracy can be applied to inland frontiers. To test whether the Green River pioneers carried capitalism with them, or whether they suffered privatization when the frontier passed, this essay looks at the first wave of permanent settlement in an area south of the Green River around the present-day towns of Eddyville and Princeton. The migrants into this area came to acquire land; they came already conceiving of their rights as privatized. Perhaps because the area never went through Turner's hypothetical democratic stage, no new hierarchy emerged. The leaders of the Green River pioneers had established their elite, slaveholding status before setting foot in western Kentucky. The frontier experience did not, could not, shake things up.

The language of Virginia's laws authorizing settlement of Kentucky lands suggests that legislators wanted to dispense land to sturdy folk committed to self-sufficiency rather than to avarice. In 1705 they required each claimant to build on his site a wood house no smaller than twelve feet square and to clear, plant, and tend one acre. In 1779 another Virginia law sought to reward bona fide settlers.[11] But, despite the intentions of lawmakers, Virginians commonly hired land jobbers to establish claims by building cabins, clearing fields, and planting corn. Outlyers made cabin improvements on the best land and sold the improvements. The 1779 law reserved land south of the Green River for veterans of the Revolutionary War. Officers and soldiers entitled to this land generally hired others to survey it for them.[12]

Virginia law sent petit capitalists into Kentucky, and those pilgrims brought law and lawyering with them. At first, though, the frontier seemed lawless; violence characterized it. And Eastern courts could do little to protect pioneers from the Indians they encountered. Although Virginia's statutes directed settlers toward land "not legally occupied," the territory that whites claimed in Kentucky was inhabited. In his memoir, Peter Cartwright writes that "savages . . . murdered and scalped" "many thousands" of white immigrants. Whites traveled to Kentucky in caravans, rarely passing a day without seeing the corpses of earlier travelers, killed by Indians. Cartwright remembered passing a tense night in a place called Camp Defeat, where a party of white families had been killed shortly before. Feeling solemn and gloomy, the travelers quaked with fear through the night.[13]

Bloody vigilantism characterized western Kentucky from the beginning. Peter Cartwright described Logan County as a "Rogues' Harbor." According to Cartwright, murderers and thieves actually formed a majority of its population. The courts charged these brigands, but "they would swear each other clear" and escape justice. No one has carefully studied Cartwright's assertions, and his narrative sounds like the classic justification for vigilantism. The criminals' strength and the weakness of the courts, Cartwright said, drove the honest citizens to become "Regulators" who fought pitched battles against the rogues; many lives were lost on both sides. Cartwright concluded his narrative by calling it "but a partial view of frontier life." Still, vigilantism plagued western Kentucky for more than a hundred years after the Regulators drove the rogues from Logan County.[14]

Actually, despite all the violence and lawlessness, pioneers traveling to Kentucky brought Virginia law with them. For settlers seeking land in Kentucky, the 1795 law and subsequent statutes copied the procedures outlined in Virginia's 1705 and 1779 laws. Settlers located a desirable tract of which they registered a minimal description with the state auditor or, later, the county clerk. Thomas Thompson's initial description of his tract simply said, "Beginning on the SW. Corner of John Ward, Running Northerly & Easterly for quantity." In Livingston County these certificates often measured four by eight inches. Although the descriptions said little, certificates could be bought and sold, and settlers traded them like currency.

At some point the holder of the certificate persuaded the county surveyor to make a survey, with friends and neighbors acting as chain carriers. The surveyor made a more precise description, trying, but not always succeeding, to avoid existing claims and surveys. Even the more precise descriptions written by surveyors relied on trees, rocks, streams, and other transitory geographic features. It is a measure of settlers' commitment to private property that they felt surveyed land "belonged" to them. In western Kentucky surveys had value and could be bought and sold; some changed hands several times. William Purkins surveyed a hundred-acre tract on March 21, 1803. Two years later he sold the half-page document to Richard Lee, who sold it to James George in 1807. In a place with little cash and a lot of land, the pioneers used land as a kind of currency.

In fact, holders of completed surveys did not yet own their land; title transferred from the state only after the governor, drawing from the description given by the survey, issued a patent or grant. Once the governor patented a tract, the holder could continue to trade and sell it, but the process was more formal, requiring a deed.[15]

Just as Virginians had speculated in central Kentucky under their state's 1705 and 1779 laws, hiring jobbers or establishing claims for sale, some of the pioneers traveling to western Kentucky made contracts to survey land claims for those unwilling or unable to make the journey. In 1792 Virginian John Craig hired Joseph Colville of Bourbon County, Kentucky, to go to western Kentucky "to enter locate & survey 2000 acres of land." Colville signed a contract not only to acquire the land, but to find land well-watered and timbered. When Colville did not do what Craig wanted, the Virginian sued him.[16] In another case, Tennessean David Looney hired Justinian Cartwright to establish title to three hundred acres on Lick Creek. Looney died before Cartwright performed the contracted services, but he still willed his Kentucky lands to his sons.[17]

Not only did settlers immediately trade land in a free market, they also bought and sold privately owned chattel. Through the nineteenth century and into the twentieth, Kentuckians allowed their stock, especially hogs, to run loose on open ranges. But this does not mean they did not jealously guard their property rights. When John Atcheson and Jesse Kuykendall called their neighbor, John Dobbins, a hog thief, saying their "hogs cannot go down the creek but what he [Dobbins] makes pork of them," Dobbins hired a lawyer and sued. The Livingston County Circuit Court investigated and found that the two men had lied about Dobbins, damaging his reputation. On September 8, 1803, both slanderers apologized.[18] In Kentucky, the hogs roamed free on public lands, but everyone tended their title to pork. Doing what some historians have postulated, that is, freely sharing the "neighborhood's" pork, could get a resident in trouble. In fact, just saying a neighbor freely shared in private property could land a person in court, fighting a slander suit. The Green River pioneers not only pursued their private rights in court, they saw their reputation for respecting those rights as something also worth protecting in court.

Green River migrants traded debts just as they exchanged land certificates and surveys. Promises to pay passed from hand to hand, with a new assignation scribbled on the back as the note passed to a new owner. In the absence of banks, these petit capitalists created their own money, which functioned as a medium of exchange, and the legal system's role in making debtors pay kept the economic system afloat. From the beginning, courts enforced debt repayment. Justices of the peace served as debt collectors should anyone prove recalcitrant. William C. Rodgers contracted with Joshua Scott, promising to pay Scott 112 gallons and 3 quarts of merchantable whiskey.[19] When Rodgers failed to provide the whiskey, Scott expected the courts to force payment. David Davidson promised to pay Matthew Lyon $41.06 in merchantable pork, delivered on foot. When Davidson did not pay, Lyon took him to court.[20] In these and similar suits, Green River pioneers assigned debts and sued to enforce paper obligations. They fought over private property in court, using lawyers and judges to enforce contracts.

The ease with which pioneers sold and traded land indicates an impressive respect for private property on the frontier, a fact not diminished by the largely egalitarian nature of land distribution in western Kentucky. Kentucky's 1795 and 1797 laws for the relief of settlers made for a remarkably equitable distribution of land. Of those Christian County residents taxed in 1799, 94 percent had between one hundred and four hundred acres: 68 percent owned exactly two hundred acres, the quantity authorized by the legislature.[21] In 1800, a third of Livingston County's taxable population owned two-hundred-acre tracts. And in other Green River counties, as much as three-quarters of landowners held the legislatively sanctioned acreage. The transition to landowner could be quick on the Green River. All claimants appearing on 1797 and 1798 Christian County tax lists had no land. But by 1799, after they had tended the corn crop required in the 1797 statute, the tax list credited 84 percent of them with land holdings, almost always two hundred acres.[22] All of this suggests the kind of frontier democracy Turner mythologized and Aron documented, a place where a poor man could make something of himself.

Still, for the poor of western Kentucky, opportunity hardly equaled achievement. Christopher Hammond probably left South Carolina's rough backcountry for Tennessee and then Kentucky because he heard that good land could be had for sixty cents an acre. Hammond had fought in the Revolutionary War, but seems to have owned no land in South Carolina. In 1790, when Hammond arrived in Washington County, Tennessee, economic conditions were terrible. He languished in tenancy until 1794, when he purchased a hundred acres and became a freeholder for the first time.[23]

In 1798 Hammond came to Kentucky, where he immediately had twice as much land as he had ever owned in eastern Tennessee. Settling on what would eventually be called Hammond Creek in present-day Lyon County, Hammond rapidly accumulated property. In 1799, he paid taxes on two hundred acres; in 1803, four hundred acres; in 1809, he purchased his first slave. Along with economic competence came political participation. Authorities repeatedly called on Hammond to serve as juror, grand juror, and road surveyor. Eventually, he came to own ten slaves (valued in excess of twenty-five hundred dollars), more than double the average number of bondsmen held by the slaveholding quarter of the population.[24]

But the frontier did not give Hammond political power. He never became a justice of the peace or a sheriff. The one time he served as foreman of a jury, he failed to understand the nature of the case and miswrote the verdict.[25] Nor did Hammond create a legacy that he could pass to the next generation. None of Hammond's sons who stayed in the area matched their father's wealth. Only one, Joshua, managed to retain his inherited slave.[26] In a culture devoted to honor, the creation of a family estate was a high priority; it gave a father authority over his children and other dependents that he would not otherwise have wielded. Heirs could be made to wait for their inheritance. Good land at sixty cents an acre promised more than "reputation for the living," it implied a heritage for the next generation, one that could be awarded at the pleasure of the patriarch.[27] But Christopher Hammond's biography illustrates the limits of frontier democracy in advancing poor men to a higher status. Although he achieved some success on the frontier, the final prize—creation of a legacy—escaped this would-be patriarch's grasp.

Not everyone found success on the frontier. In Livingston County, almost half of the taxable population had no land.[28] Two hundred acres surveyed for James Smart on Skinframe Creek in 1799 did not keep the pioneer from losing everything but his horse by 1822. Like Smart, James Thompson seems never to have accumulated more than his initial two hundred acres, but unlike Smart, he did have four slaves by 1809. His slaves, however, did not guarantee his success. Later that same year he sold a slave woman named Hannah and her child to David and John Doom for five hundred dollars. In 1818 his taxable holdings included just two horses, and two years later, just one worth forty dollars. Likewise, the fortunes of a growing number of migrants living in Caldwell County declined as the years passed. In 1800, 15 percent of migrants that could be located on tax lists had no land. By 1820, the landless had risen to 29 percent.[29]

A large number of the pioneers disappeared from tax lists after a few years. By 1810 more than half of all landowners no longer showed up on tax lists. Some never appeared in the first place. Lawyer Samuel Caldwell of Logan County claimed land in Livingston County, but only as a speculator; he never intended to farm it. Some migrants never actually claimed land, appearing in the records only as chain carriers for the actual surveyors. They may never have owned any property in Kentucky, and tax collectors missed them as they drifted through. Some simply moved on. Joshua Delaplane went to Indiana Territory. George Gordon went down the Natchez Trace to Saint Helena Parish, Louisiana. James Lusk Alcorn, a future Mississippi governor, migrated to the Yazoo-Mississippi Delta from Livingston County, as did several of his cousins and an uncle who had been Livingston County sheriff. One visitor to the area in 1810 wrote that "a great many are dissatisfied, and wish to emigrate west of the Ohio, and south of the Tennessee River."[30]

While some failed on the frontier, others did very well. Ten percent had four hundred acres or more. Historians describing the Green River country as the "best poor man's country" should wonder how 10 percent of the population became so wealthy so fast. Slaveholding made a huge difference. An examination of estate inventories of those who died between 1800 and 1803 reveals that slaveholders' estates averaged $1,381.45, while nonslaveholders' property amounted to an average of $338.73.[31] Only a small percentage of migrants into Green River country brought slaves with them. In Livingston County, a mere 11 percent had slaves when they came to Kentucky. Most who brought slaves had only one or two. With twelve slaves, David Caldwell was the exception, not the rule. And others who brought slaves with them failed. About half the slaveholders traveling to Livingston County either did not increase their stock of slaves or lost the ones they did have.[32]

For some, the slaves they brought to Kentucky gave them a leg up on their neighbors. William Bond had four slaves when he came, but twenty by 1804. Owning slaves enhanced political opportunities. Only a tiny percentage of the migrants into western Kentucky achieved any kind of political leadership status, but the ones who did almost always owned slaves. Men who brought slave wealth with them when they migrated into western Kentucky became the seven original justices of the peace in Livingston County. Of those who came with seven or more slaves, most served either as justice of the peace or as judge. Others like Isaac Bullard, who brought eight slaves, did not find status in judicial positions, but he operated a tavern, a mill, and a ferry and speculated in discounted notes. Perhaps the influence he garnered through his economic activities proved more profitable than that which he could have exerted politically. William Miles paid taxes on seven slaves in 1799, the same year he took office as one of Livingston County's first justices of the peace. David Caldwell had been Logan County Clerk before being taxed on twelve slaves in Livingston County, where he became a judge of the Court of Quarter Sessions.[33]

By 1820, most of the original western Kentucky settlers owned slaves. Their taxable property averaged over two thousand dollars. The most successful of these survivors, Mercer Wadlington, had surveyed two hundred acres on "bigg Eddy" on April 10, 1799. But for several years his fortunes did not improve beyond his initial headright. By 1812, though, he had 5 slaves and, by 1818, he had 360 acres and 10 slaves. Two years later, he claimed nearly eight thousand dollars in taxable property; four years after that he surpassed the eight-thousand-dollar mark. James Wadlington Jr. and William Wadlington did almost as well as Mercer. In 1820 James Junior paid taxes on $5,920 in property, including three slaves, while William's six slaves and other property were valued at $5,263. While none of these three success stories came to Kentucky with slaves, all were heirs of James Wadlington Sr., who died in 1800. James Senior had traveled with William Prince, another migrant who had established his wealth in South Carolina and Tennessee before coming to Kentucky. Like Prince, James Senior brought slaves with him when he migrated.[34]

Green River settlers William Bond and his son Winfrey also appear on the 1820 Caldwell County tax list. In 1799, William Bond owned four slaves and, with six hundred acres, was one of the largest slaveholders in his county. By the next year, William owned seventeen slaves, and at his death in 1825, his estate included one "musical gold watch" and "London silver."[35] Not surprisingly, Winfrey benefited from his father's financial success. While he initially held only one hundred acres and no slaves, by 1814 he had eight slaves; four years later he held twelve. By 1826, Winfrey's fifteen slaves and eight hundred acres were valued at seventy-five hundred dollars. Most of the immigrants who survived to 1820 and accumulated four thousand dollars or more in property had been slaveholders when they came to Kentucky or were the sons of migrating slaveholders.[36]

Historians have generally described self-sufficient cultivators as "yeomen," suggesting a kind of sturdy self-reliance. Such personality traits will generally remain beyond the grasp of the researcher, but few Green River pioneers were yeomen if that term implies a commitment to agricultural self-sufficiency over capitalistic competition. They came to western Kentucky with motives that, at some level, must be described as avaricious, if not capitalistic. In Caldwell County, antebellum circuit court grand jury records designated defendants and grand jurors as "farmers" or "yeomen." When the names of those identified as farmers and yeomen are matched with tax lists, it becomes clear that yeomen had no fewer slaves or acres than farmers. Neither group shied away from acquiring property.[37]

However independent Green River yeomen and farmers may have been, they followed certain political leaders. These leaders probably should not be characterized as aristocrats, but they may well have expected the kind of deference that they had once accorded their betters on the East Coast.[38] William Prince, who had accompanied James Wadlington Sr. to western Kentucky, was a Revolutionary War veteran and a leader of the South Carolinians who settled around Eddy Creek. In 1782, Prince left Spartanburg County, South Carolina, for present-day Montgomery County, Tennessee, where he established Prince's Station on the Cumberland River. He then led his close-knit community of followers to Kentucky, where they helped each other survey land for their farms in the last months of 1798 and the beginning of 1799. Prince himself became one of the leading farmers of the county, holding ten slaves and seven hundred acres, operating a tavern, and becoming a judge. His son Enoch became Livingston County Clerk.[39]

South Carolinian Edward Mitchison had also established himself before moving to Kentucky. He obtained some or all of his slaves from the estate of John Drury Chew, a South Carolinian killed in the Revolutionary War. Executor of Chew's estate, Mitchison left for Kentucky with Chew's slaves. Chew's children brought suit, but apparently Mitchison's absence from the state made it impossible for them to pursue him in court. In Kentucky Mitchison became deputy sheriff after his brother became sheriff and served as a major in the militia as well.[40]

One faction of Green River pioneers came from Vermont, refugees from the 1798 Sedition Act. The leader of these Vermont Republicans had established himself as a politically active entrepreneur long before setting foot in Kentucky. Matthew Lyon, the outspoken leader of these migrants, chose to come to Kentucky after having been jailed, fined, and indicted a second time for criticizing President John Adams. A merchant and newspaper editor in Vermont, founder of the town of Fairhaven, the first American to use wood pulp in the manufacture of paper, Lyon did not make himself over on the Kentucky frontier. Instead, he brought a familiarity with the "civilized life and the benefits of commerce" to Kentucky.[41]

In the fall of 1799 Lyon set out across Pennsylvania for Kentucky, accompanied by the children of his first marriage and "several other adventurers." Lyon's second wife and their family remained in Vermont. The migrants wintered in New Geneva, Pennsylvania, on the Monongahela.[42] Lyon brought "considerable" property with him from New England, which he increased in Pennsylvania by selling his teams for iron, mill stones, and grind stones. When he left his followers, they were "fixing their boats and making preparations." He instructed them to follow the Ohio River to the Cumberland, looking for the most suitable place. "I have given them," he wrote Andrew Jackson, "latitude to go up as far as they choose."[43]

When Lyon left his followers on the Monongahela, he returned to Congress to represent his Vermont district. Federalist leaders in Congress must have been chagrined to see their nemesis return after having once confined him to jail and then hatching a scheme to send him back. Lyon himself certainly wondered what kind of reception he would get. But the Federalists may also have begun to recognize that their campaign against Republican newspaper editors had backfired with the voters. For whatever reason, they apparently gave Lyon little trouble. Lyon described this session of Congress as "much more moderate" than the one before. For his part, Lyon was already thinking about his new home. He planned to head west the minute Congress recessed.[44]

Congress adjourned May 14, 1800. By July, Lyon had gone down the Ohio to the mouth of the Cumberland and followed that river to Eddy Creek. Like the South Carolinians, Lyon found he had to squeeze his own land claims between vast tracts of land claimed by earlier arrivals. These earlier claims, Lyon wrote, had been made without any acknowledgment of Indian rights to the land, which seemed to explain the Indians' often "insolent and troublesome" attitudes.[45] Lyon apparently felt some sympathy for the Native Americans he encountered. When whites murdered an Indian in a tavern, Lyon pressed for prosecution of the killers. But he continued to work for the expansion of white settlement to the detriment of the Indians.[46]

On July 1, 1800, Lyon made his first land purchase in Kentucky. "For value received," William C. Rodgers assigned a certificate to Lyon entitling the Vermonter to two hundred acres.[47] This certificate had changed hands several times before it reached Lyon, once having been sold at public auction. Thus, Lyon found himself involved in western Kentucky's land traffic immediately upon his arrival.[48]

But Lyon was not satisfied with buying surveyed lands with so much vacant territory available. On July 17, he set out with a surveyor, two chain carriers, and a marker to survey the land described on his certificate. On August 18, Lyon purchased and made five more surveys on lands with entries or certificates made by other persons. On August 29, he purchased yet another two hundred acres on Clifty Creek, now known as Hammonds

Creek. Lyon made these purchases while suffering what he called "seasoning," adjusting his health to harsh frontier conditions. Only the ousting of his political nemesis raised his spirits; Lyon wrote that he remained ill until Jefferson's election as president.[49]

After a summer of land buying in Kentucky, Lyon returned to Philadelphia to finish his term as a Vermont congressman. He helped to elect Jefferson after the 1800 election went to the House of Representatives. In April 1801, Lyon was in the federal city, writing that some unspecified "piece of business" had taken him "this far out of any road from here to N. Geneva."[50]

Turner asserted that the frontier promoted independence. But Matthew Lyon recognized the important role played by the federal government in promoting settlement, especially its regulation of Indian activities and its establishment of post roads. When Lyon returned to Kentucky on June 15, he noticed that the population had "five folded" since his first visit.[51] "This tranquility," Lyon explained, "has been attributed in some measure to the posts on the Ohio below the mouth of these rivers and to the constant communication between them and the posts above."[52]

Lyon described the whites he encountered in Kentucky as "a kind of Arabs from the back part of the Carolinas."[53] He and his fellow Vermonters felt more comfortable in town than did the South Carolinians, who preferred a farming life. But while the Vermonters transformed Eddyville into a commercial center, the Republican leader did not "found" the town of Eddyville as he had Fairhaven, Vermont.[54] By 1802, Lyon operated a mill and a store, and he purchased pork and cotton for resale in Nashville. His establishment connected interior farmers with the world market. Vermonter Gideon D. Cobb and his sons also became important merchants and landholders in Livingston County. Cobb's frontier cabin could be a wild place. One traveler wrote that he "took a frolick at Mr. Cobb's tavern and jumpt out an upper window to get Clear of the party."[55] Lyon, Cobb, and the other Vermonters brought a commercial mentality formed far from Kentucky to the frontier. They had little patience with the poor men they encountered.

In 1801 Lyon wrote with satisfaction that "Civilization is fast gaining ground." The destitute, he explained, have left "& their places have been filled up by people of more property and industry; people possessed of some knowledge of the comforts [of] civilized life and the benefits of commerce."[56] His son Chittenden, for whom Lyon County was named, became a large landowner and, like his father, a congressman. Lyon's descendants intermarried with the Skinner, O'Hara, Cobb, and Gracey families. By 1850, at least half of Eddyville's merchants had familial connections with Matthew Lyon.[57] As in Vermont, he became a prominent politician in western Kentucky, where voters sent him to the state legislature and then to the United States Congress. Contrary to Turner's assertion, the frontier did not place fresh faces in government.

Nor did the frontier generate a new governing structure. Matthew Lyon, William Prince, Edward Mitchison, and other frontier leaders in Livingston County governed under a county court system inherited from Virginia. Virginia's earliest laws empowered justices of the peace appointed by the governor to oversee each county. Meeting in county courts, these magistrates had wide-ranging powers. They built bridges and collected taxes, established and maintained roads, probated wills and estates, heard criminal cases, regulated church wardens and blacksmiths, posted rewards for wolves, established ferries, and controlled the prices charged by ferry and tavern operators. In short, they governed their counties.[58] In creating their own county courts, Kentucky lawmakers borrowed the language of Virginia statute books.[59] County courts in Kentucky as in Virginia were undemocratic, self-perpetuating, aristocratic, oligarchic, and nepotistic. Virginia law directed governors to select "the most able, honest and judicious persons of the county."[60] In practice, governors selected members of the local gentry with wealth and power, allowing them to dispense patronage and accumulate additional riches. This happened in Virginia and it repeated in Kentucky.[61]

Kentucky's frontier generated no new elite, and the old elite governed on a Virginia model. But while all this suggests continuity, Kentucky's Great Revival clearly challenged the existing order, threatening the power of leaders like Prince, Mitchison, and Lyon. In her memoir of frontier Kentucky, Lyon's daughter described her father as only superficially a friend of religion. He professed belief in an all-wise creator, warmly welcomed ministers into his home, and encouraged his hands to attend church. But Lyon's family habitually wore the richest of apparel—a public indication of an absence of religiosity. Since revivalists promoted plain dressing, clothing was the easiest way to distinguish the evangelicals from their opponents. At revivals the saved sometimes tore the ruffles and ribbons from their garments. When Lyon's daughter joined the evangelicals, she began wearing unadorned clothing. Her rejection of his aristocratic values made her father most uneasy.[62]

But the Great Revival promoted rather than threatened existing capitalistic values. When Kentuckians ripped the ruffles from their shirts, they did not, in fact, reject consumerism or private rights or economic competition. Rather, they wanted a purer form of capitalist competition, one in which the participants competed on more equal terms. The evangelicals challenged the prevailing honor code by attacking profane swearing. Western Kentucky men often used vigorous, manly oral expression—profanity—to assert their honor for community approval. Those who had been "reborn," however, became gentler and more home-centered, "all tenderness" in the words of one evangelical. Moreover, evangelicals followed the lead of Partisans, people committed to a more democratic society. The Partisan political movement condemned speculation and regarded its opponents' skill at acquiring large tracts of land as sure signs of aristocratic corruption, what we might call "insider trading."[63] They objected to the way aristocrats played the game, not to the game itself.

At the end of the 1790s, and after, Kentucky grand jurors showed their dissatisfaction with elite leadership by presenting profane swearers in court, where they had to pay a small fine. In Caldwell County the most wealthy swearers proved to be the ones most likely to return to court for a second or even a third taste of evangelical justice. Matthew Lyon apparently controlled his tongue within earshot of roving grand jurors, but they caught his son Chittenden twice. Anyone could be fined for profanity, but jurors delighted in presenting old-style aristocrats in court.[64]

A new breed of popular politician that promoted egalitarianism emerged to take the place of traditional leaders, whom evangelicals attacked. But these men also heralded a commitment to entrepreneurial energy, often coupled with religious passion. The Great Revival legitimized enterprise, the impersonal marketplace, and moneymaking by non-elites. It hardly created these values, and most likely, pioneers understood that capitalism and commercialism helped make the Revival possible. The Great Revival represented no last gasp of some lost utopia, nor did it signal an abrupt break with the past. Instead, evangelicals promoted the same values most pioneers brought with them as they passed "South of the Green."[65]

The ghost of Frederick Jackson Turner must forever haunt western studies. But his picture of sturdy yeomen hostile to institutionalized authority does not stand well in western Kentucky. It seems most unlikely that anyone coming to western Kentucky in response to the 1795 and 1797 land statutes came for any motive that could not be described as capitalistic. Nor did the western Kentucky frontier experience upset existing political hierarchies. The men who emerged to lead western Kentuckians had achieved elite status before coming to the region. The pioneers who dragged surveying chains through the woods south of the Green River did not "lose" the West. Nor did they shift their economic thinking away from communal and toward private property. Some property remained communal even at the end of the nineteenth century, but the central tendency was always toward private property rights.

It may well be useful for historians to focus on the rise of capitalism in the early republic.[66] But no matter how this slippery concept is defined, capitalism had permeated the consciousness of the Green River pioneers before they crossed into Kentucky. That Green River settlers shared some customary common rights does not mean they did not value private property and economic competition more.

This has meaning for western Kentucky's regional identity. Stephen Aron has argued that the Green River country turned "blue," meaning that the area became "a facsimile" of central Kentucky's Bluegrass plantation system.[67] It could also be said, however, that the Green River country turned "black," eventually becoming known as the Black Patch for the dark variety of tobacco grown there. In those portions of the Black Patch around Hopkinsville, large plantations reminiscent of the Bluegrass did prevail, so that during the Civil War the whole region—more than the rest of Kentucky—favored the Confederacy. But on the western edge of this area, the region this essay has examined, small farms were more common. And more than one hundred years after the vigilante violence Peter Cartwright described in Logan County's Rogue's Harbor, Black Patchers again turned to murderous night-riding violence. Black Patch courts refused to punish the offenders. Horrified, denizens of the Bluegrass shook their heads. The Black Patch, they realized, was a world apart.

Notes

The author wishes to thank Tom Appleton who read most of this material in a different form. Craig Friend's comments and criticisms helped make this a better work.

1. *Acts Passed at the Session of the General Assembly for the Commonwealth of Kentucky* (Frankfort: John Bradford, 1795), 79-81; *Acts Passed at the Session of the General Assembly for the Commonwealth of Kentucky* (Frankfort: John Bradford, 1797), 184-87.

2. Stephen Aron, *How the West Was Lost: The Transformation of Kentucky from Daniel Boone to Henry Clay* (Baltimore: Johns Hopkins Univ. Press, 1996), 153.

3. Few today would claim that those of European descent represented "civilization" while the "savages" did not. But Turner's definition of frontier, shorn of its insensitive

language, still holds. The frontier was the western edge of white settlement, the place where whites, and their slaves, met Native Americans.

4. Frederick J. Turner, "The Significance of the Frontier in American History," *Annual Report of the American Historical Association for the Year 1893* (Washington, D.C.: Government Printing Office, 1894), 199-227. See also Martin Ridge, "Turner the Historian: A Long Shadow," *Journal of the Early Republic* 13 (1993): 133-44.

5. Turner, "Significance of the Frontier," 199, 227. Legal historians sometimes find Turner less appealing. For scholars arguing that legal discourse, not environmental or social factors, primarily shaped legal institutions, see William E. Nelson, *Americanization of the Common Law: The Impact of Legal Change on Massachusetts Society, 1760-1830* (1975; reprint, Athens: Univ. of Georgia Press, 1994); John Phillip Reid, *Law for the Elephant: Property and Social Behavior on the Overland Trail* (San Marino, Calif.: Huntington Library, 1980). Similarly, cultural historians argue against Turner's environmental and social factors. See David Hackett Fischer, *Albion's Seed: Four British Folkways in America* (New York: Oxford Univ. Press, 1989); Bertram Wyatt-Brown, *Southern Honor: Ethics and Behavior in the Old South* (New York: Oxford Univ. Press, 1982).

6. Hayden White, *Metahistory: The Historical Imagination in Nineteenth-Century Europe* (Baltimore: Johns Hopkins Univ. Press, 1973), 22-29. Perhaps the most famous Marxist proclamation of a "pre-capitalist" society came from Eugene Genovese. See *Roll, Jordan, Roll: The World the Slaves Made* (New York: Vintage Books, 1974). For the "privatization" of the southern backcountry, see Steven Hahn, *The Roots of Southern Populism: Yeoman Farmers and the Transformation of the Georgia Upcountry, 1850-1890* (New York: Oxford Univ. Press, 1983); Crawford King Jr., "The Closing of the Southern Range: An Exploratory Study," *Journal of Southern History* 43 (1982): 53-70; Shawn Everett Kantor and J. Morgan Kousser, "Common Sense or Commonwealth? The Fence Law and Institutional Change in the Postbellum South," *Journal of Southern History* 59 (1993): 201-42; Steven Hahn, "A Response: Common Cents or Historical Sense?" *Journal of Southern History* 59 (1993): 243-58. Three 1970s articles launched the current assault on capitalism as a constant. Michael Merrill, "'Cash is Good to Eat': Self-Sufficiency and Exchange in the Rural Economy of the United States," *Radical History Review* 4 (1977): 42-71; Robert E. Mutch, "Yeoman and Merchant in Pre-Industrial America: Eighteenth-Century Massachusetts as a Case Study," *Societas* 7 (1977): 279-302; James A. Henretta, "Families and Farms: *Mentalité* in Pre-Industrial America," *William and Mary Quarterly*, 3d ser., 35 (1978): 3-32.

7. Thomas Perkins Abernathy, *From Frontier to Plantation in Tennessee: A Study in Frontier Democracy* (1932; reprint, University: Univ. of Alabama Press, 1967), 162, 359. Subsequent writers have agreed with Abernathy that successful pioneers called on family wealth or eastern connections. Ralph Mann, "Frontier Opportunity and the New Social History," *Pacific Historical Review* 53 (1984): 463-91; Lacy K. Ford Jr., "Frontier Democracy: The Turner Thesis Revisited," *Journal of the Early Republic* 13 (1993): 144-63.

8. Aron, *How the West Was Lost*, 150-69.

9. Ibid., 41-59.

10. Edmund S. Morgan, *American Slavery, American Freedom: The Ordeal of Colonial Virginia* (New York: W.W. Norton, 1975), 63, 83-84; Thad W. Tate and David L. Ammerman, eds., *The Chesapeake in the Seventeenth Century: Essays in Anglo-American*

Society (New York: W.W. Norton, 1979), especially essays by Lois Green Carr and Russell R. Menard, "Immigration and Opportunity: The Freedman in Early Colonial Maryland," 206-42; David W. Jordan, "Political Stability and the Emergence of a Native Elite in Maryland," 243-73; and Carole Shammas, "English-Born and Creole Elites in Turn-of-the-Century Virginia." See also Lorena S. Walsh, "Servitude and Opportunity in Charles County, Maryland, 1658-1705," in *Law, Society, and Politics in Early Maryland*, eds. Aubrey C. Land, Lois Green Carr, and Edward C. Papenfuse (Baltimore: Johns Hopkins Univ. Press, 1977), 111-30.

For the role of theory in social science research, see Stanley Lieberson, *Making it Count: The Improvement of Social Research and Theory* (Berkeley: Univ. of California Press, 1985), 116-17, 195-96, 229-31; Darrett B. Rutman with Anita H. Rutman, "By Way of Prologue: Historians' Imperatives of an Empiricist in a Marxist Den," in *Small Worlds, Large Questions: Explorations in Early American Social History, 1600-1850* (Charlottesville: Univ. Press of Virginia, 1994), 3-15.

11. William Waller Hening, *Statutes at Large: Being a Collection of All the Laws of Virginia*, 13 vols. (Richmond: private printing, 1822-23), 3: 304-29; 10: 35-50.

12. Ibid., 10: 35-50; Neal O. Hammon, "Land Acquisition on the Kentucky Frontier," *Register of the Kentucky Historical Society* 78 (1980): 297-321; idem, "Settlers, Land Jobbers, and Outlyers: A Quantitative Analysis of Land Acquisition on the Kentucky Frontier," *Register of the Kentucky Historical Society* 84 (1986): 241-62.

13. W.P. Strickland, ed., *Autobiography of Peter Cartwright: The Backwoods Preacher* (Freeport, N.Y.: Books for Libraries Press, 1972), 17-18.

14. Ibid., 24-25. Some historians continue to assert, if not prove, the justification for vigilantism, claiming the Black Patch to be a naturally violent place. See Suzanne Marshall, *Violence: In the Black Patch of Kentucky and Tennessee* (Columbia: Univ. of Missouri Press, 1994).

15. Thomas Thompson, certificate 1225, 5 November 1805, Livingston County Clerk's Office, Smithland, Ky.; Thomas Thompson survey 4836, 15 June 1807, Kentucky Historical Society, Frankfort; Christopher Greenup grant to Thomas Thompson, book 5: 257-58, Kentucky Historical Society, microfilm; William Purkins survey 11656, 24 March 1803, Kentucky Historical Society. Caldwell County's deed book "A" has been published; see Ukua Earle Fowler, comp., "Caldwell County, Ky. Records—Abstracts from Deed Book A," *Register of the Kentucky Historical Society* 34 (1936): 160-72.

16. *James Craig v. Joseph Colville*, Livingston County Order Book, 1803-1805, 179, Circuit Court Clerk's Office, Smithland, Ky. The suit was abated when Colville died.

17. *David Looney v. Justinian Cartwright*, Livingston Circuit Court Papers, Smithland, Ky. Looney's will, dated 1 May 1801, is included in the case file.

18. *John Dobbins v. John Atcheson*, *John Dobbins v. Jesse Kuykendall*, Livingston Circuit Court Papers; Livingston County Order Book, 1803-1805, 99.

19. *Joshua Scott v. William C. Rodgers*, Livingston Circuit Court Papers.

20. *Matthew Lyon v. David Davidson*, Livingston Circuit Court Papers.

21. Christian County tax lists, 1797, 1798, 1799, Kentucky Historical Society, microfilm.

22. Christian County tax lists, 1797, 1798; Livingston County tax list, 1799.

23. Christopher Waldrep, "Immigration and Opportunity along the Cumberland River in Western Kentucky," *Register of the Kentucky Historical Society* 80 (1982): 392-407.

24. In 1815, 22.6 percent of the taxable population owned slaves. On average, they owned 3.27 slaves. In 1830, when Hammond died, 25.8 percent of the taxable population owned an average of 4.76 slaves; Caldwell County tax list, Kentucky Historical Society, microfilm. Biographical information on Christopher Hammond is from *Audited Account of Christopher Hammond,* South Carolina Department of Archives and History, Columbia; Washington County, Tennessee, tax list, Tennessee State Library and Archives, Nashville, microfilm; and Caldwell County Will Book "A," 428-29.

25. *Commonwealth v. Peter Cartwright*, Livingston County Circuit Court bundles, Livingston County Court Clerk's Office, Smithland.

26. Joshua Hammond's inventory, Lyon County Inventory Book "A," County Clerk's Office, Eddyville, Ky., 330-32. Joshua's slave, Cupid Hammons, was born c. 1828 and died between 1870 and 1880.

27. Bertram Wyatt-Brown, "The Ideal Typology and Antebellum Southern History: A Testing of a New Approach," *Societas* 5 (1985): 5; idem, *Southern Honor*, 117-98.

28. Aron, *How the West Was Lost*, 152-53; Livingston County tax list, 1800.

29. Caldwell County tax list, Kentucky Historical Society, microfilm.

30. Analysis of the disposition of Green River settlers is based on examination of the careers of 209 individuals drawn from 140 state land records or surveys made in the settlement of what became, almost entirely, Caldwell County when that county was divided from Livingston in 1809. Only surveys dated 1798, 1799, or 1800 are included. For a fuller analysis of this study data, see Waldrep, "Immigration and Opportunity," 392-407; Caldwell County Deed Book "A," 89; Ermine Northcutt Marshall, *Gordons of the Deep South* (Austin, Texas: private printing, 1961), 47-48; Lillian A. Pereyra, *James Lusk Alcorn: The Persistent Whig* (Baton Rouge: Louisiana State Univ. Press, 1966), 4-5, 20-21; Edward S., Joynes, ed., "Memoranda Made by Thomas R. Joynes on a Journey to the States of Ohio and Kentucky, 1810," *William and Mary Quarterly*, 1st ser., 10 (1902): 222.

31. Livingston County Order Books "A" and "B," Livingston County Clerk's Office, Smithland.

32. In most cases we can only wonder how slaveholders lost their slaves. But court records document Thomas Hawkins's shift to nonslaveholder status. Authorities charged him and his wife with murdering their only slave. Livingston County Circuit Court bundles.

33. Boynton Merrill Jr., *Jefferson's Nephews: A Frontier Tragedy* (Princeton: Princeton Univ. Press, 1976), 295n; Livingston County Court Order Book "A," 35, 43, 85, 192.

34. Mercer Wadlington survey, 436, Surveys South of the Green River, State Land Office Records, Kentucky Historical Society, microfilm; Livingston County Will Book "A," 2-4; W.D. Snively Jr. and Louanna Furbee, *Satan's Ferryman: A True Tale of the Old Frontier* (New York: Frederick Ungar Publishing, 1968), 25.

35. Caldwell County Inventory Book I, 191-95, County Clerk's Office, Princeton, Ky.

36. Caldwell County Inventory Book I, 191-95; Caldwell County tax lists, 1809, 1811, 1814, 1818, 1820, 1822, Kentucky Historical Society, microfilm; Livingston County tax lists, 1799, 1800, Kentucky Historical Society, microfilm.

37. Caldwell County Circuit Court case files, 1809-1843, Circuit Court Clerk's Office, Princeton.

38. For the transition to capitalism, see especially Gordon S. Wood, "The Enemy is Us: Democratic Capitalism in the Early Republic," *Journal of the Early Republic* 16 (1996):

293-308. Historians disagree over the alleged decline of deference. Albert H. Tillson Jr., in *Gentry and Common Folk: Political Culture on a Virginia Frontier, 1740-1789* (Lexington: Univ. Press of Kentucky, 1991), argues that deference declined after the Revolution, while Jack Greene, "Independence, Improvement, and Authority: Toward a Framework for Understanding the Histor*ies* of the Southern Backcountry during the Era of the American Revolution," in *An Uncivil War: The Southern Backcountry during the American Revolution*, eds. Ronald Hoffman, Thad W. Tate, and Peter J. Albert (Charlottesville: Univ. Press of Virginia, 1985), 3-36, argues that the Revolution produced no change in traditional deference. For pioneer consumerism in Kentucky, see Elizabeth A. Perkins, "The Consumer Frontier: Household Consumption in Early Kentucky," *Journal of American History* 78 (1991): 486-510.

39. Ursula Smith Beach, *Along the Warioto* (Nashville: McQuidy Press, 1964), 22-23; Livingston County Tax List, 1800.

40. James E. Wooley, *Collection of Upper South Carolina Genealogical and Family Records* (Easley, S.C.: Southern Historical Press, 1982), 3: 54; Samuel W. Steger, *Caldwell County, Kentucky, History* (Paducah, Ky.: Turner Publishing, 1987), 37, 323-24.

41. Matthew Lyon to Thomas Jefferson, 12 August 1801, Jefferson Papers, Manuscripts Division, Library of Congress; Aleine Austin, *Matthew Lyon: "New Man" of the Democratic Revolution, 1749-1822* (University Park: Pennsylvania State Univ. Press, 1981), 30-44; Estelle Messenger Harrington, *A History of the Messenger Family: Genealogy of the Ancestry and Descendants of John Messenger and His Wife, Anne Lyon Messenger, and Allied Families of Col. Matthew Lyon and Capt. James Piggot* (St. Louis: private printing, 1934).

42. Lyon to Andrew Jackson, 28 February 1800, Jackson Papers, Manuscripts Division, Library of Congress.

43. Lyon to John Messinger, 17 August 1799, John Messinger Papers, Illinois Historical Society, Springfield; Lyon to Jackson, 28 February 1800.

44. Lyon to Jackson, 28 February 1800.

45. Lyon to Jefferson, 12 August 1801.

46. *Commonwealth v. Reuben Cook et al.*, Livingston County Circuit Court bundles; Merrill, *Jefferson's Nephews*, 226-27.

47. The original entry for this certificate had been made by Daniel Hazleton. The certificate is on file with Lyon's survey 3512 at the Kentucky Historical Society.

48. Reuben Durrett, "Early Banking in Kentucky," unpublished manuscript (1892), Filson Club, Louisville.

49. Surveys 2943, 2944, 2945, 2946, 2250, and one assigned to Chittenden Lyon, which has not yet been located, Kentucky Historical Society; Lyon to Jefferson, 12 August 1801, Jefferson Papers.

50. Lyon to Jefferson, 4 April 1801.

51. Lyon to Jefferson, 12 August 1801.

52. Ibid.

53. Ibid.

54. Robert Lee Blackwell, "Matthew Lyon, a Forgotten Patriot Recalled," *Filson Club History Quarterly* 46 (1972): 237, described Lyon's arrival at "what was to become Eddyville." Boynton Merrill Jr., in *Jefferson's Nephews*, 116, wrote that Eddyville "had been planned and built on the land of . . . Matthew Lyon." Lyon's descendants sometimes gave

him too much credit for Eddyville. See Mary Marshall to "Frank," 22 September 1879, Special Collections, Margaret I. King Library, University of Kentucky, Lexington; Elizabeth A. Roe, *Aunt Leanna or Early Scenes in Kentucky* (Chicago: private printing, 1855), 37. For references to Eddyville, or "Eddy Cabbins," before Lyon's arrival, see Christian County Order Book "A," 27, Christian County Clerk's Office, Hopkinsville, Ky.; William Littell, *The Statute Law of Kentucky*, 5 vols. (Frankfort: William Hunter, 1809-19), 2: 213.

55. William Joseph Clark, "Diary," *Register of the Kentucky Historical Society* 25 (1927): 195.

56. Lyon to Jefferson, 12 August 1801.

57. Seventh United States Census (1850), Caldwell County, National Archives, Washington, D.C., microfilm; J.H. Battle, W.H. Perrin, and G.C. Kniffin, *Kentucky, A History of the State* (Louisville: F.A. Battey, 1885).

58. Hening, *Statutes at Large*, 1: 302-3, 447, 310, 328, 456, 348, 411, 522; 2: 11, 69-71; 3: 220; 5: 175. See also Charles Sydnor, *Gentlemen Freeholders: Political Practices in Washington's Virginia* (Chapel Hill: Univ. of North Carolina Press, 1952), 78-93; A.G. Roeber, *Faithful Magistrates and Republican Lawyers: Creators of Virginia Legal Culture, 1680-1810* (Chapel Hill: Univ. of North Carolina Press, 1981), 42-130.

59. Littell, *Statute Law of Kentucky*, 1: 90-93.

60. Hening, *Statutes at Large*, 2: 69.

61. Robert M. Ireland, *The County Courts in Antebellum Kentucky* (Lexington: Univ. of Kentucky Press, 1972); Robert M. Ireland, "Aristocrats All: The Politics of County Government in Antebellum Kentucky," *Review of Politics* 32 (1970): 367; Christopher Waldrep, "An Interloper in the Oligarchy: Livingston County's County Seat Controversy of 1806-1809," *Register of the Kentucky Historical Society* 78 (1980): 115-22.

62. Elizabeth A. Roe, *Recollections of Frontier Life* (Rockford, Ill.: private printing, 1885), 35-48.

63. E. Merton Coulter, "Early Frontier Democracy in the First Kentucky Constitution," *Political Science Quarterly* 39 (1924): 665-77; Patricia Watlington, *The Partisan Spirit, 1779-1792* (New York: Atheneum Press, 1972), 43- 47; Thomas Perkins Abernathy, *Three Virginia Frontiers* (Baton Rouge: Louisiana State Univ. Press, 1940), 63-96; Richard E. Ellis, *The Jeffersonian Crisis: Courts and Politics in the Young Republic* (New York: W.W. Norton, 1971), 123-38.

64. Caldwell County Circuit Court files, 1809-1843, Circuit Clerk's office, Princeton.

65. Gordon S. Wood, *The Radicalism of the American Revolution* (New York: Alfred A. Knopf, 1992), 229-369.

66. The literature is immense. See, for starters, Paul A. Gilje, "The Rise of Capitalism in the Early Republic," *Journal of the Early Republic* 16 (1996): 159-82.

67. Aron, *How the West Was Lost*, 168.

Workingmen supplied labor for the most dangerous urban jobs of the early republic. John Robert Shaw, a well-digger in Lexington, had several narrow escapes from the explosives used in his occupation. By 1806, his multiple injuries included the loss of an eye, five fingers, and seven toes. John Robert Shaw, *A Narrative of the Life & Travels of John Robert Shaw* (Lexington: Daniel Bradford, 1807)

"The Poor Men to Starve"
The Lives and Times of Workingmen in Early Lexington

STEPHEN ARON

In the *Kentucky Gazette* of November 27, 1806, an advertisement announced the forthcoming publication of John Robert Shaw's autobiography. *The Life and Travels of John Robert Shaw* promised to be a unique narrative, for the author, as the announcement boasted, had been "five different times a soldier, three times shipwrecked, 12 months a prisoner of war and four times blown up," and had actually lived to tell about it.[1]

Shaw, as readers of his autobiography learn, had arrived in Kentucky in 1791 after being discharged from the American army in Ohio. Because he had not received his pay, Shaw set out from Fort Washington (Cincinnati) a near penniless man. In these straitened circumstances, he had no choice but to work "for my victuals and whatever other compensation my employer thought proper." Performing odd jobs in exchange for a shirt and a pair of shoes, he quickly graduated into the business of blasting rock for wells. At this, he had some experience; in Pennsylvania the ability "to hunt water . . . got [Shaw] the name of a water witch." He expected this talent would be much appreciated in Kentucky, whose springs and streams could not meet the water needs of the tens of thousands of pioneers then settling the Bluegrass region.[2]

His well-digging and blasting skills were indeed in much demand, but Shaw did not yet own the tools of his trade. That made him a "dependent," which, on the Kentucky frontier in the 1790s, was an unenvied, though not uncommon, status for an adult man. As a dependent, Shaw was vulnerable to the whims of his employers. Sure enough, his first Kentucky contractor "endeavored to defraud" him. "Considering half a loaf better than no bread," Shaw unhappily accepted partial payment and moved on to Lexington where he hoped to find better times. In Lexington, which was just then establishing itself as the principal town in Kentucky, he found work quarrying stone for a tavern keeper. Once again, the wages were low, and his employer "strove by every means in his power to take advantage of me."[3]

Shaw's woes were just beginning. In an inadvertent explosion, he was left for dead, but recovered. Shortly after returning to well-digging, Shaw was blown up once more. Miraculously, he emerged unscathed, save for some splinters. But he was not so fortunate the next time; after a poorly timed blast, Shaw's "brains [were] running out," and he lay senseless for twenty-one hours before his Lazarus-like luck returned.[4]

Having survived the avarice of his employers and the hazards of his occupation, Shaw fared less well in his battles with "bottle fever." Drinking induced visions that aided divining, or so Shaw contended. More important, it steadied nerves. Given the dangers, it is not surprising that Shaw imbibed corn whiskey—both on the job and off. But on many occasions, inebriation separated Shaw from his senses. Often, he brawled. Sometimes, he bargained. The latter was truly costly, for drunkenness repeatedly robbed Shaw of his business acumen. Seeking to avoid any future mistakes, he placed an advertisement in the *Kentucky Gazette* warning persons "from crediting me when intoxicated by liquor, as I am determined not to discharge contracts in such cases."[5]

Yet Shaw persevered and prospered, at least economically. Guaranteeing that he would find water if he were allowed "choice of place," Shaw promised to "take nothing for labor" if he failed. The ploy evidently worked. After a decade in Kentucky, he had saved enough money to buy a farm in Shelby County, land-ownership being the usual course by which a man established his independence. But farm life bored Shaw, and he soon moved back to Lexington, where his business flourished. Shaw was now an employer, immensely proud of his ability "to hire as many hands as I wanted." With the handsome profits of his trade, he acquired a five-acre quarry near Lexington, as well as a couple of pairs of oxen, a cart, and a wagon. In his autobiography, Shaw estimated his worth at an impressive four thousand dollars—gained over the previous fifteen years by the sweat of his brow and at the cost of one eye, five fingers, and seven toes.[6]

What, then, does Shaw's life tell us of his times? Beyond his singular combustibility, how unusual was his career? Were his struggles and successes typical of other Lexington residents who lived by their hands? Strictly speaking, that delineation encompassed almost all of the people passing through Lexington during Shaw's time there. Only a small minority of the inhabitants in and around Lexington qualified as gentlemen who lived entirely off the toils of their slaves and tenants. The term "hands," however, by late eighteenth- and early nineteenth-century understanding, did not include all manual laborers; property-owning farmers, for instance, did not fall into this category. Rather, hands referred more specifically to those in the employ of others—to those who were, in the parlance of the day, "dependents."

This inquiry into the expectations and experiences of dependents does not concern itself with all hands. Though women and children were by definition dependents, this essay focuses only on adult males. Females had almost no chance to escape their dependence. By contrast, men like Shaw came to Kentucky precisely because its fabled reputation promised them the opportunity to become independent, to cease being hands.[7]

In some respects, at least, the trajectory of Shaw's life conformed with broader social patterns. During the last decade of the eighteenth century and the first decade of the nineteenth, many of the white artisans and laborers who joined Shaw in Lexington found improved circumstances. Certainly, too, Shaw's taste for alcohol and his fondness for fighting were endemic practices among the company he kept.

But in other ways, Shaw's narrative deceives. Even in Lexington's boom years before the War of 1812, few hands acquired property to the extent that Shaw did. And shortly after the publication of Shaw's autobiography, the economy busted. With that postwar downturn, the fortunes of most white workingmen suffered.

For his part, Shaw blamed the competition from black labor for harder times, a sentiment likely shared by many of Lexington's white workingmen. Of course, what was unwelcome competition to Shaw offered some hope for African American hands. For black men, slave and free, employment in the households, shops, and manufactories of Lexington opened a possibility of greater independence. But through good times and bad, the opportunities for black hands were never so promising as were Shaw's.

Founded in 1779, the town of Lexington quickly became the cutting edge of trans-Appalachia's "urban frontier." In the mid-1780s, Lexington still consisted of only three rows of log cabins. But building (and population) took off in the last half of the 1780s and continued into the 1790s. By the end of the eighteenth century, the town probably consisted of one hundred houses, including some of brick. The town did not, as its promoters hoped, become the political capital of the state of Kentucky. But it reigned until the War of 1812 as the economic capital of the trans-Appalachian country, "the greatest inland city of the western world." As long as it held that status, Lexington was a land of relative opportunity.[8]

More quickly than anywhere in the "western country," Lexington shed its log cabin origins. From Lexington radiated a vibrant commercialism that captured the trade of a vast hinterland. Already, when Shaw arrived, the town boasted more than a dozen general stores, stocked with an array of briskly selling commodities. The hustle and bustle of daily life in *fin de siècle* Lexington reminded commentators of Market Street in Philadelphia. These boom times enriched at least some of the merchants of Lexington and lent an air of opulence to the "Philadelphia of the West," especially to the outskirts of town where merchants and other wealthy gentlemen built their grand brick residences. Taking note of these fashionable homes and well-groomed estates, the author of an early nineteenth-century guidebook declaimed that "nowhere in America has the almost instantaneous change, from an uncultivated waste to the elegances of civilization, been so striking" as in Lexington and its vicinity.[9]

In addition to traditional investments in conspicuous display and land speculation, Lexington merchants established enterprises that turned the town into the western country's leading manufacturing center. In 1800, five rope-making factories operated in the town whose population had reached eighteen hundred. By 1810, the population had increased to forty-three hundred, and the number of establishments in Lexington and surrounding Fayette County that made hemp into rope had risen to thirteen. Lexington and its immediate environs were also home to five manufactories devoted to the conversion of hemp into bagging for cotton. Together ropewalks and cotton bagging operations annually turned out nearly six hundred thousand dollars worth of hemp products, a forty-fold increase in a single decade.[10]

An expanding economy and a dearth of master craftsmen made Lexington an inviting place for skilled artisans, especially those who could be their own bosses—or better still, the employers of others. The good news, John Melish related after visiting Lexington in 1806, was that "industrious journeymen very soon become masters." Though opportunity and wages varied considerably between crafts, a correspondent to *Niles' Weekly Register* reported that "mechanics of all descriptions receive nearly double the price for their labor that they get to the eastward."[11]

The comparatively low cost of living in Lexington added to the town's advantages for skilled and unskilled hands. In New York and Philadelphia, the French traveler François André Michaux figured that artisans toiled four days to pay their boarding charges and meet other basic needs. In Lexington, however, where boarders paid only one to two dollars per week for room and food, single journeymen "can subsist a week with the produce of one day's labour."[12]

In his memoir, the papermaker Ebenezer Stedman recalled the turn of the century as a golden age for artisans and laborers in central Kentucky. In those years, claimed Stedman, workingmen were respected, and so was their "Good[,] Substantial work." Stedman remembered that his father, a skilled mechanic, was "looked upon as a man of more than ordinary Importance. Men of the Highest Standing Sought his acquaintance." The son waxed nostalgic for his father's day when there were "no overgrown wealthy Capitalist[s] to Screw down the wages of honest workmen & cause them to Slight their work."[13]

To be sure, the age was less golden than Stedman recollected. In a cash-poor economy, collecting payments from customers and wages from employers involved many complications. Showing his penchant for poetry, Shaw tried the whimsical approach in presenting his terms to the purchases of his well-digging services: "When the stone they all are laid, the goods and money must be paid; for I must have cash in hand, to pay my hands what they demand." Shaw knew that workingmen did not always get what they demanded, much less what they had been promised. He, after all, had been cheated on his first job in Kentucky. For men like the elder Stedman, the benefits of relatively high wages and rubbed elbows did not translate into the security that Kentucky men sought. Ownership of land, widely considered the cornerstone of personal independence, remained elusive. In fact, few turn-of-the-century artisans achieved the propertied standing that Shaw had. Inequality in the distribution of land surfaced early in Lexington, and it was more pronounced than anywhere else in Kentucky. At the end of the eighteenth century, more than three-quarters of the town's taxpayers owned no real estate. By 1805, the proportion of landowners dropped below one in five. Less than one in ten craftsmen listed in the 1806 Lexington directory owned a single acre.[14]

For landless men especially, chronic underemployment heightened the insecurities of dependence and gave Lexington life a transient character. In many crafts, seasonal or sporadic employment frequently idled workers. For occupations requiring waterpower, in which Lexington was notably deficient, itinerance became a necessity. When the paper mill in which Ebenezer Stedman and his father worked shut for want of flowing water, the two, along with other papermakers, hit the road. Father and son traveled on foot from mill to mill all the way to Ohio, hoping to find enough work to avoid starvation. Back in Lexington, the younger Stedman found temporary residence in a boarding house. Though rates were affordable, the nickname of the house, "Cold Comfort," suggested the meager accommodations and monotonous fare that transients endured. No wonder many boarders turned to the bottle for warmth and solace. According to Ebenezer Stedman, men "thought they could not work without whiskey."[15]

Nor, he might have added, did men think they could play without alcohol. To judge from Shaw's and Stedman's memoirs, drinking saturated the days and nights of Lexington workingmen. Corn whiskey lubricated their working lives and animated the rough play that workingmen favored. Their spirits raised, Lexington's hands mocked those who sought to take away their liquor and tenderize their tough manhood.[16]

Chief among the critics of the drinking and general roughness of Lexington workingmen were the country's clergy. Indeed, while clergymen encountered menacing men in all corners of Kentucky, they thought the concentration of heathens greatest at the center, in Lexington. As the revival of 1801 gained momentum in the surrounding Bluegrass countryside, "poor L[exingto]n" remained "this Sodom," its inhabitants scornful of evangelical entreaties. The events at Cane Ridge, where more than ten thousand gathered in August 1801, did become the talk of the town in late summer; it did not, however, make evangelists any more welcome. In October, a revival meeting drew about four thousand people, twice Lexington's population. But the carnivalesque appeal of the assembly seemed, in this instance, a primary attraction. The crowd, according to the Presbyterian minister John Lyle, was "very disorderly." Rowdy men taunted the few who fell and drunkenly mocked the gesticulations of preachers.[17]

After the outpouring of religious enthusiasm in 1801, the lives of Lexington's workingmen remained unreformed. True, revivalism made some inroads. After a "singular dream" in which a voice warned him to repent, John Robert Shaw joined the Methodist church and swore off strong drink. His conversion, though, was short-lived. Blaming the "religious controversies [that] began to disseminate in this the dawning of my spiritual salvation," Shaw explained away "the backsliding of a number with myself." While sectarian rivalry accounted for some of the reversions, the defection of Shaw (and thousands of others) owed more to the continuing hold of secular attractions. In the years following the Great Revival, expulsions for betting, dancing, drinking, defrauding, swearing, fighting, fornicating, and the catch-all "immoral conduct" dominated church records. Some of these transgressions obviously required men and women, yet exclusions often pertained to conduct—gambling, drinking, fighting, and swearing—that were distinguishing attributes of rough manhood. Consequently, disciplinary actions involved far more men than women, and backsliding left churches with many more female than male members. That imbalance reflected the difficulties of workingmen in adapting to an evangelical culture that exalted tenderness over toughness.[18]

Touring Lexington in 1806, the Englishman Thomas Ashe found profane customs the order of the day. To Ashe's dismay, the men of Lexington treated the Sabbath as a day to give "loose to their dispositions and exhibit many traits that should exclusively belong to savages." Two years later, the Presbyterian minister Joshua Wilson concurred that Lexington was still home to "the blackest atheism," a place filled with "boasters" and "blasphemers." But what Ashe and Wilson found so objectionable were to white workingmen the signature of an imperfect, but still on later reflection, golden age.[19]

The gilding began to crack shortly after the publication of Shaw's narrative, but the full impact of the economic slump was not felt until the end of the War of 1812. That downturn in the Lexington economy injured both rich and poor. But working people, who lived nearer the margins of subsistence, suffered the greater privations. In these hard times, white artisans and laborers faced threats to their livelihoods and to their ways of life.

A decline in hemp prices beginning in 1809 signaled trouble ahead and spurred Bluegrass planters and Lexington merchants to call for protection against foreign rope. The war, which temporarily removed British competition, suspended the tariff campaign mounted by Lexington's congressional representative, Henry Clay. The war also briefly restored at least the appearance of prosperity. By 1814, however, Lexington merchant-manufacturers complained anew of "gloomy" prospects. Peace brought a flood of cheap British goods, deepening the crisis for Lexington manufactories. The hemp industry suffered a terrible blow from which it never fully recovered. By the middle of 1815, all fourteen ropewalks in Lexington had shut down. Most did not reopen or resumed operation on a much smaller scale. In other industries, a similar contraction occurred. By 1819, factories in the vicinity of Lexington representing five hundred thousand dollars in capital investment were idled. The manufacturing census of 1820 revealed the magnitude of the depression in Lexington. Discontinued or drastically diminished operations characterized virtually every industry.[20]

The simultaneous collapse in commercial volume amplified the severity of Lexington's postwar plummet. The proliferation of steamboats on western waters after the War of 1812 doomed inland Lexington's reign as the entrêpot of the Ohio Valley. Regional trade formerly handled by Lexington merchants shifted to the river cities of Cincinnati and Louisville. To stem the decline, Lexington merchants launched canal proposals and lobbied anew for government encouragement of domestic manufactures. Henry Clay heard the call of his most influential constituents and stepped up his campaign to obtain federal funding of internal improvements. Even had these efforts of Clay's succeeded, Lexington's pre-steamboat preeminence was gone forever.[21]

Investments in lands in and around Lexington partially insulated merchants and manufacturers from the shock of failing industries and languishing commerce. Fueled by the liberal loan policies of western banks, speculation in trans-Appalachian lands reached a frenzy in the years after the War of 1812. Across the Ohio Valley, land values skyrocketed, with the most exorbitant bids recorded for urban real estate. In Lexington, land prices climbed as high as four hundred dollars per acre. For wealthy investors, who reaped a bonanza from the sale of Lexington lots, the tremendous increase in property values postponed the impact of the economic downturn.[22]

Workingmen had no cushion against the postwar crash. The closing of manufactories and the decrease in trade threw hundreds of mechanics out of work. Land speculation permitted merchant-manufacturers to maintain a genteel standard of living, but "poor people," acknowledged one manager of a hemp manufactory, had "great difficulties in making a living for their families."[23]

Nor did the reopening of some manufacturing operations restore prewar conditions for Lexington's free workforce. Snapping up bankrupt enterprises at reduced prices made good sense to merchant-manufacturers with bank notes to spare. After the cotton and woolen factory built by Lewis Sanders at a reported cost of $150,000 defaulted on bank loans in 1816, a group of merchant-manufacturers purchased the property at the bargain price of $21,000. But the new board of directors understood that returning the Sanders property to profitability required changes in management, changes that would alter the circumstances and composition of the labor force. Before resuming operation, the directors hired George Lockebie to restructure the organization of the factory.[24]

Lockebie forwarded a remarkably prescient proposal in February 1818. In his report, Lockebie invoked time-honored cliches, urging the directors to operate the plant with the "utmost economy," reminding them that the "loss of time is loss of profit." This was standard advice, repeated endlessly in every country almanac. What was new in Lockebie's exposition were the details of his plan to minimize waste and maximize economy. Likening a factory to "a busy hive," Lockebie maintained that it was crucial to arrange operations so "that no part may be standing still on account of another part having fallen behind." His vision of an integrated workplace, in which each operative performed a specific task, went far beyond the decidedly unscientific management that had been the rule in Lexington craft shops and manufactories. To make the enterprise function "with as much precision as a military corps," Lockebie advocated closer supervision of all hands. Denying the humanity of the labor force, the manager argued that a tardy or absent worker "ought to be dismissed as [a] piece of machinery that does not answer the ends proposed." Lockebie also advised the directors to open a store convenient to the manufactory to "obviate the necessity of paying all the wages in ready cash" and to augment the control that employers exerted over their employees.[25]

These intentions challenged the traditions of Lexington workingmen, as did the Sunday school that the new managers established for their hands. Still, organized resistance was slow to develop. While master craftsmen often cooperated to fix prices, ordinary mechanics mounted just one effort to raise wages through collective action. In 1811, twenty-one journeymen cordwainers banded together to protest unfair wages. At a meeting in February of that year, the assembled shoemakers resolved not to work for any master paying substandard wages nor to associate with any journeyman violating the accord.[26]

Low persistence rates, however, made enforcement of a compact among Bluegrass journeymen difficult in the best of times; maintaining those standards became impossible when the economy of Lexington slid after the War of 1812. Hard times intensified transience. Just 51 of the 138 craftsmen enumerated in the town's 1806 directory were still carrying on the same business twelve years later when an updated volume was published. And the persistent minority tended to be master craftsmen who had already graduated to the top of the artisanal hierarchy and who were far more likely to own property.[27]

The majority of ordinary mechanics and day laborers moved on. Many undoubtedly sought employment in the river cities that had supplanted Lexington as places of relative opportunity. Those who stayed behind struggled to get by in the uncertain present. And had they read Lockebie's confidential prescription for industrial recovery, most would have shuddered for the future in which dehumanized employees were to do as they were told, in which hands were to have no minds of their own.

Lockebie's vision of the future workplace made no mention of slavery. That was odd, for slaves were an established and growing part of the Lexington labor system. From farm to factory, the cultivation of hemp and its conversion into rope and bagging material fell increasingly to African Americans. Slaves came to dominate Lexington's leading industries, sparking friction between white and black hands.

Unfriendly competition between slave and free labor dated to the first settlement of Lexington and the surrounding Bluegrass countryside. During the 1780s gentry landowners typically sent dependents ahead to do the hazardous and arduous tasks of pioneering—to take possession of tracts, clear fields, construct fences, and raise shelters. A typical practice among absentee owners was to lease tracts to landless men and their families. Leasing kept squatters off property, and the improvements made by tenants enhanced the value of claims. Still, the precarious situation of the Kentucky frontier, added to the usual difficulties of opening a farmstead, necessitated that generous terms be offered to renters; typically, tenants negotiated agreements that deferred payments for the first year or two of a four- or five-year lease and kept subsequent rents relatively light. From this perspective, slave labor was attractive, for African American hands lacked the bargaining power of free (and armed) tenants. Some slaveholders expressed misgivings about the practice of putting their slaves in danger. One agonized about the morality of "send[ing] a parcel of poor slaves where I dare not go myself." But this master, like other slaveholders, reconciled himself to having slaves smooth the way for his family.[28]

Competition from slaves did not sit well with landless white men. They had not come to Kentucky to be tenants, no matter how generous the terms of dependence. They had expected that tenancy would be a brief station, a steppingstone to landowning independence. Slaves, however, curtailed the opportunities of tenants, and that recognition alone inspired broad opposition to the introduction of unfree laborers into central Kentucky. In constitutional conventions, legislative assemblies, and (most important) church pulpits, opponents of slavery spoke of the immorality of holding people in bondage. But among white hands fear of displacement spoke louder than spiritual concerns. Antislavery appealed to propertyless men who anticipated that elimination of unfree competitors would encourage the breakup of large plantations and improve tenants' chances to acquire lands of their own.[29]

Opponents of slave labor, however, lost their battles and, in many cases, made their peace. Instead of prohibiting slavery, the state's constitutions of 1792 and 1799 explicitly protected the property of slaveholders. That the second constitution upheld slavery was especially noteworthy, for opposition to slavery galvanized the movement for constitutional revision. Unlike the 1792 charter, the new constitution was to be drafted by delegates elected by the voters of the state. Given that three-quarters of the electorate owned no slaves, emancipationists expected that they would win the majority of seats. But the returns represented a decisive setback for antislavery candidates. Without reading too much into these results, it is clear that many nonslaveholding voters abandoned the antislavery cause. Part of the explanation may lie in the rising percentage of landholders during the 1790s, which abated the competition between tenants and slaves. At the same time, the percentage of slaveholders also edged upward. More important, while only about one in four households counted black hands among their property, this statistic caused the pervasiveness of slavery to be underestimated. Many farmers, for example, chose to "hire out" slaves on a seasonal or annual basis. These short-term arrangements permitted small farmers and even tenants to take advantage of otherwise unaffordable slave labor. By turning unfree labor from competitor to contributor, hiring out won slavery support from nonslaveholders and gained the system a more secure base.[30]

Hiring out was prevalent in town as well as countryside. Renting slaves allowed employers flexibility to expand and contract their labor force in response to changing demand. One-year contracts were typical, but shorter terms were also occasionally negotiated.[31]

Lexington manufacturers eagerly seized the advantages of owning and hiring slave labor. At one cotton bagging factory employing between sixty and one hundred "negroes of all ages," a skeptical observer came away impressed with the performance of the laborers, who showed "more skill in the management of their machinery than I had supposed the slaves possessed."[32]

Work in cotton bagging factories and ropewalks offered opportunities to slaves, for whom the experience sometimes brought "a taste of freedom." In contrast to plantation overseers, factory supervisors downplayed coercive methods in favor of a task system with daily quotas. To motivate hands to meet and exceed their minimums, managers paid bonuses for any "overwork." According to a New England visitor to a Lexington hemp manufactory, the incentive stimulated the ambition of slaves and left them "happier" than any "set of workmen" he had ever seen. Without hesitation, the New Englander affirmed that "there is more health, wealth, strength and happiness, more real freedom of body, and quite as much independence of mind among the slaves of Kentucky, as there is in Blackburn, Sheffield, Birmingham or Paisley."[33]

For slaves who turned their taste of freedom into something permanent, work in Lexington shops provided an unparalleled opportunity. Buying freedom was an expensive proposition. Before manumitting slaves, owners received all of the annual hiring-out fees. Masters also exacted up to one thousand dollars in over-work earnings, though the market value of adult bondsmen did not approach that level. Accumulating that sum of money took slaves years of overtime toil. Even then, nothing was certain, for chattel had no recourse against masters who forgot or broke promises of emancipation. Yet some slaves were diligent—and lucky; in a handful of instances, the most fortunate amassed enough savings to free spouses and children, too.[34]

Unfortunately, very few tasted this kind of legal freedom. In 1800, Lexington's "free blacks" numbered only twenty-three, little more than 1 percent of the town's population. By contrast, Lexington's slave census was 439. Over the next decade, the number of free blacks jumped to 85, but this figure represented less than 2 percent of the town's population and was dwarfed by the 1,509 African Americans who were then enslaved. By 1820, the free black community counted 115 persons, but the proportions remained about the same.[35]

Through these years free blacks found their freedom severely constrained. Lacking the capital or credit to start businesses of their own, free black men expected that they would have to continue to work for others. Nonetheless, according to one visitor to Lexington, they tried to avoid jobs as waiters and valets, which reminded them of servility. But in a world of limited employment choices, most settled for whatever day-laboring jobs were available.[36]

Always they were the subjects of repression and surveillance. Legal and extralegal pressures encouraged manumitted slaves to leave Kentucky and prevented "free Negroes and Mulattoes" from migrating to Kentucky. Those who stayed confronted a host of discriminations. While the 1792 constitution permitted free blacks to vote, its 1799 successor disfranchised them. It also deprived them of their right to bear arms and serve in the militia. Additional legislation curtailed the ability of free blacks to assemble and required them to observe curfews that made no distinction between free and enslaved. These distinctions were further blurred by laws ordering free blacks to carry certificates attesting to their status and employment, and by Lexington's night watchmen, who vigorously enforced vagrancy statutes.[37]

Suspicion, surveillance, and harassment intensified whenever a crime was unsolved or a rumor of a slave insurrection circulated. News in 1800 of "Gabriel's Conspiracy" in Richmond, Virginia, prompted Lexington's trustees to reinstate the patrols of night watchmen. Ten years later, the discovery of a supposed plot involving free and enslaved blacks in Lexington sent whites into "an uproar," renewing demands for better policing. Talk of closer regulation, if not elimination, of hiring out also followed, for the practice was said to give slaves too much freedom.[38]

A rash of fires that consumed nine manufactories in Lexington in the half-dozen years before the War of 1812 added to the fears of white residents. The hemp works owned by John Wesley Hunt, the richest of the town's merchant-manufacturers, was victimized by incendiaries twice in less than five years. On the first occasion in November 1807, a hired slave boy was convicted of arson. In January 1812, a second fire caused twenty thousand dollars' worth of damage to the rebuilt factory. The same week three other blazes damaged Lexington manufacturing establishments. Within two weeks of the conflagrations, two male slaves under fifteen charged with torching Hunt's establishment were sentenced to be hanged. Citing the age of the convicts, the governor commuted the sentences. The reprieve outraged manufacturers, who saw it as sending the message that "boys may burn houses with impunity."[39]

Of course, the guilt of those convicted was by no means certain. True, the fires may have been the actions of the accused. Slaves and free blacks, after all, resisted as they could. For slaves, flight was the most direct form of protest, but smaller and less overt acts of defiance were more common. In manufactories, hired slaves sometimes resisted efforts to speed their work. Complaints by factory managers of slaves "falling behind" indicated that enslaved black laborers, like their free white counterparts, slowed the pace of work to a schedule of their own and not their employers' choosing. Whether the convicted arsonists intended to strike a bigger blow against an oppressive regime, we do not know, for the record omits their views.[40]

We do know, however, not to trust the verdicts of Kentucky juries in cases such as this. The factories that burned employed large numbers of slaves and few free laborers. These operations exemplified the displacement of white by black labor. Thus, they stirred the animosity of white mechanics, who believed that any opportunities enjoyed by slaves (or free blacks) came at the expense of white workers who were not hired. Such thinking was deeply ingrained among white hands. Nothing, summarized the *Kentucky Gazette*, rankled these men more than the sight of slaves "clad in better attire than honest white persons who labour for their living." A verse in one of John Robert Shaw's advertisements put the resentment of white workers almost in rhyme: "The great men are determin'd/ All the negroes to have/ To work in their factories/ The poor men to starve."[41]

Two years after the appearance of this advertisement and six years after the publication of John Robert Shaw's autobiography, his luck ran out. On August 30, 1813, Shaw was blown up a fifth time. The accident occurred in Lexington at the bottom of the well of one Robert Wilson, and there Shaw died. The *Lexington Reporter* carried a brief account of the incident, which concluded with a one-sentence tribute to the deceased: "He was an honest, industrious citizen of Lexington for twenty years."[42]

Figuratively, Shaw's fortunes resembled those of other Lexington workingmen. While Shaw's rise took him further than other dependents and his demise was more tragic, the trajectory of his career mirrored the fate of Lexington's hands. His twenty-two years in Lexington coincided with the town's most spectacular growth. Life was rough, but the favorable economic climate of the era enabled Shaw to ascend from rags to respectability. Likewise, Lexington in those years provided skilled mechanics and even unskilled laborers with advantages unknown to hands in towns to the east. Shaw's death, however, came at a time of increasing economic trouble for Lexington's hands. As commercial traffic shifted away from inland Lexington and hemp manufactories closed their doors, workingmen lamented the good times gone.

Even before the economic climate soured, Shaw scapegoated African American hands. In this, he was hardly alone. Across the neighboring Bluegrass countryside and far beyond, the most vulnerable of white men had long vented their rage against even more vulnerable slaves and free blacks. For enslaved men, hiring out, a cornerstone of the Lexington economy, promised some relief from the most extreme rage of their masters and from the most abject dependence. But discrimination, intimidation, and injustice usually betrayed the hopes of the hired-out and too often left free blacks free in name only.

Notes

1. *Lexington Kentucky Gazette*, 27 November 1806.

2. Quoted in Odessa M. Teagarden and Jeanne L. Crabtree, eds., *John Robert Shaw: An Autobiography of Thirty Years, 1777-1807* (Athens: Ohio Univ. Press, 1992), 119, 128.

3. Ibid., 129.

4. Ibid., 147.

5. Ibid., 129; *Kentucky Gazette*, 20 June 1798. See also the advertisement, "Answer a Fool according to his folly," in which one of Shaw's critics had his own poetic say about drinking and divining; *Lexington Independent Gazetteer*, 15 February 1805.

6. Teagarden and Crabtree, *John Robert Shaw*, 146; Shaw advertisement in *Independent Gazetteer*, 19 October 1804.

7. On Kentucky's reputation as a promised land of patriarchal independence, see Stephen Aron, *How the West Was Lost: The Transformation of Kentucky from Daniel Boone to Henry Clay* (Baltimore: Johns Hopkins Univ. Press, 1996), 64-73; Patricia J. Watlington, *The Partisan Spirit: Kentucky Politics, 1779-1792* (New York: Atheneum, 1972), 3-34.

8. *Niles' Weekly Register*, 28 January 1815. For more on the settlement and early economic development of Lexington, see Lee Shai Weissbach, "The Peopling of Lexington, Kentucky: Growth and Mobility in a Frontier Town," *Register of the Kentucky Historical Society* 81 (1983): 115-33; Bernard Mayo, "Lexington: Frontier Metropolis," in *Historiography and Urbanization: Essays in Honor of W. Stull Holt*, ed. Eric F. Goldman (Port Washington, N.Y.: Kennikat Press, 1968), 21-42; Charles R. Staples, *The History of Pioneer Lexington, 1779-1806*, rev. ed. (Lexington: Univ. of Kentucky Press, 1996); Richard C. Wade, *The Urban Frontier: Pioneer Life in Early Pittsburgh, Cincinnati, Lexington, Louisville, and St. Louis* (Chicago: Univ. of Chicago Press, 1959); George W. Ranck, *History of Lexington, Kentucky: Its Early Annals and Recent Progress including Biographical Sketches and Personal Reminiscences of the Pioneering Settlers, Notes of Prominent Citizens, Etc., Etc.* (Cincinnati: Robert Clarke, 1872); J. Winston Coleman, Jr., *The Squire's Sketches of Lexington* (Lexington: Henry Clay Press, 1972), 19-26; Craig T. Friend, "Inheriting Eden: The Creation of Society and Community in Early Kentucky, 1792-1812" (Ph.D. diss., University of Kentucky, 1995), 180-223.

9. William Darby, *The Emigrant's Guide to the Western and Southwestern States and Territories* (New York: Kirk and Mercein, 1818), 206. For other witnesses to Lexington's boom times, see Nedham Parry Diary, 1794, John Lyman Draper Manuscript Collection 14CC2, State Historical Society of Wisconsin, Madison; Bayard Still, ed., "The Westward Migration of a Planter Pioneer in 1796," *William and Mary Quarterly*, 2d ser., 21 (1941): 343; Lewis Condict, "Journal of a Trip to Kentucky in 1795," *Proceedings of the New Jersey Historical Society* 4 (1919): 120; John Shane Interview with John Coons, Draper Manuscript Collection, 12CC130; John Melish, *Travels in the United States of America in the Years 1806 and 1807, and 1809, 1810, and 1811*, 2 vols. (Philadelphia: Thomas and George Palmer, 1812), 2: 185; Josiah Murdoch Espy, *Memorandums of a Tour Made by Josiah Espy in the States of Ohio and Kentucky and Indiana Territory in 1805* (Cincinnati: Robert Clarke, 1871), 8; John Breathitt, "Commencement of a Journal from Kentucky to the State of Pennsylvania," *Register of the Kentucky Historical Society* 52 (1954): 7-8; Fortescue Cuming, *Sketches of a Tour to the Western Country, through the States of Ohio and Kentucky*, in *Early Western Travels, 1748-1846*, ed. R.G. Thwaites, 32 vols. (Cleveland: Arthur H. Clark, 1904-1907), 4: 183-88; James McBride, "Journey to Lexington, Kentucky by James McBride of Hamilton, Ohio, Related in Letter to Margaret Poe, 1810," *Quarterly Publications of the Historical and Philosophical Society of Ohio* 5 (1910): 20-25; Edward S. Joynes, ed., "Memoranda Made by Thomas R. Joynes on a Journey to the States of Ohio and Kentucky, 1810," *William and Mary Quarterly*, 1st ser., 10 (1902): 225; "Kentucky Manufactures, Extract of a Letter from a Gentleman in Lexington, Ken. to His Friend in Charleston, S.C., Dated May 1, 1810," in *Travels in the Old South: Selected from Periodicals of the Time*, ed. Eugene L. Schwaab, 2 vols. (Lexington: Univ. of Kentucky Press, 1973), 1: 66-67.

10. *Lexington Kentucky Gazette*, 12 April 1794, 18 September 1810, 19 February 1811;

William Leavy, "A Memoir of Lexington and Its Vicinity," *Register of the Kentucky Historical Society* 40 (1942): 118-19, 259-60, 374; Tench Coxe, comp., *A Statement of the Arts and Manufactures of the United States of America for the Year 1810* (Philadelphia: A. Cornman, 1814), 121-28; James F. Hopkins, "A History of the Hemp Industry in Kentucky" (M.A. thesis, University of Kentucky, 1938), 57-70.

11. Melish, *Travels in the United States*, 188; *Niles' Weekly Register*, 28 January 1815.

12. Francois André Michaux, *Travels to the West of the Alleghany Mountains, in the States of Ohio, Kentucky, and Tennessee, and Back to Charleston, by the Upper Carolines*, in Thwaites, *Early Western Travels*, 3: 201; Ida Earle Fowler, ed., "Kentucky 150 Years Ago as Seen through the Eyes of an English Emigrant Told in Two Letters Written by Henry Alderson, Dated September 10, 1801," *Register of the Kentucky Historical Society* 49 (1951): 56; Melish, *Travels in the United States of America*, 2: 181; *Niles' Weekly Register*, 11 June 1814; Margaret M. Bridwell, "Kentucky Silversmiths before 1850," *Filson Club History Quarterly* 46 (1942): 114; Frances L.S. Dugan and Jacqueline P. Bull, eds., *Bluegrass Craftsman: Being the Reminiscences of Ebenezer Hiram Stedman, Papermaker, 1808-1885* (Lexington: Univ. of Kentucky Press, 1959), 20-21.

13. Dugan and Bull, *Bluegrass Craftsman*, 14, 23.

14. Shaw advertisement in *Lexington Kentucky Gazette*, 12 March 1811. Of 267 taxpayers in 1797, 65 (24.3 percent) owned land. The median holding was 1,093 acres. In 1805, tax lists showed 415 taxpayers in Lexington, of which 77 (18.6 percent) owned land. The acreage owned by Lexington taxpayers totaled 257,274 acres. The 6 largest landowners, all of whom possessed at least 10,000 acres, paid taxes on 164,564 acres. The 42 taxpayers with the largest land holdings owned over 250,000 acres. Figures calculated from Fayette County Tax List, 1797, 1805, Kentucky Historical Society, Frankfort, microfilm. One hundred five craftsmen listed in *Lexington Directory, Taken for Charless' Almanac for 1806*, Special Collections, Margaret I. King Library, University of Kentucky, Lexington, also appeared in the Fayette County Tax List for 1805. Of these 105 artisans, 10 owned land. Except for one silversmith with holdings of 1,499 acres, all of the other artisan-landowners claimed less than 300 acres.

15. Dugan and Bull, *Bluegrass Craftsman*, 40; also see 41-45, 103-4.

16. On the evangelicals' challenge to "rough" manhood, see Christopher Waldrep, "The Making of a Border State Society: James McGready, the Great Revival, and the Prosecution of Profanity in Kentucky," *American Historical Review* 99 (1994): 767-84.

17. Quoted in "Extract of a Letter from a Gentleman to His Friend at the City of Washington, Dated Lexington, Kentucky, 9 March 1801," in *Religion on the American Frontier: The Baptists, 1783-1830*, ed. William Warren Sweet (New York: H. Holt, 1931), 610; John Lyle Diary, 1801-3, Kentucky Historical Society, 51; Joshua L. Wilson to Mrs. Sally Wilson, 14 March 1808, Joshua L. Wilson Papers, Reuben Durrett Collection, University of Chicago Library. For more on origins, spread, and significance of the Great Revival in Kentucky, see Paul Conkin, *Cane Ridge: America's Pentecost* (Madison: Univ. of Wisconsin Press, 1990); James S. Dalton, "The Kentucky Camp Meeting Revivals of 1797-1805 as Rites of Initiation" (Ph.D. diss., University of Chicago, 1973); John D. Boles, *The Great Revival, 1797-1805: The Origins of the Southern Evangelical Mind* (Lexington: Univ. Press of Kentucky, 1972); Ellen T. Eslinger, "The Great Revival in Bourbon County, Kentucky" (Ph.D. diss., University of Chicago, 1988).

18. Teagarden and Crabtree, *John Robert Shaw*, 4. On "backsliding," see Fred J. Hood, "Restoration of Community: The Great Revival in Four Baptist Churches in Central Kentucky," *Quarterly Review* 39 (1978), 73-83; Aron, *How the West Was Lost*, 184-89.

19. Thomas Ashe, *Travels in America, Performed in 1806, for the Purpose of Exploring the Rivers Alleghany, Monongahela, Ohio, and Mississippi, and Ascertaining the Produce and Condition of Their Banks and Vicinity* (London: E.M. Blunt, 1808), 191; Joshua L. Wilson to Mrs. Sally Wilson, 14 March 1808, James L. Wilson Papers.

20. *The Memorial of the Mechanics and Manufacturers of Lexington, Kentucky, to Congress* (Washington, D.C.: R.C. Weightman, 1811); John Brown to Margaretta Brown, 10 March 1811, John Mason Brown Family Papers, Special Collections, University of Kentucky; William A. Leavy, "A Memoir of Lexington and Its Vicinity," *Register of the Kentucky State Historical Society* 41 (1943): 317-18; William Barry to Catherine A. Barry, 20 February 1815, William Taylor Barry Letters, Manuscripts Division, Filson Club, Louisville; James Weir to John Henderson, 28 October 1814, Draper Manuscript Collection, 21CC113; Weir to Bartlett and Cox, 22 December 1814, Draper Manuscript Collection, 21CC118; Weir to Adams, Knox, and Nixon, 1 June 1815, Draper Manuscript Collection, 21CC126; Weir to Henderson, 25 July 1816, Draper Manuscript Collection, 22CC2-3; Weir to John P. Pleasants, 2 February 1817, Draper Manuscript Collection, 22CC19; Weir to Henderson, 6 December 1817, Draper Manuscript Collection, 22CC248; *Kentucky Gazette*, 7 May 1819; *Digest of Accounts of Manufacturing Establishment in the United States and of Their Manufactures* (Washington, D.C.: n.p., 1823), 24-25.

21. *Kentucky Gazette*, 23 August 1817, 11 October 1817, 30 April 1818; Mayo, "Lexington," 21-42; Wade, *The Urban Frontier*, 169; Aron, *How the West Was Lost*, 133-39.

22. Leavy, "A Memoir of Lexington," 126-27, 318; Samuel R. Brown, *The Western Gazetteer; or Emigrants Directory* (Auburn, N.Y.: H.C. Southwick, 1817), 94; Stuart Seely Sprague, "Town Making in the Era of Good Feelings: Kentucky, 1814-1820," *Register of the Kentucky Historical Society* 72 (1974): 337-41; Wade, *The Urban Frontier*, 170.

23. John Brand to Father and Mother, 24 January 1820, John Brand Letterbooks, Special Collections, University of Kentucky, microfilm; John Brown to Orlando Brown, 14 March 1820, Brown Family Papers; John Palmer, *Journal of Travels in the United States of North America, and in Lower Canada, Performed in the Year 1817* (London: Sherwood, Neely, and Jones, 1818), 105-8.

24. *Kentucky Gazette*, 7 May 1819; Dale Maurice Royalty, "Banking, Politics, and the Commonwealth: Kentucky, 1800-1825" (Ph.D. diss., University of Kentucky, 1971), 203-4.

25. George Lockebie to the Directors of the Sanders Manufacturing Company, 14 February 1818, Sanders Family Papers, Manuscripts Division, Filson Club, Louisville.

26. *Kentucky Gazette*, 17 September 1819, 26 March 1796, 21 August 1810, 26 February 1811, 5 March 1811.

27. The persistence figure was calculated by comparing the names in the *Lexington Directory, Taken for Charless' Almanac for 1806* with those in *Directory for 1818 of the Town of Lexington, Kentucky, from Worsley and Smith's Almanac*, Special Collections, University of Kentucky.

28. Thomas Hart to Nathaniel Hart, 3 August 1780, in "Shane Collection of Documents: The Hart Papers," *Journal of the Presbyterian Historical Society* 14 (1931): 343-44.

On tenancy, see Fredrika J. Teute, "Land, Liberty, and Labor in the Post-Revolutionary Era: Kentucky as the Promised Land" (Ph.D. diss., Johns Hopkins University, 1988), 207-12.

29. On antislavery as a political, religious, and social movement, see Asa Earl Martin, *The Anti-Slavery Movement in Kentucky prior to 1850* (Louisville: Standard Printing, 1918); Jeffrey Brooke Allen, "Were Southern White Critics of Slavery Racists? Kentucky and the Upper South, 1791-1824," *Journal of Southern History* 44 (1978): 169-90; Aron, *How the West Was Lost*, 89-95.

30. Joan Wells Coward, *Kentucky in the New Republic: The Process of Constitution Making* (Lexington: Univ. Press of Kentucky, 1979), 63; Marion B. Lucas, *A History of Blacks in Kentucky: Volume 1: From Slavery to Segregation, 1760-1891* (Frankfort: Kentucky Historical Society, 1992), xv-xvi, 101-7; Ellen Eslinger, "The Shape of Slavery on the Kentucky Frontier, 1775-1800," *Register of the Kentucky Historical Society* 92 (1994): 1-23. As Daniel Drake remembered, his "father never purchased a slave for two substantial reasons: *first*, he had not the means; & *second*, [he] was so opposed to slavery that he would not have accepted the best negro in Kentucky." But "now & then," when family labor was insufficient, "he hired one" from a neighboring slaveholder. Renting slaves, it seemed, was amenable to antislavery men of pliant principles; Daniel Drake, *Pioneer Life in Kentucky, 1785-1800*, ed. Emmet Field Horine (New York: Henry Schuman, 1948), 93.

31. James McBride, "Journey to Lexington, Kentucky by James McBride of Hamilton, Ohio, Related in Letter to Margaret Poe, 1810," *Quarterly Publication of the Historical and Philosophical Society of Ohio* 5 (1910): 24-25; Agreement between John Wesley Hunt and John Brand, 5 January 1803, John Wesley Hunt Papers, Manuscripts Division, Transylvania University Library, Lexington; James A. Ramage, *John Wesley Hunt: Pioneer, Merchant, Manufacturer, and Financier* (Lexington: Univ. Press of Kentucky, 1974), 61; Lucas, *A History of Blacks in Kentucky*, 8-11.

32. *Louisville Daily Journal*, 29 November 1830, Manuscripts Division, Filson Club; McBride, "Journey to Lexington, 24-25.

33. Lewis Clarke, "Leaves from a Slave's Journal of Life," in *Slave Testimony: Two Centuries of Letters, Speeches, Interviews, and Autobiographies*, ed. John W. Blassingame, (Baton Rouge: Louisiana State Univ. Press, 1977), 152; *Daily Journal*, 29 November 1830; J. Winston Coleman Jr., "John W. Coleman: Early Kentucky Hemp Manufacturer," *Filson Club History Quarterly* 24 (1950): 40-42; Clement Eaton, "Slave-Hiring in the Upper South: A Step Toward Freedom," *Mississippi Valley Historical Review* 46 (1960): 663-78.

34. See, for example, the interviews with Tab Gross, Lewis Smith, Washington Spradling, and Mrs. Lewis Bibb in Blassingame, *Slave Testimony*, 346-53, 385-86, 446. See also the manumission agreements in Michael L. Cook and Bettie A. Cook, eds., *Fayette County Kentucky Records*, 5 vols. (Evansville, Ind.: Cook Publications, 1985), 2: 19-20, 118, 302, 349, 368. For the exceptional biography of one Kentucky slave who managed to purchase the freedom of sixteen family members, see Juliet E.K. Walker, *Free Frank: A Black Pioneer on the Antebellum Frontier* (Lexington: Univ. Press of Kentucky, 1983).

35. Population figures compiled from *Second Census of the United States* (Washington: n.p., 1801); *Aggregate Amount of Persons within the United States in the Year 1810* (Washington: n.p., 1811); *United States Census for 1820* (Washington: n.p., 1821).

36. McBride, "Journey to Lexington," 25; James Flint, *Letters from America, Contain-*

ing Observations of the Climate and Agriculture of the Western States, the Manners of the People, the Prospects of Emigrants, &c., &c. (Edinburgh: W. and C. Tait, 1822), 137.

37. William Littell, ed., *The Statute Laws of Kentucky*, 3 vols. (Frankfort: William Hunter, 1811-1919), 1: 343-45; Juliet E.K. Walker, "The Legal Status of Free Blacks in Early Kentucky, 1792-1825," *Filson Club History Quarterly* 57 (1983): 382-95; Lucas, *A History of Blacks in Kentucky*, 107-17.

38. Lucas, *A History of Blacks in Kentucky*, 59; *Kentucky Gazette*, 31 July 1800, 29 September 1800; Joseph Underwood to Edmund Rogers, 26 December 1810, Underwood Collection, Kentucky Library, Western Kentucky University, Bowling Green; John Brown to Margaretta Brown, 20 January 1811, 17 February 1811, Brown Family Papers; Harry M. Ward, *Charles Scott and the "Spirit of '76"* (Charlottesville: Univ. Press of Virginia, 1988), 154; Clement Eaton, "A Law Student at Transylvania University in 1810-1812," *Filson Club History Quarterly* 31 (1957): 270.

39. *Kentucky Gazette*, 25 February 1812, 14 January 1812, 21 January 1812; John Brown to Margaretta Brown, 17 February 1811, Brown Family Papers; Underwood to Rogers, 13 February 1812, Underwood Collection; Ramage, *John Wesley Hunt*, 64- 65.

40. John Brand to John Wesley Hunt, 2 September 1810, Hunt-Morgan Papers, Special Collections, University of Kentucky; Thomas H. Burbridge to Hunt, 29 June 1813, John Wesley Hunt Papers, Manuscripts Division, Filson Club.

41. *Kentucky Gazette*, 16 January 1823; for Shaw advertisement, see 12 February 1811.

42. Quoted in Teagarden and Crabtree, *John Robert Shaw*, 5.

PART THREE

A Revised Promised Land

The condition of slavery drained many African-Americans of their joy for life. In this sketch by an unknown artist, both male and female slaves are moved across country for sale. The revivalism of the early 1800s, however, offered new opportunities for slaves to experience some control over their lives. J. Winston Coleman, Jr., *Slavery Times in Kentucky* (1940; renewed, University of North Carolina Press, 1968)

The Beginnings of Afro-American Christianity Among Kentucky Baptists

ELLEN ESLINGER

The beginnings of African American Christianity are believed to lie somewhere in the latter half of the eighteenth century in the wake of several broad cultural developments. Perhaps the most important of these developments was what one author has described as a "religious renaissance," a general strengthening of Christian institutions that led slaveholders to become less indifferent to religion and less resistant to the conversion of their slaves. Much of the religious growth was also due to a second development, the emergence of a new evangelical style of religious worship, one that shared central beliefs, stylistic preferences, and rituals with African cultures. Probably equally significant, this new evangelical culture offered a more egalitarian fellowship than did established religions or society at large. In addition, scholars have noted important changes within the colonial black population. As the proportion of African-born slaves diminished, assimilation into Anglo-American culture increased. Early black converts are believed to have included a high proportion of slaves owned by church members or slaves who had frequent contact with Anglo-American culture such as those living in small quarters or working as house servants and crafts workers.[1] The growth of evangelicalism and the assimilation of American slaves combined to produce a black population that was more receptive to Christianity.

Because these developments were stronger in Virginia than elsewhere in the South, and because the slave population was quite large, the earliest significant emergence of black Christianity occurred there in the aftermath of the Great Awakening. By the end of the colonial era, quite a number of Baptist congregations in Virginia included significant black membership; in about a half-dozen, blacks comprised a majority. Probably even more numerous, but impossible to gauge, were the blacks who attended worship in these congregations without ever undertaking membership. And, while the Baptists were probably more successful in attracting black adherents, other dissenting denominations also experienced noticeble increases of blacks among their memberships during this period. By the end of the eighteenth century,

Christianity had gained a firm foothold among Virginia's black population.[2]

Historians have perhaps gone as far as the Virginia records will allow, at least for the present. Fortunately, following Virginia Baptists to the Kentucky Bluegrass frontier offers a fresh opportunity for further research. According to one estimate, approximately one-quarter of Virginia's Baptists migrated to Kentucky following the end of the Revolutionary War, propelled in part by a desire to escape religious harassment in the Old Dominion.[3] Though recorded amidst a dangerous frontier setting, their church minute books rival, if not surpass, the detail of Virginia minute books during this period, permitting a more thorough analysis. Thirteen fairly complete church minute books have been located for the late eighteenth century, four of which date to the mid-1780s. In many respects, the patterns and practices portrayed in these records resemble those of their Virginia counterparts. They also, however, raise important questions concerning the underlying motives for black church membership during this period. In particular, the Kentucky records suggest that from the very beginning, well before the appearance of separate black churches, Christianity provided local black populations with an important institutional structure.

The Baptist congregations analyzed in this study lay primarily in the Bluegrass counties surrounding Lexington, where the lush quality of the land attracted the first concentration of settlers. Contrary to popular impressions about frontier society, the virtually insatiable labor requirements of newly settled areas made the frontier extremely hospitable to slavery. This was especially true for areas like the Bluegrass with obvious potential for staple agriculture. Fayette County, which in 1787 encompassed the Baptist congregations of Bryan's Station, Marble Creek, Great Crossings, and Providence, included 2,136 slaves, nearly 1,000 of whom were age 16 or older. At a time when Kentuckians were still vulnerable to Indian attacks, Fayette County slave levels were not far behind those found in many more settled areas of Virginia. Frederick County in the lower Shenandoah Valley, for instance, had 3,203 slaves (1,554 aged 16 or older).[4]

Moreover, western slavery grew at a tremendous rate throughout the period, especially in the Bluegrass region. In 1800, the federal population census counted 4,225 slaves in Fayette County, more than in any other place in the western settlements (despite a geographic area much smaller than in 1787). Scott County, one of several counties that had been carved out of Fayette County and home to Great Crossings Baptist Church, had 1,910 slaves. On the eastern edges of the Bluegrass region, where Providence Baptist Church was located, Clark County had 1,561 slaves. Bourbon County, dominated by the congregation at Cooper's Run, included 2,136 slaves. In Kentucky as a whole, the number of slaves increased from 12,430 in 1790 to 40,343 in 1800. Approximately one-quarter of all Kentucky householders owned at least one slave, and in the Bluegrass counties, the rate was approximately one-third.[5] Thus, western Baptists did not lack potential black converts.

Not only did the Bluegrass region contain a sizable black population, but Kentucky Baptists generally owned slaves at rates surpassing local averages. At Great Crossings Baptist Church near the modern town of Georgetown in Scott County, twenty (41.7 percent) of the white males recorded as members in 1790 owned slaves, and seventeen (35.4 percent) did not, while eleven others could not be located on extant tax lists. By 1800, more than half of the white male members were slaveholders. A few miles to the south at Bryan's Station Baptist Church, the proportion of slaveholding members was almost exactly half in 1800 (forty-seven, or 50.5 percent of ninety-three white male members). Farther east, at Cooper's Run Baptist Church in Bourbon County, approximately 36 percent of the white male members owned slaves in 1800. In the small congregation of Marble Creek, with members distributed in both Jessamine County and southern Fayette County, at least twelve (44.4 percent) of the twenty-seven white male members in 1800 owned slaves.[6] In all of these neighborhoods, the local proportion of slaveholding in 1800 was significantly lower, ranging between 27.1 percent of the householders in Bourbon County and 34.0 percent of those in Fayette County, to 39.7 percent in Scott County and 40.7 percent in Jessamine County (the latter, incidentally, the highest level in the state). As these figures suggest, no longer could Baptists be described as poor, outcast dissenters.[7]

Although western Baptists were heavily involved with slavery, many struggled to resolve the contrast between earthly distinctions and heavenly equality. Marble Creek, for example, wondered about the status of slave marriages. Should the moral standards for white members be equally applied to black couples when slave marriages were illegal? A decade later the Marble Creek Baptists debated whether slavery was a moral evil. Likewise, in 1796, a member of Severn's Valley Baptist congregation asked, "Is slavery oppression or not?" The membership, which at the time included hardly any blacks, concluded that it was. This shortly led to a second question: "Can we as a church have fellowship with those that hold w.[ith] the righteousnis of perpetual slavery?" The people of Severn's Valley decided that, no, they could not. And, in 1796, the congregation decided that slaveholding members were obliged to let their slaves buy themselves out of bondage.[8]

While most other Baptist congregations in Kentucky could not bring themselves to go this far, many still made notable efforts toward egalitarian fellowship. Minutes concerning repairs for the gallery in the Dick's River meetinghouse suggest that church seating may have been more integrated than became common in the nineteenth century. The congregation ordered repairs in 1793, "so as to make it convenient for women to pass into Sd. Gallery." Apparently the seating area was not yet relegated to black members, as became the common practice later. Egalitarianism is also sometimes suggested in the format followed by church records. For example, the membership list kept by the congregation at Marble Creek distinguished between the sexes, but recorded black and white members together.[9] Church discipline, in sharp contrast to civil procedure, allowed black members to offer evidence in cases involving white infractions, or even submit accusations themselves against white wrongdoing. This included complaints against masters, if they too belonged to the church. In the Bryan's Station congregation, for example, Brother Arch lodged a complaint against his master, one of the more prominent members of the congregation, "for refusing to suffer Sd. Black Bro. to Speak to him and for raising a Stick against him." The master confessed his fault publicly and received a reprimand.[10] Reverend William Hickman recalled in his memoirs that at the Forks of Elkhorn Baptist Church, "slaves were received by the congregation, in the spirit of religious equality, partaking of all the privileges of full membership."[11] Reverend Hickman may have exaggerated, but his comments so many years later nonetheless indicate the seriousness with which eighteenth-century Baptists regarded this issue.

Any slaves who thought that professing Christianity would make life easier, however, were in for a rude surprise. In addition to satisfying the usual duties of a slave, church members had to avoid "disorderly behavior" such as drinking, dancing, and swearing. Failure to do so could be divulged to the congregation not only by the master, but also by other white and black church members. For example, in 1799 Brother Hodgen reported to Severn's Valley congregation in Nelson County that he had received information from a person named McMahon that a church member named Ceasor had been spreading an "evil report about his daughter & then denied it." In the congregation of Cooper's Run, a slave member named Jacob accused another of the black brethren, named Billy Murry, of "swearing and drinking to excess." Murry confessed and was excluded from fellowship. Church rules seemed unreasonable at times, as when Cooper's Run cited a slave named George for playing the fiddle so others could dance and George told the church elders "he saw no evil in Fiddling and dancing."[12] Sexual relations probably presented the greatest difficulty. Blacks were not legally allowed to marry, but church members had to behave as if they were. Thus, in 1787 Elkhorn Baptist Association received a query from a member congregation asking "Whether it is lawful for a slave being an orderly [church] member and compelled to leave his wife and move with his master about five hundred mile[s] then to take another wife?"[13] Held to the same high standards as whites but facing more obstacles, black Baptists often found church membership difficult.

Neither did joining a Baptist congregation guarantee equal treatment. Cooper's Run did not allow black members to vote in church matters, and challenges to this policy in 1792 and 1802 brought no change. The congregations of Great Crossings and Stamping Ground carefully distinguished between black and white members by keeping separate lists. At Mayslick Baptist Church, black and white members did not sit together at the communion table until 1805. The lesser status of black believers is perhaps most glaringly apparent in occasional failures to refer to them by personal name. At Marble Creek, for example, the clerk recorded in 1800 that the church had received "a Black woman of Mr Richard Yonge." Likewise, black members were sometimes completely overlooked. No blacks were listed with the constituting members when Stamping Ground Baptist Church was founded in September 1795, yet the very next month "Brother Duke" approached the congregation for permission to marry. Likewise, the first mention of "Sister Rachel" was when she was cited in 1798 for "Dancing and keeping Bad company."[14] These incidents and many others like them suggest that most early Baptist congregations fell short of practicing undifferentiated Christian fellowship.

A quick look at minute books for Baptist congregations in Virginia during this period reveals that these shortcomings did not represent a new western departure from church practice. Blacks comprised a significant portion of the Baptist church at Broad Run in Fauquier County, yet a membership list in 1785 named twelve white males and twenty-two white females. Black members were collectively dismissed with the following notation: "Besides several Negros, whose names are recorded in the former part of this book; and need not be repeated here." Mill Swamp Baptist church was probably more egalitarian than most, yet in 1799 received a query, "Has the free Male members (of the Blacks) an equal right to sit with us in Conference, or not?" Sure to stir controversy, discussion of the query was postponed for several months and was then rejected by a "large majority." A disciplinary action in 1786 involving a white member who tried to sit amongst the black brethren reveals that Water Lick Baptist Church in Shenandoah County also carefully distinguished between black and white members. These examples indicate that in Virginia, as in Kentucky, egalitarian church organization may have existed more as an ideal than as an actual practice.[15] Its importance in attracting black adherents was probably limited.

The Baptist position on emancipation lends additional support for this point. Many Baptist settlers had brought with them to Kentucky an opposition to hereditary slavery, which Revolutionary ideology of natural rights further reinforced.[16] The practically insatiable demand for labor on the frontier, however, placed opponents of slavery under strong pressure.[17] Nearly every western congregation found itself struggling to accommodate opposing views at one time or another. Western church leaders, anxious to preserve the peace and unity of their fledgling congregations, sidestepped the issue whenever possible. Thus, when Bryan's Station Baptist Church debated in 1791, "Is perpetual slavery consistent with Christianity and the Gospel of Christ or not?" and could not reach a consensus, the congregation preserved harmony by referring the question to the Elkhorn Association of regional churches.[18] After extensive debate, the Elkhorn Association declared slavery to be inconsistent with the principles of Christianity. Several member churches reacted so negatively, however, that the association quickly called a special meeting and retracted its statement.[19] Feeling on both sides remained high, and refusing to take a stand did not necessarily prevent discord. For example, when Kentucky's Salem Association hesitated to declare itself opposed to slavery, the Rolling Fork church withdrew in protest. Likewise, two families withdrew from the church at Cooper's Run in Bourbon County because they objected to holding fellowship with slaveholders. At Marble Creek the pastor was nearly deposed because of his rigid opposition to slavery.[20] Few other issues wielded greater divisive power during the post-Revolutionary era than did slavery.

Valuing peace over principle, Kentucky Baptists eventually gravitated toward a policy of noninterference. The change became especially apparent after the campaign for delegates to the second state constitutional convention in 1799, in which emancipation emerged as a key issue. The outcome of the election was so decidedly against emancipation that westerners thereafter generally regarded slavery as a civil matter rather than a moral one.[21] This was also true among Kentucky Baptists. By 1805, the Elkhorn Association of Baptist churches, which encompassed most of the Bluegrass, accepted that it was "improper for ministers[,] Churches, or Associations to meddle with emancipation from Slavery or any other political Subject." In another section of Kentucky, Bracken Association issued a similar statement the same year: "It is our Opinion that as An ass'n we have nothing to do with Slavery, seeing that it involves political questions, but do advise every soul to be subject to the higher powers." Despite a few stubborn holdouts, the Reverend David Barrow being perhaps the most notorious, the Baptist movement against slavery was essentially over by the beginning of the nineteenth century.[22]

The retreat from emancipation had little effect upon black membership in Baptist congregations, however, because no western congregation included more than a handful of black members during this early period. Bryan's Station Baptist Church near Lexington in the heart of the lush Bluegrass region, one of the largest congregations in Kentucky, included only sixteen black members five years after its 1791 founding. This increased to 21 by mid-1800, but blacks still comprised no more than 9.1 percent of the church's 230 members. Other large congregations had even fewer black members. At Great Crossings Baptist Church, located a few miles north of Bryan's Station, the 107 church members in 1800 included only 7 male and 5 female black members (11.2 percent). Similarly, the ninety-nine church members at Marble Creek Baptist Church, founded in 1787, included only fifteen black members in good standing by August 1791. By 1800, when the congregation totaled fifty-nine, black members numbered no more than nineteen (four were recorded as dead on an early membership list, but with no accompanying date). When Providence congregation subdivided in 1790, the church included approximately 134 white members but only 3 blacks. By August 1800, the black membership in the church's Howard's Creek branch had gained a little ground: seven black males compared with ninety-seven white males, and seven black females compared with eighty-one white females (7.9 percent). Cooper's Run, located in a denser area of slaveholding, did little better, increasing from four black members in 1790 to merely seventeen a decade later. Most remarkable is the composition of members at Severn's Valley, which had staked out the most vigorous opposition to slavery. Severn's Valley included eighteen white males and twenty-eight white women in 1800, but only four blacks.[23]

The low proportion of black Baptists in the western congregations might seem unremarkable except that in Virginia, where nearly all of the Kentucky Baptists originated, the situation was very different by this time. Of the twenty-two Baptist congregations in Virginia for which minutes survive, blacks outnumbered whites in at least six. Boar Swamp Baptist Church, for example, had 108 black members and 75 whites in 1787. Blacks formed significant minorities in many others.[24] The weaker black presence in Kentucky congregations was, moreover, readily apparent. A Baptist preacher named John Gregg who visited Kentucky in 1796 as a prospective settler recorded in his journal after attending Sunday services at David's Fork that "the communion was pretty large, and only one black partaker." Similarly, Gregg noted at Town Fork meetinghouse, "There was present a number of people, . . . and but few negroes to what I have generally seen at such meetings in Virginia."[25] Gregg's observation is all the more telling because it indicates that western blacks were not only failing to join churches, they were not even attending services.

Particularly interesting is that comparison with other religious denominations indicates that the regional difference was not because of internal differences between Virginia and Kentucky Baptists. Early Kentucky was dominated by three denominations: the Baptists were the most numerous, followed by the Presbyterians and the Methodists. Although local records for the two latter denominations are essentially nonexistent, the Methodists did keep cumulative membership figures during this period. These figures reveal a similar regional orientation as that among Baptists. Despite considerable success in attracting blacks elsewhere in the United States, Methodism too claimed disproportionately fewer black members in the western settlements. The western preaching circuits included 1,052 white members and 107 (10.16 percent) black members in 1790. By contrast, the Virginia circuits (including mountainous circuits where slaveholding levels were low) reported an average black membership of 24.9 percent. The regional contrast was still very apparent in 1800. In the annual minutes for that year, the Virginia circuits included a total of 13,390 members, of whom 23.3 percent were black. By contrast, black membership in the circuits of Kentucky and Tennessee stood at only 7 percent (1,626 white, 115 black), actually lower than a decade earlier.[26] In addition to confirming the reliability of the Baptist data, the Methodist figures indicate that the diminished presence of blacks in western congregations was more likely a result of regional differences in slavery than of internal denominational factors.

Black church membership in Kentucky's Baptist congregations remained low until the Great Revival that swept the western settlements in 1800.[27] Although the Great Revival is usually associated with the emergence of camp meeting revivalism among Presbyterians and Methodists, western Baptists experienced a major surge in religious interest as well. The number of black

Table 1. Racial Breakdown of Great Revival Converts in Selected Baptist Congregations

Congregation	Dates	BLACKS Males/Females/%	WHITES Males/Females/%
Bryan's Station	9/1800-8/1801	77/66/39.0	121/104/61.0
Providence	5/1801-1/1802	13/14/21.9	46/50/78.1
Great Crossings	8/1800-8/1801	35/38/19.4	total 303/80.6
Cooper's Run	5/1801-10/1801	8/14/59.4	7/9/43.2
Forks of Elkhorn	11/1800	7/6/20.6	26/24/79.4

Baptists suddenly soared, especially in the Bluegrass congregations (see table 1). Providence congregation, for example, received new members through baptism between May 1801 and the end of the year, 27 of whom (21.9 percent) were black. Similarly, from November 1799 to April 1800, Forks of Elkhorn congregation received twenty-six white men, twenty-four white women, plus seven black men and six black women (20.6 percent). The congregation at Great Crossings also experienced a massive revival, receiving 376 new members by baptism between the association meetings of 1800 and 1801, of whom 73 (19.4 percent) were black (35 male, 38 female). Cooper's Run, where the revival operated somewhat more briefly, received more new black members than it did whites. At Bryan's Station, the only Baptist congregation with more than a handful of blacks before the revivals, the influx of new black members was especially dramatic. The first signs of a revival in the Bryan's Station Baptist Church followed the annual meeting of the Elkhorn Association in August 1800. By November the surge in new members led the clerk to begin numbering them. By the next meeting of the Elkhorn Association in August 1801, Bryan's Station had admitted no less than 367 new members, of whom 143 (39.0 percent) were black. The black component of the congregation was now 29.0 percent, compared with only 12.3 percent before the revival. The level of black membership in the western Baptist churches had gone from one of underrepresentation to one of overrepresentation in a matter of months.[28]

The sudden black interest in religion was not, however, a universal phenomenon. Whereas approximately 20 percent of western Baptist congregations were black by 1805, only about 3 percent of the western Methodists were—a rate actually lower than before the Great Revival.[29] This diverging pattern is somewhat surprising in view of the more egalitarian religious culture of the Methodists and their greater opposition to slavery during this period. That this did not necessarily translate into more success in attracting black converts implies that other factors may have wielded more influence.

One possible explanation is that many western Baptists owned slaves, whereas Methodists tended not to; thus, the master and his family may have exerted a spiritual influence. Every Baptist family head was expected to lead the household, slaves included, in daily family prayer and to provide religious instruction. Some masters may have gone further. At Bryan's Station the spiritual responsibility of masters to their slaves surfaced in 1796 as a matter of general church concern. The congregation concluded after extended discussion that masters should use "Every possible argument of persuasion and Endeavours" short of corporeal punishment. At Cooper's Run, slaveholding members were obliged to teach their slaves to read Scripture.[30] Spiritual influence may have worked in other ways as well, such as requiring that slaves accompany their masters' family to religious services.

Glimpses at local patterns of membership, however, suggest that the religious status of masters exerted minor influence in attracting blacks to Baptist congregations. Of thirty-two blacks admitted to Bryan's Station church before 1800, only twelve apparently had Baptist owners. Similarly, at Marble Creek, only fourteen (28.6 percent) of forty-nine blacks who joined during the height of the revival (between August of 1800 and August of 1801) belonged to Baptist masters. These figures may slightly underestimate the influence of masters because some black Baptists belonged to households where the master was not a church member but the mistress was. This may have been a factor for three female slaves who joined Cooper's Run church in 1801. Their master, Jacob Spears, was not a church member, but his wife Betsy had joined a decade earlier.[31] Yet even if more female members could be traced, the contrast between the size of Baptist slaveholdings and the meager number of black church members would probably remain.

The degree of influence wielded by masters and mistresses is also questionable because, when alternatives existed nearby, some blacks chose not to join the congregation of their master. John Branham, for example, was among the founding members at Stamping Ground Baptist Church in 1795. His slave Harry joined the same congregation in December 1800, but another of his slaves, Sarah, joined the nearby congregation at Great Crossings in February 1801. Similarly, a slave named Nelly joined the Stamping Ground Church in 1801 while her master, Thomas Ficklin, belonged to Great Crossings. Christian slaves might also have chosen to join a different denomination, as in the case of Phyllis and Ned, two slaves who joined Bryan's Station

Baptist Church in 1791, but who belonged to a prominent Presbyterian layman named Levi Todd.[32] The lack of demonstrable influence from masters is all the more notable because the size of average slaveholdings in Kentucky was small compared with that in Virginia and presumably created greater opportunities for personal contact. The urgings of a Baptist master or mistress probably did influence some slaves, but the opportunity for Christian fellowship with their white owners apparently carried only mild appeal.

Most interesting of all, Kentucky Baptist records suggest that the slaves most likely to join a congregation were those who came from larger slave units where they would have had less contact with whites. The blacks who were accepted for membership in Great Crossings during the revival of 1800 were distributed among forty-two masters, of whom thirty-one can be located on county tax lists for that year. The masters owned an average of 8.74 slaves, compared with a neighborhood average of 5.27. In neighboring Stamping Ground Baptist Church, the slave members were distributed among thirty-three masters, of whom twenty-eight could be traced to local tax lists. Their slaveholdings averaged 10.11 compared with a neighborhood average of 7.38. In both Great Crossings and Stamping Ground, more than three-quarters of the masters owned at least five slaves. Similarly, in Cooper's Run Baptist Church in Bourbon County, ten of fourteen masters in the congregation could be traced to local tax lists. All but one owned at least five slaves. The slaves who joined Cooper's Run came from holdings that averaged 19.1 slaves, whereas the local average was barely 2.[33]

Moreover, and probably more relevant, early black Baptists tended to come from slaveholdings having more adults. This observation is especially significant because the population in recently settled areas such as Kentucky skewed toward youth among both whites and blacks.[34] Thus, many sizable slaveholdings comprised mainly children. Black church members nonetheless tended to come from those holdings that included other black adults. The slaves who joined Great Crossings lived in units with an average 4.2 adults, and slaves who joined Stamping Ground lived with 3.2 adults, versus local averages of only 2.67 and 2.13. For blacks in Cooper's Run, the contrast was even more distinct. Black members came from holdings that averaged 5.9 adult slaves, compared with a local pattern of less than 1.[35] Most western congregations do not have records that permit this level of analysis, but the data from these few that do are extremely consistent.

The tendency for the first generation of slave converts to come from larger holdings runs contrary to historical assertions about the importance of cultural assimilation. But had assimilation been the driving force behind black church membership, early black Baptists would have come from small and more socially isolated holdings. That they came instead from larger slaveholdings, especially those with other adults, raises the possibility that their decision to join a church was in some way connected to the development (or reestablishment) of an Afro-American community. The idea that Christianity offered black adherents more than simply a belief system is, of course, hardly novel, at least for the nineteenth century. For some time, historians believed that regular social contact and other preconditions necessary for an Afro-American subculture or community did not exist during earlier times. Recently, however, several studies have shown that the size of slave units, age profiles, and other characteristics that structured slavery in the Chesapeake region may have allowed for an African American subculture considerably earlier.[36] This development, as much as the growth and spread of evangelicalism, may help explain why Virginia Baptists attracted considerable numbers of black adherents in the 1760s, while Kentucky congregations did not do so until nearly a generation after first settlement, with the Great Revival of 1800. Unfortunately, Virginia records are unable to support parallel analysis.[37]

Pressure from black church members for autonomous group worship lends further support to the idea that slave church membership was related to the emergence of an Afro-American subculture. Virtually every Kentucky congregation able to attract a few black church members soon faced this issue. Some congregations responded by appointing a black male "to have Watch Care of the Black Brethren," but they all uniformly resisted efforts to organize separate black worship. In 1789, Billy Murry, a black member of Cooper's Run, was cited for preaching to groups of slaves. The church gave Murry a chance to demonstrate his abilities as a preacher, as was standard for all who sought authority to preach, but decided that "his Gift was not for the Glory of God . . . nor for the Edification of the Church." Murry may not have had much preaching ability, but it is perhaps telling that the others who applied for permission to preach were white and all were approved. While Murry painfully submitted, other black preachers accepted expulsion. At Mayslick in Mason County, a slave named Abraham was admitted to fellowship in 1798, and by the end of the year, was preaching without authorization. When told to desist, he resented the order, but complied. Yet a few months later a white member reported that Brother Abraham "has attempted to preach in publick in direct opposition to the unanimous judgment of the church." This time he refused to obey and was therefore excluded. Apparently

Brother Abraham placed more importance upon his identity as a preacher to blacks than as a fellow Christian among whites.[38]

Bryan's Station may be the only Kentucky congregation where blacks had regular access to separate worship before the Great Revival. Even so, Bryan's Station closely regulated the activities of its slave members. The first reference to autonomous group worship dates to early 1790, when disciplinary action was taken against a slave, owned by Brother George Boswell, named Simon. Simon "had been exercising a publick gift." After considerable deliberation the church decided to "Stop him from holding Publick meetings." Upon hearing this, Simon reportedly spoke strong words against the church and challenged its authority, creating further trouble. At the disciplinary proceedings Simon readily confessed, but apparently without much remorse, for he was subsequently excluded.[39]

Whether Simon continued to preach is impossible to determine from the church minutes, but blacks at Bryan's Station received their own preacher a short while after the difficulty involving Simon. In 1791, a slave member named Sam, property of Major Hall, was given leave to exhort and appoint meetings on a trial basis. Sam was not the only black preacher active in the neighborhood. Bryan's Station cited a slave named James, property of John Rogers, for discipline because he had "appointed meetings and Exercised a Gift contrary to our Order and likewise undertakes to Marry Negroes." James, finally able to attend a disciplinary meeting in July 1792, agreed to cease his preachings. Three years later, in 1795, Brother Sam was cited for the same reasons. He too came forward, but, giving satisfaction for his behavior, the committee allowed him to continue his restricted ministry among the black members. Yet, in 1799, Sam was again in trouble, this time for supposedly hearing conversion experiences, performing baptisms, and conducting communion services without authorization. Cited with him was a slave named Daniel, property of Mr. Ransdell. Sam initially refused to attend the church session and was excluded, but both he and Daniel eventually came forward and "gave satisfaction" for their activities. These two men found it necessary to appease the white members who controlled the congregation. Although allowed to exhort, they could not conduct other ministerial services. Nonetheless, their ability to preserve opportunities for separate black worship probably accounts for Bryan Station's high proportion of black members, roughly 40 percent, twice that of most other Baptist congregations in 1800.[40]

The desire for separate black worship surfaced more frequently following the infusion of black members during the Great Revival. Of all the different possible benefits of church membership—disciplinary measures against harsh masters, full and equal participation in church matters, church support for emancipation—none surfaced as often as did the desire for separate black worship. Virtually every Baptist congregation that gained black members during the Great Revival faced this issue at some point in the years immediately afterward. As a new season of evangelical outreach commenced at Providence meetinghouse in May 1802, questions arose about whether black members should preach without the approbation of the church. When this question was taken up again in June, the congregation concluded, "we are of opinion that the Laws of the State is Shuch that the Church has no wright to approbate a Slave as a precher without the Consent of their owner." Slaves who wished to preach or exhort also had to be reviewed by a committee of at least six male members. In this instance, George G. Taylor gave permission for his slave George to "be at liberty to exercise his gift of exhortation among his brethren."[41] Elsewhere black church members were less successful and always closely monitored by the main (white) body of the congregation.[42] Separate black worship would remain a rarity until around 1820. It was a hard-fought privilege, initiated by blacks rather than whites. Meanwhile, black Christians learned how to organize "invisible institutions," beyond the purview of the white master.

Thus, the beginnings of black Christianity in Kentucky indicate a complex process at work. It was not simply an extension of the process in Virginia, even though so many western Baptists, black and white, came from that state. In Kentucky, blacks sought church membership in substantial numbers not with the appearance of a sympathetic evangelical culture, nor with the development of a predominantly Creole population, nor as the result of close and sustained contact with white masters. All of these conditions existed from the very beginning of Kentucky settlement. Not until the Great Revival of 1800, nearly a generation after initial settlement, did Kentucky blacks adopt Christianity in significant numbers. Most interesting of all, the individuals who constituted this first big wave of black church membership usually belonged to larger slaveholdings, often with other adults, where a semi-independent Afro-American society would have found better opportunities for developing. The institutional structure may have appealed to people in such situations. The numerous efforts, quickly initiated, to establish autonomous black worship are consistent with an emphasis on community development.

The process outlined here probably applies to Virginia as well, but is not so readily apparent because there, the emergence of Afro-American culture and the development of evangelical Protestantism so closely coincided.[43] Rather than reducing the significance of Virginia's role in black Christianity, the Kentucky model suggests the need for more local studies. Instead of a primary event in Virginia, which then dispersed to other slave areas, black Christianity may have had multiple beginnings. Such studies may eventually confirm that black desire for autonomous community life had always been an important factor in Afro-American religion, even in the eighteenth century, thereby bringing its origins into better alignment with the historical understanding of later periods.

Notes

Earlier versions of this essay were presented in 1992 at the annual meeting of the Society for the History of the Early American Republic and, more recently, at the Newberry Library Seminar in Early American History. The author would like to thank Andrew Cayton, John Boles, Alfred Young, and other participants for their thoughtful comments.

1. Donald G. Mathews, *Religion in the Old South* (Chicago: Univ. of Chicago Press, 1977); Albert J. Raboteau, *Slave Religion: The "Invisible Institution" in the Antebellum South* (New York: Oxford Univ. Press, 1978), 132-49; Mechal Sobel, *Trablin' On: The Slave Journey to an Afro-American Faith* (Westport, Conn.: Greenwood Press, 1979); Eugene Genovese, *Roll, Jordan, Roll: The World the Slaves Made* (New York: Vintage Books, 1976); James D. Essig, *The Bonds of Wickedness: American Evangelicals against Slavery, 1770-1808* (Philadelphia: Temple Univ. Press, 1982); David T. Bailey, *Shadow on the Church: Southwestern Evangelicals, Religion, and the Issues of Slavery, 1783-1860* (Ithaca: Cornell Univ. Press, 1985); John B. Boles, ed., *Masters and Slaves in the House of the Lord: Race and Religion in the American South, 1740-1870* (Lexington: Univ. Press of Kentucky, 1988).

2. Sobel, *Trablin' On*; and idem, *The World They Made Together: Black and White Values in Eighteenth-Century Virginia* (Princeton: Princeton Univ. Press, 1987); Rhys Isaac, *The Transformation of Virginia, 1740-1790: Community, Religion, and Authority* (Chapel Hill: Univ. of North Carolina Press, 1982); Harrison W. Daniel, "Virginia Baptists and the Negro in the Early Republic," *Virginia Magazine of History and Biography* 72 (1972): 60-69.

3. On the early history of Kentucky Baptists, see John Taylor, *A History of the Ten Baptist Churches, of Which the Author Has Been Alternately a Member: In Which Will Be Seen Something of a Journal of the Author's Life for More Than Fifty Years, Also: A Comment on Some Parts of Scripture in Which the Author Takes the Liberty to Differ from Other Expositors* (Bloomfield, Ky.: William A. Holmes, 1827); John H. Spencer, *A History of Kentucky Baptists, from 1769 to 1885, including More Than Eight Hundred Biographical Sketches*, 2 vols. (Cincinnati: J. R. Baumes, 1885); Robert B. Semple, *A History of the Rise*

and Progress of the Baptists in Virginia by Robert B. Semple, Minister of the Gospel in King and Queen County, Virginia (Richmond: private printing, 1810); George W. Ranck, "The Travelling Church," *Register of the Kentucky Historical Society* 79 (1981): 240-65.

4. Netti Schreiner-Yantis and Florene Speakman Love, comps., *The 1787 Census of Virginia*, 3 vols. (Springfield, Va.: Genealogical Books in Print, 1987). On slavery in early Kentucky, see Gail S. Terry, "Sustaining the Bonds of Kinship in a Trans-Appalachian Migration, 1790-1811: The Cabell-Breckinridge Slaves Move West," *Virginia Magazine of History and Biography* 102 (1994): 455-76; and Ellen Eslinger, "The Shape of Slavery on the Kentucky Frontier, 1775-1800," *Register of the Kentucky Historical Society* 92 (1994): 1-23. A slightly expanded version of the latter, titled "The Shape of Slavery on Virginia's Kentucky Frontier, 1775-1800," is included in *Diversity and Accommodation: Essays on the Cultural Composition of the Virginia Frontier*, ed. Michael J. Puglisi (Knoxville: Univ. of Tennessee Press, 1997), 172-93.

5. Charles Brunk Heineman and Gaius Marcus Brumbaugh, *"First Census" of Kentucky, 1790* (Washington, D.C.: Gaius Marcus Brumbaugh, 1938), 3-4; G. Glenn Clift, *"Second Census" of Kentucky, 1800* (Frankfort: Kentucky Historical Society, 1954), v-vi.

6. Leland Winfield Meyer, ed., "Great Crossings Church Records," *Register of the Kentucky Historical Society* 34 (1936): 3-21 and 171-95; "Bryan's Station Church Book," Kentucky Historical Society, Frankfort; Cooper's Run Church Minute Book, John Fox Jr. Library, Duncan Tavern, Paris, Ky.; "Marble Creek Church (Baptist), 1787-1842," unpublished manuscript, Kentucky Historical Society.

7. Statewide, approximately one-quarter of all Kentucky householders owned slaves. Joan Wells Coward, *Kentucky in the New Republic: The Process of Constitution Making* (Lexington: Univ. Press of Kentucky, 1979), 63. On the prosperity and status of Kentucky Baptists during this period, see Fred J. Hood, "The Restoration of Community: The Great Revival in Four Baptist Churches in Central Kentucky," *Baptist Quarterly Review* 39 (1978): 75-77. As might be expected, a similar transition was under way among Virginia Baptists as well; see Janet Moore Lindman, "A World of Baptists: Gender, Race, and Religious Community in Pennsylvania and Virginia, 1689-1825" (Ph.D. diss., University of Minnesota, 1994).

8. "Marble Creek Church," 4 September 1789 and 6 April 1799; Minutes of the Severn's Valley Baptist Church, Elizabethtown, Kentucky, July 1788-Aug. 1803, 23 January 1796, 27 February 1799, and April 1796, Kentucky Historical Society, 32-33. See also Stamping Ground Baptist Church Book, Kentucky Historical Society, 11.

9. Bryan's Station Church Book; "Marble Creek Church." The Dick's River church was a sister congregation to Bryan's Station. Discussion of the meetinghouse gallery repairs may be found on page 59 of the Bryan's Station minutes.

10. Blacks gave evidence against white brethren in Marble Creek Church Minutes, 7 August 1794. Stamping Ground Baptist Church disciplined a white man and a black woman on the basis of evidence provided by a black male in 1798; see Stamping Ground Church Book, 11. The incident involving Brother Arch is from Bryan's Station Church Book, 50.

11. G.C. Downing, "Forks of Elkhorn Church," *Register of the Kentucky Historical Society* 4 (1906): 35-42.

12. Minutes of the Severn's Valley Baptist Church, 25 May 1799, 42; Cooper's Run Church Minute Book, 19 July 1799, 40 and 55.

13. Church discipline of black members is discussed extensively in Sobel, *Trablin'*

On; William Warren Sweet, ed., "Minutes of the Elkhorn Baptist Association," *Religion on the American Frontier: The Baptists, 1783-1830* (New York: Henry Holt, 1931), 423, 437; Bryan's Station Church Book, 50-52.

14. Cooper's Run Church Minutes Book, 33-35, 48, 102-3; "Great Crossings Church Records"; Stamping Ground Baptist Church Book; "Mayslick United Baptist Church of Jesus Christ Minutes," 12 July 1805 and 14 September 1805, Special Collections, Margaret I. King Library, University of Kentucky, Lexington, microfilm; "Marble Creek Church," 8 November 1800; see also 10 January 1801. For other examples of failure to record black members by name, see "A Transcript of the First Record Book of Providence Church, Clark County, Kentucky," 12 September 1801, Kentucky Historical Society; Stamping Ground Baptist Church Book, 1 and 16.

15. Broad Run Church Minute Book, 1762-1872, Virginia Baptist Historical Society, Richmond; Mill Swamp (Isle of Wight) Baptist Church Minute Book, 1774-1811, Virginia Baptist Historical Society, 14 September 1799 and 14 March 1800; Water Lick Baptist Church Minute Book, 1787-1817, Virginia Baptist Historical Society, 25 May 1786. The characterization of Virginia Baptists as racially egalitarian is slowly coming under reexamination. See Jewel L. Spangler, "Salvation was Not Liberty: Baptists and Slavery in Revolutionary Virginia," *American Baptist Quarterly* 13 (1994): 221-36; and Lindman, "A World of Baptists."

16. David Brion Davis, *The Problem of Slavery in the Age of Revolution* (Ithaca: Cornell Univ. Press, 1975); Essig, *Bonds of Wickedness*; Sobel, *The World They Made Together*, 209-10; Bailey, *Shadow on the Church*; W. Harrison Daniel, "Virginia Baptists in the Early Republic," *Virginia Magazine of History and Biography* 80 (1972): 60-69.

17. Eslinger, "The Shape of Slavery in Kentucky." The evidence presented by Spangler for Virginia Baptists also shows less support for emancipation in recently settled areas; "Salvation was Not Liberty," 227.

18. Bryan's Station Church Book, 38-39. A similar retreat occurred among Baptists in Virginia and elsewhere. Sylvia R. Frey, *Water From the Rock: Black Resistance in a Revolutionary Age* (Princeton: Princeton Univ. Press, 1991), 243-62.

19. Minutes of Elkhorn Association, 27 August 1791, Southern Baptist Theological Seminary, Louisville.

20. Spencer, *A History of Kentucky Baptists*, 1: 184; Whitley, "Footnotes to Local History," *Paris (Ky.) Kentuckian-Citizen*, 21 June 1957; Marble Creek Church Minutes, 1 March 1799, 6 April 1799, 3 May 1799, 1 June 1799.

21. The classic study of the 1799 state constitution is Coward, *Kentucky in the New Republic*, especially 118-23 and 107-8.

22. Sweet, "Minutes of the Elkhorn Baptist Association," 508; *Kentucky Pioneers and Their Descendants* (Frankfort: Kentucky Society, Daughters of Colonial Wars, 1951), 257; Essig, *Bonds of Wickedness*, 145-46. Barrow headed one of Kentucky's earliest antislavery organizations and authored a pamphlet titled *Involuntary, Unmerited, Absolute, Hereditary, Slavery Examined* (Lexington, Ky.: D.C. Bradford, 1808).

23. Church minute books indicate that nearly all western black Baptists were converts rather than transferees from other congregations. Worth noting as well is a fairly balanced gender pattern, also true of the white membership during this period. Bryan's Station Church Book; Meyer, "The Great Crossings Church Records"; "Marble Creek Church"; "A Transcript of the First Record Book of Providence Church"; Sweet, "Minutes of the Elkhorn Baptist Association," 484; Cooper's Run Church Minute Book; Severn's

Valley Baptist Church Minutes. Due to the inadequate nature of the sources, no effort has been made here to adjust for the loss of members due to death, only to dismissal or exclusion.

24. Sobel, *Trablin' On*, 189, 298 n. 48; Lindman, "A World of Baptists," 178, 180-81.

25. Journal of John Gregg, in Kentucky, 1796, Reuben T. Durrett Collection, Department of Special Collections, University of Chicago Library, 17 and 27.

26. *Minutes of the Annual Conferences of the Methodist Episcopal Church for the Years 1773-1828*, 7 vols. (New York: T. Mason and G. Lane, 1840), 1: 94-95 and 240-42.

27. The literature on this event is extensive, but see especially John B. Boles, *The Great Revival, 1797-1805: The Origins of the Southern Evangelical Mind* (Lexington: Univ. Press of Kentucky, 1972); Paul K. Conkin, *Cane Ridge: America's Pentecost* (Madison: Univ. of Wisconsin Press, 1990). For the Baptist experience during the Great Revival, see Hood, "The Restoration of Community," and Ellen Eslinger, "The Great Revival in Bourbon County, Kentucky" (Ph.D. diss., University of Chicago, 1988), 325-30.

28. "A Transcript of the First Record Book of Providence Church," Forks of Elkhorn Baptist Church Minute Book, Kentucky Historical Society; "Great Crossings Church Records"; Bryan's Station Church Book; Sweet, "Minutes of the Elkhorn Baptist Association," 484-87. The figures for Bryan's Station omit one black male and one female who were excluded within the revival period.

29. *Minutes of the Annual Conferences*, 1: 240-42.

30. Bryan's Station Church Book, 87-88; Cooper's Run Church Minute Book, 60 and 63.

31. Cooper's Run Church Minute Book. Betsy Spears joined in 1791. The few such situations that can be located raise the possibility that spiritual concerns tended to follow gender lines. It should be noted that, unlike later in the nineteenth century, the gender breakdown among white church members was relatively balanced.

32. Stamping Ground Baptist Church Book, 28 and 34; "Great Crossings Church Records," 194; Bryan's Station Church Book, 37.

33. The statistics cited here are based on the two tax districts where most of the Great Crossings and Stamping Ground members resided. Similarly for Bourbon County, the local figures are drawn for the district in which most church members resided. Scott County Tax Lists, 1800, Kentucky Historical Society, microfilm; Bourbon County Tax Lists, 1801, Kentucky Historical Society, microfilm.

34. U.S. Bureau of the Census, *A Century of Population Growth* (Baltimore: Genealogical Publishing, 1970), 94. On the age structure of western slaves during this period, see Eslinger, "The Shape of Slavery in Kentucky," 13-15.

35. "Great Crossings Church Records"; Stamping Ground Baptist Church Book; Cooper's Run Church Minute Book. The size of slave units in the local district was determined through county tax lists. Unfortunately, a similar analysis has proven elusive for Virginia Baptists during this period.

36. Allan Kulikoff, *Tobacco and Slaves: The Development of Southern Cultures in the Chesapeake, 1680-1800* (Chapel Hill: Univ. of North Carolina Press, 1986); Jean Butenhoff Lee, "The Problem of Slave Community in the Eighteenth-Century Chesapeake," *William and Mary Quarterly*, 3d ser., 43 (1986): 333-61; Ira Berlin, "Time, Space, and the Evolution of Afro-American Society on British Mainland North America," *American Historical Review* 85 (1980): 47-78; Frey, *Water From the Rock*, has come closest to linking the formation of an African American subculture with the adoption of Christianity.

37. A number of Baptist congregations in Virginia have left detailed minutes, but in too many instances, they do not have a complete list of black members or do not list the full name of the slaveholder. The few that do are unfortunately located in counties for which no personal property tax list survives.

38. Marble Creek Church Minutes, 7 May 1793; Cooper's Run Church Minute Book, 12 and 14; Mayslick United Baptist Church of Jesus Christ Minutes, 8 December 1798, 9 February 1799, 8 June 1799, and 13 July 1799.

39. Bryan's Station Church Book, 27-28.

40. Ibid., 41, 49, 82, 84, 102, 103, and 131.

41. "A Transcript of the First Record Book of Providence Church," 44-46.

42. An exception may be a slave preacher named Peter, better known as "Old Captain" and credited with organizing the "first African Baptist Church in Lexington." The slave of Reverend Joseph Craig, Old Captain supposedly belonged to Boone's Creek Baptist Church before living on the property of William Maxwell, where he centered his ministerial efforts. Early minutes of Boone's Creek (founded in 1795) do not mention him. His ministry probably began after the Great Revival. Robert H. Bishop, *An Outline of the History of the Church in the State of Kentucky, during a Period of Forty Years: Containing the Memoirs of Rev. David Rice, and Sketches of the Origin and Present State of Particular Churches, and of the Lives and Labours of a Number of Men Who Were Eminent and Useful in Their Day* (Lexington, Ky.: Thomas T. Skillman, 1824), 230-34; Ranck, "The Travelling Church," 253; Boone's Creek Baptist Church Minutes, Southern Baptist Theological Seminary, Louisville.

43. Another hindrance is the quality of Virginia records, which limits the tracing of individual black church members.

The Cane Ridge revival of 1801 was attended by thousands of men and women, black and white, slave and free, whose experiences opened for them new perspectives on their lives and cultures. Women, in particular, were enabled to participate more fully in religious life. Courtesy of New-York Historical Society, New York

"I Cannot Believe the Gospel That Is So Much Preached"
Gender, Belief, and Discipline in Baptist Religious Culture

BLAIR A. POGUE

"I wish you to give me a letter or a dismission in any way you think proper," Betsy Payne wrote the Great Crossings Baptist Church in Scott County, Kentucky, sometime between 1826 and 1842; "I am dissatisfied with the doctrin I under stand is preached there. I also understand," she continued, "that some of your favorite preachers considers all that believes the doctrine I do is Stumbling blocks in the way of makeing all the people Christians and I do not wish to be in the way of makeing Christians." After quoting from Galatians in the New Testament and Exodus in the Old, and making clear her distress at having to leave the church community, Payne came to the heart of the matter. "I am afflicted in body and mind not in body as much as in mind," she poignantly revealed. "Because this boddy will have an end I mourn on account of sin I ask the Lord to teach me the way in truth and Holyness. . . . I am Ready to be a witness against those would not obey the gospel, I cannot believe the gospel that is so much preached."[1]

Betsy Payne's letter to the Great Crossings Church challenges historians' current assumptions about white Baptists' gender conventions. Recent studies have argued that women were powerless in Baptist churches. Women worshiped in churches governed by men, who filled all major church leadership roles by serving as ministers, elders, deacons, moderators, treasurers, and clerks. In both the North and the South the American Revolution was a watershed for female Baptists. Before the Revolution, Baptist communities were more egalitarian; women voted on church affairs with greater frequency, served as deaconesses and exhorters, and played larger roles in church government. After the Revolution, church structures and language became more patriarchal. While before the Revolution, white women were often defined as members, afterward, "member" was constructed to mean "male," and more often, "white male." Scholarship has also indicated that after the Revolution sin was "feminized," as the transgressions committed by women were deemed most threatening to Baptist communities, and churches cracked down on "disorderly women" in order to reassert their patriarchal authority and achieve social respectability.[2] Yet Betsy Payne, by examining and rejecting her church's doctrine, was not made passive by her subordinate status in the congregation. Payne's beliefs allowed her to transcend earthly gendered barriers to challenge and ultimately reject the views of church fathers.

Examining the full implications of women's religious beliefs rather than focusing on institutional gender conventions enables us to see post-Revolutionary Kentucky Baptists in a more complex and accurate light. Without an understanding of the centrality of belief, women's willing participation in evangelical communities is puzzling at best. In *Masters of Small Worlds*, for example, Stephanie McCurry observes that women crowded into antebellum South Carolina low-country churches governed exclusively by men. While McCurry finds the attraction of white yeoman men to evangelicalism obvious, she notes that "the tremendous numbers of yeoman women drawn to the church is another matter altogether."[3] Similarly, Jean Friedman's exclusive focus on the effects of kin networks and church discipline on southern evangelical women prevents her from seeing churches as much more than "enclosed gardens." According to Friedman, churches strengthened patriarchal families, inhibited women's autonomy, and deterred the formation of independent women's organizations by regulating women's sexuality through enforcement of a double standard of church discipline.[4] Work of this sort renders southern women "victims" of their churches and of the societies in which their churches participated. It treats white Baptist women's failure to fight back and their willing participation in the lives of their churches as contributing to their own victimization. This is an unsatisfactory thesis at best. Despite the increasingly conservative faith and orientation of white Baptists, the pursuit of religious truth had potentially radical consequences. The individual quest for godly knowledge and the desire to translate that knowledge into action brought about social situations and alliances that at times turned the gender assumptions of Baptists and Kentuckians upside down.[5]

As Payne's case illustrates, religious convictions enabled women and men to transcend earthly, historically constructed boundaries. Religious beliefs also motivated them to act in seemingly paradoxical ways, contrary to what would seem to be in their own self-interest. In Kentucky so many Baptist women voluntarily adhered to a hierarchical social vision that to understand fully their world view or the impetus behind many of their words and actions, belief must be taken into account. In order to understand the full range of Kentucky Baptists' gender relations, this essay explores four aspects of their religious culture: the importance of religious belief, the gendered language used by Baptists to describe their individual and collective faiths, the occasional inversions of gender norms, and the practical working out of belief through disciplinary practices.

Kentucky Baptist women were active participants in the ideological struggles of their congregations and denominations. This observation is in stark contrast to Susan Juster's argument in *Disorderly Women* that post-Revolutionary New England Baptist women contributed little to the theological debates of their day. Whereas Juster portrays these debates as "a struggle over lay control," in Kentucky they were primarily ideological. Theological disputes were critical and highly charged because they were battles over the meaning of godly truth. To evangelicals there was no contest more important. In Kentucky, the importance of ideological orthodoxy and the democratization of Christianity worked to women's benefit. An emphasis on doctrinal purity, denominations' competition for converts, and the spiritual marketplace's broad array of choices gave women spiritual and social leverage.[6] Between 1780 and 1860 this leverage manifested itself in the fact that significant numbers of white Baptist women were courted by other evangelical denominations and left their Baptist communities of faith.

In this essay I use the term "patriarchy" to mean male leadership in families, churches, and society. I use this term cautiously. While Kentucky Baptists believed white men to be the biblically ordained leaders of families and religious communities, and most women supported their leadership, an examination of the dynamics of power in day-to-day encounters, church business meetings, and worship services must take into account the complexities inherent in relationships between men and women. As Linda Gordon astutely observes, "we need concepts of male supremacy that can explain . . . the extremely complex struggles, negotiations, and cooperation with which the sexes have faced each other and the social/cultural institutions that define gender relations."[7] Understanding the dynamics causing Baptist men and women to think and act in radical ways despite their overall conservativism elucidates the ambiguities and seemingly apparent contradictions with which Baptists lived and worshiped. Such an approach also demonstrates why a focus on the controlling aspects of patriarchy alone is misleading. As David G. Hackett notes, "religious traditions are themselves settings for discord and improvisation . . . theology, ritual, and religious institutions both shape and are shaped by relations between men and women."[8]

Kentucky was a region deeply molded by the revivalism of the early nineteenth century. Within its changing religious and cultural landscape, Baptist, Methodist, and Presbyterian congregations shaped the lives of men and women and in turn were influenced by them.[9] Because the beliefs and practices arising from Kentucky revivalism played a profound role in the development of southern religion and culture, study of the interplay of religious culture, society, belief, and gender there has wider ramifications.[10] This essay sheds light on relationships between men and women in a region both southern and western by examining one of the few institutions in which women could participate publicly alongside men—church congregations. Despite their subordinate status, evangelical churches offered women greater equality with men than was available elsewhere in society. Church meetings were places to win respect and occasionally to obtain protection from physical and mental abuse. For white women and men, the intense nature of evangelical community fostered new models of friendship between the sexes often unavailable in the larger society. Belief-based, supportive friendships between husbands and wives, and between ministers and their female congregants, lessened tensions between the sexes.

While most members of Kentucky Baptist churches were white and female, and were increasingly so over time, white men continued to hold all major positions of power.[11] Despite their preponderance, females supported male leadership. That they did so, and were at the same time active participants in their congregations, is seen in church minute books, diaries, and letters of women such as Betsy Payne. When women disagreed with positions taken by particular churches they spoke their minds and sometimes left their Baptist communities of faith. More often than not, these critics rebelled against the ideas endorsed by male leaders and church members, not against the leadership of males.

Despite some disagreements between different groups of Kentucky Baptists, most shared a few basic beliefs. They cohered around three main axes: the role of the individual, the definition of "church," and church practice.[12] While Baptists deemed participation in a community of like-minded believers essential to spiritual growth and development, so too was the independent relationship between an individual and God paramount. Belief that the Holy Spirit would inspire, guide, and sustain believers led many Baptists to place more emphasis on the individual's responsibility to God than on their loyalty to a church. As "man" had fallen in the Garden of Eden, so too human institutions including churches were ever prone to corruption. In keeping with the Protestant Reformation, individual Baptists claimed the right to read and interpret the Bible for themselves. Many church divisions arose from the assumptions that there was one true interpretation of each biblical passage and that individuals, inspired by the Holy Spirit, could arrive at biblical truth without clerical guidance. While some biblical passages could easily be interpreted in a socially conservative light, others, especially the commands of Jesus Christ and the words of the prophets, were radical in their ethical demands. The combination of an emphasis on the role of the individual believer in working out her fate and the radical commands of the prophets and Jesus was potentially volatile.

North American Baptist churches, as distinct from state-supported American and European models, were voluntary communities of believers. Baptists did not come together on the basis of geographical proximity alone, but more often on the basis of shared religious convictions.[13] While some believers and enquirers gathered for social reasons including entertainment, religious purposes were often primary. In theory, Baptists sought "pure" churches composed of individuals who had made public professions of the saving work and grace of Jesus Christ in their lives, known as conversion experiences, and had undergone public baptisms. Each church represented the Universal Church and was to embody harmonious Christian community. Church membership, not granted or entered into lightly, brought an individual into a supportive "family" of like-minded believers. A community in which male and female members referred to others as "brothers" and "sisters" provided a place to worship God, to share and refine beliefs, to get and give support for the desire to live a Christian life, and, when necessary, to receive guidance and correction. In their desire to see that churches had the necessary independence to be pure and prophetic, Kentucky Baptists initially did everything possible to prevent the development of institutional hierarchies and dependencies. These efforts, including the refusal to support a "hireling clergy," forced many ministers, especially before the antebellum period, to earn their livelihood in other ways—often as small farmers.

Like Baptists generally, Kentucky Baptists believed that every religious practice required biblical precedent or justification. The four rituals most frequently employed in Baptist churches—the public recounting of conversion narratives, public baptism, communion, and church discipline—were all biblically based. One of the most important rites, composed of a multitude of individual practices and assumptions, was church discipline or "correction." To keep Baptists individually and corporately pure, as well as to keep them "walking" in a way that would serve in the larger society as a positive "witness" to their faith, members vigorously scrutinized each other's words and actions.

The theological and practical differences between the two main groups of Baptists, Regulars and Separates, were much less pronounced in Kentucky than in other states, including Virginia. By the time significant numbers of Virginia Baptists began migrating to Kentucky in the late 1780s and '90s, enough similarities existed between the two groups that many ministers affiliated with the Separates in Virginia referred to themselves as Regulars once in Kentucky. According to J.H. Spencer, these Virginia Separate ministers were "more Calvinistic" and were willing to adopt the Philadelphia Confession of Faith accepted by all Regular congregations. A desire for greater respectability may also have played into this decision. From their first appearances in Virginia in 1754 and in North Carolina in 1755, Separate Baptists were perceived by Regulars and non-Baptists as more disorderly and emotional, and less refined than Regulars. Separates' use of eldresses, deaconesses, and an occasional female exhorter also discredited them in the eyes of many Regulars, Virginians, and North Carolinians. Additionally, by the time most Baptists relocated to Kentucky soil, the Regulars and Separates in their home states had already joined forces as United Baptists. In Kentucky, the two groups united in 1801; the revivals of 1800 and 1801 facilitated the union. The desire to save souls motivated Regulars and Separates to work together.[14]

Some Baptist beliefs could have radical consequences, especially their understanding of scripture as the ultimate source of religious authority and their commitment to the notion that the individual is responsible to God before "man." While the Bible upheld an essentially patriarchal view of the social order, especially in the Old Testament and in the writings of Paul, a message of liberation was also there for the taking, most vividly in passages such as Galatians 3:28: "there is neither Jew nor Greek, there is neither bond nor free, there is neither male nor female: for ye are all one in Christ Jesus."[15] Such egalitarian passages, interpreted by individuals with guidance from the Holy Spirit, could raise critical questions about participation in church affairs. Did being "one in Christ Jesus" mean that women were to participate in church life as visibly and freely as their male counterparts?

Although piety was an essential component of Kentucky evangelicalism, especially after the Great Revival in 1801, men and women from a variety of socio-economic and educational backgrounds struggled vigorously with questions of orthodoxy. The fact that a conversion-centered pietistic theology played an influential role in southern religious development did not mean that men and women ignored the doctrinal particulars of their faith and the churches they chose to join. Even though some members urged their ministers to "stop preaching John Calvin and James Arminius and preach

Jesus Christ," many more grappled with the theological stances taken by Kentucky's competing denominations.[16] Initially, revivalism caused many Baptists to pare down their doctrinal stance to its theological basics. Preaching to and speaking individually with seekers, ministers and lay evangelicals concentrated on the meaning of Christ's death and resurrection. They also stressed the consequences of failure to respond to the Christian message. This did not mean, however, that theology became less important to the converts, or that, once converted, they refrained from theological speculation and debate.[17]

Theologically based struggles greatly influenced post-Revolutionary Kentucky Baptist religious culture. Powerful competition provided first by the Methodists, and later by the Disciples of Christ, forced even those men and women who had not been overly concerned about theological matters to take a doctrinal stand. Calvinists, Arminians, Antinomians, and sometimes even Arians tried to alter or eliminate creeds and define the agendas of particular congregations.[18] Since Truth meant "correct" knowledge of God and salvation, battles over Truth were often fierce. In such a climate, the orthodoxy of male and female church members, not their sex, was of paramount importance. Baptists debated matters, formed alliances, left congregations, and were excluded on the basis of belief.

To understand Baptist religious culture as well as the complexities inherent in relations between Baptist men and women, one must grasp the tension between the brands of orthodoxy demanded by churches and associations, and the pursuit of Truth by autonomous individuals. Despite emphasis on the pietistic side of faith, doctrinal orthodoxy was often what brought men and women into or drove them out of Baptist churches. All individuals desiring to join Baptist churches for the first time were required to come before the church and relate the story of their journey to salvation. Individuals coming from Baptist churches "of a different faith and order" were asked for a statement of their "principles" or theological beliefs. As the Burks Branch church in Shelby County noted in its 1801 rules of decorum, "strict enquiry" was to "be made of all persons professing to unite in Membership of a work of grace on their hearts their principals of faith in the Doctrines of the Gospel the uprightness of their lives Except Members from other churches who bring letters of Dismission from sister churches."[19] Church members were often free to question applicants on theological particulars, including any ambiguous statements made. An incident that took place in Boone's Creek Baptist Church of Fayette County in the latter part of the 1780s illustrates the seriousness with which Baptists took this procedure.

Although a "raw Irishman" named Watson "related a good work," and the minister "asked him all the questions necessary," two brethren objected to his reception into the church. They were not yet convinced that he was a Christian. One of the objectors, a minister named Brother Tanner, asked Watson "some deep questions on eternal decrees." After further discussion with Watson following the service, Brother Tanner professed himself satisfied that Watson was indeed a Christian.[20]

Attempts to maintain orthodoxy were manifest also in an insistence upon letters of dismission—certificates of good behavior and standing from an individual's former church. In addition to providing a character reference, an important security measure in mobile, rapidly changing communities, a letter of dismission informed the church receiving it of the major theological positions embraced by the applicant's former congregation. Sometimes churches found it necessary to elaborate their doctrinal concerns, especially with reference to missions and creeds. Migration raised a host of new situations for Baptists, provoking uncertainty about the biblical ways of handling them. Although migration to the colonial backcountry had already given many Baptists exposure to life in a transitional community of faith, this had not completely prepared them for migration to Kentucky. Some Kentucky Baptists arrived with their pastor and former church members; others knew each other from prior acquaintance; many others were meeting fellow Baptists for the first time. Knowledge of individuals' faith and character from long acquaintance was not always possible. With these concerns in mind, the Elkhorn Association attempted to answer a 1787 query "what rule are we to receive Baptist members by from the old country or elsewhere not of our association?" The association responded, "all members coming from churches of our faith and order bringing an orderly letter of dismission from said orderly church, we advise to be admitted, and all baptists coming from churches of other order by experience."[21] The majority of individuals leaving churches requested letters of dismission. Churches deemed departures without such letters actions worthy of censure, sometimes exclusion.

Ministers and church leaders urged members to engage in biblical study and reflection. Believing that the Bible possessed clear truths available to all believers through the guidance of God's Holy Spirit, churches encouraged men and women to read the Bible daily and to reflect upon the lessons contained therein. As minister James Stone wrote to his sister Sarah, "your bible, or at least a bible that I shall present you—will teach and instruct you what you are to do; search it well, every opportunity: not neglecting those things which it is necessary for you to do in this life."[22] Men and women were instructed to read the Bible in the "family circle" and to meditate upon its words when alone in their "closet." Those men and women who could not read acquired their religious beliefs from public readings of the Bible, circular letters, and newspapers, as well as from sermons, hymns, prayer meetings, and discussions with friends. Many individuals unable to read memorized particular biblical verses or even chapters. Diaries, letters, and church records reveal numerous accounts of men and women avidly striving for and often struggling over the exact meaning of godly Truth.

Attainment of Truth and its daily application was the means by which individuals hoped to achieve the end of salvation. For men and women awakened to their "inherent sinfulness" at protracted meetings, in church, or in conversation with committed Baptists, salvation was everything. Making correct theological commitments was literally a matter of life and death. As the sermon from I Timothy 4:16 delivered to Bethel Baptist Church in Washington County so clearly conveyed, "take heed unto thyself and unto thy doctrine; continue in them for in so doing this thou shall both save thyself, and them that here thee."[23] Numerous accounts in diaries and letters make clear the paralyzing effects awareness of their sinfulness had on men and women. In this respect, pursuit of salvation was a leveling mechanism; assurance of salvation did not depend upon one's sex.

Doctrinal unity bound Baptist communities together; doctrinal disputes tore many communities apart. While congregational loyalties and friendships played important roles in keeping congregations intact, they were often unable to prevent doctrine-based divisions. This was especially true in the antebellum period when religious competition was intense, and Methodists and Disciples reached most locales through itinerant preaching, protracted meetings, camp meetings, and the establishment of churches. The pursuit of Truth ironically worked against the very ministers who had encouraged it, complicating the goal of communal orthodoxy. As Betsy Payne remarked, "I try to ask the Lord to keep his people from being deceived by false Teachers. The Teachers of the people causes them to sin."[24] Antinomian sentiments were sometimes the result.

Commitment to a biblically based Christianity caused a development disturbing to orthodox Baptists, especially in the 1840s. Just as Betsy Payne was dissatisfied with the "doctrin" preached at the Great Crossings Baptist Church, so too were many others, especially white women. Antebellum Kentucky church records reveal that significant numbers of white women left churches and were often excluded for their faith-based choices. An in-depth statistical sampling of eight Kentucky Baptist churches reveals that joining another denomination was one of the largest disciplinary categories for white women.[25] Between 1780 and 1860, 92 women out of a total of 433, or 21 percent, were charged with joining another denomination. This figure is actually a low estimate because many women accused of joining the Disciples of Christ or Reformers, or as critics derogatorially referred to them, the Campbellites, were listed in church minute books as "joining a society in disorder," "joining a society not in union with church," and dissatisfied with church "government." The majority of these charges, forty-six, took place between 1841 and 1850.[26] Of the ninety-two women charged with joining another denomination, thirty-three, or 36 percent, were charged with joining the Reformers and their predecessors, the Christians or Stoneites. An additional twelve women, or 13 percent, were charged with joining the Methodists. In comparison, only 34 men out of a total of 1,137, or 3 percent, were charged with joining another denomination. From this small number sixteen men were accused of joining the Reformers, and six of joining the Methodists. Very few men or women joined the Episcopalians or Shakers, and none joined the Presbyterians.[27]

More than one-fourth of the women recorded as joining another denomination chose the Disciples of Christ, a more socially conservative sect than most Baptist congregations. Disciples renounced all "human compositions," including creeds and benevolent societies. Participation in missionary organizations and other benevolent groups had the potential to widen women's spheres of "appropriate" activity, as has been demonstrated in the works of Nancy Cott, Barbara Berg, and Mary Ryan. Those women who abandoned the Baptists for the Disciples when other denominations were available to them prized conviction over social opportunity. The Methodists, for example, competed simultaneously for converts, offering women leadership roles in female class and prayer meetings. Yet, many women chose the Disciples, suggesting that for some devout women issues of belief outweighed opportunities for greater participation.

While most women leaving Baptist churches for other denominations were excluded, expulsion followed their departures. In these cases, exclusions were responses to women's independent actions. Belief gave white women spiritual and thus intellectual and social agency. On this front, the Kentucky scenario differed from that of New England, where Juster found that post-Revolutionary New England Baptists purged their congregations of "marginal adherents," who were increasingly female, in order to "attack at the root the disorder that seemed endemic to their institution."[28] Kentucky Baptist women were not victims of a "purge"; more often than not they left churches of their own volition.

For those who remained in Baptist churches, the pursuit of truth flew in the face of gender hierarchies.[29] Any member holding religious opinions differing from those of the church was vulnerable to charges of "heresy." White men, especially white male ministers, were as vulnerable to exclusion for erroneous sentiments as were white women. The case of Brother John Mulkey, minister of Mill Creek Baptist Church in Monroe County, illustrates this point. At a church business meeting the second Saturday in August 1809, church members agreed to send for "helps" from other churches to assist them in evaluating charges against Brother Mulkey. Although he had been both a founder of and pastor to the Mill Creek church, Mulkey's importance did not exempt him from congregational scrutiny. On the second Saturday in October 1809, after hearing and debating the charges against him, the church agreed "that he denied the ["our Esteem tho" crossed out] Esentisal doctrine of the Gospel such as denying in our Esteem that Jesus Christ satisfied the demands of Law and Justice for his people or died as our surety or that any man is saved by the Righteousness of Jesus Christ imputed to him. . . ." Although Mulkey refused to give them up, the church demanded his preaching "credentials."[30]

Reclaiming those pursuing false doctrine was a difficult, often impossible task. In January 1844, for example, members attending the business meeting of Middle Creek Baptist Church in Boone County learned that Sister Agness Stephens had attached herself to the "Universal" Church. The Middle Creek church promptly appointed two white male brethren to have an "interview" with her and request her attendance at the next meeting. At the February meeting, both brothers reported that Sister Stephens "stated that the reports was true and that she felt satisfied in the course she had taken and that she firmly believes the doctrine she has embraced." The church excluded her on the ground that "she has departed from original principles and the true faith of the gospel."[31]

An 1817 entry from the Dry Ridge Church minute book in Grant County sheds light on yet another dimension of theological debates among Baptists: heresy was often a family affair. Although in conflict with Baptist "brothers" and "sisters," dissenting Baptists frequently had the support of spouses, children, and kin. As the clerk noted, "Henry Childers Sr., Mary Childers, Thomas Childers, S[ere]ah Childers, William C. Childers, Elizabeth Childers, Major Childers, William Childers, James Thomas, M[a]ry L?ch? & Elizabeth Lay are Excluded having refused to be corrected by the Church & having refused to Recant the Heresy that Salvation is by the free will of Man." He added, "may the Power of All Mighty God lead them back to the Eternal Truth of Sovereign Grace."[32] While women often joined churches on their own, the significantly larger number of women on church membership lists suggests that women also joined those churches in much the same manner, either with female kin or alone.

The gendered language that reflected belief blurred sexual distinctions. Although Christian females, especially from the Jacksonian period on, were privy to the demands of the "cult of true womanhood," they were often praised by male Baptists for exhibiting manly qualities. Minister John Taylor, for example, praised old Sister Arnold's "natural strength of judgement" and "masculine fortitude."[33] Similarly, the 1852 obituary of Amanda Malona Morris of Elizabethtown noted approvingly that during a revival in 1851 "she took up her cross as an old soldier, conversing with mourners, seeking out and exhorting her impenitent friends, and using all diligence to advance the cause of the redeemer."[34] Many other obituaries praised women for their activities as "soldiers" of the gospel.

Although Baptists and the wider culture in which they operated considered male leadership essential, the Christian qualities deemed most desirable were considered to be female. Baptists were encouraged in circular letters to "be not high minded," but lowly, to "imitate Christ's acts of condescension and mercy," to not prosper at the expense of others, and to trust God "and lean not unto your own understandings." Admonitions like these, biblical in origin, appeared throughout the period.

Even ministers were urged to exhibit "female" qualities. An 1851 essay by James Pendleton titled "An Able Ministry" exhorted ministers to follow the apostle Paul's example by exhibiting "feminine" piety. According to Pendleton, when Paul thought about the enemies of Christianity, "his manliness became the most effeminate tenderness; he exhibited all the softness of the gentler sex, and he wept like a tender-hearted child." Paul also spoke of "travailing in birth" for the Galatians. According to Pendleton, Paul's example was an "emphatic refutation" that a strong intellect and a devout, pious heart are incompatible.[35]

Promoting "feminine" traits in men and praising "male" qualities in females combined with religious zeal and the social realities of a numerically feminized faith to bring about repeated inversions of the gender hierarchy. Religious enthusiasm and independent female spiritual reflection, for example, sometimes resulted in confrontations between ministers and female congregants. Assertive female behavior was tolerated and even encouraged if it was thought to be motivated by spiritual impulses. Taylor, for instance, remembered that Hannah Graves of Clear Creek Church in Woodford County was known for her occasional "blunt dealings" with preachers. When a minister whom she greatly respected decided no longer to serve her congregation, Hannah "asked him if he was going to prove that he was only a hireling, seeing he fled when the wolf came and seemed not to care for the sheep."[36]

Numerical feminization resulted in Baptist churches having a large number of female members whose husbands were less zealous, were not members, and did not attend church. Such situations introduced complications into Baptists' domestic vision of female submission to male "headship." When the wife, not the husband, was a committed Christian, Baptists had to come to terms with issues including the degree to which the wife should answer to the husband and who should lead services of family worship.

Although white males were supposed to have the final word in church and at home, real-life situations did not always work out so neatly. Soon after her baptism, Polly Rice asked her husband, a Baptist before their marriage, to direct family worship with their children and servants. After he declined to do so, she proposed "with his consent" to lead her family in reading the Bible, song, and prayer. According to Taylor, "this was yielded to for awhile, and perhaps would have been more sufferable, if company did not come." Although her husband later "threw discouragements in her way" Polly would not be deterred, especially when praying for her children.[37] In other situations, husbands solicited their wives' religious opinions and instructions, and asked for their wives' prayers, sometimes on their knees.[38]

Women's increased spiritual authority in the home coincided with a similar trend in the community. White men were thought to be the natural leaders in church and at home. They were also considered to be the stronger gender emotionally and constitutionally. White women, supposed to be emotionally and constitutionally weaker than white men, were assumed to be more pious. As the more "spiritual" gender women were held responsible for communal purity. Although men alone were to occupy all significant positions of authority, they were also believed to be more disorderly than women. Thus, as churches were feminized numerically a shrinking pool of men continued to govern a growing number of more "pious," "orderly" women. Additionally, over time, and especially from the 1830s on, evolution of the ideas and assumptions comprising what Donald Mathews calls "evangelical womanhood" further increased Baptist women's importance to the religious community. While white women's presence and cooperation were always vital to Baptist success, their importance took on new dimensions in the antebellum period when domestic activities were perceived as having important communal repercussions. As their importance increased, so too did their authority.[39]

Commitment to a common belief system and the intense nature of evangelical community fostered supportive friendships between white men and women. Throughout the period, such relationships were less common in the larger society. Often found between Baptist husbands and wives, and between ministers and their female congregants, relationships of this type lessened the potential for conflict between the sexes. In addition to shared beliefs, Baptists' encouragement of strong, fervent women and humble, expressive men made these friendships possible.[40]

Male and female Baptists gave their conversion narratives and exposed their private failings in front of one another, and frequently worked toward common spiritual goals. In their churches and homes, women and men shared their most deeply held beliefs. Extant correspondence between women and their ministers reveals the depth of these ties. In a letter from Newport, Kentucky, dated 1820 to "My Worthy Friend & Brother," Sister Rebecca Lindsey attempted to comfort a minister mourning the death of his daughter. In the body of her letter, she provided words of exhortation and encouragement similar to those dispensed by ministers. "What a gracious God do we serve," Lindsey proclaimed, "that is not only able but willing to s[u]pport us under the heavy and trying afflictions which we, incident to our fallen nature or in his wisdom he sees necessary to lay upon us as a tender Father correcting his darling child for his own benefit." In the course of her letter she expressed hope that "my good friend & his dear wife has been enabled to exercise resignation to the will of heaven." Most significant, Lindsey signed her three-page letter in the same way as many other married and widowed Baptist sisters writing to their "brothers." Without a prefix identifying her as another's wife, she signed her letter "your Friend & Sister in the Gospel Rebecca Lindsey."[41] Spiritually based relationships between the sexes enabled Baptists, and especially white women, to identify themselves as autonomous individuals worthy of friendship in their own right. These friendships evolved not from kin or business connections, but from shared beliefs. Social worthiness was based more upon one's faith and Christian "walk" than upon family connections or wealth.

Minister James Stone's letter to Sister Mary Singleton also reveals the importance of extrafamilial relations between Baptist brothers and sisters. In his epistle, Stone apologized for his "misunderstanding" with her husband a few days earlier when he "acted tho under the influence of passion." In addition to expressing remorse for dishonoring "God & his religion," Stone was concerned he had offended Singleton. He desired, although his hope was not expressed explicitly, that she would mediate the conflict. "Thinking you might be ["somewhat" is crossed out] hurt at me, on hearing of the transaction, I ["have" crossed out] address ["ed" crossed out] this to you and I hoping you will be satisfied, and forgive any wrong that you may conceive I have been guilty of[.] I hoped also that Mr Singleton will think no more of it as I wish to be at peace with all men. I bear no enmity or no malice, against him or any other person." He concluded the letter, "but Let me still remain as your ["?" crossed out] Brother in christ Jesus our Lord Jas. E. Stone."[42]

Saturday meetings of church discipline provided a forum where belief was translated into action. At these meetings, "acceptable" and "unacceptable" behavior was defined for men and women. They are thus an instructive place to study Baptists' changing and static notions of appropriate and inappropriate behavior for both sexes over time. Because disciplinary meetings were sites of individual and communal conflict and harmony, records of these meetings are the best sources for examining the complex relationships between Baptist men and women. The meetings also provided an arena where situations and beliefs that threatened individual salvation and communal purity were debated and resolved.

Between 1780 and 1860, church discipline meetings served as surrogate courts where male and female Baptists brought charges against each other. Baptists were expected to use church courts before using those of the "world" to obtain godly verdicts and to avoid giving those outside the church evidence that might discredit the entire community. Procedures used in evaluating charges against individuals were well defined and consistently observed. Church members were confident that their methods of correction worked in the best spiritual interests of the individual and the community; discipline attempted to keep both pure.

Transgressions (activities defined by Baptists as sinful) were divided into two main categories—private and public. These terms did not necessarily mean trespasses committed in the private or public realms. Rather, private transgressions were those committed against an individual, while public transgressions were crimes committed against the community. For example, although occurring in private, adultery, whipping one's wife, and leaving one's spouse were labeled as public, because they reflected badly upon the characters of the individuals committing them, and thus on the congregation. Private transgressions tended to involve disputes between individuals over such matters as land, wills, payment of debts, and slander.

In cases of private trespass, the aggrieved individual, following instructions given in Matthew 18:15-17, was first to meet with the person by whom he or she felt injured. If the two parties were not able to make amends, especially if the person causing the conflict did not respond favorably, the injured party was then to bring along two to three church members to a second meeting with the transgressor. If this procedure failed, the matter was then brought before the church.[43]

Public transgressions usually arose from reports of "disorderly" conduct given to the church in person or by letter. The accused was generally "charged" if present or "cited" to come before the church to explain the case or to confess to wrongdoing. Often, committees composed of white men, sometimes of white women, and less often of white men and women together, were appointed to investigate particular cases and to cite the accused if the evidence became convincing. During periods of growth and bureaucratization, usually in the antebellum period, some churches directed that public trespasses first be brought before a church committee composed of white males, and appear before the church only if the committee was unable to resolve the dispute, or if the verdict was challenged by one of the parties involved.

An examination of individual transgressions reveals that although they were often gendered, only during very few decades or distinct historical periods did churches crack down on men or women for a specific "sin." The only transgression associated with a specific decade and sex was that of joining another denomination. This trespass was brought most frequently against white women in the 1840s when the Disciples of Christ were wreaking havoc on Kentucky Baptist churches.

While sexual identification was important, many of the men and women participating in church "trials" would have identified themselves as Christians or as Baptists before acknowledging their gender. Although Baptists grew in size and strength between the 1780s and 1850s, joining this fundamentally conservative movement was still a radical step. It took much effort and self-discipline to become and to remain a Baptist. If men and women took their commitment lightly, they were excluded. For Baptists of both sexes, the purity of their lives, as well as those of other brothers and sisters, was of the utmost importance; obtaining the truth was what most mattered. That church records contain examples of women bringing charges against members of their own sex is difficult to comprehend without an understanding of the dedication to godly purity. To focus on gender alliances at the expense of belief is to misunderstand the central dynamic of Baptist religious culture before the Civil War.

The findings here are based on a sample of eight Baptist church records from 1780 to 1860 containing a total of 1,570 charges and 856 exclusions.[44] Although waning at times, church discipline continued to be enforced. The first decade of the nineteenth century contained the most charges. In that decade 420 men and women faced the discipline of the church, compared with 342 between 1841 and 1850, and 194 between 1811 and 1820. By contrast, the decade 1841-1850 contained the most exclusions, 225, while the second largest number, 196, took place between 1801 and 1810, and the third largest number, 113, between 1851 and 1860.

The prevalence of charges, citations, and exclusions in these decades resulted from two larger events. First, Kentucky churches were most vigilant in the decade following the Great Revival of 1801. Spiritual zeal and a commitment to godly purity encouraged churches to eradicate vigorously all traces of sin. Despite a desire for new converts (and a desire to keep those converts from joining the Methodists and Presbyterians), Baptists sought only members committed to God and to their views of faith and baptism. Second, the 1840s was a decade of intense denominational competition. Although churches hoped to keep individual Baptists within their fold, they wished to retain only orthodox members.

Men were charged more often than women for their transgressions. Since the leadership of white males was thought essential for the successful functioning of churches and households, their behavior was observed with the greatest vigilance. In almost every decade, the numbers of white males charged with various trespasses were more than twice those of white females. In two decades, the 1780s and the 1800s, white male citations and charges were more than triple those of their female counterparts. These were decades when white females tended to outnumber white males in membership by more than two to one.

While men were thought to be more disorderly than women, women's transgressions were viewed more seriously, as evinced by a low rate of restoration.[45] An individual was generally "restored" to church membership after coming before the church, acknowledging deep sorrow for sins committed, and promising to live a more godly life. The assumption that white women were more spiritual than men and were thus responsible for church and family purity made their transgressions seem that much more glaring. The crimes with which women were most often charged, sexual transgressions and joining another denomination, were perceived as the female activities most threatening to communal purity and harmony.

Although men were excluded less often than women relative to the number of charges placed against them, they were actually expelled with the greater frequency based on the total number of exclusions. While white males filled all major leadership positions and voted in all disciplinary cases, they charged and excluded themselves more often. Therefore, any interpretation of disciplinary patterns as revealing only gender conflicts, domination, and submission does not tell the whole story.

As church members, white women had access to church "courts." They brought disputes involving wills, estates, and slander before the church; they also used the tribunals to guarantee payment for domestic goods sold, such as fabric. In a number of cases, women acted as evangelical "deputy husbands," speaking on behalf of spouses, fathers, or sons wronged by male Baptists.[46] In most of these instances, the female deputy husband or deputy relative was a church member, while her spouse or male relative was not. Such a situation took place in the Mount Tabor church on June 17, 1809. At that meeting, Sister Judith Rogers brought charges against Brother Benjamin Crenshaw for "a failure of his promise relative to some hogs he purchased from Mr. Elijah Rogers, also for his refusing to pay Interest upon money which he borrowed from Said Rogers also of his neglecting to meet her Father at September court according to promise and likewise of his saying that he paid her Father Captn Buford two hundred dollars, which she believes he never did." Although, in the course of the "trial" an unidentified individual asked whether or not it appeared "that Sister Rogers hath been guilty of sin in the above case, saving [sic] in her suffering her passion to rise too high etc," the church answered "no" and eventually placed Brother Crenshaw under her censure.[47]

Baptists' beliefs about the proper roles of husbands and wives, as well as the institution of marriage, were evident in decisions involving domestic conflict and abuse. Some of the most difficult cases coming before churches were those between spouses. In virtually every instance, churches attempted to reconcile the testimony and evidence of Christian "brothers" and "sisters" with assumptions about "appropriate" marital roles and interactions. Additionally, churches had to take into account the fact that one spouse was usually more devout than the other, or was a family's only Baptist.

To Baptists, marriage was a sacred institution designed by God and the cornerstone upon which rested the entire Baptist and social edifice. Baptists' vision of the marital relationship, and of the husband and wife's role in it, was based largely on Ephesians 5:22-33 in which the wife was to submit to her husband and the husband was to love his wife as Christ loved the church. The husband was to be the head of the household and guide his wife and family on the pathway to godliness.[48]

Despite Baptists' ideas about the proper roles of husbands and wives, and men and women, church decisions were not so clear. Although Baptists held assumptions about the stronger and weaker sexes, churches also took the specifics of cases into account. Rebecca Shepherd, for example, was brought before the Severn's Valley Baptist Church in Elizabethtown, Kentucky, by Brother Isaac Kenneth, who was "aggrieved with her for leaving her husband and refusing to live with him any longer." After a full hearing, the Church decided in Sister Shepherd's favor. As the clerk noted, "she being present after hearing her reasons also the evidence of several of the members who are well acquainted with the circumstance after a full investigation of the subject the Church exprest by her vote an opinion that they think her excuseable and are willing to bear with her." Additionally, not only men brought charges of marital discord against women. Many Baptist women shared the assumptions about husbands and wives held by their male counterparts. Women, as well as men, brought charges against church sisters for leaving their husbands.[49]

Without an understanding of the implications of religious conviction it is difficult to comprehend cases where women brought charges against themselves. In January 1793 such a case took place in the Severn's Valley church when Sister Betty McCluer came forward of her own volition "and acknowledged herself guilty of the fault of fornication viz of being with the child by the person whom she married at the time she was married to him." Fortunately for McCluer the church agreed to restore her membership at a subsequent meeting since she "shewed so much tokens of repentance both to the Church and the world."[50]

Churches occasionally brought husbands and male relatives to account for domestic transgressions. Physical and verbal abuse of wives and children, including "unsavory language," "getting in a passn," "misuseing" a wife, and "being disagreeable," were all considered offenses requiring a church hearing. In this way, churches sometimes protected women from exploitation and abuse. This was especially important because most Baptist women did not have the economic means to escape. The only drawback was that men accused of abusing their wives were more often censured than excluded or excommunicated. All husbands had to do to obtain restoration was to confess their mistake and demonstrate repentance.

A complete portrait of Baptist religious culture in early Kentucky requires a thorough understanding of the centrality of belief. Such knowledge is also critical to an accurate interpretation of the gender dynamics within that culture. Leaving belief out of the picture makes Baptist men and women much less complex and, thus, less human and interesting. For men and women such as Betsy Payne, belief was often the motivation behind membership in specific religious communities and the termination of membership in these communities. The importance of belief is especially evident in those cases where individuals felt compelled to leave communities with whom they felt deep ties. As Payne noted in her letter, "I am distressed to say fare well to the Great Crossings Church, I have a feeling for that church that will never leave me in this life. . . . I think of you in the night when I suppose you are all asleep."[51]

Historians of gender, generally dismissive of religious belief and often unwilling to take men and women's religious expressions at face value, are unable to explain why white women remained in churches led by white males in such overwhelming numbers. Although some white women surely joined churches primarily for social reasons, many more did so for spiritual ones. Kentucky Baptist men and women desired intimacy, community, and acceptance. They also hungered for true knowledge of God; and they were willing to endorse radical ideas and act in radical ways, often unknowingly, to obtain it.

Notes

The author wishes to thank the PEW Foundation for the Study of Religion and American History at Yale University, and specifically Jonathan Butler and Harry Stout, for a summer dissertation fellowship which supported the writing of this essay. Thanks are also due to the College of William and Mary's Department of History for financial support. Finally, the author wishes to express her gratitude to the following individuals for reading earlier drafts of this essay and offering their expert and insightful suggestions: Michael McGiffert, James Whittenburg, Patricia Bonomi, Janet Lindman, Beth Schweiger, Jewel Spangler, Eva Sheppard, Lynn Nelson, and Antoinette vanZelm.

1. Betsy Payne, "To the Baptist church at the Crossings," n.d., Great Crossings Baptist Church (Scott County) miscellaneous papers, Southern Baptist Theological Seminary, Louisville, Ky. No disciplinary case involving Payne was recorded in the church minute book, so we cannot know if she was excluded from fellowship after writing this letter. An Elizabeth Payne was listed on a December 2, 1826, membership list, but not on the next list appearing in the minute book, that for 1842. It is likely, on the basis of similar cases, that her letter was read at a Saturday church business meeting. During this period, Kentucky Baptists held business meetings once a month on the Saturday preceding a Sunday meeting of worship. When female members were charged by a church for their doctrinal views, they were requested to appear before the church or to send a letter

explaining their case. The letter of dismissal was used by Baptists throughout the United States as a letter of spiritual recommendation.

2. This summary of Baptists' gender conventions is derived from the following studies: Jean E. Friedman, *The Enclosed Garden: Women and Community in the Evangelical South, 1830-1900* (Chapel Hill: Univ. Press of North Carolina, 1986); Susan Juster, *Disorderly Women: Sexual Politics and Evangelicalism in Revolutionary New England* (Ithaca: Cornell Univ. Press, 1994); and Stephanie McCurry, *Masters of Small Worlds: Yeoman Households, Gender Relations, and the Political Culture of the Antebellum South Carolina Low Country* (New York: Oxford Univ. Press, 1995). Recent work, such as that by Janet Lindman on Virgina and Pennsylvania Baptists, challenges Susan Juster's assertion that by 1780 women were increasingly targeted by churches as sources of disorder. Lindman argues that there was a decline in female discipline by the end of the eighteenth century. Perhaps this difference was regional. See Janet Moore Lindman, "A World of Baptists: Gender, Race, and Religious Community in Pennsylvania and Virginia, 1689-1825" (Ph.D. diss., University of Minnesota, 1994).

3. McCurry, *Masters of Small Worlds*, 180-81.

4. Friedman, *The Enclosed Garden*, 9.

5. White Baptists were conservative because their beliefs and practices attempted to preserve a traditional expression of Christianity in which white men were the divinely ordained rulers over all creation, including women. This conservatism considered social, gender, and racial hierarchies as natural and as part of the created order. Radical consequences were those that overturned conservative notions of what was "true" and "proper."

6. Juster, *Disorderly Women*, 167. For a discussion of the ways Christianity was "democratized" and became more competitive after the Revolution see Nathan O. Hatch, *The Democratization of American Christianity* (New Haven: Yale Univ. Press, 1989); and R. Laurence Moore, *Selling God: American Religion in the Marketplace of Culture* (New York: Oxford Univ. Press, 1994).

7. Linda Gordon, *Heroes of Their Own Lives: The Politics and History of Family Violence, Boston 1880-1960* (New York: Viking Press, 1988), vi. Patriarchy is also a problematic analytical device because its strength or weakness varies by time, place, region, class, and race. Additionally, over time such developments as evangelicalism muted and smoothed over its harsher manifestations.

8. David G. Hackett, "Gender and Religion in American Culture, 1870-1930," *Religion and American Culture: A Journal of Interpretation* 5 (1995): 142.

9. By "congregations" I mean the gatherings of church members and nonmembers, Christians and the unconverted, for worship, for prayer, and often to hear a sermon.

10. The chronology of this study is also significant. As Moore notes, "In the most objectively measurable terms, the great age of religion in the United States was not the seventeenth century, however remarkable the theological inventiveness of the Puritans, but the nineteenth century"; Moore, *Selling God*, 10.

11. In fourteen churches with only one membership list before 1861, white females outnumbered white males in every church but two. In these two churches the numbers of white men and women were relatively equal. Mount Tabor Baptist Church in Barren County had 137 white male and 127 white female members, and Brashear's Creek in Shelby County had 15 white males and 13 white females. In eighteen churches with more than one complete church list before 1861, white females eventually outnumbered white

males in every church but two. In the case of West Fork Baptist Church in Washington County, white females outnumbered white males fewer than two years after the church was founded. In four churches, Boone's Creek in Fayette County, Severn's Valley in Hardin County, Great Crossings in Scott County, and Corn Creek in Gallatin County, the ratio of women to men was eventually almost two to one, while at Middle Creek in Boone County, the ratio of women to men was slightly more than two to one. In those churches where white men eventually outnumbered white women, King's Baptist Church in Taylorsville and First Baptist Church in Leitchfield, there are no surviving membership lists for the period after 1813. It is thus possible that their male to female ratios may have differed before 1861.

12. For Baptists' beliefs see Robert G. Torbet, *A History of the Baptists*, 3rd ed. (Valley Forge, Penn.: Judson, 1993); H. Leon McBeth, *The Baptist Heritage* (Nashville: Broadman Press, 1987); and William Henry Brackney, *The Baptists* (New York: Greenwood Press, 1988).

13. This was especially evident in nineteenth-century Kentucky, and specifically the antebellum era, when Methodist and Disciples of Christ gatherings gave Baptists serious theological competition.

14. J.H. Spencer, *A History of the Kentucky Baptists: From 1769 to 1885*, 2 vols. (1885; reprint, Gallatin, Tenn.: Church History Research and Archives, 1984), 1: 482. Information about initial differences between Regular and Separate Baptists in Virginia, North Carolina, and Kentucky, and their 1801 union in Kentucky, can be found in Spencer, *A History of Kentucky Baptists*, 102-11, 482-87, 544-47; William L. Lumpkin, *Baptist Foundations in the South: Tracing through the Separates the Influence of the Great Awakening, 1754-1787* (Nashville: Broadman Press, 1961), 29, 38-40; Robert Baylor Semple, *History of the Baptists in Virginia* (Lafayette, Tenn.: 1810; reprint, Church History Research and Archives, 1976), 13-16; and Frank Masters, *A History of Baptists in Kentucky* (Louisville: Kentucky Baptist Historical Society, 1953), 158-59.

15. *The New Testament of Our Lord and Saviour Jesus Christ, Translated out of the Original Greek and with the Former Translations Diligently Compared and Revised. By the Special Command of King James I of England* (Philadelphia: Mathew Carey, 1802), Special Collections, University of Virginia, 863.

16. According to Spencer, this comment was made by an "aged widow"; *A History of the Kentucky Baptists*, 1: 663.

17. In his study of Georgia Baptists, Gregory Wills notes a similar development. He observes that although "not always well-informed, the laity often felt a keen interest in theology, especially in times of controversy. They took sides in public debates, formed factions in their churches, and expected sound theology from their ministers"; Gregory A. Wills, *Democratic Religion: Freedom, Authority, and Church Discipline in the Baptist South, 1785-1900* (New York: Oxford Univ. Press, 1997), 5. My sources reveal two distinct phases of spiritual development in the lives of male and female Baptists. Initially, Baptists underwent a conversion experience based more in the emotive than in the intellectual faculties (although seekers did enquire after godly knowledge during this stage). After conversion, although the emotions still played an important role in their spiritual life and worship, converts focused more on godly ideas and the practical working out of those ideas in their lives and in the life of the gathered church.

18. An Antinomian is "[A] person who maintains that the moral law is not binding on Christians"; an Arian is one who adheres to the fourth-century doctrine of Arius "who denied that Christ was *Consubstantial*" or of the same substance as God; a Calvinist is one who embraces the doctrines of sixteenth-century Protestant reformer John Calvin, including particular election, particular redemption, moral inability in a fallen state, irresistible grace, and final perseverance; and an Arminian is one who agrees with the sixteenth-century views of Protestant theologian James Arminius, who opposed the views of Calvin, especially predestination; *The Oxford English Dictionary*, 1: 89, 113, 115; 2: 799.

19. Minute Book of Burks Branch Baptist Church, Shelby County, vol. 1, July 1801, Southern Baptist Theological Seminary.

20. William Hickman, "A Short Account of My Life and Travels, For More Than Fifty Years; A Professed Servant of Jesus Christ. To Which Is Added a Narrative of the Rise and Progress of Religion in the Early Settlement of Kentucky; Giving an Account of the Difficulties We Had To Encounter, &c," Southern Baptist Theological Seminary, transcript.

21. Minutes of the Elkhorn Baptist Association, 6 August 1787, Southern Baptist Theological Seminary. Unfortunately, the Elkhorn Association minutes for 1787 do not mention the church from which the query originated.

22. James E. Stone to Sarah Ann Stone, 24 October 1828, Bush-Beauchamp Family Papers, Filson Club, Louisville.

23. Minute Book of Bethel Baptist Church (Washington County), July 1817, Southern Baptist Theological Seminary, transcript.

24. Betsy Payne to the Great Crossings Baptist Church, Southern Baptist Theological Seminary.

25. The eight Baptist church minute books from which the following information was extracted are Severn's Valley, Hardin County; Cox's Creek (New Salem), Nelson County; Great Crossings, Scott County; Forks of Elkhorn, Franklin County; Marble Creek (East Hickman), Fayette County; Mill Creek (Tompkinsville), Monroe County; Middle Creek (Belleview), Boone County; and Mount Tabor, Barren County. Records were selected for their chronological length and detail. When possible, they were also selected for geographic diversity. The majority are available on microfilm from the Historical Commission of the Southern Baptist Convention. The Great Crossings, Forks of Elkhorn, Marble Creek, and Mount Tabor records are at the Southern Baptist Theological Seminary archives. A transcript of the Marble Creek minute book from 1787 to 1842 is available at Special Collections, Margaret I. King Library, University of Kentucky, Lexington.

26. The term "charge" includes accusations brought against men and women at church business meetings as well as accusations brought by individuals against themselves. Charges were also brought against absent individuals. Absent members were usually "cited" to come before the church. In a sample of thirty Mississippi evangelical church and circuit records with a total of twelve hundred disciplinary cases, Randy Sparks found that 17.3 percent (twenty-six cases) of all charges against white women were for joining another denomination. He attributes this statistic to "women who wed husbands from another denomination." While some Kentucky women left Baptist churches to join their spouses, the majority left because of disagreements over doctrine and the practical application of doctrine. They also left to be with family members who shared their views. Very few Kentucky Baptist women were listed as leaving a church to join their husband's

denomination. Randy J. Sparks, *On Jordan's Stormy Banks: Evangelicalism in Mississippi, 1773-1876* (Athens: Univ. of Georgia Press, 1994), 161.

27. Additional women charged with joining another denomination or a "society in disorder" included: one for joining the Unitarians, one for joining the Universalists, eighteen for following a minister supportive of missions, one for joining the Hard Side Baptists, one for joining the Separate Baptists, one for joining the Episcopalians, and two for joining the Shakers. White men were also charged for the following: one for joining a missionary church, fourteen for following a minister supportive of missions, and one for joining the Separate Baptists. No men or women were charged with joining the Presbyterians. Of all the individuals charged, seventy-seven women, or 84 percent, and thirty-one men, or 91 percent, were excluded for joining another denomination.

28. Juster, *Disorderly Women*, 147.

29. The term "gender hierarchies" is derived from Janet Lindman's phrase "hierarchies of gender and race"; see Lindman, "A World of Baptists."

30. Minute Book of Mill Creek Baptist Church, August and October 1809, and October and December 1810.

31. Minute Book of Middle Creek Baptist Church, January 1844.

32. Minute Book of Dry Ridge Baptist Church, Grant County, October 1817, Southern Baptist Theological Seminary, photocopy.

33. John Taylor, *A History of Ten Baptist Churches* (New York: Arno Press, 1980), 96. Although there is no way to know exactly when Taylor made this observation about Sister Arnold, it is recorded after events taking place in the early 1820s. His *History* was first published in 1823. According to Barbara Welter, the essential qualities comprising "True Womanhood" were "piety, purity, submissiveness and domesticity." Barbara Welter, "The Cult of True Womanhood: 1820-1860," *American Quarterly* 18 (1966): 151-74.

34. *Louisville Western Recorder*, January 14, 1852, 11.

35. Ibid., 1851.

36. Taylor, *History*, 106.

37. Ibid., 103.

38. A wonderful example of one such husband-wife encounter in which female spiritual authority triumphed over male "headship" is related by John Taylor in his *History*. After a "Mrs. Reese" was baptized, with her husband's permission, in front of the members of Clear Creek Baptist Church in Woodford County, Mr. Reese "concluded his wife disregarded him and therefore had left him and joined the Baptists, and they were all hypocrits [*sic*] together." After he flew into a rage, declaring that he would no longer live with his wife, and riding off on his horse without his wife and child, Mrs. Reese found him loudly bemoaning his actions. According to Taylor "when he was ready to ask her a thousand pardons, hoped she would forgive him, left his horse, dropped on his knees in the mud, and entreated his wife to pray for him"; ibid., 74.

39. Donald G. Mathews, *Religion in the Old South* (Chicago: Univ. of Chicago Press, 1977), 112-24.

40. Frederick A. Bode finds a similar development in antebellum Georgia. He argues that "the religious, and especially the evangelical, impulse in the South may actually have resisted in subtle ways the constraints of hierarchy, at least as far as the relations between white men and women were concerned. . . . Religion became a common sphere in which men and women frequently acted together to save souls, nurture chil-

dren, and perform works of benevolence"; Frederick A. Bode, "A Common Sphere: White Evangelicals and Gender in Antebellum Georgia," *Georgia Historical Quarterly* 79 (1995): 779.

41. Rebecca Lindsey to her minister, 5 February 1820, Bush-Beauchamp Family Papers.

42. James E. Stone to Sister Mary Singleton, [c. 1820s], Bush-Beauchamp Family Papers.

43. The text of Matthew 18:15-17 is as follows: "Moreover if thy brother shall trespass against thee, go and tell him his fault between thee and him alone: if he shall hear thee, thou hast gained thy brother. But if he will not hear *thee, then* take with thee one or two more, that in the mouth of two or three witnesses every word may be established. And if he shall neglect to hear them, tell *it* unto the Church: but if he neglect to hear the church, let him be unto thee as an heathen man and a publican"; *The New Testament*, 740.

44. See note 25.

45. While 433 women were charged with various transgressions between 1780 and 1860, and 279 were excluded, only 40, or 14 percent, were restored. By comparison, 577 men out of 1,137 charged were excluded, and 113, or 20 percent, were restored.

46. The term "deputy husband" is taken from Laurel Thatcher Ulrich's study of New England women. *Good Wives: Image and Reality in the Lives of Women in Northern New England, 1650-1750* (New York: Oxford Univ. Press, 1983).

47. Minute Book of Mount Tabor Baptist Church, June-October 1809.

48. For example, Ephesians 5:22-25 reads: "Wives, submit yourselves unto your own husbands, as unto the Lord. For the husband is the head of the wife, even as Christ is the head of the Church: and he is the Saviour of the body. Therefore as the church is subject unto Christ, so *let* the wives *be* to their own husbands, in every thing. Husbands, love your wives, even as Christ also loved the church, and gave himself for it"; *The New Testament*, 868.

49. Minute Book of Severn's Valley Baptist Church, December 1826.

50. Minute Book of Severn's Valley Baptist Church, January and March 1793.

51. Betsy Payne to the Great Crossings Baptist Church, Southern Baptist Theological Seminary.

25 DOLLARS REWARD.

The subscribers will give for the apprehension and return of a colored man, named THORNTON, who absconded from our employ on the 3d or 4th of July, inst. Said Thornton is about 5 feet, 9 or 10 inches high; stout made, and of a yellow complexion; light eyes, and of good address; had on when he left, a blue cloth coat and pantaloons, boots, and a black hat.

july 7 WURTS & REINHARD.

Proximity to large numbers of free blacks and other hired-out slaves often served to inspire Kentucky's urban slaves to escape bondage. On 3 July 1831, Thornton Blackburn and his wife fled Louisville for freedom. This notice appeared four days later in the local newspaper. *Louisville Public Advertiser*, 7 July 1831

“There We Were in Darkness, —Here We Are in Light”
Kentucky Slaves and the Promised Land

KAROLYN E. SMARDZ

On the evening of July 3, 1831, Thornton and Lucie Blackburn left Louisville for a new home in the north. They crossed the Ohio River and flagged down the *Versailles,* a steamboat just departing Louisville on its upstream cruise. The Blackburns rode as far as Cincinnati where they boarded a stagecoach to Sandusky, Ohio. There they switched coaches and headed to their new home in Detroit, Michigan Territory. Thornton found work with a local stonemason. Although happy and well liked in their new community, the couple encountered legal difficulties and moved across the border to Amherstburg, Ontario. A year later the Blackburns once again relocated, this time to Toronto where they built a small frame house and rose to prominence for their charitable aid to other American immigrants resettling in British-ruled Canada. When Thornton and Lucie opened the city's first taxi business, their yellow and red cab became a familiar sight on Toronto streets and the symbol of success at the end of their long journey. In the 1890s, these transplanted Kentuckians died childless, but far from friendless. They were buried in the Toronto Necropolis Cemetery. Their house was torn down; their property became part of a neighborhood schoolyard. Slowly, the Blackburns faded from memory and, a century later, the large marble obelisk that marks their common grave relates very little of their story:

> In memory of Thornton Blackburn
> Died Feb. 26, 1890, age 76 years
> A native of Maysville, Kentucky, U.S.A.
> Blessed are the dead which die in the Lord.

Overall, the Blackburns' story does not seem particularly extraordinary. Their journey was unremarkable. People easily and commonly crossed the border between Canada and the United States in those days, and Americans were not indifferent to the opportunities to be found in developing cities like

Detroit and Toronto. What does make this story exceptional, however, is that Thornton and Lucie Blackburn were African Americans who had escaped slavery in Kentucky to find freedom in "the promised land."[1]

The Blackburn story is rare in the amount of historical detail available and, therefore, provides superb insight into the fugitive slave issue. Thornton and Lucie's decision to leave Louisville for Canada eventually led to Detroit's first racial upheaval: the so-called "Blackburn Riots of 1833." The consequences of their flight into Canada were legal and diplomatic decisions that dictated Canada's relationship with the United States on the matter of fugitive slaves for decades to come. The Blackburn case—one of the first peacetime extradition hearings between the two nations—set the precedent for fugitive slave extradition cases for nearly thirty years.

The Blackburn story was unearthed in a 1985 archaeological excavation at the site of the couple's Toronto home.[2] The Thornton and Lucie Blackburn Public Archaeology Project generated enormous popular interest in the four short months of its operation. As the only fugitive slave site ever excavated in the Province of Ontario, the dig has been the subject of an award-winning documentary, popular and scholarly articles, television and radio interviews, and a grade-six curriculum available in Toronto schools. Yet, despite the growing volume of archaeological evidence, investigations uncovered little about the cabby and his wife. Street directories list the original owner of the property as "Thornton Blackburn, cabman, coloured."[3] A late-nineteenth-century *Toronto Telegram* article, "The First Cab in the City," described the Blackburns' house, barn, and cab company, but provided little insight into their private lives.

To understand the reason for the great popular interest in this fugitive slave couple and their life story, one must look back from Toronto, through Detroit, to Kentucky, where the tale begins. The first clue leading to Kentucky is the gravestone in the Toronto Necropolis Cemetery. Etched across its granite face is a list of the graves' occupants:

Thornton Blackburn
aged 76 died Feb. 26, 1890 born Maysville, Ky.
Lucie Blackburn
aged 90 died Feb. 6, 1895 born U.S.
Alfred Blackburn
aged 55 died June 10, 1863 born U.S.
Libby Blackburn
aged 80 died Oct. 27, 1855 born Virginia U.S.

Ann M. Jackson
aged 70 died Jan. 28, 1880 born U.S.
Richard Jackson
aged 38 died June 2, 1885 born U.S.[4]

Although the relationship of Ann and Richard Jackson to Thornton and Lucie Blackburn remains puzzling, the others in their family plot are more easily identified. When the Blackburns arrived in Toronto in 1834, they found Alfred Blackburn employed as a carpenter; he lived only two blocks from the plot of land where Thornton and Lucie chose to build their modest home. Born circa 1813, Alfred is thought to have been either Thornton's brother or cousin. The identity of Libby Blackburn is more problematic, but not impossible. In both Detroit and Toronto, oral history relates that in the 1840s Thornton Blackburn returned to Kentucky to rescue his mother.[5] Given the extraordinary events that surrounded Thornton's owners' attempts to retrieve him after his escape, a return to Kentucky would seem either foolhardy or extraordinarily brave. Still, a lady of appropriate age to Thornton's mother is buried in the family plot in Toronto.

Libby Blackburn's identity as Thornton's mother makes great sense. At the time of Thornton's birth, Maysville, Kentucky, was a major gateway to the West. By 1811, literally thousands of families, often accompanied by their slaves, traveled in flatboats from Maysville down the Ohio River into more remote parts of the state.[6] Since Libby Blackburn's birthplace was Virginia, one might conjecture that as her owners passed through Maysville on their way west, Libby gave birth to Thornton. His birth to a slave woman in a slave state immediately thrust Thornton into slavery.

Like Thornton's owners, many of the earliest migrants to Kentucky came from the tidewater region of Virginia and Maryland and were convinced of the central role of slavery to the rural southern economy. Not willing to sacrifice the advantages of enslaved labor as they migrated to the newly opened lands of the West, these southerners brought thousands of slaves with them to clear the land, work the fields, construct homes and factories, and provide domestic services. Of Kentucky's 73,677 residents in 1790, some 12,430 persons were African American slaves. Twenty years later 80,560 of the state's 406,511 residents were enslaved blacks.[7] While this did not compare with the hundreds of thousands of slaves who inhabited the Carolinas and Virginia, it contrasted markedly with the 3,417 slaves in Tennessee. Over the next three decades, the numbers continued to increase dramatically. Only in the two decades before the Civil War did the slave population of Kentucky begin to decline.[8]

Yet, while Kentucky was well established as a slave state, slaves were not evenly distributed within its borders. The vast majority toiled in the Bluegrass region, where a milder climate and fertile soil made hemp production and other agricultural pursuits more profitable. The presence of urban population centers like Lexington and Louisville also encouraged the use of slaves as domestic servants, factory laborers, dock workers, and mill hands. Historians have interpreted slavery in Kentucky as relatively moderate when compared with patterns in the Deep South. So did contemporaries; "Perhaps the mildest form of the system of slavery is to be seen in the State of Kentucky," declared Harriet Beecher Stowe in her famed *Uncle Tom's Cabin.*[9] Indeed, Kentucky slaveholders seemingly believed they were unique in their kindliness toward slaves and convinced themselves that Kentucky's slaves were more content than those elsewhere.[10]

The demands of slavery, as "mild" as it might have been in Kentucky, were too harsh for many. Upper Canadian census records for the period 1830 through 1860 reveal that dozens of fugitive slaves who immigrated to Canada claimed a Kentucky birthplace. Slaves did not appreciate the moderate conditions of their servitude to the extent that slaveholders might have wished. Sold with estates, mortgaged for debts, and mistreated at the whim of owners without recourse to law, Kentucky's slaves faced the same dehumanizing situations found in all the slave states—an absence of freedom. Further, they feared the prospect of being taken to the markets of New Orleans and Natchez for sale in the Deep South. The threat, therefore, "to be sold down the river"— an expression first coined in Kentucky—suggests quite well why so many Kentucky slaves like Thornton and Lucie Blackburn sought safety north of the forty-ninth parallel.

In 1829, Thornton Blackburn resurfaced in the historical record as domestic servant to the recently deceased Dr. Gideon Brown, a prominent resident who operated a "doctor's shop" in Hardinsburg, Kentucky, and a small farm on the outskirts of town.[11] Brown's wife, Susan, was the daughter of Clayton Talbot, a prominent Huntsville, Alabama, businessman. Susan had followed her sister to the Hardinsburg area and now, with her husband's death, she came to rely increasingly on her brother-in-law, John Pope Oldham.[12] Her father and brother-in-law served as executors and oversaw the operations of widow Brown's estate, which she held in trust for her "five infant children." The inventory of the late doctor's estate included seven slaves, two of whom were male: Thornton, valued at $400, and Bob, who was worth $350.[13] Apparently, Susan Brown decided to retain all seven and, a year or so later, when she and her children moved to a farm outside Louisville, the slaves went with her.[14] And so did the Oldhams. They purchased extensive property southeast of Louisville as well as a townhouse. Shortly thereafter, John became the city's postmaster, a stepping-stone to his eventual position as district judge.

Within two years, Susan Brown hired out Thornton in downtown Louisville. In Kentucky, as in all of the slave states, it had become common practice to hire out slaves not needed at home in order to produce extra income. While generally illegal, the practice flourished because it was profitable and because it satisfied the labor needs of individuals and companies faced with shortages of white urban laborers.[15] In Louisville, slaves worked at manufacturing and other arduous tasks that in northern states were the province of Irish and other immigrant workers. The greatest need for hired-out slaves was at the dockyards, where they labored as day men. They also helped to build canals and railroads, and toiled in the ropewalks.[16]

Often owners hired out their slaves on yearly contracts, with provisions that required the lessor to provide adequate clothing, food, and medical care. Naturally, owners received the wages due their slaves, but occasionally, the slave could keep extra money from overtime work and tips. Some slaves saved enough to purchase not only their own freedom but also that of their families.

Of course, the practice did not please all slaveholders. Contemporary critics warned of the inevitable weakening of patriarchal control over slaves. "They [hired-out slaves] scarcely know that they are slaves," complained the editor of the *Louisville Public Advertiser*.[17] Out from under the watchful eye of the slaveholder, hired-out slaves came into contact with undesirable influences like abolitionists, freedmen, and discontented slaves. Hiring out broke down the close supervisory relationship that was usual on a plantation or in cramped urban neighborhoods, further eroding the slaveholders' presence and control.[18] In particular, it allowed for the development of community among blacks: they organized churches, schools, and other associations where the freed and the enslaved mingled within the welcoming anonymity of the urban context.

In the spring of 1831, Susan Brown hired out Thornton to the Wurts and Reinhard Dry Goods Store in downtown Louisville.[19] Because his owner lived on a farm with her children and other slaves, Thornton most likely "lived out" in Louisville as well. Almost certainly Thornton met his future wife during these days. She was a Creole West Indian slave woman.[20] Her name in slavery was "Ruthie" or "Rutha," but throughout her life in Detroit and Toronto, she was known as "Lucie" Blackburn. When Thornton met her, she worked as a nurse for George and Charlotte Backus, of Backus and Bell Drygoods Company in Louisville. Both owners had died, and Ruthie was increasingly nervous with her situation, and with good reason.[21] The Backus estate was sold; probate records indicate the sale of Ruthie to a recently arrived businessman, Virgil McKnight, a highly respected figure in Louisville society and future president of the Bank of Kentucky.[22]

Perhaps Ruthie was upset at being sold away from family and friends. Possibly, Thornton had experienced enough freedom to want it fully. There is no recorded cause for the Blackburns' flight. Whatever the reason, on "the day before Independence Day" in 1831, Thornton and Ruthie took the first step on the long road that took them to Canada and freedom. They crossed the river to Jeffersonville, Indiana, on July 3. By their manners and attire—Lucie wore a black silk dress and was described as a very handsome woman by the boat's captain—the Blackburns convinced the officers of the *Versailles* of their free status and headed toward the promised land.[23]

As slaves, neither Thornton nor Lucie had legitimate claim to remove from the state or even from the city; they were the legal properties of the Brown and McKnight families, respectively. In fact, had either been caught in the journey, punishment would have been swift and sure, and most certainly would have included a return to slave status. Thus, their journey to Cincinnati—and then to Sandusky, Detroit, and eventually Toronto—was far more arduous than the opening sketch indicated. The Blackburns' escape to the promised land represented a journey from slavery to freedom. As another fugitive slave explained, "There we were in darkness,—here we are in light."[24]

No one knows how many slaves escaped the bondage of the South or how many freed people left the overt racism of the North. According to estimates, thirty thousand to sixty thousand individuals fled to Canada in the years before the Civil War. Slaves and freed people, particularly in Kentucky, found ample opportunity to seek a haven by running northward. The state's proximity to Ohio and Indiana, and the activities of abolitionists, contributed to the out-migration of hundreds, if not thousands.

Most refugees made their way with the guidance of the North Star; others depended on the Underground Railroad system through the northern states. When successful in their escape, fugitive slaves like Harriet Tubman and Henry Box Brown provided models for thousands of others. Still, many faced capture only a few miles from their homes; others stood only a few yards from their destinations as local magistrates arrested them. On their flight north, Thornton and Lucie Blackburn appeared destined for the ranks of the recaptured.

Four days after their departure, a notice appeared in the *Louisville Public Advertiser* requesting information about the runaway "Thornton": "stout made, and of a yellow complexion; light eyes, and of good address."[25] The advertisement was too late. Susan Brown's nephew, William Oldham, caught the very next steamboat headed for Cincinnati. He discovered their names in a logbook for the stagecoach to Sandusky. William, convinced they were en route to Canada, decided that he could not overtake them before they reached the border; he returned to Louisville.[26] The Blackburns continued to Sandusky, and thence to Detroit.

When William Oldham returned without the fugitives, his father and Virgil McKnight sued the steamboat company that had carried the Blackburns to Cincinnati. The case centered around the fact that, although the Blackburns boarded the steamboat *Versailles* on the Jeffersonville, Indiana, side of the river, the entire Ohio River was considered Kentucky and, therefore, slave territory. Hence, the steamboat company had, albeit inadvertently, aided two fugitive slaves to escape. The captain of the *Versailles* acknowledged that he had taken on "persons of color, whom he had supposed to be free," and regretted that "they have been lost to their owners."[27] The case dragged on until 1846, however, and created an inordinate number of documents and depositions. When the case finally ended, the steamboat company owners and captain had lost: the judge awarded Virgil McKnight and Susan Brown four hundred dollars each.[28]

Meanwhile, Thornton and Lucie Blackburn arrived in Detroit on July 18. Thornton found employment with the local stonemason, Thomas Coquillard.[29] For the next two years, the Blackburns attended church, created a circle of friends, and enjoyed a life of freedom. By all accounts, the couple were model citizens.

But disaster awaited the Blackburns. Within the year, Thomas Rogers arrived in Detroit. A friend of Susan Brown who had known Thornton from Wurts and Reinhard's store, Rogers recognized Thornton on the street and feigned concern to ascertain whether Ruthie was in Detroit as well. When Rogers returned south to Louisville with reports of the escaped slaves' location, the couple's erstwhile owners lost no time. Another of Oldham's sons, Clayton Talbot Oldham, departed for Detroit with the family lawyer, Benjamin Weir.[30]

At the request of the Kentuckians, the Detroit sheriff imprisoned Thornton and Lucie pending a trial where the onus was on the couple to prove their freedom. The case was clear: according to the Fugitive Slave Law of 1793 and supported by the Territorial Act of 1827, Michigan had to send any proven runaways back to their southern owners.[31]

The possibility of Thornton and Lucie's deportation surprised local citizens. "Thornton is a respectable, honest and industrious man," editorialized the *Detroit Courier*, "the kind of person who has numerous friends."[32] Detroit's black community was incensed. Not only were the Blackburns well liked, but many other members of the community had no more claim to free status than did the Kentucky couple. If the courts decided in Clayton Oldham's favor, no fugitive slave would be safe in Michigan.[33]

As the trial progressed, the city became increasingly restless. While a proportion of the white community expressed unhappiness with the willingness of territorial officials to return individuals to a state of bondage, the black community teetered on rebellion. Angry African Americans filled the balconies of the courtroom and threatened to burn the town if the Blackburns lost.[34] Judge Henry Chipman had little inclination to test the Territorial Act of 1827, however, and turned over Thornton and Lucie Blackburn to Oldham.

As a precaution against increasing unrest, Sheriff John Wilson housed the Blackburns in the city jail pending the arrival of a steamboat to carry them back to Kentucky and slavery. For three days, angry crowds of blacks armed with clubs, sticks, pistols, and even rocks milled about the commons and the jail. Newspapers reported that people traveled from as far as Fort Malden in Ontario to protest the Blackburns' deportation.[35]

Eventually, not content to see any of their community returned to a state of bondage, several black citizens took matters into their own hands. Meeting at the home of prominent barber and landowner Benjamin Willoughby on the evening of June 15, 1833, the conspirators hatched a plot to free the Blackburns. They did little to keep the plan secret; as a white resident noted, "There is but little doubt that a systematic organization existed among the negroes, and that a regular plan of operation was laid for the rescue of Thornton. Indeed, there was no concealment of the fact by the negroes themselves."[36]

The first phase of the plan was to free Lucie. To appease the angry crowd, Sheriff Wilson allowed the wives of two leaders of the black Baptist Church in Detroit, Mrs. George French and Mrs. Madison Mason, into the jail to visit the Blackburns. As their stay lingered into the evening, Mrs. French changed clothes with Lucie, who then departed the jail in the company of Mrs. Mason. Friends immediately spirited Lucie across the Detroit River and into Canada. In Detroit, George French freed his wife by obtaining a writ of habeas corpus just before her departure as Lucie Blackburn.[37]

Although his wife was safe in Canada and especially because her escape had been so successful, Thornton's plight appeared more grim. On the morning of June 17, 1833, Blackburn stood at the door of the Detroit jail in manacles, waiting for a cart to the steamboat docks. Sheriff Wilson and his deputy, Lemeul Goodall, cautiously guarded the prisoner.

Down by the riverside, Detroit's black citizenry, bolstered by reinforcements from throughout Michigan Territory and Canada, gathered about the steamboat docks where the *Ohio* had made its arrival. A crowd upwards of four hundred people slowly moved toward the jail, an elderly woman carrying a stake wrapped with a white rag, leading it.[38] Goodall ran back into the jail and locked the door, abandoning Wilson to face the mob alone.[39] A melee ensued. Wilson was "borne down by the crowd, and beaten with clubs, having in vain endeavored to defend himself by discharging his pistols."[40] He died a year later from his wounds.

A half-dozen of the rioters commandeered a nearby wagon and, with Thornton aboard, they began a wild race toward the Detroit River. With a posse forming at the jail, Thornton and his rescuers abandoned the cart several blocks from the river and hid in the woods. Breaking Thornton's chains with an axe and silencing his manacled ankles with rags, the group headed toward the riverbank only to discover upon arrival that none of them had money to pay the boatman. Finally, one of the conspirators sacrificed his gold watch. Thornton and eight others rode across the river to safety in Canada.[41]

Canada had a long history of accepting and protecting American fugitive slaves. In the early days of settlement both the British and the French regarded African and Native Canadian slavery as necessary for the development of the new colonies. Climatic conditions, however, made slavery uneconomical as an agrarian labor source. Most slaves worked as domestics, and the system never really took root as it did in the southern United States.

Upper Canada (later the Province of Ontario) and the Maritime Provinces were the two major areas of black settlement in British North America. During the American Revolutionary War, black Loyalists received land and freedom in return for military action. In 1793, Upper Canada became the first part of the British Empire to legislate against slavery. The province's first lieutenant governor, Sir John Graves Simcoe, was an ardent abolitionist who was instrumental in the passage of a nonimportation bill that further required the freeing of all slave children by the age of twenty-five. It did not free those already enslaved, but guaranteed the end of slavery within a generation.[42] News spread south of the border that if slaves followed the North Star and reached "The Land of the Drinking Gourd," they would be free. Between the 1770s and the outbreak of the Civil War, black Canadian communities swelled with thousands of African American fugitives who sought freedom in the "Land of Canaan."[43] By the 1840s, an active Underground Railroad assisted runaways with an organized system of "stations" and "conductors" who assisted fugitive slaves on the way to Canada. Free black communities arose in the Ontario cities of Toronto, Chatham, Saint Catherines (for a while, home to Harriet Tubman, the "Black Moses" who led so many people to freedom), Hamilton, and Windsor. Blacks also created homes in myriad smaller places including Wilberforce, a colony founded by Cincinnati African American emigrants in Buddulph Township in 1829, and the highly successful Elgin Settlement, south of Chatham, at what is now North and South Buxton.

After the passage of the Fugitive Slave Law of 1850, immigration increased dramatically. Thousands of freed people and fugitives who, before midcentury, had established businesses and farms in the northern United States, left everything behind and sought a new life for their families in the promised land.[44] The majority of fugitive slaves who arrived in Ontario came from the border states of Kentucky, Missouri, Virginia, Maryland, and Delaware. Two of the best known fugitive slaves came from Kentucky: Henry Bibb, author, publisher of the *Voice of the Fugitive* antislavery newspaper, leader of the Refugee Home Society Settlement, and an extremely active antislavery advocate; and his contemporary, Josiah Henson, settler and historian of the Dawn Settlement near Dresden, Ontario, and one of the founders of the British-American Institute.[45] Proximity to free territory, as well as the active work of abolitionists in adjacent states such as Pennsylvania and Ohio, doomed border-state slavery to a relentless winnowing of numbers.

In 1833, when the ringleaders of the Blackburn Riots transported Thornton to Canada, they followed a long tradition of those who aided fugitive slaves to find a safe haven across the border. But upon arrival, the Blackburns had not yet reached the promised land. In February of that same year, the governments of Canada and the United States had signed their first extradition treaty; the Blackburn incident was to be its first test.

The riot that aided Thornton and Lucie's escape continued to disrupt Detroit society. When unrest broke out, Lewis Cass, secretary of war in President Andrew Jackson's cabinet, happened to be visiting nearby Fort Gratiot. To restore order in the frontier town, Cass called out the troops, imposed a curfew, and arrested several members of the city's black community. Both conspirators and innocents served up to six months at hard labor as a result. Yet arrests and curfews did not stabilize the community. Eliza Mason wrote to her sister-in-law on June 20, 1833, that several blacks had set fire to "a large barn near the nail [manufactory] containing a horse, cow and other property, . . . they have threatened to burn the city unless the prisoners are set at liberty."[46] Dozens of Detroit's black residents moved en masse across the river to Canada hoping to avoid the inevitable retaliation by the white community.[47]

Even the city's active abolitionists condemned the destruction of property and hastily disassociated themselves from it. In the *Detroit Journal and Advertiser* of July 19, 1833, former white supporters of the black community seemingly reversed their position on the Blackburn incident. "While we hold personal liberty as sacred and inalienable right," the editorial explained, "when the property of the master is clearly proven in the slave, it becomes our duty to see that the laws be maintained and that no riotous mob be allowed to violate them."[48]

Sensing a weakness in the coalition of abolitionists and blacks, the acting governor, a twenty-one-year-old named George Mason, drafted a request for the extradition of Thornton and Lucie Blackburn and sent it to Upper Canada's lieutenant governor, Sir John Colborne. Mason's demand was the first of many American efforts to convince Canadian authorities to return fugitive slaves; all but one would be futile.

It was also the first test case of the Fugitive Offenders Act of 1833.[49] Under the terms of the treaty, fugitives could be extradited only if they had committed a capital crime as recognized by the nation in which they were captured. This was a neat loophole drafted into the agreement by Colborne and his executive council. Escaping from slavery was not a crime in Canada and, therefore, the Canadian government was in no way obligated to return fugitive slaves to the American judiciary.[50] As the attorney general explained, "[escaping from slavery] is an offense which could not be committed in this Province [of Upper Canada] in any case."[51]

But Mason and his advisors planned for this provision. They accused the Blackburns of inciting the very riot that had freed Thornton. Colborne's response was characteristically acerbic, and much followed the tone of his response in 1829 when the Cincinnati black community, facing increased oppression, asked for asylum in Canada. He said, "Tell the Republicans on your side of the line that we do not know men by their colour."[52] In 1833, Colborne pointed out the difficulty with understanding how Lucie could have incited a riot that occurred after her arrival in Canada. He also enquired how Thornton could have done so from within a Detroit jail cell. Colborne was a known abolitionist, as were several members of his executive council, and he had no intention of returning anyone to bondage. He denounced the Michigan governor's thinly veiled attempts to return the Blackburns to their Kentucky owners, pointing out that no crime existed for which the British government of Canada considered enslavement an appropriate punishment.[53] Colborne and the Upper Canadian attorney general, Robert Simpson Jamieson, were unequivocal in their rejection of the extradition request.

The resolution of the Canadian government meant that the Blackburns were free to create a new life in Canada.[54] Thornton and Lucie first settled in Amherstburg, Ontario, but in 1834 they moved farther inland to the newly incorporated City of Toronto, where they constructed a small frame house on the outskirts of the city. After working as a waiter for some years, Thornton decided to open a cab company, the first in Upper Canada. He sent to Montreal for the design of a hackney cab and hired a local mechanic, Paul Bishop, to construct it. He painted the cab red and yellow and christened it, *The City*. For several years, Thornton Blackburn monopolized Toronto's cab business.

Thornton and Lucie also became noted throughout Toronto for expending much of the company's profits on various black self-help movements that had arisen to deal with the ever-increasing number of fugitive slaves arriving in southern Ontario. The Blackburns became active in the local abolitionist cause. Thornton appeared as a delegate to the Convention of Coloured Freedmen held at Saint Lawrence Hall in Toronto in September 1831. They helped to develop make-work projects for fugitive slaves. The *Voice of the Fugitive* noted that Thornton was vice president of the Canadian Mill and Mercantile Association. The company built a sawmill, gristmill, and general store at the Elgin Settlement in Raleigh Township and supplied jobs to scores of new Canadian residents.

In the 1860s, the Blackburns retired from the cab business and enjoyed a quiet life of gardening, hunting, and fishing in the marshes at the mouth of the Don River. Thornton passed away in 1890; Lucie followed some five years later. Their estate, after more than twenty years of retirement, amounted to more than seventeen thousand dollars, a small fortune in those days.

Thornton and Lucie Blackburn's journey from Louisville, Kentucky, was longer and more arduous than distance alone suggests. They left behind everything familiar and dear, as well as the hated state of bondage. The couple fled north in search of freedom—to live as they wished, receive pay for their labor, own a home and business, and have control of their very bodies, free from any service save that which they chose for their own livelihood. Their long struggle and their success typified the experiences of many fugitive slaves who fled Kentucky for the freedom of Canada. Yet, the Blackburns' story is only one of thousands yet to be unearthed. Still, it provides a representative example of just how dear the concept of freedom was to the enslaved, and the lengths to which they were willing to go to attain it.

Notes

For their readings and responses to the manuscript, as well as for their ongoing and enthusiastic support for my research into the lives of Thornton and Lucie Blackburn, the author would like to thank Bruce Heyding, who always believed; John Leverton; Peter Hamalainen; and John McCarthy. For support and encouragement in the lengthy journey from archaeological dig to book, of which this article is a part, special thanks are due the staff of the now-closed Archaeological Resources Centre; Paul Anderson, Glace Lawrence, and the members of the Ontario Black History Society; Donald Nethery and Arlene Tanz of the Toronto Board of Education; and Dr. Jim Walker of the University of Waterloo. Financial support for the more than ten years of "research in my spare time" that contributed to the story detailed here was provided in part by grants and fellowships from Multiculturalism Canada, the Ontario Heritage Foundation, the Virginia Historical Society, and the Anderson Center for Interdisciplinary Studies at Red Wing, Minnesota.

A very special thanks is due Bryan Prince and Alice Newby, chair and curator, respectively, of the Raleigh Township Centennial Museum of North Buxton, Ontario. Because the museum commemorates the Elgin Settlement that harbored hundreds of fugitive slaves before the Civil War, it is most important to the author that the members of the North Buxton community be acknowledged for their part in the research and narration of the Blackburn story. Gwendolyn and John Robinson of Chatham, Ontario, my friends and much-admired colleagues, have done much to ensure that Ontario's fugitive slave heritage is remembered as well as having aided in this telling of the Blackburn story. Finally, I must mention Dr. Norman McRae of Detroit, Michigan, whose article, "Crossing the Detroit River to Find Freedom," was my first clue to Thornton and Lucie's exciting history.

1. This was one of several names used in gospel music, local folklore, and the code of the Underground Railroad to describe Canada. Others included "The Land of Canaan" and "The Land of the Drinking Gourd"; the latter referred to the configuration of the Big Dipper, or Drinking Gourd, with the North Star often serving as lonely fugitives' only guide to their destination.

2. The Ontario Ministry of Culture, Tourism, and Recreation cosponsored the excavation with the Toronto Board of Education to illuminate the city's long heritage as a haven for fugitive slaves and as a center for abolitionist activities in the first half of the nineteenth century. It was carried out in partnership with the Ontario Black History Society.

3. Toronto Street Directory, 1846.

4. Toronto General Burying Ground, Section E, Lot 100.

5. Reginald R. Larrie, *Makin' Free: African-Americans in the Northwest Territory* (Detroit: Blaime Ethridge Books, 1981), 20.

6. Lewis Collins, *Historical Sketches of Kentucky* (Cincinnati: U.P. James, 1847), 431.

7. Ibid., 151.

8. John Hope Franklin and Alfred A. Moss Jr., *From Slavery to Freedom: A History of Negro Americans* (New York: Alfred A. Knopf, 1980), 80.

9. Harriet Beecher Stowe quoted in James Lane Allen, *The Blue-grass Region of Kentucky and Other Kentucky Articles* (New York: Harper & Brothers, 1892), 52.

10. Steven A. Channing, *Kentucky: A Bicentennial History* (New York: W.W. Norton, 1977), n. 18.

11. Indenture of 9 June 1829 between David Murray and his wife Martha and the heirs of Dr. Gideon Brown, Deed Book IV, Breckinridge County Archives, Hardinsburg, Ky.

12. Extensive research has so far failed to establish firmly a birthplace or family connections for Dr. Brown. It is likely that he was related to Dr. William Brown of Charles County, Maryland, a Revolutionary War veteran and an attending physician at the death of George Washington. Several members of the Maryland Browns moved to Breckinridge County in the first decades of the nineteenth century, together with their relatiies, the Alexanders of Alexandria, Virginia. Dr. Gideon Brown's name occurs in various documents relating to these families. For documents on Brown's trusteeship of Gustavus R.A. Brown's children, see Breckinridge County Circuit Court Order Book No. 11, 1842, Breckinridge County Archives. For the Talbots, see Robert Howe Fletcher, ed., *Genealogical Sketch of Certain of the American Descendents of Matthew Talbot, Gentleman* (Richmond, Va.: private printing, 1956), 35-36. Oldham was the son of William Oldham, a very early Virginian settler in Kentucky who had been involved in a series of engagements under the command of George Rogers Clark against Native Americans; Lyman Draper Manuscript Collection, 37J115, State Historical Society of Wisconsin, Madison.

13. Inventory of Appraisement of Gideon Brown's House, 9 June 1829, Breckinridge County Estate Book 3, Breckinridge County Archives.

14. John P. Oldham and Mrs. Brown indenture, Breckinridge County Deeds, 20 June 1832, Box 6, Folder 7, Breckinridge County Archives. Also, Fletcher, 36-37, 44-46.

15. Jacob P. Wheeler, *A Practical Treatise on the Law of Slavery* (1837; reprint, New York: Negro Universities Press, 1968), 152.

16. Channing, 96.

17. *Louisville Public Advertiser*, 30 November 1835.

18. For further discussion, see Hanford Dozier Stafford, "Slavery in a Border City: Louisville, 1790-1860" (Ph.D. diss., University of Kentucky, 1982); also Richard C. Wade, *Slavery in the Cities: The South, 1820-1860* (New York: Oxford Univ. Press, 1964), 29, 68.

19. Norman McRae, "Crossing the Detroit River to Find Freedom," *Michigan History* 67 (1983): 35.

20. "Report of the Committee," *Detroit Courier*, 19 June 1833.

21. Obituary of Charlotte S. Backus, "wife of George Bachus [sic] of the firm Bachus and Bell," *Louisville Daily Focus*, 16 April 1831.

22. Will of George Backus, Book 9, 228, and Book 8, 502-5, Probate Records,

Jefferson County Courthouse, Louisville, Ky. According to the Louisville Directories at the time, McKnight occupied a house on Fifth Street between Walnut and Green, and operated a dry goods business. He became president of the Bank of Kentucky in 1843.

23. Depositions of Thornton Bayliss Quarrier, *McKnight v. Quarrier* (1832) and *Oldham v. Quarrier* (1832), Chancery Court Record Nos. 2221 and 2222, Public Records Division, Kentucky Department for Libraries and Archives, Frankfort.

24. Testimony of Mrs. Isaac Riley, one of the first settlers in the fugitive slave colony known as the Elgin Settlement, now Buxton, Ontario, quoted in Benjamin Drew, *The Refugee: or the Narratives of Fugitive Slaves in Canada* (1856; reprint, Toronto: Coles Publishing, 1972), 301.

25. "Fugitive slave notice for the escaped slave, THORNTON," *Louisville Public Advertiser*, 7 July 1831.

26. Deposition of William Oldham, *McKnight v. Quarrier.*

27. *McFarland et al. v. McKnight*, in Ben Munroe, *Reports of Cases at Common Law and in Equity Decided in the Court of Appeals of Kentucky* (Cincinnati: Robert Clark, 1846), 4: 502-3.

28. The steamboat company owners and captain lost the case and were required to pay the sum of four hundred dollars for "Ruthy's" loss to Virgil McKnight and a similar sum to Susan Brown for Thornton. Interestingly, several of the depositions grant Thornton, husband of "Ruthy," the courtesy of the last name "Blackburn," contrary to the more accepted custom of identifying slaves with only a first name; *Judicial Case, Concerning Slavery*, 375.

29. "Report of the Committee," *Detroit Journal and Advertiser*, 19 July 1833.

30. McRae, "Crossing the Detroit River," 39. The events of "The Blackburn Case" are extremely well documented. Not only are there several extant eyewitness accounts of the trial, ensuing civil unrest, and the riots themselves, but there is also a series of legal and diplomatic documents referring to the court case and the later attempt to convince the government of Upper Canada to extradite the Blackburns after they had crossed the border. In particular, see "Thornton Blackburn, Fugitive Slave, 1833," Papers of the Secretary of State, record groups 56-26, box 198, folder 9, Michigan State Archives, Lansing.

31. *Laws of the Territory of Michigan* (Detroit: State Printing Office, 1827); *Journal of the Legislative Council of the Territory of Michigan* (Detroit: State Printing Office, 1827).

32. "Trouble among the Blacks," *Detroit Courier*, 19 June 1833.

33. Arthur Raymond Kooker, "The Anti-Slavery Movement in Michigan, 1796-1840" (Ph.D. diss., University of Michigan, 1941), 56, 64.

34. *Detroit Journal and Advertiser*, 19 July 1822.

35. McRae, "Crossing the Detroit River," 37; also David M. Katzman, *Before the Ghetto: Black Detroit in the Nineteenth Century* (Urbana: Univ. of Illinois Press, 1973).

36. Eliza B. Mason to Catherine Mason, 22 June 1833, John Mason Papers, Burton Historical Collection, Detroit Public Library, Detroit; also McRae, "Crossing the Detroit River," 37.

37. Clipping from *Detroit Post*, 1870, in Friend Palmer's Scrapbook, vol. 3, Burton Historical Collection.

38. Kooker, "Anti-Slavery Movement in Michigan," n. 67.

39. Deposition of Lemeul Goodall, "Thornton Blackburn, Fugitive Slave, 1833."

40. McRae, "Crossing the Detroit River," 37-38; *Detroit Journal and Advertiser*, 19 June 1833.

41. Kooker, "Anti-Slavery Movement in Michigan," 69.

42. *Statutes of Canada*, 1793, 33 George 3, c. 7.

43. For a full discussion, see Daniel Hill, *The Freedom Seekers: Blacks in Early Canada* (Toronto: Book Society of Canada, 1984). On maritime immigrants, see James St. George Walker, *The Black Loyalists: The Search for a Promised Land in Nova Scotia and Sierra Leone, 1783-1870* (Toronto: Univ. of Toronto Press, 1992).

44. J. Winston Coleman, Jr., *Slavery Times in Kentucky* (Chapel Hill: Univ. of North Carolina Press, 1940), 207. For the story of the Cincinnati black community's request to Colborne for land and freedom in Canada, eventually given to them north of London, Ontario, for use as the Wilberforce Settlement, not the town of Lucan, see Robin Winks, *The Blacks in Canada* (Montreal: McGill Univ. Press, 1971), 155.

45. Josiah Henson, *The Life of Josiah Henson, Formerly a Slave, Now an Inhabitant of Canada: Narrated by Himself* (Boston: n.p., 1849). Some authorities consider Hensen the model for Harriet Beecher Stowe's Uncle Tom; see Winks, *Blacks in Canada*, 185.

46. Eliza B. Mason to Catherine Mason, 20 July 1833, John Mason Papers.

47. *Detroit Tribune*, 28 June 1896; McRae, "Crossing the Detroit River," 39; Kooker, "Anti-Slavery Movement in Michigan," 70; *Detroit Courier*, 26 June 1833.

48. *Detroit Journal and Advertiser*, 19 July 1833.

49. Upper Canada Sundries, 1830, Public Archives of Ontario, Toronto, microfilm; also, "Thornton Blackburn, Fugitive Slave, 1833."

50. Winks, *Blacks in Canada*, 168-69.

51. Robert S. Jamieson, Attorney General of Upper Canada to Lieutenant Colonel Rowan, Secretary to Lieutenant Governor Sir John Colborne, 12 July 1833, Upper Canada Sundries, Public Archives of Canada, microfilm.

52. Sir John Colborne, Lieutenant Governor of Upper Canada, when asylum was requested by the Cincinnati black community in 1829; see Winks, *Blacks in Canada*, 155, 180.

53. Upper Canada Sundries, 1830, 212 ff.

54. "Thornton Blackburn, Fugitive Slave, 1833."

About the Contributors

STEPHEN A. ARON is associate professor of history at the University of California at Los Angeles. He is author of *How the West Was Lost: The Transformation of Kentucky from Daniel Boone to Henry Clay* (Baltimore: Johns Hopkins Univ. Press, 1996); "Significance of the Frontier in the Transition to Capitalism," *The History Teacher* 27 (1994): 271-76; "The Significance of the Kentucky Frontier," *Register of the Kentucky Historical Society* 91 (1993): 298- 323; and "Pioneers and Profiteers: Land Speculation and the Homestead Ethic in Frontier Kentucky," *Western Historical Quarterly* 23 (1992): 179-98.

ELLEN ESLINGER is associate professor of history at DePaul University in Chicago. She is author of "The Shape of Slavery on the Kentucky Frontier, 1775-1800," *Register of the Kentucky Historical Society* 92 (1994): 1-23; "Some Notes on the History of Cane Ridge Prior to the Great Revival," *Register of the Kentucky Historical Society* 91 (1993): 1-23; and "Migration and Kinship on the Trans-Appalachian Frontier: Strode's Station, Kentucky," *Filson Club History Quarterly* 62 (1988): 52-66.

CRAIG THOMPSON FRIEND is assistant professor of history at Georgetown College in Georgetown, Kentucky. He is author of "Merchants and Markethouses: Reflections on Moral Economy in Early Kentucky," *Journal of the Early Republic* 17 (1997): 553-74; and "'Fond Illusions' and Environmental Transformations along the Maysville-Lexington Road," *Register of the Kentucky Historical Society* 94 (1996): 4-32.

A. GWYNN HENDERSON is archaeology education coordinator for the Kentucky Archaeological Survey at the University of Kentucky in Lexington. She is author of "Dispelling the Myth: Seventeenth- and Eighteenth-Century Indian Life in Kentucky," *Register of the Kentucky Historical Society* 90 (1992): 1-25; *Kentuckians Before Boone* (Lexington: Univ. Press of Kentucky, 1992); and editor of *Fort Ancient Cultural Dynamics in the Middle Ohio Valley*, Monographs in World Archaeology #8 (Madison, Wis.: Prehistory Press, 1992).

NANCY O'MALLEY is staff archaeologist for the Department of Anthropology at the University of Kentucky in Lexington. She is author of *A New Village Named Washington* (Washington, Ky.: Old Washington, 1992); *Searching for Boonesborough* (Lexington: University of Kentucky Department of Anthropology, 1990); and *"Stockading Up": A Study of Pioneer Stations in the Inner Bluegrass Region of Kentucky* (Lexington: University of Kentucky Department of Anthropology, 1987).

BLAIR A. POGUE is a doctoral candidate at the College of William and Mary. Her current project is on Baptist religious culture in Virginia and Kentucky during the early republic and antebellum years.

KAROLYN E. SMARDZ is manager of the public archaeology and heritage series at the Institute for Minnesota Archaeology in Minneapolis. Her current project is a book-length study of Thornton and Lucie Blackburn.

DANIEL BLAKE SMITH is professor of history at the University of Kentucky in Lexington. He wrote the screenplay for *Alamance*, produced by Lue Simopoulos, 55 mins., University of North Carolina Center for Public Television, 1996; and is author of *Inside the Great House: Planter Family Life in Eighteenth- Century Chesapeake Society* (Ithaca: Cornell Univ. Press, 1980); and "The Study of Family in Early America: Trends, Problems, and Prospects," *William and Mary Quarterly* 39 (1982): 3-28.

CHRISTOPHER WALDREP is associate professor of history at Eastern Illinois University in Charleston. He is author of "The Making of a Border State Society: James McGready, the Great Revival, and the Prosecution of Profanity in Kentucky," *American Historical Review* 99 (1994): 767-84; and *Night Riders: Defending Community in the Black Patch, 1890-1915* (1993). His current project is *Roots of Disorder: Race and Criminal Justice in the American South, 1817-1880.*

MARION NELSON WINSHIP is a doctoral candidate at the University of Pennsylvania. She is author of "The Land of Connected Men: A New Migration Story from the Early American Republic," *Pennsylvania History* 64 (special supplemental issue, 1997): 88-104. Her current project is on the western careers and operations of a cadre of Virginia-born Jeffersonian Republicans.

Index

Select Baptist Churches, 1790-1830

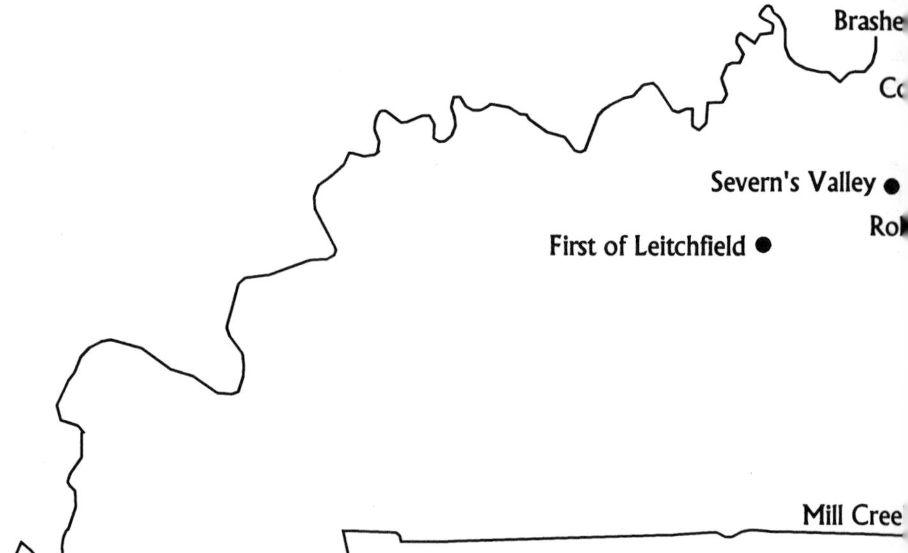